环球雅思学校雅思（IELTS）考试
培生教育集团旗下品牌

环球教育

MW01687691

雅思阅读官方题库

全球10位
著名雅思考官

联合推荐

→ 杨凡◎编著

南京大学出版社

图书在版编目（CIP）数据

雅思阅读官方题库 / 杨凡编著. -- 南京：南京大学出版社, 2012.5（2014.5重印）

ISBN 978-7-305-09829-1

Ⅰ.①雅… Ⅱ.①杨… Ⅲ.①IELTS－阅读教学－习题集 Ⅳ.①H319.4-44

中国版本图书馆CIP数据核字(2012)第069424号

出版发行 南京大学出版社
社　　址 南京市汉口路22号　　邮　　编 210093
网　　址 http://www.NjupCo.com
出 版 人 左　健

书　　名 雅思阅读官方题库
编　　著 杨　凡
责任编辑 王慧玉　吕颜辉　蒋桂琴　　编辑热线 010-62127297
审读编辑 董　颖　朱小旭

印　　刷 北京天宇万达印刷有限公司
开　　本 787×1092　1/16　　印　　张 25　　字　　数 530千
版　　次 2012年5月第1版　　2014年5月第5次印刷
印　　数 18001—21000
ISBN 978-7-305-09829-1
定　　价 59.80 元

发行热线 010-62127297
电子邮箱 Press@NjupCo.com
Sales@NjupCo.com（市场部）

环球雅思图书编委会核心小组

推荐序

我与杨凡老师在环球雅思学校共事多年，其独特的语言教学法和对英语理论、应试英语的理解，在全国可谓独树一帜。能够将其教学理论和授课实践的精华撰写成书以帮助更多的“烤鸭”，一直是我和他所教授的学生们的夙愿。

许多见过杨凡老师的人都觉得他有点“文弱书生”的感觉，其实“初见谈吐静如水，三句过后起波澜”是他教学中最鲜明的特点。杨凡老师的才思敏捷和风趣幽默吸引了无数学生，他博览群书，这一点在其教学内容的精炼通俗上得到了充分的体现。多年相处，我觉得无论是教学风格还是行事风格，用“以柔克刚”一词来形容杨凡其人最为贴切。

据悉杨凡老师早前编写的《雅思写作官方题库范文大全》一书，一经推出便受到了广大雅思考生的欢迎且好评如潮，该书对考生写作成绩的提高和英语水平的巩固均起到了绝佳的帮助。鉴于《雅思写作官方题库范文大全》给考生带来的切实帮助，为了能在雅思阅读方面也能令更多的考生受益，杨凡老师在百忙之中倾力编写了《雅思阅读官方题库》，为了达到最为真实的考题效果，成书前杨凡老师做了大量的考题信息搜集和分析工作，结合对雅思阅读的考试题型、难度和出题思路等方面的理解，编写出与真题考点、题型及难度等都极为接近的考题，相信书中12套高质量的阅读考题、精炼的题型分析和考题精解定能帮助考生实现雅思高分的梦想。

杨凡老师作为“环球雅思教学委员会GTRC”的主要发起人之一，一直积极推动将优秀教学成果转化为学术教材并向全国推广。他致力于促进学生及教师的相互学术交流，及时沟通考试动态，随时总结发展应试英语学习法，不断超越自我，提升雅思教学水平，让广大考生得到优秀教师的精髓和真传，这些都确立了他在语言及教学行业中的至高地位。愿杨凡老师和他的这本书能够成为广大考生的良师益友！

借此感谢广大师生多年来对环球雅思学校的信赖，使我们很荣幸地成为数十万学子人生脚下的前进大道。祝愿环球卓尔文化公司再创历史新辉煌！

环球雅思学校总校长

环球天下教育科技集团总裁

张永琪

2012年4月

前 言

今闻《雅思阅读官方题库》备受广大雅思考生青睐，上市仅两个多月即获加印，倍感欣慰。时至今日，笔者已在雅思培训行业执教十余载。能够助更多怀揣出国梦想的年轻人一臂之力，是我在这条道路上继续前进的不竭动力。也正因如此，我在三尺讲台上传道授业解惑的同时，也力求将自己多年的教学心得和所知最大限度地传播开去。

基于此愿，在繁忙的教学工作的同时，我开始进行《雅思阅读官方题库》的编写工作。成书前我用了近一年的时间进行了大量的资料收集和考题分析工作，结合对雅思阅读的考试题型、难度和出题思路等方面的理解，编写出12套与真题考点、题型及难度等都极为接近的考题。希望笔者的诚意之作能够帮助考生取得理想的成绩。

本书的主要内容有：

1. 雅思阅读题型技巧

雅思阅读考试有很多技巧可循，而掌握这些技巧，是考生能否取得理想成绩的关键。本书对几种雅思阅读常考题型做了精炼的讲解与分析，力求令考生快速掌握每种题型的解题技巧。

2. 最新雅思阅读试题

备考雅思阅读，真题虽是最好的材料，无奈题数有限。为了达到最为真实的考题效果，让广大雅思考生充分感受真题氛围，笔者做了大量的试题研究和分析工作，最终编写出12套与真题极为接近的学术类考题。值得一提的是，这12套试题均经过雅思考官的严格审定，从而使试题的质量得到了保证。

3. 考题详解及参考译文

本书在每套题后都提供了考题精解和参考译文以帮助考生更透彻地理解考题和关键信息点，把握文章的逻辑层次，同时扫清阅读障碍。

4. 最新雅思阅读机经

鉴于每年的雅思阅读考试都有重复考查的话题，且这些话题重复出现的次数较多，考生有必要熟悉这些话题。所以本书在最后的附录中提供了近百个阅读机经考题回忆，帮助考生熟悉高频话题，了解相关背景知识。

汗水浇灌硕果，付出总有回报，备考雅思的道路上难免会遇到挫折与困难，但只要挺过艰难的时刻，积极面对困境，冲破黎明前的黑暗，终会看到属于自己的灿烂阳光。最后，祝广大考生雅思考试取得成功！

感谢环球教育集团总裁张永琪先生以及环球卓尔公司刘海华总经理多年来对我的支持与帮助。同时，还要感谢环球卓尔公司的编辑同仁，本书从调研论证、编写完成到出版，前后历时一年多，经过无数次的讨论、否定、修改与校验，她们为本书的出版付出了辛勤的劳动。

在本书的编辑过程中，李铁戎、李钧、郑兰宾、赵伯兰、李铁成、郑芝梅、陈光平、郑芝真、杨维勤、朱海霞、郑珊珊、李桂枝、张宝娟、冯光辉、杨林、林桂珍、张瑞娟、朱倩雨、陈培君、文苑、朱晋枫、王悫、杨希玙、陈曦、杨艳萍、赵梦、郭晓倩、朱际休、郭笑苗、王珏、赵鹏、陈成、蓝雅颖、瞿文伊、王斐也参与了资料收集及部分编写工作，在此一并致谢。

杨凡

2012年7月

目录
Contents

第一部分 雅思阅读综述

第二部分 最新雅思阅读题库

PART 1

第一部分

雅思阅读综述

一、雅思阅读概况

1. 考试时间

雅思阅读考试的时间为60分钟。

★注意：雅思听力考试中，考生在正常的答题时间之外，会有额外的10分钟时间来将答案誊写在答题纸上，而阅读考试的60分钟则将读文章、做题以及誊写答案全部包括在内，所以请考生一定要计划好时间。

2. 试题分类

雅思阅读考试分为A类（Academic，即学术类）和G类（General Training，即移民类）两类。A类和G类均分为三个部分。A类是三篇长文章，分别称为Reading Passage 1，Reading Passage 2和 Reading Passage 3，每篇文章在1 000字左右。G类的三个部分分别称为Section 1, Section 2和Section 3。Section 1是两至三篇短文章，Section 2是两篇中等长度的文章，Section 3是一篇在长度和难度上与A类相似的文章。

3. 题目的数量

雅思阅读的题数在40道题左右。40道题是出现频率最多的，有时还可能出现38、39、41甚至42道题。一般情况下，三篇文章的题数分配比较平均，每篇11–15道题。

4. 评分标准

根据答对题目的数量评定分数，各题无论难易，分值都是一样的，具体评分标准见下表：

正确题数	分数
15–19	5
20–23	5.5
24–26	6
27–29	6.5
30–32	7
33–34	7.5
35–37	8
38–39	8.5
40	9

5. 试题特点

与国内其他英语类考试相比，雅思阅读有如下两个特点：

（1）阅读量大

考生要在60分钟的时间内读完三篇难度不等总字数在2 400–3 000左右的文章，完成40道题。由于题量大、时间短，考生如不能合理安排好时间，很可能会出现答不完题的状况。

（2）题型多样

与大学英语四、六级和考研等标准化考试不同，雅思阅读考试具有题型灵活多样，测试点全面等特点，能够全面、真实地反映考生的英语运用能力。所涉及的题型共有十种。

虽然阅读量大，题型也多，但雅思阅读的评分标准并不高，从上面列出的评分标准表格中可以看出：只要答对50%（即20题），就能得5.5分；答对60%（即24题），就能得6分；答对75%（即30题），就能得7分。

雅思官方统计数据表明，每次考试，阅读的平均分是四项（听力、阅读、写作和口语）中最高的，取得6分以上、7分以上成绩的比例也是四项中最高的，甚至，每次考试都会出现有考生取得满分9分的情况。所以，也请考生树立信心，只要有一定的基础，掌握正确的答题方法，做足够数量的练习，就能取得令自己满意的分数。

二、雅思阅读四要素

1. 词汇

词汇对于雅思阅读来说“既重要，也不重要”。一方面，词汇是阅读的核心，没有一定的词汇量，阅读免谈。另一方面，没有必要花很多时间在准备词汇上。有的考生把准备阅读的一半的时间都用在背单词上，而且记了很多偏、难、怪词，其实这样不但浪费时间效果也不理想，应该集中精力突破雅思阅读高频词汇。

2. 技巧

雅思阅读考试的最大特点是题型多样，考查重点往往聚焦在对文章主旨结构的理解以及考生定位和理解文章细节的能力上。而不同的题型有着不同的特点，考生在备考过程中要认真学习并掌握雅思阅读各题型的特点和做题技巧。

3. 做题

许多考生在备考时，倾向于搞题海战术，希望能从大量的做题中提高自己的信心，他们觉得做完题对完答案就万事大吉了，不愿做分析总结，所以很多时候他们并不十分清楚自己错在什么地方。其实，在复习的时候错的那些题永远要比对的那些题来得有价值，如果没有及时分析原因，到真正考试的时候可能还会在同样的地方犯错。因此，考生在做完本书的每套题后，都应该对自己做错的题目进行总结和分析，这样可有针对性地克服相对薄弱的题型。

4．机经

由于雅思考试很频繁，几乎每个星期都会举行，研发考题的速度远远跟不上考试的频度，所以，雅思考试题目是重复出现的。而参加考试的考生回忆，就弥足珍贵。因为，很有可能你在考试中遇到的题目就是这些考生考过的题目。考生的考试回忆，俗称为“机经”。看阅读机经，就像看中文科普小说一样，花的时间很少，却能起到锦上添花的作用。对于一些基础薄弱的考生，可能还会起到决定性的作用。

三、雅思阅读的时间分配

正确的时间分配有助于考生在考场上最大限度地发挥自己的实际水平，提高整体正确率。合理的时间安排，原则上是20分钟一篇，但是考生都有自己熟悉的话题和有把握的题材。所以，在正式开始做题之前，考生不妨通过标题浏览等方式Skim三篇文章，按照自己的实际情况对三篇文章的难易程度进行定位，确定哪篇文章是自己把握比较大的，对于这种比较有把握的文章一定要保证时间充足，这样有助于整体正确率的提升。但是每一篇文章原则上最多不超过25分钟，否则考生是没有办法有效率地完成40道题目的。

四、双向式阅读法

雅思阅读文章大都比较长，信息量大。这样一篇带着10余个题目的长文章摆在面前，到底应该怎样阅读和做题呢？

许多考生选择先将文章从头到尾细读一遍，然后做题。这种方法虽然准确率较高，但却很浪费时间，即使英语基础好的考生，通常在考试时间内，也会做不完题。

下面，我们来介绍一下“双向式阅读法”，这种方法的阅读步骤如下：

Step 1　先读一下文章的标题。

文章的标题所表达的是文章的大意，在做题前，读文章的标题，了解文章的主要内容，用时不多，效果很好。

Step 2　开始做题，参照各题型技巧依次做题。

做题与读文章同步进行，这样在做完题的同时，也读完了文章。鉴于雅思阅读题型众多，掌握各题型的解题技巧对于考生来说十分必要。关于各题型的解题技巧，后面会有讲解。

一篇文章，通常会出现三种题型，也有两种甚至四、五种题型出现的情况，但不多。可以按照题型顺序依次做，也可以两种甚至更多题型一起做。对于基础一般的考生来说，适合按照题型顺序依次做，这样更清楚，更简单，准确率更高。基础较好的考生，适合两种甚至更多题型一起做，这样速度更快，能做对更多的题目。

五、各题型的解题技巧

雅思阅读考试的题型一直以来都呈现出灵活多样的特点，将其归纳起来可分成如下五大类：

- 有顺序性的细节题
- 无顺序性的细节题
- 段落标题配对题
- 全文主旨题
- 特殊题型

下面，我们来分别讲解这五大类的解题技巧。

1. 顺序性的细节题

“顺序性”是指题目的顺序与原文的顺序一致。“顺序性的细节题”具体包括如下六种题型：

- 判断题（True / False / Not Given）
- 简答题（Short Answer Question）
- 摘要填空题（Summary Completion）
- 选择题（Multiple Choice）
- 图表填空题（Diagram / Table / Flow Chart）
- 句子填空题（Sentence Completion）

鉴于这六种题型的答案对应信息在文中出现都有一定的顺序性，在做题时可按题目顺序从前往后依次做。做每道题时，分三步：

Step 1　读题

仔细阅读题干，读懂题干的大致意思，划出其中的关键词（可能不只一个词）。

Step 2 定位

根据划出的关键词，在原文中找出能和题干相对应的一句话或者几句话，多为一句话，少数情况下，是原文中连续的几句话。

有两种定位方法：

（1）特殊词定位法

题干中如果包含年代、人名、地名、数字、专有名词和特别生僻的词，这些词肯定是关键词，因为在设题时一般不会对这些词做改变，依据这些词考生不需要阅读全文，就能直接对应到原文的某一句话。

（2）顺序性定位法

由于这六种题型是有顺序性的，所以第1题的答案应在文章的前部，第2题的答案应在第1题的答案之后，在第3题的答案之前。这个规律虽有助于考生确定答案的位置，但需要考生阅读原文，读懂原文各段落或句子的大意。

Step 3 确定答案

仔细阅读定位出来的句子，读懂其大意，结合题干，确定正确答案。

2. 无顺序性的细节题

“无顺序性的细节题”与“顺序性的细节题”最主要的区别是：题目的顺序与原文的顺序不一致。“无顺序性的细节题”分为以下三种类型：

- 事物及其特征的搭配
- 作者及其观点的搭配
- 信息及段落的搭配

这三种题型的解题方法相同，如下：

（1）先将此题型的所有题干都看一遍，读懂每个题干的大意。

（2）快速阅读原文，并不断与题干相对照，确定正确答案。

因为在读原文之前，已了解了各种题干的大体信息，所以最好只读一遍文章就能做出绝大多数的题目。比如一组6道题，要能找到4–5道题的答案。

由于有些题干的关键词并不明显，所以在快速阅读文章时，会有个别题干没有与原文对应上，对于这样的情况，可以有如下的解决办法：

（1）如果有印象在文章的某个部位，仔细阅读原文的该部分，确定答案。

（2）如果印象全无，但时间比较充裕，再快速读一遍原文，寻找这几个题的答案。

因为这三种题型的题目顺序与原文的顺序不一致，所以切不可按题目顺序在原文中依次定位答案，一定要带着所有题目与原文进行对照，找出正确答案。

3．段落标题配对题

段落标题配对题是雅思阅读考试中比较特别的题型，因为大部分的题型都是考查考生对细节的理解，而段落标题配对题考查的是考生对段落主旨的把握能力。这一题型是配对题中最为繁琐耗时的一个，并且出题的频率很高。其题型特点和解题步骤如下：

（1）题型特点

1）位于文章之前。

在众多雅思阅读题型中， 段落标题配对题是惟一一个位于文章之前的题型，可以将之理解为考官建议考生事先完成这种题型，因为对文章主旨的把握有助于考生更好地寻找文章中的细节。

2）选项以短语形式出现，数量大于段落数，且为乱序。

在选项列表中，每个选项都是以短语的形式出现，考生需要从中选出最能够概括段落大意或者主要内容的短语。为了干扰考生，选项中会有若干干扰选项，需要考生仔细筛选鉴别。

3）题目中会给出示例；选项不可重复使用。

一般情况下，段落标题配对题的题目中会有一个Example，会给出某一段落的答案选项。由于不可能出现一个选项使用两次的情况，因此给出的答案可以排除。

（2）解题步骤

1） 浏览文章。

如果文章有标题、副标题、图片和小标题等，一定要在做题之前仔细阅读这些信息，因为这些信息往往暗示了文章的主题，这对于考生把握全文大意，排除干扰选项会有一定的帮助。

2）划掉示例中的选项。

由于选项不可能被重复使用，因此Example中的选项不可能再次出现，故没有必要浪费时间去阅读这部分内容。所以直接在这个选项上划叉即可。

3）通读题干，划出关键词。

在关键词的选择上，谨记其unique的特点，另外主谓宾为首选，或者遵循名动形副的原则。划出之后，进行短时记忆。

4）寻找主题句，确定正确答案。

以原文段落作为解题的方向，从首段开始迅速扫描，因为段落首尾句通常是该段的主题句，所以一定要精读段首句与段尾句，泛读其他语句，尽量理解段落主题。在阅读过程中，查看是否有信息和题干中所划出的关键词吻合，进而确定正确答案。反复出现的词或专有名词一定是文章重点关注的对象。冒号、引号、及破折号后的内容常常是考点。根据含有转折、递进、因果、对比、绝对、相对之意的小词也能推断出句与句之间的逻辑关联。

主题句的特征：

a. 如果段落的第一句中包含让步状语，则该句一定是主题句。

主题句中的让步状语，常为如下句式：

Although A...，B...

While A...，B...

Despite A...，B...

中文意思是：虽然 A，但是 B。要说明的观点在B中，所以B肯定是主题句。

b. 如果段落的第一句是如下句型，则该句一定是主题句。

Doing something is not easy.

Doing something is complicated.

Doing something is difficult.

Doing something is complex.

It is not easy to do something.

It is complicated to do something.

It is difficult to do something.

It is complex to do something.

正确选项通常为：doing something或 how to do something 或 methods of doing something。

c. 如果段落的第一句是问句，它肯定不是主题句，第二句是主题句。

d. 如果段落中的某句话是以举例子的形式出现，其前面的句子是主题句。

举例子的句子，通常采用如下句型：

A..., for example, B...

A是主题句，B不是主题句。

e. 如果段落中某句话是如下句型，则该句一定是主题句。

A show that B

A showing that B

A suggest that B

A demonstrate that B

show, suggest, demonstrate是“表明”、“说明”的意思，其后的宾语从句B往往是要说明的观点，是该段话的主旨。

f. 如果段落中的最后一句话是如下句型，该句一定是主题句。

This/That is...

4．全文主旨题

此类题型要求考生找出一篇文章的主旨，即整篇文章的中心意思。关于这类题型考生应了解以下几点：

（1）题目以“四选一”或“五选一”的形式出现。

（2）题干中常有the aim of the writer（作者写文章的目的）、the title（文章的标题）、the main theme（文章的主旨）等词。

（3）通常为文章考题的最后一题。

因为这篇文章已经作了十多个题目，文章的主要意思应该是清楚的。这时，不需再看文章，即可直接做出来。一般全文主旨题还是比较简单的。

5．特殊题型

有些题型通常只在某一篇文章中出现，不能归入前面四大类中的任何一类，因此没有固定的方法和规律，做这类题型时一定要注意看清题目的要求。

PART 2

第二部分

最新雅思阅读题库

TEST 1

Candidate Number

Candidate Name

INTERNATIONAL ENGLISH LANGUAGE TESTING SYSTEM

ACADEMIC READING

TIME 1 hour

INSTRUCTIONS TO CANDIDATES

Do not open this booklet until you are told to do so.

Write your name and candidate number in the spaces at the top of this page.

Start at the beginning of the test and work through it.

You should answer **all** questions.

If you cannot do a particular question, leave it and go on to the next. You can return to it later.

All answers must be written on the answer sheet.

Do not remove this booklet from the examination room.

INFORMATION FOR CANDIDATES

There are **40** questions on this question paper.

The test is divided as follows:

Reading Passage 1	Questions 1–13
Reading Passage 2	Questions 14–26
Reading Passage 3	Questions 27–40

Reading Answer Sheet

Are you: Female? ▭ Male? ▭

Your first language code: 0 1 2 3 4 5 6 7 8 9 / 0 1 2 3 4 5 6 7 8 9 / 0 1 2 3 4 5 6 7 8 9

IELTS Reading Answer Sheet

Module taken (shade one box): Academic ▭ General Training ▭

		✓ ✗			✓ ✗
1		1	21		21
2		2	22		22
3		3	23		23
4		4	24		24
5		5	25		25
6		6	26		26
7		7	27		27
8		8	28		28
9		9	29		29
10		10	30		30
11		11	31		31
12		12	32		32
13		13	33		33
14		14	34		34
15		15	35		35
16		16	36		36
17		17	37		37
18		18	38		38
19		19	39		39
20		20	40		40

Checker's Initials		Marker's Initials		Band Score		Reading Total	

READING PASSAGE 1

*You should spend about 20 minutes on **Questions 1–13**, which are based on Reading Passage 1 below.*

The Rollfilm Revolution

The introduction of the dry plate process brought with it many advantages. Not only was it much more convenient, so that the photographer no longer needed to prepare his material in advance, but its much greater sensitivity made possible a new generation of cameras. Instantaneous exposures had been possible before, but only with some difficulty and with special equipment and conditions. Now, exposures short enough to permit the camera to be held in the hand were easily achieved. As well as fitting shutters and viewfinders to their conventional stand cameras, manufacturers began to construct smaller cameras intended specifically for hand use.

One of the first designs to be published was Thomas Bolas's "Detective" camera of 1881. Externally a plain box, quite unlike the folding bellows camera typical of the period, it could be used unobtrusively. The name caught on, and for the next decade or so almost all hand cameras were called "Detectives". Many of the new designs in the 1880s were for magazine cameras, in which a number of dry plates could be pre-loaded and changed one after another following exposure. Although much more convenient than stand cameras, still used by most serious workers, magazine plate cameras were heavy, and required access to a darkroom for loading and processing the plates. This was all changed by a young American bank clerk turned photographic manufacturer, George Eastman, from Rochester, New York.

Eastman had begun to manufacture gelatine dry plates in 1880, being one of the first to do so in America. He soon looked for ways of simplifying photography, believing that many people were put off by the complication and messiness. His first step was to develop, with the camera manufacturer William H. Walker, a holder for a long roll of paper negative "film". This could be fitted to a standard plate camera and up to forty-eight exposures made before reloading. The combined weight of the paper roll and the holder was far less than the same number of glass plates in their light-tight wooden holders. Although roll-holders had been made as early as the 1850s, none had been very successful because of the limitations of the photographic materials then available. Eastman's rollable paper film was sensitive and gave negatives of good quality; the Eastman-Walker roll-holder was a great success.

The next step was to combine the roll-holder with a small hand camera: Eastman's first design was patented with an employer F. M. Cossitt, in 1886. It was not a success. Only fifty Eastman detective cameras were made, and they were sold as a lot to a dealer in 1887; the cost was too high and the design too complicated. Eastman set about developing a new model, which was launched in June 1888. It was a small box, containing a roll of paper-based stripping film sufficient for 100 circular exposures 6 cm in diameter. Its operation was simple: set the shutter by pulling a wire string; aim the camera using the V line impression in the camera top; press the release button to activate the exposure; and turn a special key to wind on the film. A hundred exposures had to be made, so it was important to record each picture in the memorandum book provided, since there was no exposure counter. Eastman gave his camera the invented name "Kodak", which was easily pronounceable in most languages, and had two Ks which Eastman felt was a firm, uncompromising kind of letter.

The importance of Eastman's new roll-film camera was not that it was the first. There had been several earlier cameras, notably the Stirn "America", first demonstrated in the spring of 1887 and on sale from early 1888. This also used a roll of negative paper, and had such refinements as a reflecting viewfinder and an ingenious exposure marker. The real significance of the first Kodak camera was that it was backed up by a developing and printing service. Hitherto, virtually all photographers developed and printed their own pictures. This required the facilities of a darkroom and the time and inclination to handle the necessary chemicals, make the prints and so on. Eastman recognized that not everyone had the resources or the desire to do these. When a customer had made a hundred exposures in the Kodak camera, he sent it to Eastman's factory in Rochester where the film was unloaded, processed and printed, the camera reloaded and returned to the owner. "You Press the Button, We Do the Rest" ran Eastman's classic marketing slogan; photography had been brought to everyone. Everyone, that is, who could afford $25 or five guineas for the camera and $10 or two guineas for the developing and printing. A guinea ($5) was a week's wages for many at the time, so this simple camera cost the equivalent of hundreds of dollars today.

In 1889 an improved model with a new shutter design was introduced, and it was called the No. 2 Kodak camera. The paper-based stripping film was complicated to manipulate, since the processed negative image had to be stripped from the paper base for printing. At the end of 1889 Eastman launched a new roll film on a celluloid base. Clear, tough, transparent and flexible, the new film not only made the roll-film camera fully practical, but provided the raw material for the introduction of cinematography a few years later. Other, larger models were introduced, including several folding versions, one of which took pictures 21.6 cm x 16.5 cm in size. Other manufacturers in America and Europe introduced cameras to take the Kodak roll-films, and other firms began to offer developing and printing services for the benefit of the new breed of photographers.

By September 1889, over 5,000 Kodak cameras had been sold in the USA, and the company was daily printing 6,000–7,000 negatives. Holidays and special events created enormous surges in demand for processing: 900 Kodak users returned their cameras for processing and reloading in the week after the New York centennial celebration.

Questions 1–4

Do the following statements agree with the views of the writer in Reading Passage 1?

In boxes 1–4 on your answer sheet, write

YES	*if the statement agrees with the views of the writer*
NO	*if the statement contradicts the views of the writer*
NOT GIVEN	*if it is impossible to say what the writer thinks about this*

1 Before the introduction of the dry plate process short exposures could only be achieved with cameras held in the hand.

2 Stirn's "America" camera lacked Kodak's developing service.

3 The first Kodak film cost the equivalent of a week's wages to develop.

4 Some of Eastman's 1891 range of cameras could be loaded in daylight.

Questions 5–9

Complete the diagram below.

Choose ***NO MORE THAN THREE WORDS*** *from the passage for each answer.*

Write your answers in boxes 5–9 on your answer sheet.

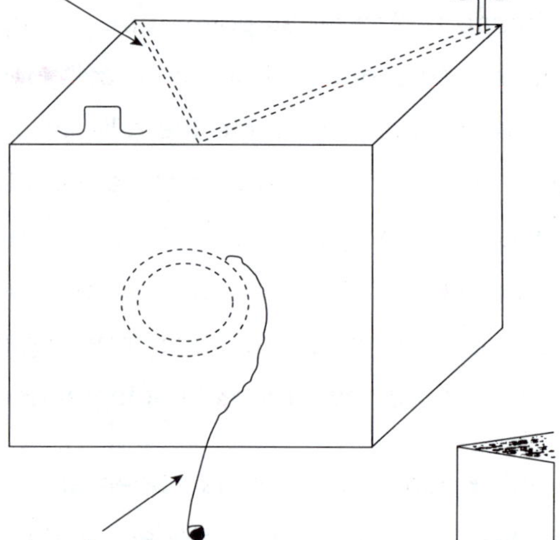

Questions 10–13

Complete the table below.

Choose ***NO MORE THAN THREE WORDS*** *from the passage for each answer.*

Write your answers in boxes 10–13 on your answer sheet.

Year	Developments	Name of Person/People
1880	Manufacture of gelatine dry plates	**10** ....
1881	Release of "Detective" camera	Thomas Bolas
11	The roll-holder combined with a **12**	Eastman and F. M. Cossitt
1889	Introduction of model with a **13**	Eastman

READING PASSAGE 2

You should spend about 20 minutes on ***Questions 14–26****, which are based on Reading Passage 2 on the following pages.*

Questions 14–18

Reading Passage 2 has seven paragraphs, **A–G**.

Choose the correct headings for paragraphs ***B–E*** *and* ***G*** *from the list of headings below.*

Write the correct number, ***i–x****, in boxes 14–18 on your answer sheet.*

List of Headings

- **i** The effect of changing demographics on organisations
- **ii** Future changes in the European workforce
- **iii** The unstructured interview and its validity
- **iv** The person-skills match approach to selection
- **v** The implications of a poor person-environment fit
- **vi** Some poor selection decisions
- **vii** The validity of selection procedures
- **viii** The person-environment fit
- **ix** Past and future demographic changes in Europe
- **x** Adequate and inadequate explanations of organisational failure

Example	***Answer***
Paragraph **A**	**x**

14 Paragraph **B**

15 Paragraph **C**

16 Paragraph **D**

17 Paragraph **E**

Example	***Answer***
Paragraph **F**	**ix**

18 Paragraph **G**

People and Organisations: the Selection Issue

A In 1991, according to the Department of Trade and Industry, a record 48,000 British companies went out of business. When businesses fail, the post-mortem analysis is traditionally undertaken by accountants and market strategists. Unarguably organisations do fail because of undercapitalisation, poor financial management, adverse market conditions etc. Yet, conversely, organisations with sound financial backing, good product ideas and market acumen often underperform and fail to meet shareholders' expectations. The complexity, degree and sustainment of organisational performance requires an explanation which goes beyond the balance sheet and the "paper conversion" of financial inputs into profit making outputs. A more complete explanation of "what went wrong" necessarily must consider the essence of what an organisation actually is and that one of the financial inputs, the most important and often the most expensive, is people.

B An organisation is only as good as the people it employs. Selecting the right person for the job involves more than identifying the essential or desirable range of skills, educational and professional qualifications necessary to perform the job and then recruiting the candidate who is most likely to possess these skills or at least is perceived to have the ability and predisposition to acquire them. This is a purely person/skills match approach to selection.

C Work invariably takes place in the presence and/or under the direction of others, in a particular organisational setting. The individual has to "fit" in with the work environment, with other employees, with the organisational climate, style of work, organisation and culture of the organisation. Different organisations have different cultures. Working as an engineer at British Aerospace will not necessarily be a similar experience to working in the same capacity at GEC or Plessey.

D Poor selection decisions are expensive. For example, the costs of training a policeman are about £20, 000. The costs of employing an unsuitable technician on an oil rig or in a nuclear plant could, in an emergency, result in millions of pounds of damage or loss of life. The disharmony of a poor person-environment fit (PE-fit) is likely to result in low job satisfaction, lack of organisational commitment and employee stress, which affect organisational outcomes i.e. productivity, high labour turnover and absenteeism, and individual outcomes i.e. physical, psychological and mental well-being.

E However, despite the importance of the recruitment decision and the range of sophisticated and more objective selection techniques available, including the use of psychometric tests, assessment centres etc., many organisations are still prepared to make this decision on the basis of a single 30 to 45 minute unstructured interview. Indeed, research has demonstrated that a selection decision is often made within the first four minutes of the interview. In the remaining time, the interviewer then attends exclusively to information that reinforces the initial "accept" or "reject" decision. Research into the validity of selection methods has consistently demonstrated that the unstructured interview, where the interviewer asks any questions he or she likes, is a poor predictor of future job performance and fares little better than more controversial methods like graphology and astrology. In times of high unemployment, recruitment becomes a "buyer's market" and this was the case in Britain during the 1980s.

F The future, we are told, is likely to be different. Detailed surveys of social and economic trends in the European Community show that Europe's population is falling and getting older. The birth rate in the Community is now only three-quarters of the level needed to ensure replacement of the existing population. By the year 2020, it is predicted that more than one in four Europeans will be aged 60 or more and barely one in five will be under 20. In a five-year period between 1983 and 1988 the Community's female workforce grew by almost six million. As a result, 51% of all women aged 14 to 64 are now economically active in the labour market compared with 78% of men.

G The changing demographics will not only affect selection ratios. They will also make it increasingly important for organisations wishing to maintain their competitive edge to be more responsive and accommodating to the changing needs of their workforce if they are to retain and develop their human resources. More flexible working hours, the opportunity to work from home or job share, the provision of childcare facilities etc., will play a major role in attracting and retaining staff in the future.

Questions 19–22

Do the following statements agree with the views of the writer in Reading Passage 2?

In boxes 19–22 on your answer sheet, write

YES	*if the statement agrees with the writer*
NO	*if the statement contradicts the views of the writer*
NOT GIVEN	*if it is impossible to say what the writer thinks about this*

19 Organisations should recognise that their employees are significant parts of their financial assets.

20 Unstructured 45-minute interviews are the best method to identify suitable employees.

21 Graphology is a good predictor of future job performance.

22 The rise in the female workforce in the European Community is a positive trend.

Questions 23–26

Complete the table below with words taken from Reading Passage 2.

Use ***NO MORE THAN TWO WORDS*** *for each answer.*

Write your answers in boxes 23–26 on your answer sheet.

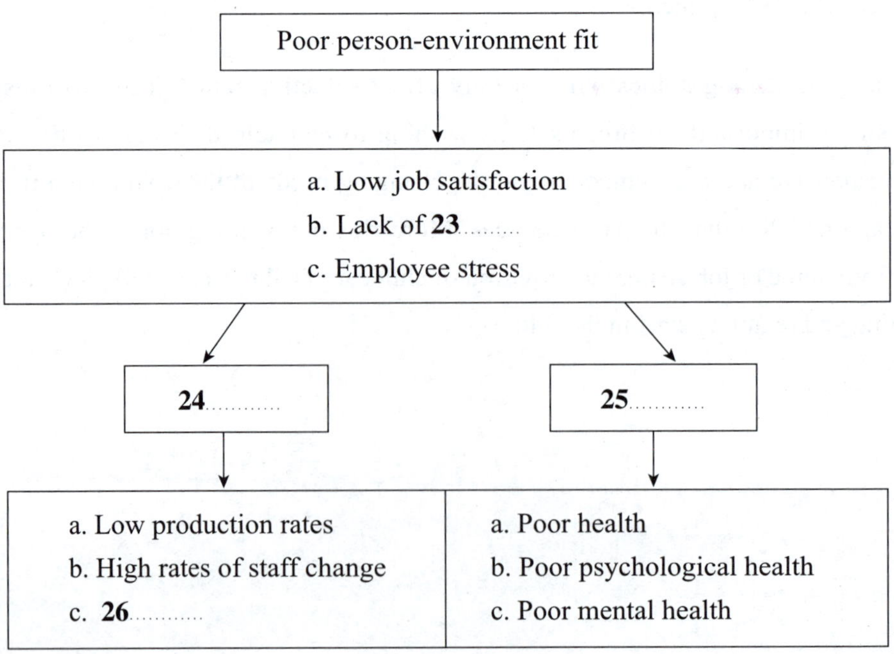

READING PASSAGE 3

*You are advised to spend about 20 minutes on **Questions 27–40**, which refer to Reading Passage 3 below.*

Why Some Women Cross the Finish Line Ahead of Men?

A Women who apply for jobs in middle or senior management have a higher success rate than men, according to an employment survey. But of course far fewer of them apply for these positions. The study, by recruitment consultants NB Selection, shows that while one in six men who appear on interview shortlists get jobs, the figure rises to one in four for women.

B The study concentrated on applications for management positions in the $45,000 to $110,000 salary range and found that women are more successful than men in both the private and public sectors. Dr Elisabeth Marx from Londonbased NB Selection described the findings as encouraging for women, in that they send a positive message to them to apply for interesting management positions. But she added, "We should not lose sight of the fact that significantly fewer women apply for senior positions in comparison with men."

C Reasons for higher success rates among women are difficult to isolate. One explanation suggested is that if a woman candidate manages to get on a shortlist, then she has probably already proved herself to be an exceptional candidate. Dr Marx said that when women apply for positions they tend to be better qualified than their male counterparts but are more selective and conservative in their job search. Women tend to research thoroughly before applying for positions or attending interviews. Men, on the other hand, seem to rely on their ability to sell themselves and to convince employers that any shortcomings they have will not prevent them from doing a good job.

D Managerial and executive progress made by women is confirmed by the annual survey of boards of directors carried out by Korn/Ferry/Carre/Orban International. This year the survey shows a doubling of the number of women serving as nonexecutive directors compared with the previous year. However, progress remains painfully slow and there were still only 18 posts filled by women out of a total of 354 nonexecutive positions surveyed. Hilary Sears, a partner with Korn/Ferry, said, women have raised the level of grades we are employed in but we have still not broken through barriers to the top.

E In Europe a recent feature of corporate life in the recession has been the delayering of management structures. Sears said that this has halted progress for women in as much as delayering has taken place either where women are working or in layers they aspire to. Sears also noted a positive trend from the recession, which has been the growing number of women who have started up on their own.

F In business as a whole, there are a number of factors encouraging the prospect of greater equality in the workforce. Demographic trends suggest that the number of women going into employment is steadily increasing. In addition a far greater number of women are now passing through higher education, making them better qualified to move into management positions.

G Organisations such as the European Women's Management Development Network provide a range of opportunities for women to enhance their skills and contacts. Through a series of both panEuropean and national workshops and conferences the barriers to women in employment are being broken down. However, Ariane Berthoin Antal, director of the International Institute for Organisational Change of Archamps in France, said that there is only anecdotal evidence of changes in recruitment patterns. And she said, "It's still so hard for women to even get on to shortlists, there are so many hurdles and barriers." Antal agreed that there have been some positive signs but said "Until there is a belief among employers, until they value the difference, nothing will change."

Questions 27–32

Reading passage 3 has seven paragraphs **A–G**.

Which paragraph contains the following information?

Write the appropriate letter, ***A–G****, in boxes 27–32 on your answer sheet.*

27 The drawbacks of current company restructuring patterns

28 Associations that provide support for professional women

29 The success rate of female job applicants for management positions

30 Male and female approaches to job applications

31 Reasons why more women are being employed in the business sector

32 The improvement in female numbers on company management structures

Questions 33–36

Look at the following statements and the list of people in the box below.

*Match each statement with the correct person **A–C**.*

*Write the correct letter **A–C** in boxes 33–36 on your answer sheet.*

33 Selection procedures do not favour women.

34 The number of female-run businesses is increasing.

35 Male applicants exceed female applicants for top posts.

36 Women hold higher positions now than they used to.

A	Dr Marx
B	Hilary Sears
C	Ariane Berthoin Antal

Questions 37–40

Answer the questions below.

*Choose **NO MORE THAN THREE WORDS** from the passage for each answer.*

Write your answers in boxes 37–40 on your answer sheet.

37 What change has there been in the number of women in top management positions detailed in the annual survey?

38 What aspect of company structuring has disadvantaged women?

39 What information tells us that more women are working nowadays?

40 Which group of people should change their attitude to recruitment?

Test 1 答案速查 Key

READING PASSAGE 1

1. NO	**2.** YES	**3.** NO
4. NOT GIVEN	**5.** A Wire String	**6.** set the shutter
7. aim the camera	**8.** (The) Memorandum Book	**9.** record each picture
10. Eastman	**11.** 1886	**12.** small hand camera
13. new shutter design		

READING PASSAGE 2

14. iv	**15.** viii
16. v	**17.** iii
18. i	**19.** YES
20. NO	**21.** NO
22. NOT GIVEN	**23.** organisational commitment
24. organisational outcomes	**25.** individual outcomes
26. absenteeism	

READING PASSAGE 3

27. E	**28.** G	**29.** A	**30.** C	**31.** F
32. D	**33.** C	**34.** B	**35.** A	**36.** B
37. doubling	**38.** delayering	**39.** demographic trends		**40.** employers

Test 1 考题精解 Detailed Explanation

READING PASSAGE 1

Questions 1–4

题型：判断题 (YES/NO/NOT GIVEN)

◆ 解析

1. NO

根据题干关键词short exposures可定位到原文第一段的第三、四句Instantaneous exposures had been possible before, but only with some difficulty and with special equipment and conditions.

Now, exposures short enough to permit the camera to be held in the hand were easily achieved.，由这两句可知瞬时曝光在以前虽能实现，但却有一定的难度，而如今，则很容易实现，而题干说短时曝光只有将相机拿在手里才能实现，此表述明显与原文不一致。另外需要提醒考生的是题干中若出现must, only, all及always一般情况下不会为YES/TRUE。

2. YES

根据题干关键词Stirn “America”，Kodak和developing service可定位到原文第五段，该段提到了两款照相机品牌Stirn “America” 和Kodak，提Stirn “America” 的目的是想说明Kodak不是第一款新型照相机，Stirn “America” 的某些功能甚至早于它就已拥有，进而引出关键句The real significance of the first Kodak camera was that it was backed up by a developing and printing service，即第一款柯达相机出现的真正意义是其拥有冲洗服务，由此可见Stirn “America” 一定是缺乏此项服务，所以答案为YES。

3. NO

根据题干关键词the equivalent of, a week 和develop可定位到原文第五段的倒数一、二句Everyone, that is, who could afford $25 or five guineas for the camera and $10 or two guineas for the developing and printing. A guinea($5) was a week's wages for many at the time, so this simple camera cost the equivalent of hundreds of dollars today，这两句主要说的是当时购买一款相机需要花费25美元或5几尼，做冲洗则需10美元或2几尼，而1几尼则相当于当时好多人一周的工资，而题干说冲胶片的花费相当于一周的工资，根据原文可知冲胶片的花费不止1几尼，也就是所需花费不止一周的工资，所以题干的说法是错的。

4. NOT GIVEN

题干所表述的1891在原文中并没出现，所以该题答案为NOT GIVEN。

Questions 5–9

题型：填图题 (DIAGRAM)

◆ 解析

5–9 A Wire String, set the shutter, aim the camera, (The) Memorandum Book, record each picture

根据图中已知的两个信息“V Linc Impression” 和 “Special Key” 可定位到原文第四段的第六、七句Its operation was simple: set the shutter by pulling a wire string; aim the camera using the V line impression in the camera top; press the release bottom to activate the exposure; and turn a special key to wind on the film. A hundred exposures had to be made, so it was important to record each picture in the memorandum book provided, since there was no exposure counter，仔细阅读不难得知，这两句是在讲述照相机曝光的操作步骤，考生只要根据句中

的描述，将每一步骤对应到图表中即可轻松找到答案。

Questions 10–13

题型：图表填空题 (TABLE COMPLETION)

◆ 解析

该题是关于时间、事件及人物的填图填表题。注意，可将时间作为定位关键词。答案要求在三个词之内。

10. Eastman

根据题干关键词1880和gelatine dry plates可定位到第三段首句Eastman had begun to manufacture gelatine dry plates in 1880, being one of the first to do so in America，由该句可知1880年胶质干片的生产者是Eastman。

11. 1886

12. small hand camera

根据题干关键词roll-holder，Eastman and F.M. Cossitt可定位到原文第四段的首句The next step was to combine the roll-holder with a small hand camera: Eastman's first design was patented with an employee, F. M. Cossitt, in 1886，由该句可知Eastman and F.M. Cossitt是于1886年将胶卷储存器与小型手持相机结合起来的。

13. new shutter design

根据题干关键词1889，introduction of model可定位到原文第六段的首句In 1889 an improved model with a new shutter design was introduced, and it was called the No. 2 Kodak camera，由该句可知1889年问世的是一款拥有全新快门设计的相机。

◎ 参考译文

胶卷革命

照相机干板照相法的引进带来了很多好处。这种方法更加方便易行，摄影师再也不用提前准备材料了，而且其更高的敏感度使得相机更新换代成为可能。瞬时曝光以前需要在特殊的装备和条件下才能够实现，操作起来也有一定的难度。如今将相机拿在手里就能进行的短时曝光已经很容易实现。除了给传统的三脚架照相机配备快门和取景器外，制造商们开始制造更小的适合手持的相机。

1881年发布的托马斯·柏拉斯的"Detective"照相机是最早的一款。该款照相机的外观就是一个简单的盒子，这与当时典型的风箱式照相机大相径庭，使用起来并不是很扎眼。"Detective"这个名字也因此变得流行起来，接下来的大约十年里几乎所有的手持式相机都被称为"Detectives"。19世纪80年代的新设计多是自动卷片照相机，在这些相机中，许多干片可以预装并在曝光后依次替换。尽管使用起来要比支架照相机方便得多，但仍只是被多数专业工作人员所采用，自动卷片干板照相机仍然笨重，并需要进入暗室进行装载和处理干片。所有这一切都被一位年轻的美国银行职员所改变，他就是后来成为摄影器材制造商的来自纽约罗契斯特的乔治·伊斯曼。

伊斯曼早在1880年就开始制造胶质干片，他也是最早在美国制作此种干片的人士之一。他认为照相机因其繁琐复杂、不易操作而不为大众接受，基于此，他很快便找到了简化摄影术的办法。他首先是与相机制造商威廉·H·沃克开发了一款能放置长卷纸质底片的装置。这个改进可以与标准的干板相机相匹配并且在重装之前可以完成多达48次曝光。纸卷和其储存器的组合重量要远远小于相同数量的玻璃板和其不透光的木质储存器的重量。尽管胶卷储存器在19世纪50年代就已被发明，但由于受当时可用的摄影器材所限，还没有人能成功地对其加以利用。伊斯曼的可卷纸质胶片非常敏感且底片质量高；伊斯曼-沃克胶卷储存器因此获得了巨大的成功。

接下来是把胶卷储存器和一个小的手持式照相机结合起来。伊斯曼的第一款设计是在1886年和一个名叫F. M. 科西特的雇员一起完成的，并被授予了专利。但此款设计并不成功。当时只生产了50台伊斯曼detective相机，并于1887年批量卖给了一个商人。相机制造的成本太高，设计也过于复杂。伊斯曼于是着手开发一款新型号的相机，并在1888年6月投产。新型相机是一个小盒子，盒子里是一卷纸基乳胶片，这些乳胶片足够进行一百次直径达6厘米的环形曝光。其操作也非常简单：拉动金属线来开动快门，利用相机顶部的V型线痕瞄准，按下释放键触发曝光，旋转特殊键来缠绕胶片。由于当时没有曝光计数器，要进行上百次曝光，在可用的记事本上记录下每一张照片就非常重要。伊斯曼用一个新造的词“Kodak”来命名他的相机，这个名字在大多数语言中都容易发音，并且有两个字母“K”，伊斯曼认为这是种牢固的、坚定的字母。

伊斯曼的新式胶卷照相机的重要之处并不在于它是第一款新型相机，之前已经有一些更早的照相机先行问世，如名动当时的Stirn“America”，它于1887年春天第一次亮相，并在1888年初上市销售。这款相机也使用了纸质底片，并有了一些诸如反射式取景窗和设计独特的曝光标志的改进。第一款柯达相机的真正意义在于它拥有冲洗服务的支持。在此之前，几乎所有的摄影师都得自己冲洗照片。这就要求摄影师要拥有一个暗室及相关设备、时间，还愿意去操作必要的化学物质和打印出照片等等。伊斯曼意识到并不是每个人都拥有那些资源和热情去做这些工作。顾客用柯达相机做了上百次曝光后，他只需将相机送到伊斯曼在罗契斯特的工厂，在那里，胶片被拆下，处理并且打印出来，而相机则被重新装好并还给机主。伊斯曼经典的销售口号是“请你按下快门，其他的事由我们来做”；摄影从此惠及了每个人。这里所说的每个人是指那些能够支付25美元或者5几尼购买相机，并能为冲洗和打印支付10美元或2几尼的人。一几尼（5美元）

在那时是大多数人一周的工资，所以这款简易相机的花费相当于现在的几百美元。

1889年，一种拥有全新快门设计的改进型相机问世了，它被称为第二代柯达相机。纸质的乳胶片操作起来比较复杂，因为打印照片需要把处理过的图像底片从纸基上取出。在1889年底，伊斯曼推出了一款新的以赛璐珞为基底的胶卷。新的胶片清晰、坚韧、透明而且可弯曲，它不仅使胶卷相机完全实用，而且为几年后电影术的推广提供了材料。另外，更大型号的相机被推广，包括几种可折叠的款式，其中一款可以拍摄尺寸为21.6 cm × 16.5cm的照片。美国和欧洲的其他制造商引进了使用柯达胶卷的照相机，而其他的公司则为了新生代摄影师的利益开始提供冲洗服务。

截止1889年9月，在美国，超过5 000个柯达相机已经被售出，而且柯达公司每天要打印6 000–7 000张底片。假日和特殊事件造成了处理胶卷需求的激增：在纽约百年庆典后的一星期里，900个柯达使用者返还了他们的相机以处理和重装。

READING PASSAGE 2

Questions 14–18

题型：段落标题配对题 (LTST OF HEADINGS)

◆ 解析

14. iv

该段主题句为尾句This is a purely person/skills match approach to selection，讲的是个人与技能配对的选拔方法，iv项与主题句表述完全一致，故为正确选项。

15. viii

该段主题句为第二句The individual has to “fit” in with the work environment, with other employees, with the organisational climate, style of work, organisation and culture of the organisation，主要讲的是个人要适应公司的环境，同事，企业文化等等，viii项与主题句表述一致，故为正确选项。

16. v

该段主题句为首句Poor selection decisions are expensive，即人员任用不当的代价是惨重的，之后一句的For example就是对用人不当后果做举例说明，v项不良的个人—环境适配的影响对该段主题做了准确的总结，故为正确答案。注意该题容易误选为vi Some poor selection decisions，而该段侧重说的是Some poor selection decisions造成的不利影响。

17. iii

该段主题句为首句However, despite the importance of the recruitment decision and the range of sophisticated and more objective selection techniques available, including the use of psychometric tests, assessment centres etc., many organisations are still prepared to make this decision on the basis of a single 30 to 45 minute unstructured interview，主要讲的是虽然任用决定很重要且有很多虽复杂但更客观的选拔方法，可很多公司仍然准备通过一个30–45分钟的不系统的面试来做决定。众选项中只有iii项有提到unstructured interview，故为正确选项。

18. i

该段主题句为第二句They will also make it increasingly important for organisations wishing to maintain in their competitive edge to be more responsive and accommodating to the changing needs of their workforce if they are to retain and develop their human resources，主要讲的是变化的人口结构对公司的影响，i项表述与本句一致，故为正确选项。

Questions 19–22

题型：判断题 (YES/NO/NOT GIVEN)

◆ 解析

19. YES

根据题干关键词organisations, employees 和 financial assets可定位到原位A段尾句A more complete explanation of "what went wrong" necessarily must consider the essence of what an organisation actually is and that one of the financial inputs, the most important and often the most expensive, is people，该句主要指出公司最重要且最昂贵的支出是人，题干表述与该句一致，故答案为YES。

20. NO

根据题干关键词unstructured 45-minute interviews可定位到原文E段倒数第二句Research into the validity of selection methods has consistently demonstrated that the unstructured interview, where the interviewer asks any questions he or she likes, is a poor predictor of future job performance and fares little better than more controversial methods like graphology and astrology，作者认为这种松散的、完全凭个人喜好提问的面试会对应聘者未来工作的表现做出不准确的预测，由此可见无系统面试并不是鉴定应聘者是否胜任工作的最佳方式，故答案为NO。

21. NO

根据题干关键词Graphology可定位到原文E段倒数第二句Research into the validity of selection methods has consistently demonstrated that the unstructured interview, where the interviewer asks any questions he or she likes, is a poor predictor of future job performance and fares little better than more controversial methods like graphology and astrology，该句中作者先是提到这种松散的、完全凭个人喜好提问的面试会对应聘者未来表现做出不准确的预测，

又说其不见得比graphology and astrology这些备受争议的方法好多少，unstructured interview已经是不好的方法了，而graphology还不如它，可见题干a good predictor of future job performance表述是错误的。

22. NOT GIVEN

根据题干关键词female workforce和European Community可定位到原位F段倒数第一、二句In a five-year period between 1983 and 1988 the Community's female workforce grew by almost six million. As a result, 51% of all women aged 14 to 64 are now economically active in the labour market compared with 78% of men，该句只是在陈述女性劳动力在增长这个事实，但并未对增长本身的趋势是消极的还是积极的做任何评价，所以答案为NOT GIVEN。

Questions 23–26

题型：表格填空题 (TABLE COMPLETION)

◆ 解析

23–26 organisational commitment, organisational outcomes, individual outcomes, absenteeism

根据已知的关键词Poor person-environment fit可定位到原文D段最后一句The disharmony of a poor person-environment fit (PE-fit) is likely to result in low job satisfaction, lack of organisational commitment and employee stress, which affect organisational outcomes i.e. productivity, high labour turnover and absenteeism, and individual outcomes i.e. physical, psychological and mental well-being，其中，原文与题干中已出现的词的对应为：

原文	题干
productivity	low production rates
high labour turnover	high rates of staff change
physical	poor health

由此很容易找到要填的词。

◎ 参考译文

人和单位：选择问题

A　据贸易与工业部称，在1991年48 000家英国公司倒闭了。关门后，照惯例会计和市场策略家对这些倒闭的公司进行了深入分析。一些公司因为资金匮乏、管理不善和不良的市场状况而宣告破产本无可厚非。然而，一些有着良好的财政支持，好的产品创意和市场眼光的公司，却也因不能满足股东的期望而纷纷破产。公司行为复杂、程度差异、渊源不同，远不是资产负债表和各种财政收支表所能说清的。要找到症结所在，我们就必须关注更本质的问题，如公司的实质是什么，以及公司最重要也是最昂贵的一项财政支出——人。

B　一个公司只有当其员工优秀了，它才能经营得好。选择适合工作岗位的员工不仅需要评定其是否拥有胜任该岗位所必需的工作能力，做这个工作所必要的教育和专业资格，还要录用可能拥有这些技能或者至少被认为拥有这些能力或有潜力开发其这些能力的人。这是纯粹的个人与技能配对的选拔方法。

C　在特定的公司背景下，员工们的工作多是在他人的指导或监督下一成不变地进行着。人们必须适应工作环境、同事、公司的风气、工作方式以及公司的结构和文化。不同的公司有着不同的企业文化。在英国航空公司当一名工程师的经历和在GEC或普莱西担任相同的职位的经历肯定是不同的。

D　人员任用不当的代价是惨重的。例如，训练一位警察的成本是大约20 000英镑。石油钻塔或核工厂在紧急情况下雇佣一位不合格的技术人员的代价是，造成数百万英镑的财产损失和人员伤亡。不和谐的人境适配可能造成很低的工作满意度，员工缺乏为公司献身的精神和工作压力，这些会影响到公司的业绩，例如，生产力低，人员流动性大和缺勤率高同时也会影响个人利益，例如，生理、心理和精神的健康。

E　然而，即使招聘的决定很重要，而且有很多虽复杂但更客观的选拔方法，这包括使用心理测试和评价中心等，但很多公司仍然准备通过一个30–45分钟的不系统的面试来做决定。的确，研究表明，选拔结果是在开始的四分钟就已经做出了。在剩下的时间里，主持面试者专门注意那些能够巩固最初的“接受”或“拒绝”决定的信息。有关选拔方法有效性进行的不断研究证明，这种松散的、完全凭个人喜好提问的面试会对应聘者未来工作的表现做出不正确的预测，并且它并不比像字系学及占星术这些备受争议的方法好多少。当遇到失业高峰时，招聘成为“买方市场”，在19世纪80年代的英国就是这种情况。

F　我们被告知未来有可能会发生变化。有关欧盟社会和经济趋势的详细调查表明欧洲的人口总数在下降并且向老龄化发展。在欧洲社会中婴儿出生率很低，只达到了维持现有人口数所需水平的3/4。据预测，截止到2020年，四个欧洲人中将有一个以上年龄在60岁或更高的人，而五个人中只有一个人是20岁以下。在1983到1988这五年间欧盟女性劳动力增长了近600万。结果是51%的14到64岁的女性在劳动力市场上活跃着，男性的这一比例是78%。

G　变化的人口结构影响的不仅是公司选拔的比例，各公司要想维系或发展他们的人力，那么，迅速调整自己以适应劳务大军的变化需求就显得日益重要。更灵活的工作时间，给予在家办公的机会，共同完成工作，提供幼托设施等，为将来吸引和留住员工起了重要作用。

READING PASSAGE 3

Questions 27–32

题型：配对题 (MATCHING)

◆ 解析

27. E

根据关键词drawbacks，company和restructuring patterns定位到E段的第一句In Europe a recent feature of corporate life in the recession has been the de-layering of management structures，三个关键词分别对应原文的delayering，corporate life和structures，题干说的是现代公司重组的缺点，原文说的是在萧条的欧洲经济背景下，公司最近的特点是管理结构层次的削减，两个信息对应，所以本题选择E。

28. G

根据关键词Associations，support对应到G段的第一句Organisations such as the European Women's Management Development Network provide a range of opportunities for women to enhance their skills and contacts，两个关键词分别对应原文的Organisations和a range of opportunities，题干说的是给职业女性提供支持，原文说的是一些像欧洲女性管理发展网这样的组织也为女性提供了一些提高她们的技能和社交关系的机会，两个信息对应，所以本题选择G。

29. A

根据关键词success rate，female job applicants 和management positions定位到A段的第一句Women who apply for jobs in middle or senior management have a higher success rate than men, according to an employment survey，三个关键词分别对应原文的success rate，Women who apply for jobs和middle or senior management，题干说的是女性申请管理职位的成功率，原文第一句说根据一项雇用调查，女性在申请中级或是高级的管理职位时比男性成功率更高，两个信息对应，所以本题选择A。

30. C

根据关键词approaches定位到原文C段第一句Reasons for higher success rates among women are difficult to isolate和最后一句Men, on the other hand, seem to rely on their ability to.... approaches对应原文的Reasons，题干说的是男性和女性申请工作的方法，原文第一句和最后一句分别说的是女性和男性申请工作的话题，所以本题选择C。

31. F

根据关键词more women和business sector定位到原文F段第一、二句In business as a whole, there are a number of factors encouraging the prospect of greater equality in the workforce. Demographic trends suggest that the number of women going into employment is steadily increasing，题干关键词与原文的the number of women going into employment is steadily increasing和In business对应，题干说的是有更多女性在公司业务部门工作的原因，原文说的是就整个市场来看，有很多因素促进劳动力市场的男女平等这一前景。人口统计学的趋势表明，女性就业的数量在稳定地增长，两个信息对应，所以本题选择F。

32. D

根据关键词numbers定位到原文D段第二句This year the survey shows a doubling of the number of women serving as non-executive directors compared with the previous year，题干说的是女性员工在公司管理职位数量的上升，原文说的是今年的调查结果显示，与上一年相比，非行政总监职位的女性数目翻番了，两个信息对应，所以本题选择D。

Questions 33–36

题型：配对题 (MATCHING)

◆ 解析

先在原文中将作者及其观点用线划出，然后依次做题。

33. C

本题的中文意思是选择过程不利于女性，与原文划线处前后一一对照，对应到原文G段中的句子However, Ariane Berthoin Antal, director of the International Institute for Organisational Change of Archamps in France, said that there is only anecdotal evidence of changes in recruitment patterns. And she said, "It's still so hard for women to even get on to shortlists, there are so many hurdles and barriers."，题干中的Selection procedures和do not favour women与原文中的recruitment patterns和so hard for women 分别对应，所以本题的观点是阿丽亚娜 · 贝图安 · 安塔尔的，故本题选择C。

34. B

本题的中文意思是女性自己开办企业的数目在增加，与原文划线处前后一一对照，对应到原文E段中的句子Sears also noted a positive trend from the recession, which has been the growing number of women who have started up on their own，题干中的female-run businesses和increasing与原文的women who have started up on their own和growing分别对应，所以本题的观点是西尔斯的，故本题选择B。

35. A

本题的中文意思是申请高级职位的男性超过女性申请者，与原文划线处前后一一对照，对应到原文B段中的句子But she added, "We should not lose sight of the fact that significantly fewer women apply for senior positions in comparison with men"，题干中的Male applicants exceed female和top posts对应原文中的significantly fewer women和senior positions，原文的这句话是由马克思博士说的，所以本题选择A项。

36. B

本题的中文意思是女性现在比以前处于更高的职位，与原文划线处前后一一对照，对应到原文D段中的句子Hilary Sears, a partner with Korn/Ferry, said, women have raised the level of grades we are employed in but we have still not broken through barriers to the top，其中hold higher positions和have raised the level of grades对应，所以本题的观点是希拉里·西尔斯的，故本题选择B。

Questions 37–40

题型：问答题 (SHORT ANSWER QUESTIONS)

◆ 解析

37. doubling

由关键词top management positions和annual survey定位到原文D段第二句This year the survey shows a doubling of the number of women serving as nonexecutive directors compared with the previous year，所以本题的答案为doubling。

38. delayering

由关键词disadvantaged women定位到原文E段首句In Europe a recent feature of corporate life in the recession has been the delayering of management structures，即对女性不利的是delayering，所以本题的答案为delayering。

39. demographic trends

由于本题没有明显的关键词，可按顺序性原则在原文第38题的答案处向后阅读，对应原文F段第二句Demographic trends suggest that the number of women going into employment is steadily increasing, suggest与题干中的tells对应，women...steadily increasing与题干的more women对应，所以本题的答案为demographic trends。

40. employers

由于本题没有明显的关键词，可按顺序性原则在原文第39题的答案处向后阅读，对应原文G段尾句Antal agreed that there have been some positive signs but said “Until there is a belief among employers, until they value the difference, nothing will change.”，其中change为原词重现，attitude to recruitment对应原文的value the difference，所以本题答案为employers。

◎ 参考译文

为什么有些妇女比男子先越过终点线?

A　根据一项雇佣调查，女性在申请中级或是高级的管理职位时比男性成功率更高。当然，她们很少去申请这些职位。一项由NB选择招聘顾问做出的研究表明，进入最后一轮面试后，男性求职者面试成功的比率为6:1，而女性则将此比率提升至了4:1。

B 这个研究集中了薪水在45 000–110 000美元的管理位置的求职申请，并且发现无论在私营机构，还是公立部门，女性求职者都更容易成功。NB选择伦敦本部的伊丽莎白·马克思博士说这个发现是可以鼓励女性的，它们发出一个积极的信息给她们去申请感兴趣的管理位置。但是她补充道，“我们不应当忽视这一值得关注的事实：和男性相比，很少有女性申请高级职位。”

C 女性高成功率的原因是很难被孤立分析出来的。一种解释是说，如果一个女性进入候选名单，那时，她可能已经被证实为一个卓越的候选者。马克思博士说，当女性申请职位时她们往往比她们的男性对手更符合资格，但是她们在选择职业时，更挑剔更保守。女性倾向于在申请职位或是参加面试前彻底研究一番。男性，相反地，更倾向于依靠他们的能力去推销自己并且使雇佣者相信他们的任何缺点都不会阻碍他们做好。

D 一个由Korn/Ferry/Carre/Orban国际完成的年度调查者排行榜证实，许多管理和行政上的进步都是由女性创造的。今年的调查结果显示，与上一年相比，非行政总监职位的女性数目翻番了。然而，进展仍然十分缓慢，在被调查的354个职位中只有18个由女性担任。Korn/Ferry的合作伙伴希拉里·西尔斯说，我们正在提高雇佣的女员工的级别，但是我们依旧没有冲破最高级别的障碍。

E 在萧条的欧洲经济背景下，公司最近的特点是管理结构层次的削减。西尔斯说，这个阻碍了女性的进步，包括现任或期望职位阶层的降低。西尔斯也提到了这种经济不景气带来的一个积极的趋势：自己创业的女性变多了。

F 就整个市场来看，有很多因素促进劳动力市场的男女平等这一前景。人口统计学的趋势表明，女性就业的数量在稳定地增长。此外，目前越来越多的女性接受过高等教育，这使得她们更有资格进入管理职位。

G 一些像欧洲女性管理发展网这样的组织也为女性提供了一些提高她们的技能和社交关系的机会。通过一系列泛欧和国家工厂双方协议，女性在雇佣过程中的障碍被打破。然而，法国国际组织变革的领导者，阿丽亚娜·贝图安·安塔尔主任说，只有零星的证据表明招聘过程中发生了改变。并且她说，女性很难在众多应聘者中脱颖而出，获得最终面试机会——这其中有太多障碍。安塔尔认为出现了一些积极的迹象，但她说：“除非雇主有信心，除非雇主能衡量出不同，否则什么都不会改变！”

Test 1 核心词汇 Core Vocabulary

READING PASSAGE 1

rollfilm *n.* 胶卷
dry plate *ph.* 干板（表面涂有感光药膜的玻璃片，用于照相，也叫硬片或干片）
instantaneous *adj.* 瞬间的，即刻的
shutter *n.*（照相机）快门
viewfinder *n.*（照相机）取景器
magazine camera 自动卷片照相机
photographic *adj.* 摄影（术）的，摄影用的；摄制的
gelatin *n.* 凝胶，白明胶
negative *n.* 底片
memorandum book 备查簿，备忘账
pronounceable *adj.* 可发音的，可断言的
ingenious *adj.* 设计独特的，制作精巧的
developing *n.* 显影
guinea *n.* 几尼（英国的旧金币，1几尼值1镑1先令）
celluloid *n.* 电影胶片
cinematography *n.* 电影术

READING PASSAGE 2

acumen *n.* 敏锐，聪明
perceive *vt.* 感觉，察觉，理解
aerospace *n.* 航空航天学；航空航天工业
absenteeism *n.* 旷工，旷课
recruitment *n.* 招募；补充
sophisticated *adj.* 复杂的；精密的，尖端的
psychometric *adj.* 心理测量的，心理测量学的
reinforce *vt.* 增强；加强
astrology *n.* 占星术
demographics *n.* 人口特征

READING PASSAGE 3

significantly *adv.* 意味深长地；值得注目地
isolate *vt.* 使隔离，使孤立，使脱离
counterpart *n.* 与对方地位相当的人，与另一方作用相当的物
managerial *adj.* 经理的；管理上的
demographic *adj.* 人口统计学的
shortlist *n.* 供最后挑选用的候选人名单

TEST 2

Candidate Number

Candidate Name ______________________

INTERNATIONAL ENGLISH LANGUAGE TESTING SYSTEM

ACADEMIC READING

TIME 1 hour

INSTRUCTIONS TO CANDIDATES

Do not open this booklet until you are told to do so.

Write your name and candidate number in the spaces at the top of this page.

Start at the beginning of the test and work through it.

You should answer **all** questions.

If you cannot do a particular question, leave it and go on to the next. You can return to it later.

All answers must be written on the answer sheet.

Do not remove this booklet from the examination room.

INFORMATION FOR CANDIDATES

There are **40** questions on this question paper.

The test is divided as follows:

Reading Passage 1	Questions 1–13
Reading Passage 2	Questions 14–28
Reading Passage 3	Questions 29–40

Reading Answer Sheet

Are you: Female? ▭ Male? ▭

Your first language code:

0	1	2	3	4	5	6	7	8	9
0	1	2	3	4	5	6	7	8	9
0	1	2	3	4	5	6	7	8	9

IELTS Reading Answer Sheet

Module taken (shade one box): Academic ▭ General Training ▭

		✓		✗			✓		✗
1		▭	1	▭	**21**		▭	21	▭
2		▭	2	▭	**22**		▭	22	▭
3		▭	3	▭	**23**		▭	23	▭
4		▭	4	▭	**24**		▭	24	▭
5		▭	5	▭	**25**		▭	25	▭
6		▭	6	▭	**26**		▭	26	▭
7		▭	7	▭	**27**		▭	27	▭
8		▭	8	▭	**28**		▭	28	▭
9		▭	9	▭	**29**		▭	29	▭
10		▭	10	▭	**30**		▭	30	▭
11		▭	11	▭	**31**		▭	31	▭
12		▭	12	▭	**32**		▭	32	▭
13		▭	13	▭	**33**		▭	33	▭
14		▭	14	▭	**34**		▭	34	▭
15		▭	15	▭	**35**		▭	35	▭
16		▭	16	▭	**36**		▭	36	▭
17		▭	17	▭	**37**		▭	37	▭
18		▭	18	▭	**38**		▭	38	▭
19		▭	19	▭	**39**		▭	39	▭
20		▭	20	▭	**40**		▭	40	▭

Checker's Initials		Marker's Initials		Band Score		Reading Total	

READING PASSAGE 1

*You should spend about 20 minutes on **Questions 1–13**, which are based on Reading Passage 1 below.*

The Spectacular Eruption of Mount St. Helens

A The eruption in May 1980 of Mount St. Helens, Washington State, astounded the world with its violence. A gigantic explosion tore much of the volcano's summit to fragments; the energy released was equal to that of 500 of the nuclear bombs that destroyed Hiroshima in 1945.

B The event occurred along the boundary of two of the moving plates that make up the Earth's crust. They meet at the junction of the North American continent and the Pacific Ocean. One edge of the continental North American plate over-rides the oceanic Juan de Fuca micro-plate, producing the volcanic Cascade range that includes Mounts Baker, Rainier and Hood, and Lassen Peak as well as Mount St. Helens.

C Until Mount St. Helens began to stir, only Mount Baker and Lassen Peak had shown signs of life during the 20th century. According to geological evidence found by the United States Geological Survey, there had been two major eruptions of Mount St. Helens in the recent (geologically speaking) past: around 1900B.C. and about A.D.1500. Since the arrival of Europeans in the region, it had experienced a single period of spasmodic activity, between 1831 and 1857. Then, for more than a century, Mount St. Helens lay dormant.

D By 1979, the Geological Survey alerted by signs of renewed activity, had been monitoring the volcano for 18 months. It warned the local population against being deceived by the mountain's outward calm, and forecast that an eruption would take place before the end of the century. The inhabitants of the area did not have to wait that long. On March 27, 1980, a few clouds of smoke formed above the summit, and slight tremors were felt. On the 28th, larger and darker clouds consisting of gas and ashes, emerged and climbed as high as 20, 000 feet. In

April a slight lull ensued, but the volcanologists remained pessimistic. Then, in early May, the northern flank of the mountain bulged, and the summit rose by 500 feet.

E Steps were taken to evacuate the population. Most campers, hikers, timber-cutters left the slopes of the mountain. Eighty-four-year-old Harry Truman, a holiday lodge owner who had lived there for more than 50 years, refused to be evacuated, in spite of official and private urging. Many members of the public, including an entire class of school children, wrote to him, begging him to leave. He never did.

F On May 18, at 8:32 in the morning, Mount St. Helens blew its top, literally. Suddenly, it was 1, 300 feet shorter than it had been before its growth had begun. Over half a cubic mile of rock had disintegrated. At the same moment, an earthquake with an intensity of 5 on the Richter scale was recorded. It triggered an avalanche of snow and ice, mixed with hot rock—the entire north face of the mountain had fallen away. A wave of scorching volcanic gas and rock fragments shot horizontally from the volcano's riven flank, at an inescapable 200 miles per hour. As the sliding ice and snow melted, it touched off devastating torrents of mud and debris, which destroyed all life in their path. Pulverised rock climbed as a dust cloud into the atmosphere. Finally, viscous lava, accompanied by burning clouds of ash and gas, welled out of the volcano's new crater, and from lesser vents and cracks in its flanks.

G Afterwards, scientists were able to analyse the sequence of events. First, magma—molten rock—at temperatures above 2, 000°F, had surged into the volcano from the Earth's mantle. The build-up was accompanied by an accumulation of gas, which increased as the mass of magma grew. It was the pressure inside the mountain that made it swell. Next, the rise in gas pressure caused a violent decompression, which ejected the shattered summit like a cork from a shaken soda bottle. With the summit gone, the molten rock within was released in a jet of gas and fragmented magma, and lava welled from the crater.

H The effects of the Mount St. Helens eruption were catastrophic. Almost all the trees of the surrounding forest, mainly Douglas firs, were flattened, and their branches and bark ripped off by the shock wave of the explosion. Ash and mud spread over nearly 200 square miles of country. All the towns and settlements in the area were smothered in an even coating of ash. Volcanic ash silted up the Columbia River 35 miles away, reducing the depth of its navigable channel from 40 feet to 14 feet, and trapping sea-going ships. The debris that accumulated at the foot of the volcano reached a depth, in places, of 200 feet.

I The eruption of Mount St. Helens was one of the most closely observed and analysed in history. Because geologists had been expecting the event, they were able to amass vast amounts of technical data when it happened. Study of atmospheric particles formed as a result of the explosion showed that droplets of sulphuric acid, acting as a screen between the Sun and the Earth's surface, caused a distinct drop in temperature. There is no doubt that the activity of Mount St. Helens and other volcanoes since 1980 has influenced our climate. Even so, it has been calculated that the quantity of dust ejected by Mount St. Helens—a quarter of a cubic mile—was negligible in comparison with that thrown out by earlier eruptions, such that of Mount Katmai in Alaska in 1912 (three cubic miles). The volcano is still active. Lava domes have formed inside the new crater, and have periodically burst. The threat of Mount St. Helens lives on.

Questions 1–3

Reading Passage 1 has nine paragraphs, **A–I**.

Which paragraph contains the following information?

*Write the appropriate letter, **A–I**, in boxes 1–3 on your answer sheet.*

1 the evacuation of people

2 the moment of the explosion of Mount St. Helens

3 compare the energy released by the eruption to that of nuclear bombs

Questions 4 and 5

What are the dates of **TWO** major eruptions of Mount St. Helens before 1980?

*Write **TWO** dates in boxes 4 and 5 on your answer sheet.*

Question 6

How do scientists know that the volcano exploded around the two dates above?

*Use **NO MORE THAN THREE WORDS** for the answer.*

Write your answer in box 6 on your answer sheet.

Questions 7–10

Complete the summary below.

Choose ***NO MORE THAN FOUR WORDS*** *from the passage for each answer.*

Write your answers in boxes 7–10 on your answer sheet.

In 1979 the Geological Survey warned **7**.................... to expect a violent eruption before the end of the century. The forecast was soon proved accurate. At the end of March there were tremors and clouds formed above the mountain. This was followed by a lull, but in early May the mountain rose by **8**.................... People were **9**.................... from around the mountain. Finally, on May 18th at **10**...................., Mount St. Helens exploded.

Questions 11 and 12

Complete the table below.

Write your answers in boxes 11 and 12 on your answer sheet.

Item	Equivalent to
The energy released by the explosion of Mount St. Helens	500 nuclear bombs
The area of land covered in mud or ash	**11**....................
The quantity of dust ejected	**12**....................

Question 13

Choose the correct letter, ***A****,* ***B****,* ***C*** *or* ***D****.*

Write the correct letter in box 13 on your answer sheet.

According to the text, the eruption of Mount St. Helens and other volcanoes has influenced our climate by

A increasing the amount of rainfall.

B heating the atmosphere.

C cooling the air temperature.

D causing atmospheric storms.

READING PASSAGE 2

You should spend about 20 minutes on ***Questions 14–28****, which are based on Reading Passage 2 below.*

Finding the Lost Freedom

A The private car is assumed to have widened our horizons and increased our mobility. When we consider our children's mobility, they can be driven to more places (and more distant places) than they could visit without access to a motor vehicle. However, allowing our cities to be dominated by cars has progressively eroded children's independent mobility. Children have lost much of their freedom to explore their own neighbourhood or city without adult supervision. In recent surveys, when parents in some cities were asked about their own childhood experiences, the majority remembered having more, or far more, opportunities for going out on their own, compared with their own children today. They had more freedom to explore their own environment.

B Children's independent access to their local streets may be important for their own personal, mental and psychological development. Allowing them to get to know their own neighbourhood and community gives them a "sense of place". This depends on "active exploration", which is not provided for when children are passengers in cars. (Such children may see more, but they learn less.) Not only is it important that children be able to get to local play areas by themselves, but walking and cycling journeys to school and to other destinations provide genuine play activities in themselves.

C There are very significant time and money costs for parents associated with transporting their children to school, sport and to other locations. Research in the United Kingdom estimated that this cost, in 1990, was between 10 billion and 20 billion pounds.

D The reduction in children's freedom may also contribute to a weakening of the sense of local community. As fewer children and adults use the streets as pedestrians, these streets become less sociable places. There is less opportunity for children and adults to have the spontaneous exchanges that help to engender a feeling of community. This in itself may exacerbate fears associated with assault and molestation of children, because there are fewer adults available who know their neighbours' children, and who can look out for their safety.

E The extra traffic involved in transporting children results in increased traffic congestion, pollution and accident risk. As our roads become more dangerous, more parents drive their children to more places, thus contributing to increased levels of danger for the remaining pedestrians. Anyone who has experienced either the reduced volume of traffic in peak hour during school holidays, or the traffic jams near schools at the end of a school day, will not need convincing about these points. Thus, there are also important environmental implications of children's loss of freedom.

F As individuals, parents strive to provide the best upbringing they can for their children. However, in doing so, (e.g. by driving their children to sport, school or recreation) parents may be contributing to a more dangerous environment for children generally. The idea that "streets are for cars and back yards and playgrounds are for children" is a strongly held belief, and parents have little choice as individuals but to keep their children off the streets if they want to protect their safety.

G In many parts of Dutch cities, and some traffic calmed precincts in Germany, residential streets are now places where cars must give way to pedestrians. In these areas, residents are accepting the view that the function of streets is not solely to provide mobility for cars. Streets may also be for social interaction, walking, cycling and playing. One of the most important aspects of these European cities, in terms of giving cities back to children, has been a range of "traffic calming" initiatives, aiming at reducing the volume speed of traffic. These initiatives have had complex interactive effects, leading to a sense that children have been able to "recapture" their local neighbourhood, and more importantly, that they have been able to do this in safety. Recent research has demonstrated that children in many German cities have significantly higher levels to freedom to travel to places in their own neighbourhood or city than children in other cities in the world.

H Modifying cities in order to enhance children's freedom will not only benefit children. Such cities will become more environmentally sustainable, as well as more sociable and more livable for all city residents. Perhaps it will be our concern for our children's welfare that convinces us that we need to challenge the dominance of the car in our cities.

Questions 14–17

Do the following statements agree with the information given in Reading Passage 2?

In boxes 14–17 on your answer sheet, write

TRUE	*if the statement agrees with the information*
FALSE	*if the statement contradicts the information*
NOT GIVEN	*if there is no information on this*

14 Children are more independent today than they used to be.

15 The private car has helped children have more opportunities to learn.

16 Children usually walk or cycle to school.

17 Parents save time and money by driving children to school.

Questions 18–22

Look at the following information (Questions 18–22) and the causes in the box below.

Match each problem with the correct cause, ***A–G****.*

Write the appropriate letter ***A–G*** *in boxes 18–22 on your answer sheet.*

NB *You may use any letter more than once.*

Problems

18 low sense of community feeling

19 streets becoming less sociable

20 fewer chances for meeting friends

21 fears of danger for children

22 higher accident risk

Causes

A few adults know local children

B fewer people use the streets as pedestrians

C increased pollution

D streets are less friendly

E less traffic in school holidays

F reduced freedom for children

G more children driven to school

Questions 23–28

Complete each sentence with the correct ending ***i–x*** *below.*

Write the correct number ***i–x*** *in boxes 23–28 on your answer sheet.*

23 By driving their children to school, parents help create

24 Children should play

25 In some German towns, pedestrians have preference right of walking

26 Streets should also be used for

27 Reducing the amount of traffic and the speed is

28 All people who live in the city will benefit if cities are

i	... a dangerous environment.
ii	... modified.
iii	... on residential streets.
iv	... modifying cities.
v	... neighbourhoods.
vi	... socialising.
vii	... in back yards.
viii	... for cars.
ix	... traffic calming.
x	... residential.

READING PASSAGE 3

*You should spend about 20 minutes on **Questions 29–40**, which are based on Reading Passage 3 below.*

New Rules for the Paper Game

A Computerised data storage and electronic mail were to have heralded the paperless office. But, contrary to expectations, paper consumption throughout the world shows no sign of abating. In fact, consumption, especially of printing and writing papers, continues to increase. World demand for paper and board is now expected to grow faster than the general economic growth in the next 15 years. Strong demand will be underpinned by the growing industrialisation of South-East Asia, the reemergence of paper packaging, greater use of facsimile machines and photocopiers, and the popularity of direct-mail advertising. In 2007, world paper and board demand reached 455 million tonnes, compared with 241 million tonnes in 1991.

B The pulp and paper industry has not been badly affected by the electronic technologies that promised a paperless society. But what has radically altered the industry's structure is pressure from another front—a more environmentally conscious society driving an irreversible move towards cleaner industrial production. The environmental consequences of antiquated pulp mill practices and technologies had marked this industry as one in need of reform. Graphic descriptions of deformed fish and thinning populations, particularly in the Baltic Sea where old pulp mills had discharged untreated effluents for 100 years, have disturbed the international community.

C Until the 1950s, it was common for pulp mills and other industries to discharge untreated effluent into rivers and seas. The environmental effects were at the time either not understood, or regarded as an acceptable cost of economic prosperity in an increasingly import-oriented world economy. But greater environmental awareness has spurred a fundamental change in attitude in the community, in government and in industry itself.

D Since the early 1980s, most of the world-scale pulp mills in Scandinavia and North America have modernised their operations, outlaying substantial amounts to improve production methods. Changes in mill design and processes have been aimed at minimising the environmental effects of effluent discharge while at the same time producing pulp with the whiteness and strength demanded by the international market. The environmental impetus is taking this industry even further, with the focus now on developing processes that may even eliminate waste-water discharges. But the ghost of the old mills continues to haunt the industry today. In Europe companies face a flood of environment-related legislation. In Germany companies are now being held responsible for the waste they create.

E Pulp is the porridge-like mass of plant fibres from which paper is made. Paper makers choose the type of plant fibre and the processing methods, depending on what the end product will be used for: whether it is a sturdy packing box, a smooth sheet of writing paper or a fragile tissue. In wood, which is the source of about 90% of the world's paper production, fibres are bound together by lignin, which gives the unbleached pulp a brown colour. The pulping stage separates the wood into fibres so they are suitable for paper making. Pulping can be done by mechanical grinding, or by chemical treatment in which woodchips are "cooked" with chemicals, or by a combination of both methods.

F Kraft pulping is the most widely used chemical process for producing pulp with the strength required by the high-quality paper market. It is now usually carried out in a continuous process in a large vessel called a digester. Woodchips are fed from a pile into the top of the digester. In the digester, the chips are cooked in a solution called white liquor, composed of caustic soda (sodium hydroxide) and sodium sulphide. The chips are cooked at high temperatures of up to 170°C for up to three hours. The pulp is then washed and separated from the spent cooking liquor which has turned dark and is now appropriately called black liquor. An important feature of kraft pulping is a chemical recovery system which recycles about 95% of the cooking chemicals and produces more than enough energy to run the mill. In a series of steps involving a furnace and tanks, some of the black liquor is transformed into energy, while some is regenerated into the original white cooking liquor. The recovery system is an integral part of production in the pulp and paper industry. The pulp that comes out has little lignin left in the fibres. Bleaching removes the last remaining lignin and brightens the pulp. Most modern mills have modified their pulping processes to remove as much of the lignin as possible before the pulp moves to the bleaching stage.

Questions 29–32

*Below is a list of possible factors, **A–G**, which will influence the amount of paper being used in the future. From the list, choose **FOUR** factors which are mentioned in the passage.*

*Write the correct letter, **A–G**, in boxes 29–32 on your answer sheet.*

List of Factors

- **A** more people read newspapers
- **B** increased use of paper bags
- **C** increased book production for education
- **D** wider use of sign post advertising
- **E** increased use of fax machines
- **F** wider use of leaflet advertising
- **G** greater use of duplicating machines

Questions 33–35

Complete the sentences below.

*Choose **NO MORE THAN THREE WORDS** from the passage for each answer.*

Write your answers in boxes 33–35 on your answer sheet.

33 The international community has begun to demand ....

34 In the past, the environmental effects of pulp mill practices, were probably a price to pay for ....

35 Some paper mills have recently modernised their mill design in order to decrease ....

Questions 36–40

*Below is a list of possible steps in the kraft process of turning wood chips into paper. They are numbered **A–H**. Only **FIVE** of the steps listed below are mentioned in the passage.*

Decide which steps are mentioned and write them in the correct order.

Write your answers in boxes 36–40 on your answer sheet.

- **A** the chips are cooked
- **B** the fibres are bound by lignin
- **C** the pulp is bleached
- **D** woodchips are put into a pile
- **E** the pulp is dried
- **F** the pulp is removed from the black liquor
- **G** the chips are put into the white liquor
- **H** the pulp is washed

Test 2 答案速查 Key

READING PASSAGE 1

1. E
2. F
3. A
4. Around 1900 B.C.
5. About A.D. 1500
6. Geological evidence
7. the local population
8. 500 feet
9. evacuated
10. 8:32 in the morning
11. 200 square miles
12. a quarter of a cubic mile
13. C

READING PASSAGE 2

14. FALSE
15. FALSE
16. NOT GIVEN
17. FALSE
18. F
19. B
20. B
21. A
22. G
23. i
24. vii
25. iii
26. vi
27. ix
28. ii

READING PASSAGE 3

29. B **30.** E **31.** F **32.** G

33. cleaner industrial production

34. economic prosperity

35. the environmental effects

36. D **37.** G **38.** A **39.** H **40.** F

Test 2 考题精解 Detailed Explanation

READING PASSAGE 1

Questions 1–3

题型：配对题 (MATCHING)

◆ 解析

1. E

题干中的关键词是evacuation，纵观全文，只在E段有提到evacuate，其首句Steps were taken to evacuate the population与题干有对应信息，所以答案为E。

2. F

题干的关键词是the moment和explosion，说的是圣海伦斯火山的爆发情况，通读全文，可知F段对圣海伦斯火山爆发的情形作了详细的描述，所以答案为F。

3. A

根据题干关键词energy和nuclear bombs可定位到A段的最后一句...the energy released was equal to that of 500 of the nuclear bombs that destroyed Hiroshima in 1945，该句将火山喷发所释放的能量与原子弹的能量作了对比，所以答案为A。

Questions 4–6

题型：简答题 (SHORT ANSWER QUESTIONS)

◆ 解析

4. Around 1900 B.C.

5. About A.D. 1500

6. Geological evidence

4题和5题的关键词是two major eruptions，根据这两个关键词可将答案定位到原文C段第二句According to geological evidence found by the United States Geological Survey, there had been two major eruptions of Mount St. Helens in the recent (geologically speaking) past: around 1900B.C. and about A.D.1500，此段明确给出two major eruptions的爆发时间为1900B.C.和A.D.1500。既而第6题所问的科学家是如何得知火山是在这两个日期爆发的，也可在该段的According to geological evidence found by the United States Geological Survey中找到答案。注意第6题要求回答字数应在三个字以内，切不可超出字数要求。

Questions 7–10

题型：摘要填空题 (SUMMARY COMPLETION)

◆ 解析

仔细阅读摘要的第一句话，根据其中的关键词1979，可定位到原文D段，各题的答案应从D段找起。

7. the local population

根据题干关键词Geological Survey可定位到原文D段第二句It warned the local population against being deceived by the mountain’s outward calm, and forecast that an eruption would take place before the end of the century，该句中的it指代Geological Survey, 而其后的warned又与空前的动词一致，由此可知原文warned后的local population 为应填答案。

8. 500 feet

根据题干关键词early May可定位到原文D段最后一句Then, in early May, the northern flank of the mountain bulged, and the summit rose by 500 feet, rose by为原词重现，故此处应填500 feet。

9. evacuated

注意摘要填空题属于顺序性细节题，当9题所需信息在D段中没有出现时，可在接下来的一段中寻找，9题信息对应E段首句Steps were taken to evacuate the population，其中population与题干中的people为同义词转换，故此处应填evacuated。

10. 8:32 in the morning

根据题干关键词on May 18th可定位到原文F段首句On May 18, at 8:32 in the morning, Mount St. Helens blew its top, literally，由此可知火山喷发的时间为8:32 in the morning。

Questions 11 and 12

题型：表格填空题 (TABLE COMPLETION)

◆ 解析

11. 200 square miles

根据题干关键词mud or ash可定位到原文H段第三句Ash and mud spread over nearly 200 square miles of country，由该句可知答案为200 square miles。

12. a quarter of a cubic mile

根据题干关键词the quantity of dust，可定位到原文I段第五句Even so, it has been calculated that the quantity of dust ejected by Mount St. Helens—a quarter of a cubic mile—was negligible in comparison with that thrown out by earlier eruptions, such that of Mount，由该句可知答案为a quarter of a cubic mile。

Question 13

题型：选择题 (MULTIPLE CHOICE)

◆ 解析

13. C

根据题干关键词influence和climate可定位到原文I段第三句Study of atmospheric particles formed as a result of the explosion showed that droplets of sulphuric acid, acting as a screen between the Sun and the Earth's surface, caused a distinct drop in temperature，其中caused a distinct drop in temperature的表述与C选项一致，所以答案选C。

◎ 参考译文

壮观的圣海伦斯火山爆发

A　1980年5月，华盛顿州的圣海伦斯火山爆发，其猛烈程度举世震惊。火山爆发的巨大威力将火山顶撕成碎片。此次爆发所释放的能量相当于500颗1945年催毁广岛的原子弹的威力。

B　此事件发生在组成地壳的两个移动板块的分界处，即北美大陆和太平洋板块的交汇处。北美大陆板块的边缘漂浮于胡安·德富卡微型板块之上，由此形成了包括贝克山，莱尼尔山和胡德山还有拉孙峰以及圣海伦斯火山在内的喀斯喀特山脉。

C　等到圣海伦斯火山开始活动时，只有贝克山和拉孙峰在20世纪期间有活动迹象。美国地质鉴定机构的证据显示，圣海伦斯火山距今最近的（就地质方面而言）两次爆发大约是在公元前1900年和公元后1500年。自从欧洲人到达此地区后，它在1831—1857年间已经历了一个独立的时断时续的活动期。此后一个多世纪以来，圣海伦斯火山处于休眠状态。

D　到1979年因火山有重新活动的迹象而引起地质鉴定机构的注意，他们一直持续观察记录该火山的活动达18个月之久，并提醒当地居民要提高警惕，不要被火山外表的平静所欺骗，该机构预测火山将会在本世纪末之前爆发。然而当地居民并没有等那么久，1980年3月27日少量烟状云层在山顶上空形成，人们感觉地面有轻微摇晃。28日，由烟和灰组成的大面积的浓云层渐渐出现并升到20 000英尺高空。接着在4月稍息，但火山专家认为情况不容乐观。之后，在5月初山体北面鼓起，山顶由此升高500英尺。

E　疏散工作逐步进行着。大多数的露营者、爬山者以及伐木工撤离了山坡。尽管政府和朋友一再催促，84岁的哈里·杜鲁门——一个住在这里50多年的假日旅馆的所有者，仍然拒绝撤离，包括学校的孩子们在内的许多民众也写信劝他离开，但他仍未离开。

F　5月18日早晨8:32分，圣海伦斯火山的山顶刹那间消失，比它生成时低了近1 300英尺。超过近半立方英里的岩石全部变成碎片，同时还伴有里氏5级的强烈地震。火山爆发引发了雪崩和冰体崩裂，且混合着滚烫的岩石，整个山的北侧表面全部脱落。滚滚热浪和岩石碎片从火山破裂的侧面以每小时200英里的速度平射过来。在滑冰和雪融化时，夹杂在其中的泥石流和岩石碎片摧毁了沿途所有的生命。成为粉状的岩石如烟云般升腾到大气层。最后，黏稠的熔岩伴随着燃烧的烟灰云从新的火山口和山体侧面的小孔和裂缝中喷出。

G　之后，科学家们能够分析出火山爆发的次序了。首先，华氏2 000℃以上的岩浆（溶化的岩石）从地幔急剧上升进入火山。伴着烟雾的逐渐堆积，大量的岩浆生成且不断增加。正是山体内部的压力致使火山膨胀。接着，气压增强导致气体急骤卸压，这使得破碎的山顶像一个从晃动的苏打水瓶上喷出的瓶塞那样喷射而出。随着山顶的消失，内部溶化的岩石以气体喷射流和碎裂的岩浆方式得以释放，熔岩从火山口流出。

H 圣海伦斯火山爆发造成了灾难性的后果。周围森林里几乎所有的树木，主要是花旗松，都被夷为平地，树枝和树皮都被爆炸引发的冲击波撕裂了。火山灰和泥浆覆盖了该地区近200多平方英里。所有的城镇和居住地都覆盖上了一层火山灰。火山灰堵塞了哥伦比亚河35英里，造成了可通航航道的深度由40英尺变为了14英尺，使远洋船陷入困境。火山脚下积聚的散落的碎片有200英尺深。

I 圣海伦斯火山爆发是史上观测分析数据最详实的一次火山爆发事件。因为地质学专家一直关注着此事，所以当火山爆发时他们能积累大量的技术数据。对爆炸时形成的大气层粒子的研究结果表明，一种酸性物质的小水滴能成功地在太阳和地球表面之间充当一个屏障，致使温度明显降低。毋庸置疑的是，自从1980年以来，圣海伦斯火山和其他火山的爆发影响了我们的气候。即使如此，据计算，由圣海伦斯火山喷出的尘埃数量（1/4立方英里）与早期例如1912年阿拉斯加的卡特迈火山（3立方英里）的火山爆发的尘埃数量相比是微不足道的。圣海伦斯火山一直很活跃，熔岩穹顶已在新的火山口内部形成，且发生周期性爆炸，圣海伦斯火山的威胁仍然存在。

READING PASSAGE 2

Questions 14–17

题型：判断题 (TRUE/FALSE/NOT GIVEN)

◆ 解析

14. FALSE

本题并无明显的关键词，仔细阅读文章，不难发现原文A段中就有关于孩子独立性的表述：However, allowing our cities to be dominated by cars has progressively eroded children's independent mobility，此句说的是汽车的普及逐渐削弱了孩子们独立出行的能力，而题干说的是孩子比以往更独立，表述完全相反，所以答案为FALSE。

15. FALSE

由关键词opportunities to learn定位到原文B段括号中的信息Such children may see more, but they learn less，此句说坐在车里的孩子虽然看到的多，但学到的却很少，而题干说的是私家车让孩子们有了更多的学习机会，表述完全相反，所以答案为FALSE。

16. NOT GIVEN

该题容易误选为FALSE，实际上原文中并没有直接提到孩子们通常是如何去上学的，所以选NOT GIVEN最为合适。

17. FALSE

由关键词time和money定位到原文C段首句There are very significant time and money costs for parents associated with transporting their children to school, sport and to other locations，此句说的是开车送孩子上学浪费了大量的时间和金钱，而题干中说的是节省时间和金钱，表述完全相反，所以答案为FALSE。

Questions 18–22

题型：配对题 (MATCHING)

◆ 解析

18. F

根据题干关键词sense of community可定位到原文D段的第一句The reduction in children's freedom may also contribute to a weakening of the sense of local community，这是一个表示因果关系的句子，有表示因果关系的动词contribute to，其中weakening of the sense of local community与题干low sense of community feeling相对应。而句中The reduction in children's freedom与选项F reduced freedom for children是对应的，所以答案为F。

19. B

根据题干关键词streets和less sociable可定位到原文D段的第二句As fewer children and adults use the streets as pedestrians, these streets become less sociable places，其中these streets become less sociable places与题干streets becoming less sociable是对应的。仔细分析这句话，首句的as在这里是表示原因的连词，答案应是fewer children and adults use the streets as pedestrians的改写，所以答案为B。

20. B

根据题干关键词fewer chances可定位到原文D段的第三句There is less opportunity for children and adults to have the spontaneous exchanges that help to engender a feeling of community，其中的less opportunity与题干中的fewer chances为同义词组转换，而have the spontaneous exchanges that help to engender a feeling of community则与meeting friends相对应，但在这句前没有说出新的原因（没有新的表示因果的词句），所以是一因多果，答案为B。

21. A

根据题干关键词fears of danger可定位到原文D段的第四句This in itself may exacerbate fear associated with assault and molestation of children, because there are fewer adults available who know their neighbors' children, and who can look out for their safety，其中的fear associated with assault and molestation of children与题干中的fears of danger for children相对应。because 是表示原因的连词，答案应是there are fewer adults available who know their neighbors' children的改写，所以答案为A。

22. G

根据题干关键词accident risk可定位到原文E段的第一句The extra traffic involved in transporting children results in increased traffic congestion, pollution and accident risk，其中的accident risk与题干中的higher accident risk相对应，注意results in表示“导致”，原因在前，结果在后，答案应是The extra traffic involved in transporting children的改写，所以答案为G。

Questions 23–28

题型：句子填空题 (SENTENCE COMPLETION)

◆ 解析

23. i

根据题干关键词By driving their children to school可定位到原文F段的第二句However, in doing so, (e.g. by driving their children to sport, school or recreation) parents may be contributing to a more dangerous environment for children generally，句中contribute to与题干create为同义词转换，句中的a more dangerous environment与i项完全对应，所以答案应为i。

24. vii

根据题干关键词Children should play可定位到原文F段第三句The idea that "streets are for cars and back yards and playgrounds are for children" is a strongly held belief，这时再看选项i–x，从中找到能与back yards and playgrounds相对应的词，所以答案应为vii。

25. iii

根据题干关键词German可定位到原文G段的第一句In many parts of Dutch cities, and some traffic calmed precincts in Germany, residential streets are now places where cars must give way to pedestrians。仔细阅读residential streets are now places where cars must give way to pedestrians这句话，大意是汽车若是在住宅区的街道上行驶必须要给行人让路，题干中说行人有在街区街道行走的优先权，而只有选项iii的信息可与题干相搭配表达正确的意思，所以答案应为iii。

26. vi

根据题干关键词Streets, also, be used for可定位到原文G段的第三句Streets may also be for social interaction，这时再看选项i–x，从中找到与social interaction相对应的词，所以答案应为vi。

27. ix

根据题干关键词Reducing the amount of和traffic and speed可定位到原文G段的第四句One of the most important aspects of these European cities, in terms of giving cities back to children, has been a range of "traffic calming" initiatives, aimed at reducing the volume and speed of traffic，仔细阅读其中的信息，不难看出，题干后接的词组应为traffic calming，所以答案应为ix。

28. ii

根据题干关键词All people, benefit可定位到原文H段的第一句Modifying cities in order to enhance children's freedom will not only benefit children. Such cities will become more environmentally sustainable, as well as more sociable and more livable for all city residents，这句话的大意是改造城市不仅孩子会受益，整个城市也会变得更融洽、更适合居住，这时再看选项，只有选项ii能与题干相连表达正确的意思，所以答案应为ii。

◎ 参考译文

寻找遗失的自由

A 人们认为私家车开阔了我们的视野并提高了我们的流动性。当考虑到孩子们的流动性时，与没有移动工具相比，拥有私家车能带他们到更多（更远）的地方。然而，私家车的普及逐渐削弱了孩子们独立出行的能力。孩子们失去了很多没有成人监管下的独自实地观察邻近地区或城市的自由。在最近的调查中，当问及一些城市的父母们关于自己的童年经历时，与他们现在自己的孩子们相对比，绝大多数父母曾有更多单独外出的机会。他们有更多的自由去探索自己周边的环境。

B 孩子们独立接触当地街道或许对他们自身的个性、智力和心理成长至关重要。让他们了解自己的邻里和社区可以给他们"方位感"，这种感觉依赖于"积极探索"，这是坐在汽车里的孩子（或许能看到更多，但学到的却很少）无法体会的。不但让孩子们自己去附近玩儿很重要，步行和骑自行车去学校及其他地方也会令孩子们真正参与到活动之中。

C 家长们将很多重要的时间及金钱花在开车送孩子们上学、做运动以及去其他地方。英国的一份研究估算了这项开销，1990年这项费用介于100亿和200亿英镑之间。

D 孩子们自由度的减少也造成地方社区感愈加薄弱。当越来越少的孩子和家长把街道作为步行街时，街道的社交性功能就变得越来越薄弱。帮助孩子和家长产生社区感的自发的交流越来越少了。这本身就可能激化了孩子们对暴力和骚扰的恐惧，因为认识自己邻居的孩子并能够注意他们安全的成人越来越少了。

E 由于送孩子而形成的额外运输量导致交通愈发拥堵，污染愈加严重，事故风险也持续增加。随着道路危险的增加，越来越多的父母亲自驾车送孩子去更多的地方，从而造成了其他行人危险系数的增加。曾体验过在学校假期期间交通高峰时运输量减少，或者经历过放学之前学校附近交通堵塞的人，肯定对此深信不疑。因此，孩子们失去出行自由的同时也牵连着重要的环境问题。

F 就个人而言，家长们力求为孩子们提供最佳的成长环境。然而，如此一来，（例如：通过开车送孩子们去运动、上学或者消遣）家长们或许会给孩子造成更加危险的环境。“街道属于汽车，而后院和操场才是孩子们的领地”是一种被普遍认知的观念，如果想要保护孩子们的安全，除了使孩子们远离街道，家长们别无他选。

G 在荷兰城市的许多地方，以及德国一些交通稳定地区，汽车若是在住宅区的街道上行驶必须要给行人让路。在这些区域，居民正逐渐接受这种观点：街道的作用不仅仅是为让汽车通行，同时它也是社交互动、步行，骑自行车和玩耍的地方。就将城市归还给孩子们而言，这些欧洲城市最重要的一项举措是出台一系列旨在降低交通容量速度的“交通舒缓”倡议。这些倡议相互影响，使孩子们产生“重新夺回”领地的感觉，更重要的是，他们能够安全地做到这些。近期研究表明，许多德国城市的孩子在自己邻里社区或城市旅行方面拥有比世界其他城市的孩子更高的自由度。

H 尽管这项城市改造旨在让孩子们获得更多的出行自由，然而受益的将不仅仅是孩子。对所有城市居民来说，改变后的城市环境可以向着可持续化方向发展，人际关系也会更加融洽，更加适宜居住。也许正是对孩子们幸福的忧心才使我们意识到该向独占城市的汽车发起挑战了。

READING PASSAGE 3

Questions 29–32

题型：选择题 (MULTIPLE CHOICE)

◆ 解析

29–32 B E F G

先读题干，通过阅读原文，不难得知题干中的一些信息可在A段中找到相应的表述：

Strong demand will be underpinned by the growing industrialisation of south-East Asia, the reemergence of paper packaging, greater use of facsimile machines and photocopiers, and the popularity of direct-mail advertising.

其中四个因素reemergence of paper packaging对应选项B；facsimile machines对应选项E；photocopiers对应选项G；the popularity of direct-mail advertising对应选项F。

Questions 33–35

题型：句子填空题 (SENTENCE COMPLETION)

◆ 解析

33. cleaner industrial production

根据题干关键词international community和demand可定位到原文B段第二句But what has radically altered the industry's structure is pressure from another front—a more environmentally conscious society driving an irreversible move towards cleaner industrial production.

原文和题干的对应如下：

原文	题干
society	international community
move towards	demand

34. economic prosperity

根据题干关键词environmental effects可定位到原文C段的第二句The environmental effects were at the time either not understood, or regarded as an acceptable cost of economic prosperity in an increasingly import-oriented world economy.

原文和题干的对应如下：

原文	题干
at the time	in the past
cost of	price to pay for

35. the environmental effects

根据题干关键词modernised和mill design可定位到原文D段的第二句Changes in mill design and processes have been aimed at minimising the environmental effects of effluent discharge while at the same time producing pulp with the whiteness and strength demanded by the international market.

原文和题干的对应如下：

原文	题干
aimed at	in order to
minimising	decrease

Questions 36–40

题型：选择题 (MULTIPLE CHOICE)

◆ 解析

D G A H F（顺序必须正确）

根据题干关键词kraft process可定位到原文F段Kraft pulping is the most widely used chemical process for producing pulp with the strength required by the high-quality paper market. It is now usually carried out in a continuous process in a large vessel called a digester. Woodchips are fed from a pile into the top of the digester. In the digester, the chips are cooked in a solution called white liquor, composed of caustic soda (sodium hydroxide) and sodium sulphide. The chips are cooked at high temperatures of up to 170℃ for up to three hours. The pulp is then washed and separated from the spent cooking liquor which has turned dark and is now appropriately called black liquor.

其中Woodchips are fed from a pile into the top of the digester对应D选项；the chips are cooked in a solution called white liquor对应A和G选项（注意在排序时按照流程发生的先后顺序G应排在A前）；The pulp is then washed and separated from the spent cooking liquor which has turned dark and is now appropriately called black liquor对应H和F选项。

注意：题中要求将选项按照文中所描述的流程的正确顺序排列，千万不要在已经找对选项的情况下，因为排序错误而失了分。

◎ 参考译文

造纸业的新规则

A 计算机数据存储和电子邮件本应成为无纸化办公的先锋，但出乎意料的是，全世界的纸张消耗量并没有表现出减少的迹象。实际上，纸张消耗量，特别是印刷和手写纸的消耗量还在连续增长。预计在接下来的15年里，世界对于纸张和纸板需求的增长将快于总体经济增长。随着东南亚工业化的发展，纸类包装的再度出现，传真机和复印机的大量使用以及直邮广告的流行都巩固了这一强烈的需求。与1991年的24 100万吨相比，在2007年全世界对于纸张及纸板的需求达到45 500万吨。

B 尽管电子科技承诺过无纸化社会，但纸浆和造纸业并未受到太大影响。使得该产业结构发生根本性改变的是来自另一面的压力——社会环保意识越来越强，无污染工业生产也必将是大势所趋。老式纸浆厂常因其做法和工艺影响而被列为需要改革的工业。关于畸形鱼和稀疏的人口的生动描述，特别是波罗的海的老式纸浆厂排放未经处理的废水已经有100年之久了，已经使国际社会感到不安。

C 直到20世纪50年代，纸浆厂和其他工业向河流和海洋排放未经处理的污水仍是很普遍的。在当时日益增长的以进口为导向的世界经济情形下，环境的影响要么不被理解，要么被看作是繁荣经济过程中一项可接受的代价。但更强大的环境意识已刺激了公众、政府以及产业本身的态度发生了根本转变。

D 自从20世纪80年代早期，大部分位于斯堪的纳维亚和北美洲的世界级纸浆厂耗费巨资提高生产工艺，从而实现了运营现代化。工厂设计和加工进程的改变旨在将排放污水给环境造成的不良影响降到最低程度的同时，生产出符合国际市场需求的洁白而且韧性强的纸张。环境因素正推动着这项产业朝着更深一步发展，该行业全力优化流程，以便使得消除废水排放成为可能。但老式工厂的“鬼魂”仍困扰着当今的产业。在欧洲，许多公司面临大量与环境有关的立法。现在德国的许多公司为他们所产生的废物承担责任。

E　制纸的纸浆是类似麦片粥似的大量的植物纤维。纸张制造者们选择植物纤维的种类和处理的方法取决于终端产品的用途：是一个坚固的填料盒、一张光滑的书写纸还是一张柔软的纸巾。世界上90%纸张的生产都选用木材作为原料，其纤维由木质素连接在一起，使未经漂白的纸浆呈褐色。制浆阶段将木头分离成纤维以使它们适合造纸。纸浆可由机械碾磨来完成；或者通过化学处理，即木头和化学药品被一同“烹饪”；或是结合两种方法来完成。

F　硫酸盐法是现在使用最广泛的生产纸浆的化学过程，可满足生产高质量纸张的市场需求。硫酸盐法通常在一个被称为蒸煮锅的大容器里持续进行。木屑通过一个管道被送入蒸煮锅的顶部。在蒸煮锅里，木屑在一种叫做白液的溶液中煮炼，白液由苛性钠（氢氧化钠）和硫化钠构成。木屑在高达170摄氏度的高温下煮炼三个小时。然后纸浆经过洗涤并与变深的废液分离，废液被贴切地称为：黑液。硫酸盐法的一个重要特征是一套化学回收系统，这套系统回收利用大约95%的烹制化学品并且生成足以运行磨粉机的能量。在一系列包括一个熔炉和煮罐的步骤中，一些黑液被转化为能量，同时还有一些黑液再生为原始的白液。此回收系统是纸浆和纸张工业生产的最主要部分。生产出的纸浆的纤维中几乎没有残留的木质素。漂白除去了最后剩余的木质素并使纸浆发亮。为了在纸浆进入漂白阶段前尽可能多地除去木质素，大多数现代工厂已经改进了制浆过程。

Test 2 核心词汇 Core Vocabulary

READING PASSAGE 1

eruption *n.*（火山）爆发

astound *vt.* 使震惊，使大吃一惊

spasmodic *adj.* 间歇的；突发性的

dormant *adj.* 休眠的；静止的

tremor *n.* 震动，颤动；地震

lull *n.* 暂停，间歇

ensue *vi.* 跟着发生，继起

evacuate *vi.* 撤离；使避难，使疏散

disintegrate *vt.* & *vi.*（使）破裂

avalanche *n.* 雪崩

scorch *vt.* & *vi.* 烧焦；烤焦

riven *adj.* 撕裂的，分裂的

inescapable *adj.* 不可避免的，逃避不了的

pulverize *vt.* 将……弄碎；摧毁，粉碎

viscous *adj.* 黏的；黏性的

magma *n.* 岩浆

swell *vt.* & *vi.* 肿胀，膨胀

eject *vt.* & *vi.* 弹出，喷出，排出

smother *vt.* 覆盖

droplet *n.* 小滴

READING PASSAGE 2

assume *vt.* 假设，臆想
erode *vt. & vi.* 侵蚀，腐蚀
engender *vt.* 产生（某种形势或状况），引起
exacerbate *vt.* 使恶化；使加重
assault *n.* 攻击，猛袭，突袭
molestation *n.* 骚扰，干扰
pedestrian *n.* 步行者
precinct *n.* 区域，行人专用

READING PASSAGE 3

herald *vi.* 预示
abate *vt.* 减少，减轻，减退
underpin *vt.* 为（论据、主张等）打下基础
facsimile *n.*（文字、图画等的）副本；传真
antiquated *adj.* 过时的，陈旧的
effluent *n.*（注入河里等的）污水
outlay *vt.* 支出，花费
impetus *n.* 推动，促进，刺激
tissue *n.* 薄纸
lignin *n.* 木质素
unbleached *adj.* 原色的，未漂白的

TEST 3

Candidate Number

Candidate Name ______________________

INTERNATIONAL ENGLISH LANGUAGE TESTING SYSTEM

ACADEMIC READING

TIME 1 hour

INSTRUCTIONS TO CANDIDATES

Do not open this booklet until you are told to do so.

Write your name and candidate number in the spaces at the top of this page.

Start at the beginning of the test and work through it.

You should answer **all** questions.

If you cannot do a particular question, leave it and go on to the next. You can return to it later.

All answers must be written on the answer sheet.

Do not remove this booklet from the examination room.

INFORMATION FOR CANDIDATES

There are **40** questions on this question paper.

The test is divided as follows:

Reading Passage 1	Questions 1–15
Reading Passage 2	Questions 16–27
Reading Passage 3	Questions 28–40

Reading Answer Sheet

Are you: Female? ▭ Male? ▭

Your first language code:

0	1	2	3	4	5	6	7	8	9
0	1	2	3	4	5	6	7	8	9
0	1	2	3	4	5	6	7	8	9

IELTS Reading Answer Sheet

Module taken (shade one box): Academic ▭ General Training ▭

		✓		✗			✓		✗
1		▭	1	▭	**21**		▭	21	▭
2		▭	2	▭	**22**		▭	22	▭
3		▭	3	▭	**23**		▭	23	▭
4		▭	4	▭	**24**		▭	24	▭
5		▭	5	▭	**25**		▭	25	▭
6		▭	6	▭	**26**		▭	26	▭
7		▭	7	▭	**27**		▭	27	▭
8		▭	8	▭	**28**		▭	28	▭
9		▭	9	▭	**29**		▭	29	▭
10		▭	10	▭	**30**		▭	30	▭
11		▭	11	▭	**31**		▭	31	▭
12		▭	12	▭	**32**		▭	32	▭
13		▭	13	▭	**33**		▭	33	▭
14		▭	14	▭	**34**		▭	34	▭
15		▭	15	▭	**35**		▭	35	▭
16		▭	16	▭	**36**		▭	36	▭
17		▭	17	▭	**37**		▭	37	▭
18		▭	18	▭	**38**		▭	38	▭
19		▭	19	▭	**39**		▭	39	▭
20		▭	20	▭	**40**		▭	40	▭

Checker's Initials		Marker's Initials		Band Score		Reading Total	

READING PASSAGE 1

*You should spend about 20 minutes on **Questions 1–15**, which are based on Reading Passage 1 below.*

Questions 1–5

Reading Passage 1 has six marked paragraphs, **A–F**.

*Choose the correct heading for paragraphs **B–F** from the list of headings below.*

*Write the correct number, **i–vi**, in boxes 1–5 on your answer sheet.*

List of Headings

i	Sydney's Location and History
ii	Residential Inner-City Suburbs
iii	Australia—Attractive to International Students
iv	Entertainment for Young and Old
v	The Harbour and Surrounding Suburbs
vi	The Cultural Climate
vii	The economy of Australia
viii	The traffic in Sydney
ix	The Education and Culture

Example	***Answer***
Paragraph **A**	**iii**

1 Paragraph **B**

2 Paragraph **C**

3 Paragraph **D**

4 Paragraph **E**

5 Paragraph **F**

Studying in Sydney, Australia—an Overview for International Students

A Australia has been a popular choice for thousands of international students over many years. Australia's universities and colleges have become increasingly recognised

overseas for their exceptionally high standard. In addition, Australia is conveniently close to South-East Asia (Jakarta, the capital of Australia's closest Asian neighbour, Indonesia, is only 5, 506 kilometres from Sydney). Revised entry procedures for overseas students have made it possible for an increasing number to study in Australia. Sydney, the largest Australian city, is the principal port of call for international airlines with services operating to Australia.

B Named after an ex-governor of New South Wales, Sydney is the State's capital city. Located on the south-east coast of Australia in the temperate zone, it enjoys a mild climate, averaging 14.5 hours of sunshine per day in summer and 10.25 hours in winter. It is also the largest, oldest, and perhaps most beautifully situated city in Australia. First established by the British as a convict settlement in 1788, it is a modern cosmopolitan city that has developed into one of the nation's major industrial, business, and manufacturing centres.

C Sydney is home to nearly 4.4 million people (as of 1997). The suburbs reach out from the city centre and harbour some 55 km to the north, 35 km to the west and 30 km to the south, creating a metropolitan area of about 3, 000 square kilometres. The 57-square-kilometre harbour is one of the largest in the world, and famous for the unmistakable 134-metre high arch of the Harbour Bridge and the graceful sails of the Opera House. It is a busy waterway with ferries, freighters, hydrofoils and pleasure craft.

D Not far from the city centre are the attractive old residential suburbs of Balmain, Glebe, and Paddington, where many people live in smart terraced houses. Art galleries, pubs, and restaurants abound in the cosy streets that tend to be quite narrow, whereas the suburbs surrounding the city's colleges and universities consist mainly of family homes and multi-unit blocks—an ideal situation for students looking for a homestay, or to rent. Sydney's newer suburbs now have a large multicultural population, and local shopping centres reflect the influences of many cultures.

E Sydney is home to the State Art Gallery of New South Wales, the State Conservatorium of Music, the Australian Opera, the Sydney Dance Company, and the Australian Ballet. The world-class Sydney Symphony Orchestra offers superb classical music all year round. Local theatre is innovative and well supported, and large-scale overseas productions tour regularly.

F As well as scores of cinemas and theatres throughout the city and suburbs, there are numerous clubs which appeal to people of all ages, and cater for all tastes. Pubs are the venue for smaller modern bands, while the big-name popular music artists, both local and international, attract capacity audiences at the huge Entertainment Centre in the heart of the city.

Dining Out

In Sydney, a vast array of ethnic and local restaurants can be found to suit all palates and pockets. In summer, café patrons often sit outside at tables under umbrellas, and enjoy the passing parade of shoppers. Students who prefer to cook at home can choose from several large weekend markets, where fresh fruit, fish, and vegetables may be bought more cheaply than at the local supermarket. Sydney also has its own Chinatown.

Shopper's Delight

In the heart of the city there are several big department stores linked by enclosed over-the-street crossings and underground walkways. Most noticeable are the towering Centrepoint complex and the Queen Victoria Building, both containing many shopping arcades, coffee shops and restaurants. Out of town, in the suburbs, there are huge regional shopping centres. At the weekend markets, bargains can be had when shopping for clothing as well as for a wide range of assorted goods.

Sporting Facilities

Australia is recognised as one of the most sports-conscious nations in the world. Sydney boasts an impressive number of facilities for all types of indoor and outdoor sporting activities. Wherever one goes, there are golf courses, cricket pitches, football ovals, tennis and squash courts, and, of course, indoor and outdoor swimming pools. Avid ice-skating and ten-pin bowling fans will find that these activities are also popular and inexpensive.

Conclusion

Whatever a student is interested in, it is certain to be available somewhere in Sydney.

Outside the colleges and universities the scope for filling the leisure hours is enormous, while on campus the choice is equally varied.

Questions 6–8

Complete the table below.

*Choose **A NUMBER ONLY** from the passage for each answer.*

Write your answers in boxes 6–8 on your answer sheet.

CLIMATE	
Summer:	
Average hours of sunshine:	14.5 hours (per day)
Winter:	
Average hours of sunshine:	**6** .... hours (per day)
SIZE	
Population (1997):	**7** .... million
Area (city & suburbs):	**8** .... square km
Sydney Harbour:	57 square km

Questions 9–15

Do the following statements agree with the information given in Reading Passage 1?

In boxes 9–15 on your answer sheet, write

TRUE	*if the statement agrees with the information*
FALSE	*if the statement contradicts the information*
NOT GIVEN	*if there is no information on this*

9 Sydney was first established as a settlement for convicted criminals.

10 Sydney Harbour is the largest harbour in the world.

11 The streets of Paddington are not very wide and contain houses arranged in rows.

12 The Entertainment Centre is only for international popular music artists who attract large audiences.

13 There is now a greater variety of restaurants to choose from in Sydney than in the past.

14 Some department stores in Sydney are joined by walkways above and below the ground.

15 Australians are sports-minded people, but it is not realised by the rest of the world.

READING PASSAGE 2

*You should spend about 20 minutes on **Questions 16–27**, which are based on Reading Passage 2 below.*

Automobiles v.s. Public Transport

Public transport plays a central role in any efficient urban transport system. In developing countries, where at least 16 cities are expected to have more than 12 million people each by the end of this decade, failing to give priority to public transport would be disastrous.

The term "public transport" covers many different types of vehicles, but most commonly refers to buses and trains. Rail services fall into four major categories: rapid rail (also called the underground, tube, metro, or subway), which operates on exclusive rights of way in tunnels or on elevated tracks; trams, which move with other traffic on regular streets; light rail, which is a quieter, more modern version of trams that can run either on exclusive rights of way or with other traffic; and suburban or regional trains, which connect a city with surrounding areas.

The recent trend in many cities is toward light rail over "heavy" rapid rail systems. Whereas metros require exclusive rights of way, which often means building costly elevated or underground lines and stations, light rail can be built on regular city streets, which means no extra expenses.

The concept of public transport also includes organised car pools, in which several people share the cost of riding together in the same private automobile. For U.S. commuters in areas with inadequate bus and train services, this is the only "public" transport option. But even where other systems are comprehensive, there is vast potential for car pooling; recent research shows that in cities the world over, private cars during commuting hours on average carry just 1.2–1.3 persons per vehicle.

Public transport modes vary in fuel use and emissions and in the space they require, but if carrying reasonable numbers of passengers, they all perform better than single occupant private cars on each of these counts.

Although energy requirements vary according to the size and design of the vehicle and how many people are on board, buses and trains require far less fuel per passenger for each kilometre of travel. In the United States, for example, a light rail vehicle needs an estimated 640BTUs of energy per passenger per kilometre; a city bus would use some 690BTUs per passenger per kilometre; and a car pool with four occupants 1,140BTUs. A single occupant automobile, by contrast, burns nearly 4, 580BTUs per passenger per kilometre.

The pollution savings from public transport are even more dramatic. Since both rapid and light rail have electric engines, pollution is measured not from the motor exhaust, but from the power plant generating electricity, which is usually located outside the city, where air quality problems are less serious. For typical U.S. commuter routes, rapid rail emits 30 grams of nitrogen oxides for every 100 kilometres each rail passenger travels, compared with 43 grams for light rail, 95 grams for transit buses, and 128 grams for single occupant automobiles. Public transport's potential for reducing hydrocarbon and carbon monoxide emissions is even greater.

Although diesel buses especially in developing countries can be heavy polluters, existing technologies, such as filters, can control their exhaust. Buses can also run on less polluting fuels such as propane (used in parts of Europe) and natural gas (used in Brazil and China). Test buses in the Netherlands that run on natural gas are estimated to emit 90 percent less nitrogen oxide and 25 percent less carbon monoxide than diesel engines do.

In addition to reducing fuel consumption and pollution, public transport saves valuable city space. Buses and trains carry more people in each vehicle and, if they operate on their own rights of way, can safely run at much higher speeds. In other words, they not only take up less space but also occupy it for a shorter time. Thus, comparing ideal conditions for each mode in one lane of traffic, an underground metro can carry 70, 000 passengers past a certain point in one hour, light rail can carry up to 35, 000 people, and a bus, just over 30, 000. By contrast, a lane of private cars with four occupants each can move only about 8, 000 people an hour, and without such carpooling the figure is, of course, far lower.

The availability and use of public transport vary widely in cities around the globe. Since variations in distances and city densities affect the total kilometres of travel, the annual number of trips each person takes by public transport provides a better standard for comparing its importance in various cities. The range of frequency of public transport use is shown in Table (see page 73).

Urban public transport has long been a government priority in Western Europe. All major cities there have high car ownership, but well-developed bus and rail systems are available, and overall public transport typically accounts for between 20 and 30 percent of passenger kilometres. In recent years, several large cities have stepped up their commitment to public transportation, combining further investments with complementary policies to restrict auto use.

Public transport also plays an important role in urban areas of developing countries. In many cities in Asia, Latin America, and Africa, buses make 50–80 percent of all motorised trips. Buses are sometimes hopelessly overcrowded; it is not uncommon to see several riders clinging to the outside. Yet most cities in developing countries have lower public transport use per person than those in Western Europe, reflecting the inability of small bus fleets to keep up with population growth.

Among the world's major cities, those in Australia and the United States make the least use of alternatives to the private car. Indeed, less than 5 percent of U.S. trips are by public transport, but in some cities such as New York City and Chicago, where service is provided extensively, it is used heavily. Indeed, nearly one quarter of the entire country's public transport trips are in New York City.

*BTUs: British Thermal Units (a measure of energy consumed)

Dependence on public transport in selected cities, 1989

City	Population	Mode	Trips*
Tokyo	11.6m	bus, tram, metro, rail	650
Buenos Aires	9.0m	bus, metro	248
Beijing	8.7m	bus, metro	107
Seoul	8.7m	bus, metro	457
Moscow	8.0m	bus, tram, metro	713
Chicago	6.8m	bus, metro, rail	101
Berlin	3.1m	bus, tram, metro, rail	356
Toronto	2.8m	bus, tram, metro	200
Melbourne	2.7m	bus, tram, rail	95
Abidjan	1.8m	bus, boat	132
Dallas	1.4m	bus	22

* trips per person per year

Questions 16–20

Answer the questions below.

Choose ***NO MORE THAN THREE WORDS*** *from the passage for each answer.*

Write your answers in boxes 16–20 on your answer sheet.

16 What is a factor that makes light rail preferable to rapid rail?

17 What is the average number of people in automobiles during commuting hours?

18 Where is the pollution measured from?

19 In which aspect does rapid rail outperform light rail?

20 What proportion of passenger kilometres is undertaken by private automobile in Western Europe?

Questions 21–27

Complete the summary using the list of words, ***A–P****, below.*

Write the correct letter, ***A–P****, in boxes 21–27 on your answer sheet.*

NB *You may use any letter more than once.*

Key Points: Automobiles v.s. Public Transport

Apart from lowering **21** .... and reducing exhaust emissions, another important benefit of public transport is the saving of the space that is taken up. It can aslo occupy the space for a shorter time, this is measured by determining the number of **22** .... that pass a particular poin under ideal conditions. As would be expected, public transport vehicles perform very well under these criteria. However, the importance of public transport depends on its **23** .... A survey in 1989 revealed that **24** .... was the city in which the greatest number of trips per person were made on an annual basis. The governments of Western Europe have attached great importance to **25** .... and in recent years, some large cities have combined further investments with **26** .... to reduce auto use. Interestingly, there is no clear correlation between acceptance of public transport and the degree of **27** .... of a country or city.

A	passengers	**I**	energy policies
B	Moscow	**J**	economic development
C	fuel efficiency	**K**	fuel consumption
D	availability of transport	**L**	decentralisation
E	vehicles per hour	**M**	frequency of use
F	Tokyo	**N**	Third World cities
G	passengers per hour	**O**	urban public transport
H	single occupant automobiles	**P**	complementary policies

READING PASSAGE 3

*You should spend about 20 minutes on **Questions 28–40**, which are based on Reading Passage 3 below.*

Pupil Size and Communication

It has already been well established that changes in pupil size are clearly associated with changes in attitude. In a typical example, when viewing photographs of food, hungry subjects experience a much greater increase in pupil diameter than do sated subjects (see figure 1). However it now appears that enlarged or constricted pupils can also affect the response of the person who observed them.

FIGURE 1
DIFFERENCES IN PUPIL RESPONSE of hungry subjects and of sated subjects to colour slides of various foods are shown. The subjects first viewed a control slide, then a slide of a food and the change in pupil size was measured.

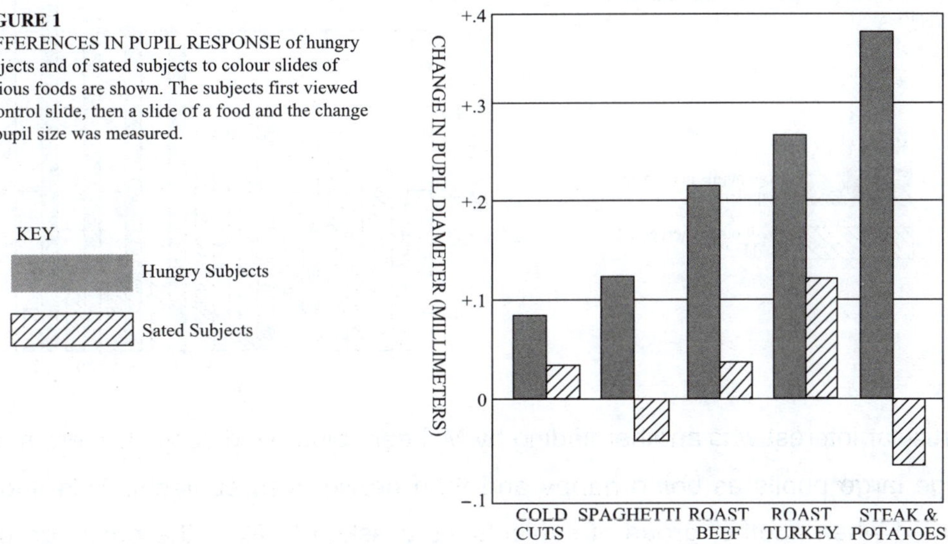

Studies of the pupil as an indicator of attitude point to the possibility that one person uses another person's pupil size as a source of information about that person's feelings or attitudes. In one experiment two photographs of an attractive young woman were shown to a group of men. The photographs were identical except that in one the woman's pupils had been retouched to make them larger and in the other they had been retouched to make them smaller. None of the men reported noticing the difference in pupil size, but when they were asked to describe the woman, they said that the women in the picture with the large pupils was "soft", "more feminine" or "pretty". The same woman in the picture with the small pupils was described as being "hard", "selfish" or "cold". There could be little doubt that the large pupils made the woman more attractive to the men.

It seems that what is appealing about large pupils in a woman is that they are an indicator of interest, which can be interpreted as sexual interest. However, when men view a picture of a woman with large pupils, their own pupils dilate. In other words, seeing large pupils gives rise to larger pupils. Interestingly, men and women showed almost no increase in pupil size when viewing photographs of members of the same sex with dilated pupils.

That the dilation response is in fact learned rather than innate is supported by experiments with children. In one experiment, subjects aged 6 to 22 were shown drawings of female faces that had different sized pupils, and asked to choose the one which was "happier". The results showed that, up to the age of 14, a person does not necessarily perceive larger pupils as being happier than smaller pupils (see figure 2).

FIGURE 2
Age differences in perceiving a face with large pupils as being happier than a face with small pupils

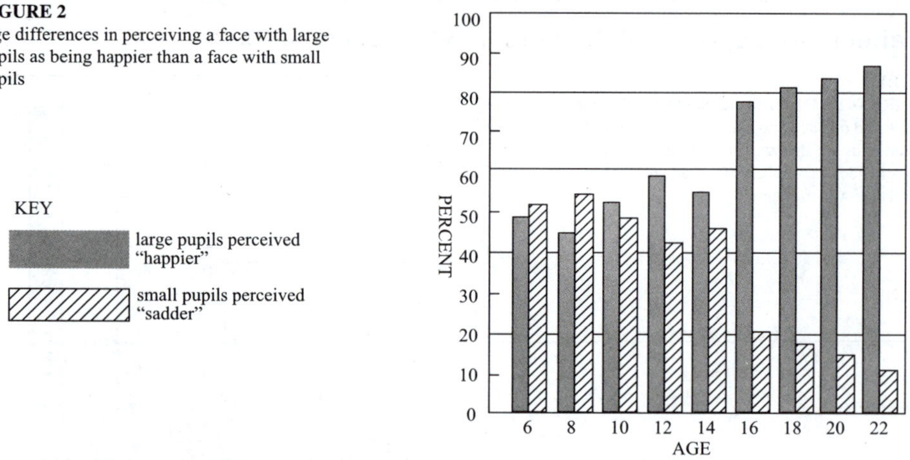

Of particular interest was another finding by McLean: blue-eyed subjects were more likely to judge large pupils as being happy and than brown-eyed subjects. This finding was confirmed when another group of subjects were asked to fill in the pupils on drawings of happy faces and angry ones: the blue-eyed subjects drew larger "happy" pupils and smaller "angry" pupils than the brown-eyed subjects (see figure 3).

FIGURE 3
BLUE-EYED SUBJECTS drew larger pupils on a sketch of a happy face and smaller pupils on a scowling face than brown-eyed subjects. In addition, when viewing a picture that normally causes dilation or constriction, blue-eyed people show a greater change in pupil size.

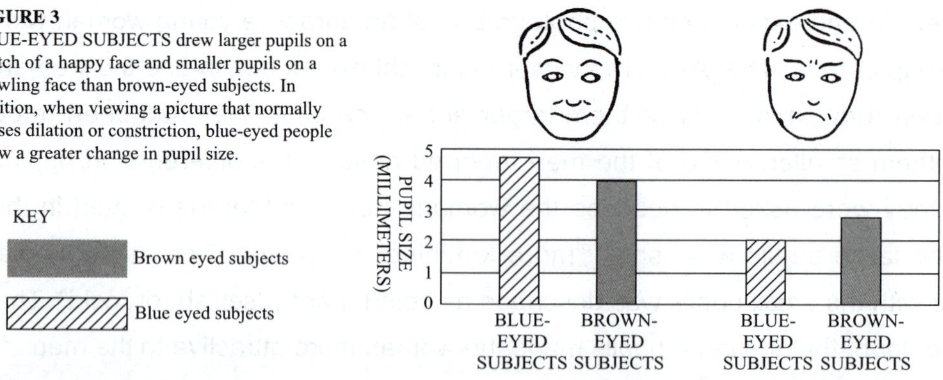

Blue-eyed people have also been found to have a stronger pupil response than brown-eyed people when they view a picture that causes pupil dilation or constriction. To be more precise, with respect to the total range of response from the smallest pupil size to the largest, the range is greater for blue-eyed people than it is for brown-eyed people.

Questions 28–35

Based on the information in Reading Passage 3, "Pupil Size and Communication", indicate the relationship between each of the two measures listed below in terms of:

PC	*if there is a positive correlation*
L/N	*if there is little or no correlation*
NI	*if there is no information*

*Write your answers(**PC, L/N, NI**)in boxes 28–35 on your answer sheet.*

	MEASURE 1	MEASURE 2
28	Changes in pupil size	Changes in attitude
29	Images of food	Pupil dilation in hungry subjects
30	Small pupil size in picture of woman	Negative response in male subject
31	Pupil dilation in picture of woman	Pupil dilation in male subject
32	Pupil dilation in picture of woman	Pupil dilation in female subject
33	Small pupil size in picture of woman	Negative response in female subject
34	Subjects under 14 years of age	Positive response to large pupils
35	Darkness of eye colour in photograph	Subject's estimate of "happiness"

Questions 36–40

Answer the questions below.

*Choose **NO MORE THAN THREE WORDS** from the passage for each answer.*

Write your answers in boxes 36–40 on your answer sheet.

36 According to the data, what kind of food do hungry people respond to most readily?

37 What interpretation is given for men's attraction to women with large pupils?

38 What conclusion can be drawn about dilation response from the phenomenon that children under 14 don't react to pupil size in other people?

39 According to figure 2, children at what age have most different responses in face-emotion perceiving?

40 How was blue-eyed subjects's response compared with brown-eyed subjects?

Test 3 答案速查 Key

READING PASSAGE 1

1. i	**2.** v	**3.** ii	**4.** vi
5. iv	**6.** 10.25	**7.** 4.4	**8.** (about) 3, 000
9. TRUE	**10.** NOT GIVEN	**11.** TRUE	**12.** FALSE
13. NOT GIVEN	**14.** TRUE	**15.** FALSE	

READING PASSAGE 2

16. no extra expenses	**17.** 1.2–1.3	**18.** power plant	**19.** less pollution
20. 70–80%	**21.** K	**22.** G	**23.** M
24. B	**25.** O	**26.** P	**27.** J

READING PASSAGE 3

28. PC	**29.** PC	**30.** PC	**31.** PC
32. L/N	**33.** NI	**34.** L/N	**35.** NI
36. steak&potatoes	**37.** sexual interest	**38.** (it is) learned	**39.** 22
40. stronger/greater			

Test 3 考题精解 Detailed Explanation

READING PASSAGE 1

Questions 1–5

题型：段落标题配对题 (LIST OF HEADINGS)

◆ 解析

1. i

通读B段，此段第二句说到了悉尼的地理位置，而由第四句中的First established...in 1788...可知该段又讲到了悉尼的历史，与i中的Location and History相符，故本题答案为i。

2. v

通读C段，本段有四句话，前两句通过具体数字说明suburbs的大小，后两句则说到harbour的大小、景观、总体评价，与v项The Harbour and Surrounding Suburbs相符，故本题答案为v。

3. ii

通读D段，可知第一句Not far from the city centre are the attractive old residential suburbs of Balmain, Glebe, and Paddington, where many people live in smart terraced houses.为主题句，由此可知本段介绍的是离市中心不远的旧居民区，与ii项Residential Inner-City Suburbs相符，故本题答案为ii。

4. vi

通读E段，本段第一句就说悉尼拥有着包括新南威尔士艺术馆、州立音乐学院……在内的艺术机构，由此可判断这段讲的是悉尼的文化，vi项The Cultural Climate与其相符，故本题答案为vi。

5. iv

通读F段，本段的第一句...there are numerous clubs which appeal to people of all ages, and cater for all tastes...为主题句，句中的all ages对应iv中的Young and Old，故本题答案为iv。

Questions 6–8

题型：表格填空题 (TABLE COMPLETION)

◆ 解析

6. 10.25

本题需要填写冬天的平均日照小时数。由关键词winter及sunshine定位到B段第二句Located on the south-east coast of Australia in the temperate zone, it enjoys a mild climate, averaging 14.5 hours of sunshine per day in summer and 10.25 hours in winter，由该句可知澳大利亚处于温带地区，气候温和，冬天平均日照时间为10.25个小时，故本题答案为10.25。

7. 4.4

本题填写人口数。文章包含的数字信息基本集中在B、C两段，而由题干关键词1997可定位到C段第一句Sydney is home to nearly 4.4 million people (as of 1997)，由此可知本题答案为4.4。

8. (about) 3, 000

由题干关键词square km可定位到原文C段第二句The suburbs reach out from the city centre and harbour some 55 km to the north, 35 km to the west and 30 km to the south, creating a metropolitan area of about 3, 000 square kilometres，本题所要填写的是市中心和郊区的总面积，故本题答案为(about) 3, 000。

Questions 9–15

题型：判断题 (TRUE/FALSE/NOT GIVEN)

◆ 解析

9. TRUE

根据题干中的关键词was first定位到原文B段第四句First established by the British as a convict settlement in 1788... 该句是题干的同义转述，故本题答案为TRUE。

10. NOT GIVEN

根据题干中的关键词Harbour定位到原文的C段第三句The 57-square-kilometre harbour is one of the largest in the world，原文只说悉尼港是世界最大的港口之一，但是否是世界最大的港口并没有提，故本题答案为NOT GIVEN。注意答此题不能凭借自己的所知，事实上，世界最大的港口是荷兰的鹿特丹，但文章中没说，所以不能答FALSE。

11. TRUE

根据题干中的关键词Paddington定位到原文D段第一句...Paddington, where many people live in smart terraced houses. Art galleries, pubs, and restaurants abound in the cosy streets that tend to be quite narrow，其中terraced对应题干中的arranged in rows, quite narrow对应题干中的not very wide，原文和题干是同义表达，故本题答案为TRUE。

12. FALSE

根据题干中的关键词Entertainment Centre定位到原文F段第二句...the big-name popular music artists, both local and international, attract capacity audiences at the huge Entertainment Centre in the heart of the city，原文说both local and international，而题干说only for international，与原文表述不符，故本题答案为FALSE。

13. NOT GIVEN

根据题干中的关键词restaurants定位到原文小标题为“Dining Out”的段落，原文中提到了悉尼有各种各样的餐馆，但并没有与过去相比，故本题答案为NOT GIVEN。

14. TRUE

根据题干中的关键词department stores定位到原文小标题为“Shopper’s Delight”的段落，该段第一句为In the heart of the city are several big department stores linked by enclosed over-the-street crossings and underground walkways，其中linked by对应题干中的joined by，原文和题干是同义表达，故本题答案为TRUE。

15. FALSE

根据题干中的关键词sports定位到原文小标题为“Sporting Facilities”的段落，该段第一句为Australia is recognised as one of the most sports-conscious nations in the world，原文说recognised，题干说not realised，recognised和realised是同义词，即句意相反，故本题答案为FALSE。

◎ 参考译文

留学在悉尼——澳大利亚概况

A　多年以来澳大利亚已经成为众多国际学生的热门选择。澳大利亚的大学和学院凭借其极高的教学水平日益蜚声海外。另外，澳大利亚毗邻东南亚，有着便利的地理位置（雅加达是印度尼西亚的首都，是距离澳大利亚最近的亚洲城市，距离悉尼仅5 506公里）。为海外学生修订的入境程序使来澳学习的人员日益增多成为可能。悉尼作为澳大利亚最大的城市，同时也是澳大利亚国际航线运营服务的主要港口。

B　悉尼是以新南威尔士州一位前总督命名，为该州首府。它位于温带地区，即澳大利亚东南海岸，气候温和，夏季平均日照时间为14.5个小时，冬天平均日照时间为10.25个小时。同时，悉尼也是澳大利亚规模最大、最古老、或许也是最美丽的城市。1788年，最初由英国人将其作为犯人流放基地而建立的悉尼如今已发展成集主要工业中心、商业中心和制造业中心于一体的现代化国际大都市。

C　悉尼约有440万人口（根据1997年的数据）。郊区最远可以由城市中心和港口向北延伸约55公里，向西延伸35公里，向南延伸30公里，占地约3 000平方公里。57平方公里的悉尼港是世界上最大的港口之一，以港口大桥那足有134米高的大拱以及悉尼歌剧院那优雅的白帆而闻名。忙碌的港口随处可见运输船、货轮、水翼船以及私人游艇。

D　距市中心不远处有三座诱人的古老村庄——巴尔曼、格利比和帕丁顿。那里有许多人都住在小型的露天平房中。随处可见的艺术馆、酒吧及餐馆使那惬意的小巷显得更加狭窄，而在学院和大学周围的村庄主要由一些居民住所和混合型社区组成——这对于那些想寻找寄宿家庭或者租房的学生来讲是一个理想的环境。悉尼较新的郊区如今拥有大量不同文化背景的人口，连当地一些购物中心也表现出受众多文化影响的特点。

E　悉尼拥有包括新南威尔士州立艺术馆、州立音乐学院、澳大利亚歌剧院、悉尼舞蹈公司以及澳大利亚芭蕾舞团在内的艺术机构。在世界上享有盛誉的悉尼交响乐团全年都会献上精彩的古典音乐。当地剧场极具创新精神而且也获得了有力的支持，经常会有大规模的海外巡回演出。

F　如同众多遍布市区及郊区的电影院和剧场一样，悉尼也拥有大量符合各年龄层和迎合各种口味的俱乐部。酒吧则是小型现代乐队的聚集地。同时，国内外著名的流行乐手也会经常在市中心的巨型娱乐中心表演节目以吸引众多观众前来观看。

饮食篇

在悉尼，可以找到众多符合各种口味及阶层的极具民族和地域特色的餐馆。在夏天，咖啡爱好者总是坐在户外阳伞下的桌旁，分享来往购物者的愉快。那些喜欢在家烹饪的学生则可以在一些大型周末集市上选择食材。在那里，新鲜的水果、鱼和蔬菜往往比当地的超市更为实惠。悉尼也拥有自己的唐人街。

购物篇

市中心有一些由封闭式天桥和地下通道连接的大型购物中心。最引人注目的是复杂塔楼型建筑以及维多利亚女王时代的建筑其内部有许多购物商场、咖啡馆以及餐馆。在城外的郊区，也有许多大型的当地购物中心。在周末集市上，衣物及其他很多商品的特价活动都随处可见。

运动篇

澳大利亚是世界公认的最有运动意识的国家之一。悉尼拥有数量相当可观的各种各样的室内外运动设施，无论你走到哪里，都可以找到高尔夫球场、板球场、足球场、网球场以及壁球场，当然，还有室内外游泳馆。那些热衷于滑雪和打保龄球的朋友们，会发现这些活动可以说既受欢迎又实惠。

总结

无论你热衷于什么，在悉尼，你都可以找到适合自己的一席之地。无论在校内还是校外，你都可以找到很多充实闲暇生活的去处。

READING PASSAGE 2

Questions 16–20

题型：简答题 (SHORT ANSWER QUESTIONS)

◆ 解析

16. no extra expenses

由题干中的关键词light rail preferable to rapid rail可定位到原文第三段的第一句The recent trend in many cities is toward light rail over "heavy" rapid rail systems，其中light rail over "heavy" rapid rail systems与题干中的关键词为同义转换。本段第二句前半部分说的是地铁需要专门的轨道，也就意味着要修建昂贵的高架铁路或者地下路线以及车站，后半句提到轻轨可以建在城市普通街道上，也就是意味着没有额外费用，由该段可知轻轨优于地铁之处在于"没有额外费用"，故本题答案为no extra expenses。

17. 1.2–1.3

由题干关键词commuting hours定位到原文第四段的最后一句...recent research shows that in cities the world over, private cars during commuting hours on average carry just 1.2–1.3 persons per vehicle，其中private cars...on average carry与题干中的the average number of people in automobiles为同义转述，故本题答案为1.2–1.3。

18. power plant

由题干中的关键词pollution定位到原文第七段的第一句The pollution savings from public transport are even more dramatic，该段第二句中有pollution is measured not from the motor exhaust, but from the power plant generating electricity，由该句可知污染不能根据汽车尾气测量，而是根据产生电力的发电厂测量，故本题答案为power plant。

19. less pollution

题干问的是地铁在哪一方面优于轻轨，由题干关键词outperform可定位到原文第七段，在该段的后半部分有提到说如果以每位旅客运行100公里为单位计算的话，地铁排放氧化氮的量为30克，轻轨为43克，由此数据可推知地铁优于轻轨的地方在于少污染，故本题答案为less pollution。

20. 70–80%

由题干中的关键词Western Europe定位到原文倒数第三段的第一句Urban public transport has long been a government priority in Western Europe，接着往下读，找到段中的句子overall public transport typically accounts for between 20 and 30 percent of passenger kilometres，注意原文说的是公共交通占20–30%，而题干问的是私人汽车所占的比例，故本题答案为70–80%。

Questions 21–27

题型：摘要填空题 (SUMMARY COMPLETION)

◆ 解析

分析选项可知，本题的所有空白处都填写名词。另外，摘要题自身符合顺序性原则，所以定位到第一道题的答案，那么后面的答案顺次寻找即可。由于摘要的前两句话与原文第九段话的第一句In addition to reducing fuel consumption and pollution, public transport saves valuable city space相对应，可知各题的答案从此处开始找。

21. K

空前为动名词lowering，缺宾语，所以可知此空填写名词。原文第九段的第一句提到reducing fuel consumption and pollution，21题空后的reducing exhaust emissions与reducing pollution同义，lowering与reducing同义，故本题答案为K。注意不要答成C，公共交通降低的是燃料的消耗，而不是燃料的效率，它提高了燃料的效率。

22. G

由空格后的pass a particular point under ideal conditions可对应到原文第九段的第四句，根据其中carry 70 000 passengers past a certain point in one hour可知答案为G，注意不要答成A，因为原文中有in one hour，此题有一定的难度，属于陷阱题。

23. M

此题是这几题中难度最大的。根据顺序原则继续浏览下文，找到原文第十段中Since variations in distances and city densities affect the total kilometres of travel, the annual number of trips each person takes by public transport provides a better standard for comparing its importance in various cities. The range of frequency of public transport use is shown in Table，这里的frequency of public transport use指的就是第一句中表述的现象，这句的中文意思是由于距离与城市密度的不同影响着出行的总公里数，每年每人利用公共交通工具出行的数值为比较公共交通工具在不同城市的重要性提供了非常好的标准。公共交通使用的频率如表所示。由此可知此空填写frequency of use，故本题答案为M。

24. B

由题干中的A survey revealed in 1989可知此题问的是后面的表格的内容，根据题干中的was the city in which the greatest number of trips per person were made on an annual basis即每年每人旅行数目最多的城市对照表格，可知是Moscow，故本题答案为B。

25. O

由题干中的Western Europe可定位到原文倒数第三段的第一句Urban public transport has long been a government priority in Western Europe，即在西欧，城市公共交通一直都是政府优先考虑的大事，have attached great importance to与原文的has been a...priority对应，所以可知本空填写urban public transport，故本题的答案为O。

26. P

由题干中的have combined further investments和reduce auto use定位到原文倒数第三段最后一句的combining further investments with complementary policies to restrict auto use，可知这里填写complementary policies，故本题的答案为P。

27. J

本题需归纳才可得出答案。原文倒数第三段的第一句Urban public transport has long been a government priority in Western Europe和原文倒数第二段的第一句Public transport also plays an important role in urban areas of developing countries分别说的是发达国家和发展中国家对公共交通的接纳程度，由此可以判断公共交通的接纳程度与经济发展程度无关，故本题答案为J。

◎ 参考译文

汽车VS公共交通

公共交通在任何有效率的城市交通系统中都发挥着核心作用。在发展中国家，当这个十年即将过去之时，至少有16个城市的人口有望达到1 200多万，不重视公共交通必然会有灾难性的后果。

“公共交通”这一术语涵盖了多种不同的交通工具，但是一般来说主要指的是公交巴士和列车。铁路交通主要分为四大类型：只在专门的隧道或者高架轨道上才能通行的地铁

（也被称为underground，tube，metro或者subway）；可以在一般的街道上同其他交通工具并行的电车；既可以在专用轨道上行驶又能与其他交通工具并行的更为安静和现代的电车——轻轨；还有连接城市与周边地区的城际或者地区列车。

近期，在很多城市都有轻轨代替“重型”地铁系统的趋势。地铁需要专用的轨道，这就意味着要修建昂贵的高架铁路或者地下路线以及车站。而轻轨可以直接在普通的城市街道上修建，这意味着没有额外的花费。

公共交通的概念还包括有组织的拼车——多人共乘一辆私家车，同时共同承担费用。在美国一些缺乏巴士以及列车服务的地区，这成了上下班人群惟一的“公共”交通选择。但是在其他公交系统丰富的地区，也极有可能出现拼车的情况。近期调查表明，全球各个城市在上下班时间平均每辆私家车上仅有1.2–1.3人。

虽然各种公共交通工具在燃料使用、尾气排放以及占地面积方面各有不同，但是如果载客人数合理，公共交通在上述问题上的优势就会大于仅有一人乘坐的私家车。

虽然能源需求会随着交通工具的尺寸、设计以及承载人数而变化，但是公共汽车和列车运行每公里距离所需要的人均燃料是非常低的。例如，在美国，一辆轻轨机车预计消耗的能量为640BTUs/人/公里；城市公共汽车需要690BTUs/人/公里；一辆承载4个人的合用车则需要1 140BTUs/人/公里。相反，单独驾驶的私家车，其消耗值达到近4 580BTUs/人/公里。

公共交通在减少污染方面发挥着巨大的作用。既然地铁与轻轨均由电力发动，环境污染就不能根据尾气排放测量，而是根据产生电力的电厂来测量。这些工厂一般设在城市外围，相对来说那里的空气质量问题不是很严重。比如典型美国的通勤线路，以每位旅客运行100公里为单位计算的话，地铁排放氧化氮的量为30克，轻轨为43克，公共汽车为95克，个人私家车为128克。公共交通在降低碳氢化合物和一氧化碳排放方面的潜力越来越大了。

虽然柴油公共汽车（多在发展中国家）污染非常严重，但是可以通过现有的技术比如过滤器来控制尾气。公共汽车也可以通过使用低污染燃料来运行，比如丙烷（多用在欧洲部分地区）和天然气（多用在巴西和中国）。目前在荷兰使用天然气的公共汽车要比使用柴油的公共汽车少排放90%的氧化氮以及25%的一氧化碳。

公共交通除了减少燃料的消耗以及污染以外，还节约了城市的有效空间。公共汽车和列车可以承载更多的旅客，如果能够在其专用的轨道上运行，他们就能以更快的速度安全地行驶。换句话说，这些公共交通工具不仅可以节约空间，而且还可以缩短所用时间。因此，如果交通路线中的各个交通模式都在理想的条件下运行，地铁可以在一个小时内将70 000名乘客运到指定地点，轻轨可以完成35 000名旅客的运载，而公共汽车的运载量大约是30 000名。相反，一条供载有四人的私家车行驶的车道一个小时内大约仅可以完成8 000

名乘客的运载，如果不是集体拼车，该数值会更低。

全球各个城市的公共交通在有效利用性和实用性上呈现出极大的不同。由于距离与城市密度的不同左右着出行的总公里数，每年每人利用公共交通工具出行的数值为比较公共交通工具在不同城市的重要性提供了非常好的标准。公共交通工具的使用频率如表所示（见下表）。

在西欧，城市公共交通一直都是政府优先考虑的大事。所有主要城市都拥有很多汽车，但其发达的公共汽车和轨道系统都得到了有效利用，全部的公交工具运行量占旅客公里数的20%–30%。近年来，很多大城市已逐步提高了对公共交通承担的责任，将进一步投资与补偿政策相结合以限制私家车的使用。

公共交通在发展中国家的城市中同样起着非常重要的作用，在亚洲、拉丁美洲以及非洲的很多城市，公共汽车占机动车旅程的50%–80%。公共汽车内经常非常拥挤，经常可以看到有人爬在汽车外面。但是与西欧相比，发展中国家城市的人均公共交通的使用率非常低，这也反映了小型公共汽车承载能力的发展无法跟上人口增长的速度。

在世界主要城市中，澳大利亚与美国私家车的替代物使用率最低。事实上，在美国，不到5%的出行是使用公共交通工具，但是在纽约和芝加哥等一些城市，由于公共交通服务系统比较完善，公共交通工具的使用率是很高的。事实上，纽约的公交使用量占整个国家的近四分之一。

几大城市公共交通工具使用频率表, 1989

城市	人口	模式	旅程*
东京	1160万	公交车，电车，地铁，火车	650
布宜诺斯艾利斯	900万	公交车，地铁	248
北京	870万	公交车，地铁	107
首尔	870万	公交车，地铁	457
莫斯科	800万	公交车，电车，地铁	713
芝加哥	680万	公交车，地铁，火车	101
柏林	310万	公交车，电车，地铁，火车	356
多伦多	280万	公交车，电车，地铁	200
墨尔本	270万	公交车，电车，火车	95
阿比让	180万	公交车，船	132
达拉斯	140万	公交车	22

READING PASSAGE 3

Questions 28–34

题型：配对题 (MATCHING)

◆ 解析

本题为配对题，问的是MEASURE 1和MEASURE 2之间是否有关系，如果正相关则写PC，如果没有或者几乎没有关系写L/N，如果原文没有提供相关信息则写NI。

28. PC

由题干关键词Changes in attitude可以定位到原文第一段的第一句It has already been well established that changes in pupil size are clearly associated with changes in attitude，即人们已经普遍认可瞳孔的尺寸变化与态度变化明显有关，可知两者正相关，故本题答案为PC。

29. PC

由题干关键词Images of food可定位到原文第一段的第二句In a typical example, when viewing photographs of food, hungry subjects experience a much greater increase in pupil diameter than do sated subjects (see figure 1)，即有一个非常典型的例子：当观察食物的图片时，饥饿受试者的瞳孔直径要远远大于饱食受试者的瞳孔直径（如图1），可知两者正相关，故本题答案为PC。

30. PC

由题干关键词Small pupil size in picture of woman可以定位到原文的第二段，由The same woman in the picture with the small pupils was described as being "hard", "selfish" or "cold"，即虽然是同一女士，只是瞳孔小一些的，他们却用"严厉"、"自私"或者"冷酷"来形容，可知两者正相关，故本题答案为PC。

31. PC

由题干关键词Pupil dilation in picture of woman和Pupil dilation in male subject可以定位到原文第三段，由However, when men view a picture of a woman with large pupils, their own pupils dilate. In other words, seeing large pupils gives rise to larger pupils，即但是，当男人们看到大瞳孔女性的图片时，他们自己的瞳孔会扩张。换句话说，看到大瞳孔能够使瞳孔变大，可知两者正相关，故本题答案为PC。

32. L/N

根据原文第三段的最后一句话Interestingly, men and women showed almost no increase in pupil size when viewing photographs of members of the same sex with dilated pupils，即有趣的是，无论是男人还是女人，在观察同性的瞳孔增大的图片时，几乎没有增加瞳孔尺寸的现象，可知同性之间没有关系，故本题答案为L/N。

33. NI

本题切忌主观猜测。根据原文第三段的最后一句：无论是男人还是女人，在观察同性的瞳孔增大的图片时，几乎没有增加瞳孔尺寸的现象，本题说的是照片中小的瞳孔，原文中没有提及这方面的内容，故本题答案为NI。

34. L/N

由题干关键词under 14 years of age可定位到原文第四段，由The results showed that, up to the age of 14, a person does not necessarily perceive larger pupils as being happier than smaller pupils (see figure 2)，即结果表明，到14岁为止，瞳孔大小与开心的感知无关（见图2），也就是说14岁以下的儿童不会对大瞳孔有积极反应，故本题答案为L/N。

35. NI

由题干关键词colour可以定位到原文的最后两段，原文说的是实验对象（就是看照片的人）的瞳孔颜色对图片反应不同，而题干说的是照片中瞳孔的颜色，故本题答案为NI。

Questions 36–40

题型：简答题 (SHORT ANSWER QUESTIONS)

◆ 解析

36. steak&potatoes

由题干中的关键词According to the data和food可定位到FIGURE 1，题干问的是饥饿的人对哪种食物反应最快，观察图1可知是steak&potatoes。

37. sexual interest

由题干关键词interpretation和men's attraction to women可定位到原文第三段的第一句It seems that what is appealing about large pupils in a woman is that they are an indicator of interest, which can be interpreted as sexual interest，可知attraction为appealing的同义转换，interpretation为interpreted的名词形式，可最终确定答案为sexual interest。

38. (it is) learned

由题干关键词dilation response和children under 14可以定位到原文第四段，由That the dilation response is in fact learned rather than innate is supported by experiments with children，可知答案为learned，或者it is learned。

39. 22

题干直接指明在figure 2中找答案，观察图片，可知反应最大的是22岁的孩子，故本题答案为22。

40. stronger/greater

由题干关键词blue-eyed subjects和brown-eyed subjects可以定位到原文最后两段，由原文最后一段的Blue-eyed people have also been found to have a stronger pupil response than brown-eyed people when they view a picture that causes pupil dilation or constriction. To be more precise, with respect to the total range of response from the smallest pupil size to the largest, the range is greater for blue-eyed people than it is for brown-eyed people，即同时发现，蓝眼睛的人群在观察瞳孔扩大或者收缩的图片时，其瞳孔的反应要比棕色眼睛的人群强烈。更精确地说，就瞳孔尺寸从最小到最大时的人群反应变化幅度而言，蓝色眼睛的人群的变化幅度要大于棕色眼睛的人群，可知正确答案为stronger或greater。

◎ 参考译文

瞳孔尺寸与交流沟通

人们已经普遍认可瞳孔的尺寸变化与态度变化明显有关。有一个非常典型的例子：当观察食物的图片时，饥饿受试者的瞳孔直径要远远大于饱食受试者的瞳孔直径（见图1）。然而，现在看来，增大或者收缩瞳孔也能影响观察它们的人的反应。

关于瞳孔可以反应态度的研究表明：一个人是可以通过观察另外一个人的瞳孔尺寸来判断其感受或者想法的。在一项实验中，向一群男士展示两张同一个年轻美丽的女性的照片。这两张照片，除了一张上的瞳孔被修正得略大，另外一张的修得小一些之外，完全一样。报告结果显示没有人发现瞳孔尺寸的差异。当要求他们描述该女士时，他们用“温柔”、“更有女人味”或者“可爱”来形容瞳孔大一些的女士。而虽然是同一女士，对于瞳孔小一些的，他们却用“严厉”、“自私”或者“冷酷”来形容。毫无疑问，瞳孔大一些的女性对于男性更有吸引力。

看来女性瞳孔大的魅力之处在于他们是兴趣的指示器，这种兴趣可被解释为性欲。但是，当男人们看到大瞳孔女性的图片时，他们自己的瞳孔会扩张。换句话说，看到大瞳孔能够使瞳孔变大。有趣的是，无论是男人还是女人，在观察同性的瞳孔增大的图片时，几乎没有增加瞳孔尺寸的现象。

以孩子作为受试者进行的实验表明，事实上，瞳孔扩大的反应是后天养成而非天生的。在一项选取6岁到22岁的受试者进行的实验中，他们会看到有着不同瞳孔尺寸的女性面部图片，要求他们选出哪一张是“开心的”。结果表明，到14岁为止，瞳孔大小与开心的感知无关（见图2）。

另外一个特别有趣的结果是麦克林发现的：蓝眼睛的受试者比棕色眼睛的受试者更倾向于将大瞳孔作为判断开心的标志。这一发现在另外一个实验中得到证实：要求一组受试者画出开心时的瞳孔和生气时的瞳孔：蓝眼睛的受试者画出了比棕色眼睛的受试者更大的“开心的”瞳孔和更小的“生气的”瞳孔（见图3）。

同时还发现，蓝眼睛的人群在观察瞳孔扩大或者收缩的图片时，其瞳孔的反应要比棕色眼睛的人群强烈。更精确地说，就瞳孔尺寸从最小到最大时的人群反应变化幅度而言，蓝色眼睛的人群的变化幅度要大于棕色眼睛的人群。

Test 3 核心词汇 Core Vocabulary

READING PASSAGE 1

exceptionally *adv.* 异常地，特殊地

principal *adj.* 首要的，主要的

temperate *adj.* （气候等）温暖的，温和的

temperate zone 温带

mild *adj.* （天气）温暖的，暖和的

cosmopolitan *adj.* 世界性的

metropolitan *adj.* 大城市的；中心地区的

freighter *n.* 货船

hydrofoil *n.* 水翼船

conservatorium *n.* 〈澳〉公立音乐学院，艺术学校

palate *n.* 味觉；品味的能力

residential *adj.* 居民的

abound *vi.* 富于，充满

innovative *adj.* 富有创造力的

patron *n.* 顾客，老主顾

avid *adj.* 渴望的，急切的

READING PASSAGE 2

category *n.* 分类

exclusive *adj.* 独有的；专一的

tunnel *n.* 隧道

elevated *n.* 高架铁路

commuter *n.* 通勤者

car pool 拼车，合伙用车

occupant *n.* 占用者

emission *n.* 散发物；排放

diesel bus 柴油汽车

READING PASSAGE 3

pupil *n.* 瞳孔

associate *vt.* 使联合

diameter *n.* 直径

constricted *adj.* 收缩的

dilation *n.* 扩大，扩张

indicator *n.* 指示物；标志

precise *adj.* 精确的，明确的

TEST 4

Candidate Number

Candidate Name ______________________

INTERNATIONAL ENGLISH LANGUAGE TESTING SYSTEM

ACADEMIC READING

TIME 1 hour

INSTRUCTIONS TO CANDIDATES

Do not open this booklet until you are told to do so.

Write your name and candidate number in the spaces at the top of this page.

Start at the beginning of the test and work through it.

You should answer **all** questions.

If you cannot do a particular question, leave it and go on to the next. You can return to it later.

All answers must be written on the answer sheet.

Do not remove this booklet from the examination room.

INFORMATION FOR CANDIDATES

There are **40** questions on this question paper.

The test is divided as follows:

Reading Passage 1	Questions 1–13
Reading Passage 2	Questions 14–27
Reading Passage 3	Questions 28–40

Reading Answer Sheet

Are you: Female? ▭ Male? ▭

Your first language code:

0 1 2 3 4 5 6 7 8 9
0 1 2 3 4 5 6 7 8 9
0 1 2 3 4 5 6 7 8 9

IELTS Reading Answer Sheet

Module taken (shade one box): Academic ▭ General Training ▭

1		✓ 1 ✗	21		✓ 21 ✗
2		2	22		22
3		3	23		23
4		4	24		24
5		5	25		25
6		6	26		26
7		7	27		27
8		8	28		28
9		9	29		29
10		10	30		30
11		11	31		31
12		12	32		32
13		13	33		33
14		14	34		34
15		15	35		35
16		16	36		36
17		17	37		37
18		18	38		38
19		19	39		39
20		20	40		40

Checker's Initials | Marker's Initials | Band Score | Reading Total

READING PASSAGE 1

*You should spend about 20 minutes on **Questions 1–13**, which are based on Reading Passage 1 below.*

Fanwall Noise Barrier

Noise generated by traffic on arterial roads and freeways is an increasing problem in Australia and there is growing concern among highways authorities in Australia about the limitations of some types of noise barriers which have been installed in this country.

The Roads and Traffic Authority (RTA) in Sydney faced a problem when it decided to proceed with the link between Concord Road at Rhodes and the F4 Freeway at Homebush (Country Road 5030) as the new arterial would deliver heavy traffic right past the backyards of suburban homes. This was because the RTA had purchased and removed a number of houses to allow the new corridor to be built, exposing to road traffic noises houses which were once located in a quiet back street.

Initially, the RTA had proposed to erect a new timber fence, replacing the existing suburban fences, to act as a noise barrier. Timber noise barriers were used quite extensively on the recently constructed F3 Freeway link from Pearce's Corner to Berowra. However, RTA engineers have become more acutely aware of noise and the problems which arise if ineffective noise barriers are installed. They also appreciate the benefits of early consultations with the affected residents and local councils.

Residents of the area were fully briefed on the appearances, the performance and the benefits of various types of noise barriers. The majority opted for the Fanwall barrier, which also provides security advantages to the householders.

The Fanwall barrier to be installed at Rhodes is the first to be erected in Australia. Fanwall barriers have been used in the United States and have been very effective at noise attenuation with up to 10 dB reduction in noise level reached at L.A. International Airport. Similar success has been achieved in various highway projects right across the USA.

In the USA, concrete has proved to be the most popular material for constructing noise barrier walls. As is happening in Australia, early barrier designs opted for low timber barriers selected largely on thc basis of cost. However, low barriers are not effective and high timber barriers have become much more expensive. In addition to this poor durability of timber fences, the combination of initial capital cost, maintenance costs and replacement cost quickly makes timber barriers very expensive.

The advantages of concrete include low capital cost and durability. Furthermore, concrete barriers can be engineered for a variety of site condition and architectural finishes can be applied to enhance aesthetics.

Fanwall is a two-component, modular, free-standing pre-cast concrete noise barrier which can be cheaply and quickly erected on a variety of foundation conditions. The wall is engineered to be stable under design wind load conditions while maintaining relatively low bearing pressures on the foundation soils. Therefore, like the timber barriers, the Fanwall barrier can be built without expensive concrete footings or piles, speeding the construction time up and reducing costs. Furthermore, Fanwall is maintenance free and it is not susceptible to damage by fire and vandalism.

Because the Fanwall barriers are engineered into a modular form, construction is easily staged. At Rhodes, the Fanwall noise barrier will be built in three stages commencing in mid August. Staging will enable further consultation with local residents and allow access to be maintained across the site via local roads. However, most importantly, the greater proportion of the barrier will be in place prior to the road corridor being constructed, reducing the effect of construction noise.

Questions 1–6

In Reading Passage 1, the writer describes a planning process, problems and issues which arise, and the steps taken to deal with them.

*From the list of situations and possible actions below (**A–I**), select the steps taken to deal with the problems and issues, as outlined in the reading passage.*

*Write the appropriate letter (**A–I**)in boxes 1–6 on your answer sheet.*

1 Problem 1

2 Cause of problem 1

3 Proposed solution to problem 1

4 Objection—potential problem 2

5 Procedure

6 The final solution to problem 1

Situations and Possible Actions	
A	RTA purchase of houses
B	Concern about the effectiveness of some noise barriers
C	Suburban houses to be exposed to heavy traffic noise
D	Erect a Fanwall noise barrier
E	Construction of a new freeway link
F	Concern about purchase of houses by the RTA
G	Consult with local residents
H	Erect a large timber noise barrier
I	Change the route of the new freeway

Questions 7–13

The author mentions a number of features of noise barriers. Some are listed below. Identify them by writing

A *if it applies to low timber barriers*

B *if it applies to high timber barriers*

C *if it applies to concrete barriers*

D *if it applies to both low timber barriers and high timber barriers*

E *if it applies to both timber barriers and concrete barriers.*

Write your answers in boxes 7–13 on your answer sheet.

7 They need to be replaced regularly.

8 They are more popular in the USA.

9 They are susceptible to damage by fire and vandalism.

10 They are not always effective noise barriers.

11 They are much more expensive to build.

12 They do not require expensive foundations.

13 They are more expensive to maintain.

READING PASSAGE 2

*You should spend about 20 minutes on **Questions 14–27**, which are based on Reading Passage 2 below.*

New-age Transport

Computerised design, advanced materials and new technologies are being used to produce machines of a type never seen before.

It looks as if it came straight from the set of *Star Wars*. It has four-wheel drive and rises above rocky surfaces. It lowers and raises its nose when going up and down hills. And when it comes to a river, it turns amphibious: two hydrojets power it along by blasting water under its body. There is room for two passengers and a driver, who sit inside a glass bubble operating electronic, aircraft-type controls. A vehicle so daring on land and water needs windscreen wipers—but it doesn't have any. Water molecules are disintegrated on the screen's surface by ultrasonic sensors.

This unusual vehicle is the Racoon. It is an invention not of Hollywood but of Renault, a rather conservative French state-owned carmaker, better known for its family hatchbacks. Renault built the Racoon to explore new freedoms for designers and engineers created by advances in materials and manufacturing processes. Renault is thinking about startlingly different cars; other producers have radical new ideas for trains, boats and aeroplanes.

The first of the new freedoms is in design. Powerful computer-aided design (CAD) systems can replace with a click of a computer mouse hours of laborious work done on thousands of drawing boards. So new products, no matter how complicated, can be developed much faster. For the first time, Boeing will not have to build a giant replica of its new airliner, the 777, to make sure all the bits fit together. Its CAD system will take care of that.

But Renault is taking CAD further. It claims the Racoon is the world's first vehicle to be designed within the digitised world of virtual reality. Complex programmes were used to simulate the vehicle and the terrain that it was expected to cross. This allowed a team led by Patrick Le Quement, Renault's industrial-design director, to "drive" it long before a prototype existed.

Renault is not alone in thinking that virtual reality will transform automotive design. In Detroit, Ford is also investigating its potential. Jack Telnac, the firm's head of design, would like designers in different parts of the world to work more closely together, linked by computers. They would do more than style cars. Virtual reality will allow engineers to peer inside the working parts of a vehicle. Designers will watch bearings move, oil flow, gears mesh and hydraulics pump. As these techniques catch on, even stranger vehicles are likely to come along.

Transforming these creations from virtual reality to actual reality will also become easier, especially with advances in materials. Firms that once bashed everything out of steel now find that new alloys or composite materials (which can be made from mixtures of plastic, resin, ceramics and metals, reinforced with fibres such as glass or carbon) are changing the rules of manufacturing. At the same time, old materials keep getting better, as their producers try to secure their place in the factory of the future. This competition is increasing the pace of development of all materials.

One company in this field is Scaled Composites. It was started in 1982 by Burt Rutan, an aviator who has devised many unusual aircraft. His company develops and tests prototypes that have ranged from business aircraft to air racers. It has also worked on composite sails for the America's Cup yacht race and on General Motors' Ultralite, a 100-miles-per-gallon experimental family car built from carbon fibre.

Again, the Racoon reflects this race between the old and the new. It uses conventional steel and what Renault describes as a new "high-limit elastic steel" in its chassis. This steel is 30% lighter than the usual kind. The Racoon also has parts made from composites. Renault plans to replace the petrol engine with a small gas turbine, which could be made from heat-resisting ceramics, and use it to run a generator that would provide power for electric motors at each wheel.

With composites it is possible to build many different parts into a single component. Fiat, Italy's biggest car maker, has worked out that it could reduce the number of components needed in one of its car bodies from 150 to 16 by using a composite shell rather than one made of steel. Aircraft and cars may increasingly be assembled as if they were plastic kits.

Advances in engine technology also make cars lighter. The Ultralite, which Scaled Composites helped to design for General Motors, uses a two-stroke engine in a "power pod" at the rear of the vehicle. The engine has been developed from an East German design and weighs 40% less than a conventional engine but produces as much power. It is expected to run cleanly enough to qualify as an ultra-low emissions vehicle under California's tough new rules.

Questions 14–18

*Choose the correct letter, **A**, **B**, **C** or **D**.*

Write the correct letter in boxes 14–18 on your answer sheet.

14 How does the Racoon cross water?

A It swims.
B It raises its nose.
C It uses hydrojets.
D It uses its four-wheel drive.

15 What is Renault most famous for?

A startlingly different cars
B family cars
C advances in design
D boat and train design

16 Why won't Boeing need a replica of the 777?

A It can use computers to check the design.
B It already has enough experience with plans.
C It will only need to upgrade the replica of the previous model.
D It can make sure all the bits fit together.

17 How did Renault test drive the Racoon?

A over rocky terrain
B in actual reality
C over French country roads
D in virtual reality

18 Which of the following is **NOT** mentioned as an ingredient of a composite?

A oil
B resin
C glass
D steel

Questions 19–21

Complete the sentences below.

Choose **NO MORE THAN THREE WORDS** *from the passage for each answer.*

Write your answers in boxes 19–21 on your answer sheet.

19 One future design feature of the Racoon might be a ……………………….

20 In the future cars might be put together like ……………………….

21 The advantage of the Ultralite engine is that it is 40% ………………………than other car engines.

Questions 22–27

Look at the following design features and list of companies.

Match each design feature with the correct company, ***A–E****.*

Write the correct letter ***A–E*** *in boxes 22–27 on your answer sheet.*

NB *You may use any letter more than once.*

22 a power pod

23 electronic controls

24 a composite body

25 elastic steel

26 aircraft prototypes

27 ultrasonic sensors

List of Companies

A Scaled Composites (SC)

B Renault

C General Motors (GM)

D Fiat

E Boeing

READING PASSAGE 3

*You should spend about 20 minutes on **Questions 28–40**, which are based on Reading Passage 3 below.*

Paper Recycling

A Paper is different from other waste produce because it comes from a sustainable resource: trees. Unlike the minerals and oil used to make plastics and metals, trees are replaceable. Paper is also biodegradable, so it does not pose as much threat to the environment when it is discarded. While 45 out of every 100 tonnes of wood fibre used to make paper in Australia comes from waste paper, the rest comes directly from virgin fibre from forests and plantations. By world standards this is a good performance since the world-wide average is 33 percent waste paper. Governments have encouraged waste paper collection and sorting schemes and at the same time, the paper industry has responded by developing new recycling technologies that have paved the way for even greater utilisation of used fibre. As a result, industry's use of recycled fibres is expected to increase at twice the rate of virgin fibre over the coming years.

B Already waste paper constitutes 70% of paper used for packaging and advances in the technology required to remove ink from the paper have allowed a higher recycled content in newsprint and writing paper. To achieve the benefits of recycling, the community must also contribute. We need to accept a change in the quality of paper products: for example stationery, may be less white and of a rougher texture. There also needs support from the community for waste paper collection programmes. Not only do we need to make the paper available to collectors but it also needs to be separated into different types and sorted from contaminants such as staples, paperclips, strings and other miscellaneous items.

C There are technical limitations to the amount of paper which can be recycled and some paper products cannot be collected for re-use. These include paper in the form of books and permanent records, photographic paper and paper which is badly contaminated. The four most common sources of paper for recycling are factories and retail stores which gather large amounts of packaging material in which goods are delivered, also offices which have unwanted business documents and computer output paper converters and printers and lastly households which discard newspapers and packaging material. The paper manufacturer pays a price for the paper and may also incur the collection cost.

D Once collected, the paper has to be sorted by hand by people trained to recognise various types of paper. This is necessary because some types of paper can only be made from particular kinds of recycled fibre. The sorted paper then has to be repulped or mixed with water and broken down into its individual fibres. This mixture is called stock and may contain a wide variety of contaminating materials particularly if it is made from mixed waste paper which has had little sorting. Various machinery is used to remove other materials from the stock. After passing through the repulsing process the fibres from printed waste paper are grey in colour because the printing ink has soaked into the individual fibres. This recycled material can only be used in products where the grey colour does not matter such as cardboard boxes but if the grey colour is not acceptable, the fibres must be deinked. This involves adding chemicals such as caustic soda or other alkalis, soaps and detergents, water-hardening agents such as calcium chloride, frothing agents and bleaching agents. Before the recycled fibres can be made into paper they must be refined or treated in such a way that they bond together.

E Most paper products must contain some virgin fibres as well as recycled fibres and unlike glass, paper cannot be recycled indefinitely. Most paper is down-cycled which means that a product made from recycled paper is of an inferior quality to the original paper. Recycling paper is beneficial in that it saves some of the energy, labour and capital that goes into producing virgin pulp. However, recycling requires the use of fossil fuel, a non-renewable energy source, to collect the waste paper from the community and to process it to produce new paper. And the recycling process still creates emissions which require treatment before they can be disposed of safely. Nevertheless, paper recycling is an important economical and environmental practice but one which must be carried out in a rational and viable manner for it to be useful to both industry, and the community.

Questions 28–34

Complete the summary of paragraphs A and B below.

Choose ***ON MORE THAN TWO WORDS*** *from paragraphs A and B for each answer.*

Write your answers in boxes 28–34 on your answer sheet.

From the point of view of recycling, paper has two advantages over other waste in that firstly it comes from a resource which is **28** .... and secondly it is less threatening to our environment when we throw it away because it is **29** .... Although Australia's record in the re-use of waste paper is good, it is still necessary to use a combination of recycled fibre and **30** .... to make new paper. The paper industry has contributed positively and people have also been encouraged by **31** .... to collect their waste on a regular basis. One major difficulty is the removal of ink from used paper but **32** .... are being made in this area. However, we need to learn to accept paper which is generally of a lower **33** .... than before and to sort our waste paper by removing **34** .... before discarding it for collection.

Questions 35–40

Look at paragraphs C and D and complete the below using the information in the passage.

Use ***NO MORE THAN TWO WORDS*** *for each answer.*

Write your answers in boxes 35–40 on your answer sheet.

Waste paper collected from factories, retail stores, **35** ...., paper coverters and printers, and **36** ....

↓

The paper is then **37** ....

↓

The paper then has to be **38** .... or added with water.

↓

If the colour is unacceptable, the fibres must be **39** ....

↓

The fibres must be **40** .... before they can be made into paper.

Test 4 答案速查 Key

READING PASSAGE 1

1. C **2.** E **3.** H **4.** B **5.** G **6.** D
7. D **8.** C **9.** D **10.** A **11.** B **12.** E
13. D

READING PASSAGE 2

14. C **15.** B **16.** A **17.** D
18. A **19.** small gas turbine **20.** plastic kits **21.** lighter
22. C **23.** B **24.** D **25.** B
26. A **27.** B

READING PASSAGE 3

28. sustainable **29.** biodegradable **30.** virgin fibre
31. governments **32.** advances **33.** quality
34. contaminants **35.** offices **36.** households
37. sorted **38.** repulped **39.** deinked
40. refined

Test 4 考题精解 Detailed Explanation

READING PASSAGE 1

Questions 1–6

题型：配对题 (MATCHING)

◆ 解析

1. C

根据顺序原则，可在第二段开头找到答案，The Roads and Traffic Authority (RTA) in Sydney faced a problem when it decided to proceed with the link between Concord Road at Rhodes and the F4 Freeway at Homebush (Country Road 5030) as the new arterial would deliver heavy traffic right past the backyards of suburban homes，即Problem 1是严重的交通压力给郊区居民带来的噪音污染，对应选项C。

2. E

根据顺序原则，在提到问题之后，第二段的后半部分This was because the RTA had purchased and removed a number of houses to allow the new corridor to be built, exposing to road traffic noises houses which were once located in a quiet back street，阐明了Cause，即道路交通署在修路时买下并拆除了大量房屋，对应选项E。

3. H

定位到原文第三段的第一句Initially, the RTA had proposed to erect a new timber fence, replacing the existing suburban fences, to act as a noise barrier，句中提出了proposed solution to problem 1，即建一道木栅栏作为隔音墙，对应选项H。

4. B

对应原文第三段第三句However, RTA engineers have become more acutely aware of noise and the problems which arise if ineffective noise barriers are installed，在提出了解决方案后，随即说明工程师的一些担忧和潜在的问题，即这些木栅栏隔音墙是否能起到预期的作用，答案为选项B。

5. G

对应原文第四段Residents of the area were fully briefed on the appearances, the performance and the benefits of various types of noise barriers. The majority opted for the Fanwall barrier, which also provides security advantages to the householders，解决这些问题的步骤是和居民协商，对应G选项。

6. D

对应原文第四段及最后一段the Fanwall noise barrier will be built in three stages commencing in mid August. Staging will enable further consultation with local residents and allow access to be maintained across the site via local roads，最终达成的方案是修建扇形隔音墙，并与居民进行进一步协商。

Questions 7–13

题型：配对题 (MATCHING)

◆ 解析

属于无顺序性的细节题，考查事物及其特征的搭配。

7. D

根据第六段：In addition to this poor durability of timber fences and the combination of initial capital cost, maintenance costs and replacement cost quickly makes timber barriers very expensive，可知木栅栏隔音墙的耐用性差，由此可推知因为耐用性不佳，需要定期更换，故答案为选项D。

8. C

对应原文第五段第二、三句Fanwall barriers have been used in the United States and have been very effective at noise attenuation with up to 10 dB reduction in noise level reached at L.A. International Airport. Similar success has been achieved in various highway projects right across the USA，此处说明扇形隔音墙在美国已经很普遍，故答案为选项C。

9. D

对应原文倒数第二段的最后两句话Therefore, like the timber barriers, the Fanwall barrier can be built without expensive concrete footings or piles, speeding the construction time up and reducing costs. Furthermore, Fanwall is maintenance free and it is not susceptible to damage by fire and vandalism，表明相比扇形隔音墙，木栅栏隔音墙易受损和防火性差，故答案为选项D。

10. A

根据原文第六段第三句However, low barriers are not effective and high timber barriers have become much more expensive，可知矮木栅栏隔音墙的隔音效果不佳，故答案为选项A。

11. B

根据原文第六段第三句However, low barriers are not effective and high timber barriers have become much more expensive，可知高木栅栏隔音墙的修建成本很高，故答案为选项B。

12. E

根据原文倒数第二段的最后两句话Therefore, like the timber barriers, the Fanwall barrier can be built without expensive concrete footings or piles, speeding the construction time up and reducing costs. Furthermore, Fanwall is maintenance free and it is not susceptible to damage by fire and vandalism，可知木栅栏隔音墙和扇形隔音墙都不需要昂贵的混凝土地基，故答案为选项E。

13. D

根据原文倒数第二段的最后两句话Therefore, like the timber barriers, the Fanwall barrier can be built without expensive concrete footings or piles, speeding the construction time up and reducing costs. Furthermore, Fanwall is maintenance free and it is not susceptible to damage by fire and vandalism，可知木栅栏隔音墙的维护成本更高，故答案为选项D。

◎ 参考译文

扇形隔音墙

在澳大利亚，主干道和高速干道交通所产生的噪音问题日益严重，澳大利亚公路主管部门正愈发关注已经安装在这个国家的一些隔音装置的局限性。

悉尼道路交通署在决定继续连接罗兹的康科德路以及霍姆布什的F4高速公路（国道5030）时遇到了麻烦，因为这条穿越郊区人家后院的新的交通动脉将带来繁忙的交通。这是因为道路交通署购买并拆除了大量房屋来修路，将原本坐落于一个安静的后街的房屋暴露于公路交通噪音之下。

起初，道路交通署提议建一道新的木栅栏作为隔音墙，以取代原有的郊区篱笆。木栅栏隔音墙最近被广泛地采用，比如连通皮尔斯角和贝洛拉的F3高速公路就采用了这种隔音墙。然而，道路交通署的工程师们更加敏锐地注意到如果安装了无效的隔音墙将会引起的噪音和其他问题。同时他们很清楚受影响的居民和当地政府之间早期达成协商的好处。

附近居民认真听取了多种涉及隔音墙外观、性能和效果的简要报告，大多数人倾向于选择能够在隔音的同时还提供安全保护功能的扇形隔音墙。

罗兹是澳大利亚第一个采用扇形隔音墙的地方。这种隔音墙在美国已经投入使用，并收到了很好的隔音效果。美国洛杉矶国际机场的扇形隔音墙达到了降低10个分贝的噪音水平。同时美国很多公路项目采用扇形隔音墙也取得了类似的成效。

在美国，混凝土已被证明是最流行的建造隔音墙的材料。在澳大利亚，早期的隔音墙设计选用矮的木栅栏，很大程度上是基于成本原因。然而，矮隔音墙隔音效果不佳，高的木栅栏隔音墙成本又很高。木栅栏隔音墙除了耐用性不佳之外，再加上初始成本、维护费用和更换花销，使得木栅栏隔音墙愈发昂贵。

混凝土的优势包括较低的成本和良好的耐用性，而且，混凝土隔音墙的设计工艺可应用于不同的施工条件。为了看着更美观可在墙体上涂漆。

扇形隔音墙是一种双组件、模块化、无需支撑的预铸混凝土隔音墙，能够以低成本在各种施工条件下快速架设。这种墙在设定的风荷载条件下非常稳固，并相对维持了地基的低承载压力。因此，它和木质隔音墙一样，无需进行昂贵的打地基和打桩，可加快施工速度，同时降低成本。此外，扇形隔音墙无需维护，并具备不易受损和防火性好的特点。

由于扇形隔音墙采用模块式设计，施工变得很容易。在罗兹，扇形隔音墙将在八月中旬分三个阶段建造。施工方将与当地居民进一步协商，在当地道路保持通畅的情况下进行施工。然而，最重要的是，在修路前将大幅度建造隔音墙，以减少施工噪音。

READING PASSAGE 2

Questions 14–18

题型：选择题 (MULTIPLE CHOICE)

◆ 解析

14. C

题干中的关键词是Racoon，Racoon首次出现在原文第二段的第一句This unusual vehicle is the Racoon，其中this unusual vehicle指的是原文第一段所描述的对象“it”，由此可知第一段说的都是罗兹的特点。阅读第一段，其中有一句when it comes to a river, it turns amphibious: two hydrojets power it along by blasting water under its body，题干中的关键词

cross water和comes to a river对应，选项C是对two hydrojets power it along by blasting water under its body的改写，故C为正确答案。

15. B

根据题干中的关键词Renault定位到原文第二段中的一句Renault, a rather conservative French state-owned carmaker, better known for its family hatchbacks，题干中的关键词most famous for和better known for对应，选项B是对family hatchbacks的改写，故B为正确答案。

16. A

根据题干中的关键词Boeing及777定位到原文第三段中的倒数第一、二句For the firt time, Boeing will not have to build a giant replica of its new airliner, the 777, to make sure all the bits fit together. Its CAD system will take care of that，此题易误选D，原文中to make sure all the bits fit together实际上是表示目的，而题干问的是原因。正确答案应来自Its CAD system will take care of that，有关CAD的描述来自该段第二句，由该句可知正确答案应为选项A。

17. D

根据题干中的关键词Rehault, how及drive定位到原文第四段中的第二、三句It claims the Racoon is the world's first vehicle to be designed within the digitised world of virtual reality. Complex programmes were used to simulate the vehicle and the terrain that it was expected to cross，故答案为选项D。

18. A

根据题干中的关键词ingredient及composite定位到原文第六段中的第二句Firms that once bashed everything out of steel now find that new alloys or composite materials (which can be made from mixtures of plastic, resin, ceramics and metals, reinforced with fibres such as glass or carbon) are changing the rules of manufacturing，注意题干中有NOT，选项B、C、D在第六段中都提到了，所以根据排除法答案为选项A。

Questions 19–21

题型：句子填空题 (SENTENCE COMPLETION)

◆ 解析

对于填空题要特别注意题目中有字数要求，本题为NO MORE THAN THREE WORDS。

19. small gas turbine

此题是三道题中最难的，首先不容易定位到具体某一个段落。这时，可以考虑运用顺序性，这种题型通常与前一种题型也构成顺序性。前一种题型选择题的最后一题的答案在原文倒数第五段，所以首先考虑从倒数第四段开始寻找答案。从倒数第四段的第一句可知，这一段的主要内容是关于Scaled Composites公司的，而题干中的关键词Racoon不是该公司的车型，而是Renault公司的（从做前面的选择题可以得出），所以答案不在该段。看下一段，倒数第三段的第一句中有Racoon，所以答案在此段的可能性很大。仔细读这一段，有的同学可能会从第二句中找到high-limit elastic steel，实际这一句与题干没有任何对应关系。正确答案应来自该段的最后一句：Renault plans to replace the petrol engine with a small gas turbine，原文中的plan（计划）对应题干中的might be（可能），都是不确定的词，故答案是small gas turbine。

20. plastic kits

根据顺序性原则向下找，答案来自倒数第二段的最后一句Aircraft and cars may increasingly be assembled as if they were plastic kits，原文中的may对应题干中的might，原文中的assembled对应题干中的put together，故答案是plastic kits。

21. lighter

通过40%，比较容易定位到最后一段中的第三句The engine has been developed from an East German design and weighs 40% less than a conventional engine，由该句可知该发动机比传统发动机轻40%，答案应符合语法规则，故应填lighter。实际上这个词在该段的第一句中也有出现。

Questions 22–27

题型：配对题 (MATCHING)

◆ 解析

属于无顺序性的细节题（事物及其特征的搭配）。先看题目的要求，选项是一些公司的名字，题目是一些设计特点。将题目从头到尾看一遍，题目中的词都比较专业，比较生僻。不用紧张，原文中出现的可能就是这些原词，比较好找。另外，选项都是专有名词，是大写字母，在阅读原文时，注意大写字母。

22. C

关键词是power pod，原文最后一段提到The Ultralite, which Scaled Composites helped to design for General Motors, uses a two-stroke engine in a “power pod” at the rear of the vehicle，由该句可知power pod出自GM。一般来讲，在原文中离题目关键词最近的选项是正确选项，GM离power pod更近。

23. B

关键词是electronic controls, 结合第一段中的There is room for two passengers and a driver, who sit inside a glass bubble operating electronic, aircraft-type controls及第二段中的This unusual vehicle is the Racoon. It is an invention not of Hollywood but of Renault可知答案应该为Renault，选B。

24. D

关键词是composite body, 根据倒数第二段中的Fiat, Italy’s biggest car maker, has worked out that it could reduce the number of components needed in one of its car bodies from 150 to 16 by using a composite shell rather than one made of steel可知答案为Fiat，选D。

25. B

关键词是elastic steel，根据倒数第三段中的Again, the Racoon reflects this race between the old and the new. It uses conventional steel and what Renault describes as a new "high-limit elastic steel" in its chassis可知答案为Renault，选B。

26. A

关键词是aircraft prototypes，根据倒数第四段中的One company in this field is Scaled Composites. It was started in 1982 by Burt Rutan, an aviator who has devised many unusual aircraft. His company develops and tests prototypes that have ranged from business aircraft to air racers可知答案为Scaled Composites, 选A。

27. B

关键词是ultrasonic sensors，根据第一段的A vehicle so daring on land and water needs windscreen wipers—but it doesn't have any. Water molecules are disintegrated on the screen's surface by ultrasonic sensors可知答案为Renault，因为通过之前做题及阅读文章已知第一段所讲的"vehicle"就是Renault。

◎ 参考译文

新时代运输

电脑化的设计、先进的材料和新型的技术正被用于生产人们从未见过的新型机器。

它看上去像直接来自《星球大战》的装置。它由四轮驱动并能从岩石表面升起。它在上山和下山时会降低和提高车头。当它遇到河流时，就变成两栖车：通过两个喷射式部件在车身下排水进行驱动。车厢内部为玻璃制泡状物，有飞行器一样的电容操控板，可容纳一名司机和两名乘客。水陆两栖交通工具需要雨刷，但它并未提供，（因为）它有一个超声波传感器保持汽车滴水不沾。

这款不同寻常的车叫"浣熊"，发明者不是好莱坞而是雷诺——一家相当保守的法国汽车制造商，因其良好的家用掀背车设计而闻名于世。雷诺设计"浣熊"是为设计师和工程师探寻最前卫的设计道路，它采用了最先进的材料和工艺。雷诺正在思索开发与众不同的车；其他的生产商也在飞机、火车和轮船方面拥有先进的新思路。

新的自由理念被融入到设计之中。强大的电脑辅助设计（CAD）系统通过点击一下鼠标即可在上千块制图板上完成需数小时人工操作才能完成的工作。所以，新产品无论多么复杂，都可以被更快速地开发。这是波音公司第一次没有建造波音777新机型的复制品以确保飞机各部件配合良好，因为其CAD系统会为其解决所有问题。

而雷诺却要在CAD上走得更远。它声称"浣熊"是现实世界中第一辆实现数字虚拟化设计的汽车。为了能够模拟出预想的汽车和所期望行驶的地形，使用了复杂的程序。这也使得由雷诺工程设计指导帕特里克·勒·奎蒙领导的团队远在汽车原型诞生前就“驾驶”了它。

不只是雷诺认为模拟现实技术将改变汽车设计。在底特律，福特汽车也在研究该技术的潜力。公司首席设计师杰克·泰尔耐克希望世界各地的设计师通过电脑聚在一起研究它。他们将不止是为汽车设计造型。模拟现实技术将使工程师们关注车的工作部件，设计师们将观察轴承的移动、汽油的流动、齿轮的啮合和水泵的运转。随着这些技术的推进，甚至也许会带来更为奇特的车型。

尤其是随着材料的进步，将这些发明从虚拟的现实变成真正的现实也会变得更加容易。曾经报怨一切都要由钢铁制造的厂商现在发现，新的合金或者其他复合材料（如塑料、树脂、陶瓷和金属的混合物，用诸如玻璃或碳纤维加固）正在改变生产的规则。同时，因为制造商要保证他们的公司在未来发展前景中占有一席之地，使得传统材料不断被优化。这种竞争也加快了所有类型材料的改良。

在这一领域中有一家叫Scaled Composites的公司。它于1982年由飞行员伯特·鲁坦创立，他之前开发了许多不同寻常的飞机。他的公司开发和测试从商用飞机到比赛用的飞机模型。它也致力于为美洲杯游艇赛研制赛船，为通用汽车100英里加仑级的家用车做碳纤维实验。

“浣熊”也反映了新旧之间的较量，它采用了传统钢材，也采用了被雷诺称为“高限度弹性钢材”的材料制作底盘。这种钢比普通钢材轻30%。“浣熊”也采用了部分复合材料。雷诺打算用燃气涡轮取代汽油机。燃气涡轮可以用隔热的陶瓷制成，用来驱动发电机带动电机使每个轮子运转。

采用复合材料，就可能把许多零件组织成一套组件。意大利最大的汽车制造商菲亚特已经找到了通过复合壳体代替纯钢的制造方法，使车身组件数量从150个减少到16个。飞机和汽车的组装将越来越像组装塑料零件那般容易。

发动机技术的进步也使得汽车变得更轻。Scaled Composites帮助通用汽车设计的Ultralite,使用的是一个安装在车尾“电池盒”中的双冲程发动机。该发动机是从一款东德设计开发而来，比传统发动机轻40%，产生的动能却没有减少。据估计它运行时也足够环保，并在低排放方面达到加利福尼亚严格的新规定。

READING PASSAGE 3

Questions 28–34

题型：摘要填空题 (SUMMARY COMPLETION)

◆ 解析

先看题干的要求，主要有以下几点：来自原文前两段，原文原词，每个答案为一个或两个字。

28. sustainable

题干要求中已经指出了摘要的出处是A段和B段，所以直接看空格前面的内容comes from a resource，原文中对应句为it comes from a sustainable resource: trees，答案有可能为sustainable或trees。哪一个是呢？trees不合语法的要求，正确答案为sustainable。原文是形容词作定语，题干中改为了定语从句。

29. biodegradable

空格前的内容it is less threatening to our environment when we throw it away because it is在原文中的对应句为Paper is also biodegradable, so it does not pose as much threat to the environment when it is discarded，所以正确答案为biodegradable。

30. virgin fibre

空格前的内容use a combination of recycled fibre和空格后的内容to make new paper在原文中的对应句为While 45 out of every 100 tonnes of wood fibre used to make paper in Australia comes from waste paper, the rest comes directly from virgin fibre from forests and plantations，正确答案为virgin fibre。

31. governments

该题是七道题中比较简单的。空格前的内容people have also been encouraged by和空格后的内容to collect their waste on a regular basis在原文中的对应句为Governments have encouraged waste paper collection and sorting schemes，所以正确答案为governments。注意不要答成government，因为答案要求是原文原词，原文中只有governments，没有government，而且government也不合乎语法规则，可数名词前必须要有限定词。

32. advances

该题是这七道题中最难的，关键是要找到空格前后的关键词，关键词removal of ink在原文中的对应句为advances in the technology required to remove ink from the paper have allowed a higher recycled content in newsprint and writing paper，其中removal of ink的对应词为remove ink，所以正确答案为advances。注意不要答成advances in the technology（字数不符）或technology advances（不能改变原文的词序）。

33. quality

空格前的内容we need to learn to accept paper which is generally of a lower和空格后的内容than before在原文中的对应句为We need to accept a change in the quality of paper products; for example stationery may be less white and of a rougher texture，正确答案为quality。注意不要答成white，它只是一个形容词，空格中应填一个名词。阅读文章中常出现for example，这个词前面的词和句子通常比较重要，可能会有考题对应。

34. contaminants

原文对应为B段最后的but it also needs to be separated into different types and sorted from contaminants such as staples, paperclips, strings and other miscellaneous items，正确答案为contaminants，是一个较生僻的词。

Questions 35–40

题型：流程图 (Flow Chart)

◆ 解析

先看题干的要求，主要有以下几点：来自原文C和D两段，原文原词，每个答案为一个或两个词，内容是关于纸张被回收再利用的流程。

35. offices

36. households

对应原文C段第三句The four most common sources of paper for recycling are factories and retail stores which gather large amounts of packaging material in which goods are delivered, also offices which have unwanted business documents and computer output, paper converters and printers and lastly households which discard newspapers and packaging material，这个句子较复杂，其中有多个定语从句。句子主干是The four sources are factories and retail stores, offices, and lastly households，由此可知35题正确答案为offices，36题正确答案为households。

37. sorted

对应原文D段的第一句Once collected, the paper has to be sorted，可知纸张在被回收之后，接下来就要被分类，故正确答案为sorted。

38. repulped

对应原文D段第三句The sorted paper then has to be repulped or mixed with water，由该句可知被分类的纸张需要再次化为纸浆或者与水混合并分解成独立的纤维，故正确答案为repulped。

39. deinked

对应原文D段第七句This recycled material can only be used in products where the grey colour does not matter such as cardboard boxes but if the grey colour is not acceptable, the fibres must be deinked，可知这种回收材料只能被应用到可以接受灰色的产品，比如纸盒，但是如果灰色是不可接受的，必须对纤维进行脱墨的工序，故答案为deinked。

40. refined

对应原文D段最后一句Before the recycled fibres can be made into paper they must be refined，可知在这些回收纤维制成纸张之前，它们必须被精炼或者用这样的方法处理，故答案为refined。

◎ 参考译文

纸张的回收再利用

A 纸张与其他废品不同，因为它来源于可持续资源：树木。与用来制造塑料、金属的矿物和油不同，树木是可替代的。另外，纸张也是可降解的，所以当它被丢弃时，对环境不会产生很大的威胁。然而在澳大利亚，用来造纸的木质纤维每100公吨里就有45公吨来自于废纸，剩余的直接来自于森林和种植园的生态纤维。按世界标准，这是一个好的表现，因为世界范围内的平均值是33%来自废纸。政府已经鼓励废纸回收和分类系统，同时，造纸业通过研发新的回收技术做出了回应，这为更加广泛地回收利用纤维铺平了道路。这样一来，在接下来的几年里，造纸业对再生纤维利用的增长预计将是生态纤维的两倍。

B 包装纸中，已经有70%来自废纸的再利用。将纸张中的油墨去除这项技术的进步，能使报纸和书写纸的回收大大增加。为了实现回收效益，社区也必须做出贡献。我们需要接受纸质产品的质量变化：比如文具或许会没那么白，并且质地较为粗糙。同样社区也需要为废纸回收项目提供支持。我们不仅需要使收集者能够收集到纸张，也需要将纸张分为不同的类型，并与污染物质诸如订书钉、曲别针、细绳和其他各种杂物进行分类。

C 由于可回收的纸张的数量存在技术局限性，有些纸质产品不能收集来重新利用，其中包括以图书和永久记录、相纸形式存在的纸张和被严重污染的纸张。最常见的用来回收的四种纸张的来源是工厂、零售店、办公室和家庭。其中工厂和零售店里积聚着大量的用来传送货物的包装纸，办公室有废弃的商业文件和电脑输出纸和打印纸，还有家庭丢弃的报纸和包装材料。造纸商花钱购买这些纸，同时也可能产生收集成本。

D 一旦被回收，纸张需要人们进行手工分类，这些人经过训练，可识别不同类型的纸张。这是必要的，因为有些类型的纸只能由特定种类的回收纤维制成。被分类的纸需要再次化为纸浆或者与水混合并分解成独立的纤维。这种混合物被称作原浆，它可能包含很多种污染物质，特别是当这个混合物是由几乎没有分类的废纸混合而成时。各种各样的机械设备被用来从原浆中除去其他的物质。经过化为纸浆的工序，打印废纸中的纤维会变为灰色，因为打印油墨浸透到了独立的纤维中。这种回收材料只能被应用到可以接受灰色的产品，比如纸盒，但是如果灰色是不可接受的，必须对纤维进行脱墨。这涉及添加如苛性钠类的化学制品或者其他碱、肥皂和去垢剂、使水硬化的物质，如氯化钙，产生泡沫和漂白的物质。在这些回收纤维可以制成纸张之前，它们必须被精炼或者用这样的方法处理，这样它们就可以溶解在一起。

E 大多数纸产品必须包含一些生态纤维和再生纤维，与玻璃不同，纸不能被无限制地循环利用。大多数纸张经回收后制成的产品比原来的纸张质量差。纸回收是有益的，因为它能节省一些能源、劳动力和资本，这些资本可以用来制造新生态的纸浆。然而，回收要求使用化石燃料—— 一种不可再生的能源来从社区收集废纸并加工它来生产新纸。回收工序仍然产生排放物，它们需要经过一些处理才能安全排放。尽管如此，纸回收是一项重要的既经济又环保的实践活动，必须用理性可行的方式实施，因为它对造纸业和整个社会都是有益处的。

Test 4 核心词汇 Core Vocabulary

READING PASSAGE 1

arterial roads 主干公路
proceed *vi.* 继续进行
corridor *n.* 通道
timber *n.* 木材，木料
brief *vt.* 向……介绍基本情况
attenuation *n.* 减少，衰减
susceptible *adj.* 易受……影响的
vandalism *n.* 破坏

READING PASSAGE 2

amphibious *adj.* 水陆两用的
blast *vt.* 喷出，爆发出
windscreen wiper 车窗雨刷
disintegrate *vt.*（使）分裂，粉碎；（使）崩溃
ultrasonic *adj.* 超音波的
digitise *vt.* 数字模拟化
prototype *n.* 原型，雏形
bearing *n.* （机器的）轴承
bash *vt.* 痛击；猛攻
composite *adj.* 合成的，复合的
elastic *adj.* 有弹性的
ceramics *n.* 陶瓷

READING PASSAGE 3

virgin *adj.* 未经利用的，原始的
scheme *n.* 方案
contaminant *n.* 污染物，致污物
staple *n.* 订书钉
paperclip *n.* 曲别针
miscellaneous *adj.* 混杂的
soak *vt.* 浸
caustic *adj.* 腐蚀性的；苛性的
alkali *n.* 碱；强碱
detergent *n.* 去垢剂

TEST 5

Candidate Number

Candidate Name ______________________

INTERNATIONAL ENGLISH LANGUAGE TESTING SYSTEM

ACADEMIC READING

TIME 1 hour

INSTRUCTIONS TO CANDIDATES

Do not open this booklet until you are told to do so.

Write your name and candidate number in the spaces at the top of this page.

Start at the beginning of the test and work through it.

You should answer **all** questions.

If you cannot do a particular question, leave it and go on to the next. You can return to it later.

All answers must be written on the answer sheet.

Do not remove this booklet from the examination room.

INFORMATION FOR CANDIDATES

There are **40** questions on this question paper.

The test is divided as follows:

Reading Passage 1	Questions 1–13
Reading Passage 2	Questions 14–27
Reading Passage 3	Questions 28–40

Reading Answer Sheet

Are you: Female? ▭ Male? ▭

Your first language code:

0	1	2	3	4	5	6	7	8	9
0	1	2	3	4	5	6	7	8	9
0	1	2	3	4	5	6	7	8	9

IELTS Reading Answer Sheet

Module taken (shade one box): Academic ▭ General Training ▭

		✓ ✗			✓ ✗
1		1	**21**		21
2		2	**22**		22
3		3	**23**		23
4		4	**24**		24
5		5	**25**		25
6		6	**26**		26
7		7	**27**		27
8		8	**28**		28
9		9	**29**		29
10		10	**30**		30
11		11	**31**		31
12		12	**32**		32
13		13	**33**		33
14		14	**34**		34
15		15	**35**		35
16		16	**36**		36
17		17	**37**		37
18		18	**38**		38
19		19	**39**		39
20		20	**40**		40

Checker's Initials		Marker's Initials		Band Score		Reading Total	

READING PASSAGE 1

You should spend about 20 minutes on ***Questions 1–13****, which are based on Reading Passage 1 below.*

Sydney 2000 Olympics

The cost of staging the year 2000 Olympics in Sydney was estimated to be a staggering $960 million, but the city was preparing to reap the financial benefits that ensued from holding such an international event by emulating the commercial success of Los Angeles, the only city yet to have made a demonstrable profit from the Games in 1984.

At precisely 4:20 am on Friday the 24th of September 1993, it was announced that Sydney had beaten four other competing cities around the world, and Australians everywhere, not only Sydneysiders, were justifiably proud of the result. But, if Sydney had lost the bid, would the taxpayers of NSW and of Australia have approved of governments spending millions of dollars in a failed and costly exercise?

There may have been some consolation in the fact that the bid came in $1 million below the revised budget and $5 million below the original budget of $29 million formulated in mid-1991. However, the final cost was the considerable sum of $24 million, the bulk of which was paid for by corporate and community contributions, merchandising, licensing, and the proceeds of lotteries, with the NSW Government, which had originally been willing to spend up to $10 million, contributing some $2 million. The Federal Government's grant of $5 million meant, in effect, that the Sydney bid was financed by every Australian taxpayer.

Prior to the announcement of the winning city, there was considerable debate about the wisdom of taking financial risks of this kind at a time of economic recession. Others argued that 70 per cent of the facilities were already in place, and all were on government-owned land, removing some potential areas of conflict which troubled previous Olympic bidders. The former NSW Premier, Mr. Nick Greiner, went on record as saying that the advantage of having the Games... "is not that you are going to have $7.4 billion in extra gross domestic product over the next 14 years... I think the real point of the Games is the psychological change, the catalyst of confidence... apart from the other more obvious reasons, such as the building of sporting facilities, tourism, and things of that nature."

However, the dubiousness of the benefits that Melbourne, an unsuccessful bidder for the 1988 Olympic Games, received at a time when the State of Victoria was still in economic turmoil meant many corporate bodies were unenthusiastic.

There is no doubt that Sydney's seductive physical charms caused the world's media to compare the city favourably to its rivals Beijing, Berlin, Manchester, and Istanbul. Mr. Godfrey Santer, the Australian Tourist Commission's Manager of Corporate Planning Services, stated that soon after the bid was made, intense media focus was already having a beneficial effect on in-bound tourism.

Developers and those responsible for community development projects eagerly pointed to the improvements taking place to the existing infrastructure of the city, the creation of employment, and especially the building of sporting facilities, all of which meet the needs of the community and help to attract more tourists. At Homebush Bay $300 million was spent providing the twin athletic arenas and the "high-tech" Aquatic Centre. However, perhaps the most impressive legacy was the new attitude shown towards both industrial relations and environmental problems. The high-profile nature of the bid; and the perception that it must proceed smoothly created a unique attitude of cooperation between the workforce and employers involved in the construction of the Olympic Village at Homebush Bay. The improvements included the lack of strikes, the breaking down of demarcation barriers, and the completion of projects within budget and ahead of time.

The Secretary of the NSW Labour Council, Mr. Michael Easson, was quoted as saying, ... "What we've achieved should become the model for the rest of the building industry... great cooperation, good management, improvement in relations between employers and employees, and a feeling of optimism ...". The lasting benefits will be first-rate sporting facilities at Homebush Bay and an industrial relations model which should impact on the rest of the building industry.

Improved negotiations and cooperation over the bid between the Greenpeace environmental group and the State Government also saw a new respect develop on both sides. Suddenly, environmentalists were no longer regarded as being radically opposed to all development, and neither was the State Government perceived as inconsiderate towards environmental concerns.

The success of Sydney's bid laid to rest much of the opposition to the gamble. Nonetheless, most economists agree that it would be wise when considering future risks of this kind to bear well in mind the financial consequences of failure.

Questions 1–8

Do the following statements agree with the information given in Reading Passage 1?

In boxes 1–8 on your answer sheet, write

TRUE	*if the statement agrees with the information*
FALSE	*if the statement contradicts the information*
NOT GIVEN	*if there is no information on this*

1 The initial estimate of the cost of the Sydney bid was $960 million.

2 The majority of the funding for the bid came from the Federal Government's grant.

3 The bid for the Games was made during a period of economic growth.

4 The potential for conflict was less because the Olympic sites were on government-owned land.

5 The former Premier of NSW claimed that the Games will bring about a feeling of confidence.

6 The world media's attitude was favourable to Sydney because of the city's friendliness towards tourists.

7 There was a positive effect on out-bound tourism not long after the bid for the Games was made.

8 The State Government and environmental group cooperated better with each other over the bid.

Questions 9–13

Answer the questions below.

*Choose **NO MORE THAN THREE WORDS** from the passage for each answer.*

Write your answers in boxes 9–13 on your answer sheet.

9 How many cities were competing in 1993 for the right to hold the 2000 Games?

10 What was the cost of the revised budget for the Sydney bid?

11 As a result of the Federal Government's $5 million grant, who also contributed towards the bid?

12 What phrase of three words in the text describes the State of Victoria when Melbourne bid for the Games?

13 How many achievements does the Secretary of the NSW Labour Council mention in his industrial relations model?

READING PASSAGE 2

*You should spend about 20 minutes on **Questions 14–27**, which are based on Reading Passage 2 on the following pages.*

Questions 14–18

Reading Passage 2 has six sections, **A–F**.

Choose the correct heading for each section from the list of headings below.

*Write the correct number, **i–x** in boxes 14–18 on your answer sheet.*

List of Headings

i The cost of adjudication
ii Handling rightsbased disputes
iii Punishing acts of aggression
iv The role of dependence in disputes
v The role of arbitrators
vi Methods of settling conflicting interests
vii Ensuring choice for consumers
viii Fulfilling employee's needs
ix The use of negotiation for different dispute types
x Advantages of negotiation over mediation
xi The role of power in settling disagreements
xii Disagreement of interests

14 Section **A**
15 Section **B**

Example	***Answer***
Section **C**	**ix**

16 Section **D**
17 Section **E**
18 Section **F**

The Nature of Disputes

To resolve a dispute means to turn opposing positions into a single outcome. The two parties may choose to focus their attention on one or more of three basic factors. They may seek to reconcile their interests, determine who is right, and/or determine who is more powerful.

Section A

Interests are needs, desires, concerns, fears—the things one cares about or wants. They provide the foundation for a person's or an organisation's position in a dispute. In a dispute, not only do the interests of one party not coincide with those of the other party, but they are in conflict. For example, the director of sales for an electronics company gets into a dispute with the director of manufacturing over the number of TV models to produce. The director of sales wants to produce more models because her interest is in selling TV sets; more models mean more choice for consumers and hence increased sales. The director of manufacturing, however, wants to produce fewer models. His interest is in decreasing manufacturing costs and more models mean higher costs.

Section B

Reconciling such interests is not easy. It involves probing for deeply rooted concerns, devising creative solutions, and making tradeoffs and compromises where interests are opposed. The most common procedure for doing this is negotiation, the act of communication intended to reach agreement. Another interests-based procedure is mediation, in which a third party assists the disputants, the two sides in the dispute, in reaching agreement.

Section C

By no means do all negotiations (or mediations) focus on reconciling interests. Some negotiations focus on determining who is right, such as when two lawyers argue about whose case has the greater merit. Other negotiations focus on determining who is more powerful, such as when quarrelling neighbours or nations exchange threats and counter threats. Often negotiations involve a mix of all three—some attempts to satisfy interests, some discussion of rights, and some references to relative power.

Section D

It is often complicated to attempt to determine who is right in a dispute. Although it is usually straightforward where rights are formalised in law, other rights take the form of unwritten but socially accepted standards of behaviour, such as reciprocity, precedent, equality, and seniority.

There are often different—and sometimes contradictory—standards that apply to rights. Reaching agreement on rights, where the outcome will determine who gets what, can often be so difficult that the parties frequently turn to a third party to determine who is right. The most typical rights procedure is adjudication, in which disputants present evidence and arguments to a neutral third party who has the power to make a decision that must be followed by both disputants. (In mediation, by contrast, the third party does not have the power to decide the dispute.) Public adjudication is provided by courts and administrative agencies. Private adjudication is provided by arbitrators.

Section E

A third way to resolve a dispute is on the basis of power. We define power, somewhat narrowly, as the ability to pressure someone to do something he would not otherwise do. Exercising power typically means imposing costs on the other side or threatening to do so. The exercise of power takes two common forms: acts of aggression, such as physical attack, and withholding the benefits that derive from a relationship, as when employees stop working in a strike.

Section F

In relationships of mutual dependence, such as between labour and management or within an organisation or a family, the question of who is more powerful turns on who is less dependent on the other. If a company needs the employees' work more than employees need the company's pay, the company is more dependent and hence less powerful. How dependent one is turns on how satisfactory the alternatives are for satisfying one's interests. The better the alternative, the less dependent one is. If it is easier for the company to replace striking employees than it is for striking employees to find new jobs, the company is less dependent and thereby more powerful. Determining who is the more powerful party without a decisive and potentially destructive power contest is difficult because power is ultimately a matter of perceptions.

Questions 19–21

Complete the sentences below.

Choose ***NO MORE THAN THREE WORDS*** *from the passage for each answer.*

Write your answers in boxes 19–21 on your answer sheet.

19 Two common procedures used in the resolution of interest-based disputes are negotiation and ....

20 When rights are ...., coming to a resolution is a relatively simple process.

21 Arbitrators and adjudicators must receive .... from the disputing parties before they can help resolve the dispute.

Questions 22–27

Classify the following disputes as relating to

A *reconciliation of interests*

B *determination of rights*

C *determination of who is more powerful*

Write the correct letter, ***A****,* ***B*** *or* ***C****, in boxes 22–27 on your answer sheet.*

22 A mother disapproves of her son's fiancee and threatens to disown her son if he marries her. The marriage goes ahead, but after some years the mother accepts it because she wants to reestablish a good relationship with her son.

23 A large company decides to buy a new computer system. The accounting department wants System X. The marketing department insists on System Y. A settlement is reached after a series of meetings between the disputants.

24 Island C is claimed by both Country A and Country B. The decision to determine whose land it is given to the United Nations, which concludes that Country A may have Island C because of stronger social and historical ties.

25 A married couple can afford only one car. The wife wants a simple transportation vehicle. The husband wants a sports car to impress his friends. A mutual friend helps them reach the agreement.

26 A divorcing couple disagreeing about who will get custody of their children go to a court of law. The court determines the mother should have custody.

27 An employer refuses to pay an employee because of poor job performance. The employee promises to improve his work.

READING PASSAGE 3

*You should spend about 20 minutes on **Questions 28–40**, which are based on Reading Passage 3 below.*

Wild Foods of Australia

Over 120 years ago, the English botanist J. D. Hooker, writing of Australian edible plants, suggested that many of them were "eatable but not worth eating". Nevertheless, the Australian flora, together with the fauna, supported the Aboriginal people well before the arrival of Europeans. The Aborigines were not farmers and were wholly dependent for life on the wild products around them. They learned to eat, often after treatment, a wide variety of plants.

The conquering Europeans displaced the Aborigines, killing many, driving others from their traditional tribal lands, and eventually settling many of the tribal remnants on government reserves, where flour and beef replaced nardoo and wallaby as staple foods. And so, gradually, the vast store of knowledge, accumulated over thousands of years, fell into disuse. Much was lost.

However, a few European men took an intelligent and even respectful interest in the people who were being displaced. Explorers, missionaries, botanists, naturalists and government officials observed, recorded and fortunately in some cases, published. Today, we can draw on these publications to form the main basis of our knowledge of the edible, natural products of Australia. The picture is no doubt mostly incomplete. We can only speculate on the number of edible plants on which no observation was recorded.

Not all our information on the subject comes from the Aborigines. Times were hard in the early days of European settlement, and traditional foods were often in short supply or impossibly expensive for a pioneer trying to establish a farm in the bush. And so necessity led to experimentation, just as it must have done for the Aborigines, and experimentation led to some lucky results. So far as is known, the Aborigines made no use of Leptospermum or Dodonaea as food plants, yet the early settlers found that one could be used as a substitute for tea and the other for hops. These plants are not closely related to the species they replaced, so their use was not based on botanical observation. Probably some experiments had less happy endings; L. J. Webb has used the expression eat, die and learn in connection with the Aboriginal experimentation, but it was the successful attempts that became widely known. It is possible that the edibility of some native plants used by the Aborigines was discovered independently by the European settlers or their descendants.

Explorers making long expeditions found it impossible to carry sufficient food for the whole journey and were forced to rely, in part, on food that they could find on the way. Still another source of information comes from the practice in other countries. There are many species from northern Australia which occur also in Southeast Asia, where they are used for food.

In general, those Aborigines living in the dry inland areas were largely dependent for their vegetable foods on seed such as those of grasses, acacias and eucalypts. They ground these seeds between flat stones to make a coarse flour. Tribes on the coast, and particularly those in the vicinity of coastal rainforests, had a more varied vegetable diet with a higher proportion of fruits and tubers. Some of the coastal plants, even if they had grown inland, probably would have been unavailable as food since they required prolonged washing or soaking to render them non-poisonous; many of the inland tribes could not obtain water in the quantities necessary for such treatment. There was also considerable variation in the edible plants available to Aborigines in different latitudes. In general, the people who lived in the moist tropical areas enjoyed a much greater variety, than those in the southern part of Australia.

With all the hundreds of plant species used for food by the Australian Aborigines, it is perhaps surprising that only one, the Queensland nut, has entered into commercial cultivation as a food plant. The reason for this probably does not lie with an intrinsic lack of potential in Australian flora, but rather with the lack of exploitation of this potential. In Europe and Asia, for example, the main food plants have had the benefit of many centuries of selection and hybridisation, which has led to the production of forms vastly superior to those in the wild. Before the Europeans came, the Aborigines practised no agriculture and so there was no opportunity for such improvement; either deliberate or unconscious, in the quality of the edible plants.

Since 1788, there has, of course, been opportunity for selection of Australian food plants which might have led to the production of varieties that were worth cultivating. But Australian plants have probably "missed the bus". Food plants from other regions were already so far in advance after a long tradition of cultivation that it seemed hardly worth starting work on Australian species. Undoubtedly, the native raspberry, for example, could, with suitable selection and breeding programmes, be made to yield a high-class fruit; but Australians already enjoy good raspberries from other areas of the world and unless some dedicated amateur plant breeder takes up the task, the Australian raspberries are likely to remain unimproved.

And so, today, as the choice of which food plants to cultivate in Australia has been largely decided, and as there is little chance of being lost for long periods in the bush. Our interest in the subject of Australian food plants tends to relate to natural history rather than to practical necessity.

Questions 28–34

Do the following statements agree with the claims of the writer in Reading Passage 3?

In boxes 28–34 on your answer sheet, write

YES	*if the statement agrees with the claims of the writer*
NO	*if the statement contradicts the claims of the writer*
NOT GIVEN	*if it is impossible to say what the writer thinks about this*

28 Most of Aboriginal knowledge of wild foods has been recovered.

29 There were few food plants unknown to Aborigines.

30 Europeans learned all of what they knew of edible wild plants from Aborigines.

31 Dodonaea is an example of a plant used for food by both Aborigines and European settlers.

32 Some Australian food plants are botanically related to plants outside Australia.

33 Aboriginal tribes closer to the coast had access to a greater variety of food plants than tribes further inland.

34 Some species of coastal food plants were also found inland.

Questions 35–37

*Choose the correct letter, **A**, **B**, **C** or **D**.*

Write the correct letter in boxes 35–37 on your answer sheet.

35 Wallaby meat

A was regularly eaten by Aborigines before European settlement.

B was given by Aborigines in exchange for foods such as flour.

C was a staple food on government reserves.

D was produced on farms before European settlement.

36 Experimentation with wild plants

A depended largely on botanical observation.

B was unavoidable for early settlers in all parts of Australia.

C led Aborigines to adopt Leptospermum as a food plant.

D sometimes had unfortunate results.

37 Wild plant used by Aborigines

A was limited to dry regions.

B was restricted to seed.

C sometimes required the use of tools.

D was more prevalent in the southern part of Australia.

Questions 38–40

Complete the summary below.

*Choose **NO MORE THAN TWO WORDS** from the passage for each answer.*

Write your answers in boxes 38–40 on your answer sheet.

Despite the large numbers of wild plants that could be used for food, only one, the **38** .... is being grown as a cash crop. Other edible plants in Australia, however much potential they have for cultivation, had not gone through the lengthy process of **39** .... that would allow their exploitation, because Aborigines were not farmers. Thus species such as the **40** ...., which would be an agricultural success if it had not had to compete with established European varieties at the time of European settlement, are of no commercial value.

Test 5 答案速查 Key

READING PASSAGE 1

1. FALSE
2. FALSE
3. FALSE
4. TRUE
5. TRUE
6. FALSE
7. NOT GIVEN
8. TRUE
9. 5/5 cities/five/five cities
10. $25 million
11. every Australian taxpayer/Australian taxpayer
12. in economic turmoil
13. 4/four

READING PASSAGE 2

14. xii
15. vi
16. ii
17. xi
18. iv
19. mediation
20. formalised in law
21. evidence and arguments
22. C
23. A
24. B
25. A
26. B
27. C

READING PASSAGE 3

28. NOT GIVEN
29. NOT GIVEN
30. NO
31. NO
32. YES
33. YES
34. NOT GIVEN
35. A
36. D
37. C
38. Queensland nut
39. selection
40. native raspberry

Test 5 考题精解 Detailed Explanation

READING PASSAGE 1

Questions 1–8

题型：判断题 (TRUE/FALSE/NOT GIVEN)

◆ 解析

1. FALSE

可采用特殊词定位法，根据题干中的关键词$960 million可以很快定位到原文第一段的第一句The cost of staging the year 2000 Olympics in Sydney is estimated to be a staggering $960 million，注意题干中说的是申办（bid）的费用，而原文$960 million说的是举办（stage）的费用。通过通读全文，可从第三段第一句... the original budget of $29 million formulated in mid-1991可知最初申报预算为$29 million，所以答案为FALSE。

2. FALSE

根据题干中的关键词Federal government grant可很快对应到原文第三段的最后一句The Federal Government's grant of $5 million meant, in effect, that the Sydney bid was financed by every Australian taxpayer，从该句中可得知联邦政府为申办拨款$5 million，在上一题中我们已知申办的总费用为$24 million，由此可知申办的大部分费用并不是来自联邦政府，所以答案为FALSE。

3. FALSE

采用顺序定位法，从原文第四段的第一句Prior to the announcement of the winning city, there was considerable debate about the wisdom of taking financial risks of this kind at a time of economic recession，可得知在宣布为获胜城市之前，人们对于在经济不景气的情况下冒着财政风险申办奥运会的举措存在巨大争议，所以题干中所说的在经济上升时期申办奥运会的说法是错误的，故答案为FALSE。

4. TRUE

采用顺序定位法，根据关键词government-owned land可对应到原文第四段的第二句Others argued that 70 per cent of the facilities were already in place, and all were on government-owned land, removing some potential areas of conflict which troubled previous Olympic bidders，该句中提到所有的运动设施均设在政府的管辖范围之内，因此排除了一些潜在的存在着危险冲突的区域，题干表述与该句相符，所以答案为TRUE。

5. TRUE

根据关键词The former Premier of NSW可定位到原文第四段最后一句I think the real point of the Games is the psychological change, the catalyst of confidence... 从该句中可得知the former Premier认为奥运会能够提升人们的自信感，所以正确答案为TRUE。

6. FALSE

采用顺序定位法，对应原文第六段的第一句There is no doubt that Sydney's seductive physical charms caused the world's media to compare the city favourably to its rivals Beijing, Berlin, Manchester, and Istanbul，从该句中可得知，为悉尼赢得各国媒体支持的是其怡人的自然风光，而非该城市对游客的友好态度，所以正确答案为FALSE。

7. NOT GIVEN

采用顺序定位法，对应原文第六段的第二句Mr. Godfrey Santer, the Australian Tourist

Commission's Manager of Corporate Planning Services, stated that soon after the bid was made, intense media focus was already having a beneficial effect on in-bound tourism，注意原文中只提到了in-bound tourism，却并未提及题干中所说的out-bound tourism，所以正确答案应为NOT GIVEN。

8. TRUE

采用顺序定位法，可对应到原文倒数第二段的第一句Improved negotiations and co-operation over the bid between the Greenpeace environmental group and the State Government also saw a new respect develop on both sides，从该句中可得知在申奥期间，绿色和平环保组织与州政府的进一步协商与合作使得双方建立了新的关系，故正确答案为TRUE。

Questions 9–13

题型：简答题 (SHORT ANSWER QUESTIONS)

◆ 解析

9. 5/5 cities/five/five cities

根据题干中的关键词1993，可快速定位到原文第二段的第一句At precisely 4:20 am on Friday the 24th of September 1993, it was announced that Sydney had beaten four other competing cities around the world...，从该句中可得知悉尼战胜了其他四个城市，赢得了奥运会的主办权，由此可知竞争2000年奥运会主办权的城市包括悉尼在内共有5个，所以答案为5/5 cities/Five/Five cities。

10. $25 million

根据题干中的关键词revised budget（生僻词）和Sydney bid可快速定位到原文第三段第一句...the bid came in $1 million below the revised budget and $5 million below the original budget of $29 million...这句话的意思是这个申办费用比revised budget少了$1 million，比最初的预算少了$5 million，最初的预算是$29 million。经过运算可知最终申办费用为$24 million，故revised budget为$25 million。revised budget意为"修改后的预算"。

11. every Australian taxpayer/Australian taxpayer

根据题干中的专有名词和数字Federal Government's $5 million grant，对应原文第三段最后一句The Federal Government's grant of $5 million meant, in effect, that the Sydney bid was financed by every Australian taxpayer，故答案为Every Australian taxpayer/Australian taxpayer。

12. in economic turmoil

根据题干中的关键词the State of Victoria和Melbourne可对应到原文第五段，该段提到当墨尔本在1988年申办奥运会时，维多利亚州仍然处在经济混乱期（in economic turmoil）。注意：题目中要求是不能超过三个词的短语。故答案为in economic turmoil。

13. 4/four

根据题干中的关键词Secretary of the NSW Labour Council，可对应到原文倒数第三段The Secretary of the NSW Labour Council, Mr. Michael Easson, was quoted as saying, ...“What we’ve achieved should become the model for the rest of the building industry... great co-operation, good management, improvement in relations between employers and employees, and a feeling of optimism ...”其中明确列出了所取得的成就：（1）great co-operation;（2）good management;（3） improvement in relations between employers and employees;（4）a feeling of optimism。故本题正确答案为4/Four。

◎ 参考译文

2000年悉尼奥运会

在悉尼举办的2000年奥运会的总花销估计高达96 000万美元，但是悉尼通过效仿洛杉矶成功的商业广告案例准备从这一国际盛事中获得财政收入——洛杉矶作为1984年奥运会举办城市，是迄今为止惟一一个从奥运会中获得切实利益的城市。

1993年9月24日星期五上午4时20分整，当宣布悉尼力压其他四个竞争城市而赢得奥运会的举办权时，不仅仅是悉尼当地人，每一个澳大利亚人都毋庸置疑为这个结果感到骄傲。但如果悉尼在这次竞争中失败了，新南威尔士和澳大利亚的所有纳税人会赞同政府为一次失败且昂贵的行动花费几百万美元吗?

实际的申办费用比修改后的预算少了100万美元，而且比在1991年最早制定的2 900万美元的最初预算少了500万美元，这也许会让人稍感安慰。然而, 最终的花费还是高达2 400万美元，其中绝大部分花在了社团和社区建设、商品经营、授权以及彩票抽奖等诸多方面。对于新南威尔士政府来说，他们最初只想花费最多不超过1 000万美元，可最后却超支了200万美元之多。而联邦政府的拨款只有500万美元，这就意味着, 事实上悉尼的申办费用要依靠每位澳大利亚纳税人的财力支持。

在宣布成为获胜城市之前, 人们对于在经济不景气的情况下冒着财政风险申办奥运会的举措存在巨大争议。还有一些人认为70% 的设施都已经到位，而且都在政府管辖范围之内，排除了一些潜在的对先前奥运会竞标者造成困扰的冲突区域。前任新南威尔士总理尼克・格雷纳先生在电视讲话中说，“举办这次奥运会的优势不仅仅在于我们的本土产品将在接下来的14年里获得74亿美元的额外收益, 即便不考虑其他更显而易见的原因，例如运动设施的建设、旅游业以及相关事物，我认为奥运会的重点是人们心理上的变化，它促使人们更加自信……”。

然而，申办1988年奥运会而失败的墨尔本所获的收益也是让人们半信半疑，当时维多利亚州还处在经济混乱期，这表明很多团体组织对于奥运会并不是很热心。

毫无疑问，悉尼诱人的自然景观使全世界的媒体在与其竞争对手北京、柏林、曼彻斯特和伊斯坦布尔相比较时，对其表现出支持。澳大利亚旅游委员会的企业规划处主管戈弗雷・森特在发言中表示在申办成功之后，极大的媒体关注度已经对国内旅游业产生了有利的影响。

开发商和那些社区开发项目的负责人兴奋地指明了现有城市基础设施会得到改善，就业机会也会有所增加，特别是运动设施建设，也会因此更上一个台阶。上述种种，一方面满足了社区需求，另一方面，也会吸引更多的游客，如在霍姆布什湾斥资3亿美元兴建的双运动员竞技场和高科技水上运动中心。然而，最动人的还当属人们在劳资关系和环保问题上观念的新转变。申奥意义重大，必须顺利实现的理念促使霍姆布什湾奥运村兴建过程中雇佣双方配合默契，和谐融洽。劳资关系有了不少改善：没有罢工，没有分界阻碍，以及按时或提前完成项目。

引用新南威尔士劳动力委员会秘书迈克尔·伊森的话："……我们所实现的应该成为其他建筑产业的典范……愉快的合作、良好的管理、雇佣关系的改进和乐观主义精神……"。最持久的收益应该是霍姆布什湾一流的运动设施和应该能对其他建筑产业产生影响的产业关系模式。

绿色和平环保组织与州政府在申奥期间的优化洽谈及合作也同样见证了双方所建立起的新关系。环境保护主义者忽然间不再被认为是反对所有进展的极端分子，州政府也不再被认为是不关心环境的自私鬼。

悉尼申奥成功之处在于消除了许多反对冒险孤注一掷的声音。然而，大多数经济学家认为考虑一下人们未来能否承受这种财政失败所带来的后果与风险也是明智之举。

READING PASSAGE 2

Questions 14–18

题型：段落标题配对题 (LIST OF HEADINGS)

◆ 解析

14. xii

通读Section A，本段主题句为前两句Interests are... the things one cares about or wants. They provide the foundation for a person's or an organisation's position in a dispute，表明利益是争议攸关的因素，利益分歧也是争议的根本。对照选项列表，只有xii的表述与主题一致，故为正确选项。

15. vi

通读Section B，在本段开头作者先提到要想使利益达成一致并不容易，要找出有效的解决方案，接着便引出了本段的主题——解决利益纷争的两种方式（协商和调解）。对照选项列表，只有vi项的表述与本段主题一致，故为正确选项。

16. ii

通读Section D，本段的主题句为首句It is often complicated to attempt to determine who is right in a dispute，通常尝试判断争议中的正确方是很复杂的。对照选项列表，只有ii项的表述与本段主题一致，故为正确选项。

17. xi

通读Section E，本段的主题句为首句 A third way to resolve a dispute is on the basis of power，第三种解决争议的方法是基于实力。对照选项列表，只有xi项的表述与本段主题一致，故为正确选项。

18. iv

通读Section F，本段的主题句为首句In relationships of mutual dependence, such as between labour and management or within an organisation or a family, the question of who is more powerful turns on who is less dependent on the other，在相互依赖的关系中，例如劳工与管理层之间或者组织以及家庭内部，谁更有实力取决于谁更少地依赖于对方。本句比较复杂，中间有一个较长的插入语，可先略去不读。对照选项列表，只有iv项的表述与本段主题一致，故为正确选项。

Questions 19–21

题型：句子填空题 (SENTENCE COMPLETION)

◆ 解析

★注意：题目中有字数要求：NO MORE THAN THREE WORDS。

19. mediation

根据题干中的关键词common procedure, interest-based和negotiation，可定位到原文Section B的第三句The most common procedure for doing this is negotiation, the act of communication intended to reach agreement，此句中出现了两种方式中的一种—— negotiation，由此可知另外一种方式应该就在下文中，从本段的第四句Another interests-based procedure is mediation, in which a third party assists the disputants, the two sides in the dispute, in reaching agreement中得知mediation为another procedure，故为正确答案。

20. formalised in law

此题较难，题干中的关键词与原文的对应并不明显，通读全文可知文中提到rights的段落为C段和D段，而C段关于rights的表述只是蜻蜓点水，D段对于rights的描述最为详细，所以可定位在D段。D段的第二句Although it is usually straightforward where rights are formalised in law中的straightforward（直截了当的）与题干中的关键词relatively simple process相对应，由此可知答案为 formalised in law。

21. evidence and arguments

题干中的关键词是arbitrators and adjudicators，与20题一样，关键词与原文的定位并不十分明显，在Section D中第二段的第三句提到最典型的判断对错的方法是仲裁，在仲裁中，争议双方把证据和论据提供给中立的第三方，由第三方来做出决定，且争议双方必须服从。题干：仲裁人和裁决人在帮助解决争议之前必须从争议双方那里得到____，由此可知在空白处应填入证据和论据（evidence and arguments）最为合适。

Questions 22–27

题型：选择题 (MULTIPLE CHOICE)

◆ 解析

本题型的设置旨在考查考生对文章的理解。文章中论述了解决争议的三种方法，分别是：

A. 利益达成一致，包括谈判(negotiation)和调解(mediation)；

B. 确定谁对谁错，通常的方法是仲裁(adjudication)；

C. 确定谁更具实力。

在调解和仲裁中，都有第三方的参与。在调解中，第三方帮助双方达成一致，但并没有权力做出决定。在仲裁中，第三方有权做出决定，双方必须服从并执行。

理清这三种方法（比较难），再弄清每个题目的意思（比较容易），这几个题目就迎刃而解了。

22. C

容易误答为A。题目中只说“母亲接受了这个婚姻，因为她想和儿子重建良好的关系”，并没有提到儿子的看法。说明，母亲更依赖于她的儿子，或者说她的儿子更具实力。母亲和儿子不一定达成一致。

23. A

属于谈判，即利益达成一致。

24. B

容易误答为C。第三方联合国做出决定：这块土地应该给国家A，因为更强大的社会和历史联系。说明，在这个问题上，国家A是对的。这个决定双方必须遵照执行，属于仲裁。

25. A

属于调解，即利益达成一致。

26. B

属于仲裁。第三方即法院有权做出决定，双方必须遵照执行。

27. C

雇员更依赖于雇主，即雇主更具实力。

◎ 参考译文

争议的本质

解决争议意味着将对立双方变为一个单一的结果。争议双方可能选择将其注意力集中在三个基本因素中的一个或者多个上。他们可能会寻求调和各自的利益、确定正确的一方或确定权威的一方。

A段

利益是人们在意或想得到的一些东西，如需求、期望、关注或者忧虑。这些决定了一个人或者一个组织在争议中的立场。在争议中，不仅仅是双方利益不一致，而且双方还处于冲突中。例如，某一电器公司的销售主管与该公司的生产主管就电视机款式的生产数量问题陷入争论。销售主管希望能够扩大生产电视机的款型，因为她所关注的利益在于销售电视机。电视机款式增多，消费者就会有更多的选择，从而销售额也将提升。而对于生产主管来说，则希望减少款式。因为他利益的重点在于降低生产成本，增多款式也就意味着增加生产成本。

B段

调解这样的利益争议并不是一件简单的事情。它涉及探寻各自根深蒂固的关注点，并想出有效的解决方案，在利益对立的时候能够折中和妥协。最常用的解决方式为谈判协商，即想要达成一致的一种交流行为。另外一种基于利益的解决方式是调解，即第三方帮助争论双方达成某种协议。

C段

并不是所有的协商（或者调解）均以协调利益为主。一些协商侧重于确定正确方，比如两个律师争论谁的案子在诉讼中处于更有利的位置。还有一些协商侧重于确认哪一方更具有权威性，比如邻居或者国家之间的相互威胁或者反威胁。通常，协商涵盖了三种形式：有些试图满足各自的利益，有些讨论正确方，有些参考相对实力。

D段

通常尝试判断争议中的正确方是很复杂的。虽然在法律正式规定的情况下很直接，但是其他的对错取决于社会认同的不成文的行为准则，比如互惠性、惯例、平等性以及资历等等。

关于对错经常会有不同（有时乃至截然相反）的标准。就对错达成共识通常是件很困难的事情，因为最终结果会确定哪一方获得何物，因此一般都会求助于第三方来确定正确的一方。典型的判定对错的程序为仲裁，即争议双方将相应的证据以及论据提供给第三方，由中立的第三方来决定，且争议双方必须服从。（相反，在调解中，第三方不具备决定争议的权力）。公开仲裁由法庭以及行政代理机构完成。个人仲裁则由仲裁人完成。

E段

第三种解决争议的方法是基于实力。狭义地定义实力，是指强制某人完成非意愿事情的能力。行使权威时一般指强加对立方所付出的代价或者威胁对立方那么做。权威的实施一般有两种方式：攻击行为，比如人身攻击以及终止基于相互关系中所获取的好处，就像员工罢工时停止工作一样。

F段

在相互依赖的关系中，比如劳工与管理层之间或者组织以及家庭内部，谁更有权力取决于谁越少地依赖于对方，如果公司对员工工作的需求大于员工对于工资的需求，那么公司就具有较大的依赖性因而权威就处于被动情况下。一方的依赖性可以转为对替代品满足的程度，以用来满足这一方的利益。替代品越好，依赖性就越小。如果公司找到替代罢工的员工比罢工的员工找到新的工作更容易，公司的依赖性就较小，因此也就更具实力。没有经过一场具有决定性的以及潜在的破坏性的实力竞赛就决定哪一方更具权威是很困难的，因为毕竟权威归根结底是一种感知因素。

READING PASSAGE 3

Questions 28–34

题型：判断题 (YES/NO/NOT GIVEN)

◆ 解析

28. NOT GIVEN

根据题干中的关键词 knowledge of wild food可定位到原文第二段的倒数第二句And so, gradually, the vast store of knowledge, accumulated over thousands of years, fell into disuse. Much was lost，关于野生食物知识的表述，题干说的是大部分已经得以恢复，而该句中只是说很多知识逐渐不再被使用，很多也已失传，但并未提及目前是否已经恢复，故答案为NOT GIVEN。

29. NOT GIVEN

采用顺序性原则阅读下文，可发现对于29题的内容原文并未提及。

30. NO

本题并无明显的可与原文对应的关键词，可根据顺序性原则，定位到第四段第一句Not all our information on the subject comes from the Aborigines，该句明确说到并不是所有的信息都来自于土著居民，由此可知题干中所说的所有关于可食用的野生植物的知识都来自于土著人这一说法太过绝对，因此答案为NO。

31. NO

根据题干中的关键词Dodonaea，可定位到原文第四段的第四句So far as is known, the Aborigines made no use of Leptospermum or Dodonaea as food plants...由此句可知土著民并没有将Dodonaea（坡柳属）作为可食用的植物，故答案为NO。

32. YES

本题并无明显的可与原文对应的关键词，根据顺序性原则，可定位到原文第五段的尾句There are many species from northern Australia which occur also in Southeast Asia, where they are used for food，此句指出许多来自澳大利亚北部的植物在东南亚也出现了，而题干表述与此句信息一致，故正确答案为YES。

33. YES

根据题干中的关键词Aboriginal tribes, coast和inland可定位到原文第六段的第一、三句In

general, those Aborigines living in the dry inland areas were largely dependent for their vegetable foods on seed such as those of grasses, acacias and eucalypts...Tribes on the coast...had a more varied vegetable diet with a higher proportion of fruits and tubers，生活在干燥内陆地带的土著人大多数是靠种子作为他们的蔬菜食物，比如青草、金合欢和桉树……在海岸边上的部落群体，特别是在沿海雨林中的部落，有更多的蔬菜食物，而且大多数是水果和茎类植物。由此可知题干中关于沿海的部落比内陆的部落拥有更多的可食用植物的表述是正确的，故答案为YES。

34. NOT GIVEN

根据题干关键词coastal food和inland可定位到原文第六段，根据顺序性原则，可定位到Some of the coastal plants, even if they had grown inland, probably would have been unavailable as food...此句虽然出现了与题干类似表述，但要注意原文句中使用了虚拟语气，并未明确说某些沿海植物在内陆也能找到，所以该题正确答案应是NOT GIVEN。

Questions 35–37

题型：选择题 (MULTIPLE CHOICE)

◆ 解析

35. A

根据题干中的关键词Wallaby可定位到原文第二段的第一句The conquering Europeans displaced the Aborigines, killing many, driving others from their traditional tribal lands, and eventually settling many of the tribal remnants on government reserves, where flour and beef replaced nardoo and wallaby as staple foods，由该句可知在欧洲人到来之前，当地土著居民是以大柄苹和小袋鼠为主食的，故答案选A。

36. D

根据题干中的关键词experimentation可定位到原文第四段的倒数第二句Probably some experiments had less happy endings; L. J. Webb has used the expression eat, die and learn in connection with the Aboriginal experimentation...，其中句首的 less happy对应D项中的unfortunate，endings对应results，故答案选D。

37. C

本题题干并无明显的关键词，可从四个选项中找，根据A中的dry region，B 中的seed以及D中的southern part of Australia可定位到原文第六段，该段第一句是说生活在干燥内陆地带的土著人大多数是靠种子作为他们的蔬菜食物。他们把那些种子放在扁平石中间磨成了粗粉。注意此句中说到的是住在干燥内陆地区的土著居民，所以A项和B项的表述过于片面，C项中加入了具有“相对意义”的sometimes，而且原文句中也提到种子要借助扁平石才能磨成粉，故答案选C。

Questions 38–40

题型：摘要填空题 (SUMMARY COMPLETION)

◆ 解析

38–40题属于从原文中选词，题目要求中并没有给出摘要的出处，仔细审读摘要的第一句话，和原文每段话的第一句进行对应，即可发现摘要出自于原文的倒数第三段。

38. Queensland nut

仔细阅读题干，然后从原文倒数第三段开始阅读，对应到该段中的首句...it is perhaps surprising that only one, the Queensland nut, has entered into commercial cultivation as a food plant，注意题干中的限定词only one也在原文中出现，其后的Queensland nut即是正确答案。

39. selection

仔细阅读题干，采用顺序性原则，可定位到倒数第二段第一句Since 1788, there has, of course, been opportunity for selection of Australian food plants which might have led to the production of varieties that were worth cultivating. But Australian plants have probably “missed the bus”，自1788年起，一些澳洲食用植物的品种有了得以生产和种植的机会。但是，这些植物或许都“错过了这班车”。故答案为selection。

40. native raspberry

仔细阅读题干，可定位到倒数第二段的倒数第二句Undoubtedly, the native raspberry, for example, could, with suitable selection and breeding programmes, be made to yield a high-class fruit...该句提到澳洲木莓在经过精心挑选和培育之后本可以成为主流水果；但是，澳大利亚人已经习惯了外来的木莓，除非一些执着的业余花匠愿意培育本土的木莓，澳洲本土木莓很难再有什么发展了。故答案为native raspberry。

◎ 参考译文

澳大利亚的野生食物

120多年前，英国植物学家J.D.胡克，在写到澳大利亚可食用的植物时，就指出植物当中有很多是可食用的，但却不值得一尝。但是，澳洲土著居民在欧洲人到来之前，一直吃的都是植物和动物。这些土著人并不是农民，他们全靠野生作物赖以生存。他们会吃很多种经过处理的野生植物。

欧洲的征服者们取代了土著居民，屠杀了很多人，把剩下的居民从他们的部落赶走，最终安置到政府保留地，在这里面粉和牛肉取代了大柄苹和小袋鼠，成为主食。因此数千年来积累下的知识逐渐不再使用，许多都已失传。

然而，一少部分欧洲人对被取代的当地土著居民产生了兴趣甚至是敬意。探险家、传教士、植物学家、自然学家和政府官员对其进行了观察和记录，而且幸运的是，有的还成为出版物。今天，我们可以根据那些出版物形成关于澳大利亚可食用自然作物的基本知识，但毫无疑问大部分是不完整的。我们只能推测那些没有被记录的可食用植物的数目。

并不是所有这方面的信息都来自于土著居民。欧洲定居者最初的岁月非常艰难，传统食物极其短缺或者对于想在一个灌木丛中建造一座农场的先驱者来说食物也极其昂贵。出于生存的需要，他们必须像土著民那样在实践中寻找食物，而且从实践中幸运地总结出了一些结果。就目前所知，土著居民不用檬茶薇和坡柳属作为食用植物，但早期的移民者发现檬茶薇可以代替茶叶，而坡柳属可以用作啤酒花。这些植物和它们所取代的物种并没有关联，所以对它们的利用并不是基于对植物的观察。实践也未必会得到好的结果，L.J.韦伯使用"吃，死亡和学习"的表达方式与土著人的实践联系起来，但只有成功的尝试才会众人皆知。澳洲土著民的食用植物很有可能只被欧洲移民或他们的子孙发现的。

即将远征的探险者发现，他们不可能把整个行程所需的食物都带上，必须在半路寻找能够吃的东西。另一种信息来源源自于其他国家的实践。在澳大利亚北部，有很多种植物在东南亚也可以找到，在那里它们也被当作食物。

通常，生活在干燥内陆地带的土著人大多数是靠种子作为他们的蔬菜食物，比如青草、金合欢和桉树。他们把那些种子放在扁平石中间磨成了粗粉。在海岸边上的部落群体，特别是在沿海雨林中的部落，有更多的蔬菜食物，而且大多数是水果和茎类植物。一些沿海植物，即使能够在内陆生长，可能也不能食用，因为他们需要长时间的冲刷和浸泡才能使它们变得无毒；许多陆地上的部落无法获得足够数量的水来进行此种处理。在不同纬度的地区，土著人吃的植物也有很大不同。通常，住在潮湿的热带地区的土著民与澳洲南部的土著民相比，在饮食种类上前者要比后者丰富得多。

尽管澳洲土著人已经把近百种植物用作食物，但令人惊奇的是，只有澳洲坚果被普遍种植。而造成这种现象的原因可能不是澳洲植物的缺乏，而是对其开发潜力的匮乏。例如，在欧洲和亚洲，食用植物得益于千百年来的优选和杂交，其生产形式要优于野生植物。在欧洲人到来之前，澳洲土著人根本就没有农业，所以没有机会去提高食用植物的质量，这也许是故意的，也许是无意识的。

自1788年起，一些澳洲食用植物的品种有了得以生产和种植的机会。但是，这些植物或许都"错过了这班车"。一些外来的可食用植物在经过长时间的种植以后，已经进入了主流，以至于澳洲食用植物很难被种植。毋庸置疑，澳洲木莓在经过精心的挑选和培育之后本可以成为主流水果；但是，澳大利亚人已经习惯了外来的木莓，除非一些执着的业余花匠愿意培育本土的木莓，澳洲本土木莓很难再有什么发展了。

如今在澳大利亚选择种哪些植物已经大部分被确定，就像不可能在灌木丛中迷路一样。而我们对于澳洲植物的兴趣在于其自然历史，而非其实用的必要性。

Test 5 核心词汇 Core Vocabulary

READING PASSAGE 1

staggering *adj.* 令人震惊的
reap *vt.* （因自己或他人所为）获得（某事物）
emulate *vt.* 模仿；与……竞争，努力赶上
consolation *n.* 安慰，慰问
catalyst *n.* 促进因素；催化剂
turmoil *n.* 混乱
seductive *adj.* 诱惑的，诱人的，富有魅力的
demarcation *n.* 定界，分界

READING PASSAGE 2

reconcile *vt.* 使和好，使和解
probe *vt.* & *vi.* 探索，探查
tradeoff *n.* 折中，权衡
mediation *n.* 调停，调解
disputant *n.* 争议人，争论者
merit *n.* 价值；优点；诉讼中处于有利地位
reciprocity *n.* 相互性；相互作用；互惠
precedent *n.* 惯例；先例
contradictory *adj.* 矛盾的；反对的
adjudication *n.* 裁定；判决
arbitrator *n.* 仲裁人
perception *n.* 感知；洞察力；观念

READING PASSAGE 3

botanist *n.* 植物学家
flora *n.* （某地区或某时期的）植物群；植物区系
fauna *n.* （某地区或某时期的）动物群
Aboriginal *adj.* 土著居民的，具有土著人特征的；澳洲土著居民的
remnant *n.* 剩余部分，残余
nardoo *n.* 一种苹属植物（产于澳洲），田菁（产于印度），大柄苹
wallaby *n.* 小袋鼠
hops *n.* 啤酒花
acacia *n.* 阿拉伯树胶；金合欢
eucalypt *n.* 桉树
vicinity *n.* 附近，邻近
intrinsic *adj.* 固有的，内在的，本质的
hybridisation *n.* 杂交，配种
raspberry *n.* 树莓，木莓

TEST 6

Candidate Number

Candidate Name ______________________

INTERNATIONAL ENGLISH LANGUAGE TESTING SYSTEM

ACADEMIC READING

TIME 1 hour

INSTRUCTIONS TO CANDIDATES

Do not open this booklet until you are told to do so.

Write your name and candidate number in the spaces at the top of this page.

Start at the beginning of the test and work through it.

You should answer **all** questions.

If you cannot do a particular question, leave it and go on to the next. You can return to it later.

All answers must be written on the answer sheet.

Do not remove this booklet from the examination room.

INFORMATION FOR CANDIDATES

There are **40** questions on this question paper.

The test is divided as follows:

Reading Passage 1	Questions 1–14
Reading Passage 2	Questions 15–27
Reading Passage 3	Questions 28–40

Reading Answer Sheet

Are you: Female? ▭ Male? ▭

Your first language code:

0 1 2 3 4 5 6 7 8 9
0 1 2 3 4 5 6 7 8 9
0 1 2 3 4 5 6 7 8 9

IELTS Reading Answer Sheet

Module taken (shade one box): Academic ▭ General Training ▭

		✓ ✗			✓ ✗
1		1	21		21
2		2	22		22
3		3	23		23
4		4	24		24
5		5	25		25
6		6	26		26
7		7	27		27
8		8	28		28
9		9	29		29
10		10	30		30
11		11	31		31
12		12	32		32
13		13	33		33
14		14	34		34
15		15	35		35
16		16	36		36
17		17	37		37
18		18	38		38
19		19	39		39
20		20	40		40

Checker's Initials		Marker's Initials		Band Score		Reading Total	

READING PASSAGE 1

*You should spend about 20 minutes on **Questions 1–14**, which are based on Reading Passage 1 below.*

Living Expenses — a Guide for Overseas Students

In the mid-1990s it is estimated that a student living alone requires on average A$12, 000 in living expenses for each year of study. Of course, these costs increase with time.

Upon arrival, students should have funds in excess of the average to cover the cost of text books and establishment expenses such as rental bond payment and basic furniture items. The amount spent on food, recreation, and entertainment expenses will vary according to requirements, budget, and location.

Those who are prepared to live in shared accommodation, which may not be suitable for all, might manage on A$10, 000 per year. It is preferable for overseas students whose English is in need of practice to take advantage of live-in situations with native-speakers whenever possible. However, sharing with friends who are easy to communicate with is probably more sensible at first.

The above figures do not include the cost of large non-essential items such as household equipment or a car. Owning and maintaining a motor vehicle is expensive in Australia. Insurance is compulsory and costly, and parking both on and off campus can be a problem requiring additional expense. It is not advisable for a student to own a car unless it is absolutely necessary. A reasonable second-hand car can cost in excess of A$4, 000.

Educational institutions are almost always serviced by reliable public transport. The university and college campuses within the major cities are well served by public buses. In addition, the larger cities have extensive train systems. For example, in Sydney, most college and university campuses are only 10 or 20 minutes from a rail station.

The summer vacation requires special financial planning. Expenses for this period must be carefully estimated and added to costs for the academic year in order to give a realistic total figure for the calendar year. They are not included in the estimated A$10, 000–A$12, 000 previously quoted. University eating facilities, and some university and college housing facilities, close during this time. As a general rule, international students should expect to spend at least as much on monthly living expenses during the summer as they do during the academic year.

Under present immigration regulations, international students are allowed to work up to 20 hours weekly during term time and full-time during vacation. It is impossible for students to expect to earn sufficient funds working part-time to pay for tuition fees and living costs. While some students are able to supplement their funds with money from part-time and/or vacation work, such work is not always regular even when available, and this can contribute to anxiety and study problems. In general, it is unrealistic to start a course with insufficient funds in the hope that "something will turn up". Students should be aware that vacation work has become more difficult to find over the last few years, but those interested can contact the Commonwealth Employment Service or the Students' Union on campus.

Warm clothes are necessary in the southern States during winter months, as night temperatures can drop to less than 10 degrees Celsius. Students should bring as much clothing from home as possible, especially if funds are limited. Information on where to buy inexpensive clothes can be obtained from the International Student Centre of most colleges and universities.

Do not rush into buying expensive text books. It is advisable to wait until your first lectures and tutorials, and then ask academic staff which are the essential purchases. There is usually a second-hand bookshop on campus, and used texts are also advertised on faculty noticeboards.

The Students' Union coordinates a number of outlets on the various university campuses that provide stationery items and other essential study equipment at reasonable prices. Some courses require specialised equipment which can be quite costly, and it is wise to check any additional costs involved with the course of your choice.

In general, those practically orientated courses tend to incur higher additional costs. Expenses for books, stationery, and equipment vary greatly, but you should allow approximately A$500-A$1, 000 a year.

Most university campuses have banks and/or credit unions. The banks issue drafts, traveller's cheques or foreign currency notes, and accept telex or airmail transactions. In some colleges and universities the credit union is the institution's own credit union. In addition to normal banking and financial services (with no transaction charges), credit unions usually provide special services for international students.

Money may be deposited or withdrawn from branches of the credit unions and banks during business hours from Monday to Friday (but not on public holidays) or 24 hours a day from the many on-campus automatic teller machines. Business hours for financial institutions vary, but credit unions are usually open from 9 am to 5 pm weekdays, and, generally, banks are open from 9:30 am to 4 pm (5 pm on Fridays). Some services are available on Saturday mornings in selected areas. While prices often compare favourably with prices overseas, because Australia is a large and exciting country, it is very easy to overspend, especially if on a tight budget.

Questions 1–9

*Complete the summary using the list of words, **A–Z**, below.*

*Write the correct letter, **A–Z**, in boxes 1–9 on your answer sheet.*

It is recommended that students have sufficient funds available to cover both the costs of living and studying while in Australia. Expenses **1** .... depending on personal requirements, budget, and location. Owning a car is not advisable nor a **2** .... for students, since universities and colleges are **3** .... by public transport. During summer vacation, international students must budget **4** ...., if they are not to exceed their allocated yearly expenses. Present immigration **5** .... enable students to work up to **6** .... per week during term time. However, work is becoming increasingly hard to obtain. If money is in short supply, clothing should be **7** .... from home, and warm clothing is necessary, especially during **8** .... Text books can be expensive, but can often be bought second-hand. On-campus banking and financial services provide extensive services, and funds are readily available from credit unions and banks, during business hours, or through automatic teller machines. However, care must be taken not to overspend if the budget is **9** ....

A spend	**H** changes	**O** restricted	**V** necessary
B bought	**I** department	**P** too high	**W** well served
C 15 per cent	**J** necessity	**Q** inexpensive	**X** nearby
D brought	**K** 20 hours	**R** 10 degrees	**Y** located
E carefully	**L** expensive	**S** regulations	**Z** 20 weeks
F available	**M** need	**T** 45 per cent	
G winter	**N** recommended	**U** vary	

Questions 10–14

*Choose the correct letter, **A**, **B**, **C** or **D**.*

Write the correct letter in boxes 10–14 on your answer sheet.

10 Sharing accommodation may be

A approximately A$10, 000 per year cheaper than living alone.

B more expensive than living alone.

C not suitable for some students.

D suitable for most students.

11 During summer vacation

A all institutional housing facilities close down.

B additional living costs are involved.

C university canteens remain open.

D monthly living expenses decrease.

12 Regular part-time work is

A always easily found.

B not always available.

C sufficient to pay for tuition fees.

D 20 hours during full-time vacation.

13 Courses that are more practical

A can require specialised equipment.

B are usually cheaper.

C cost A$500–A$1, 000 a year.

D are usually more difficult.

14 Credit unions on campus

A are open 24 hours a day.

B provide the usual financial services offered by banks.

C deduct fees for normal transactions.

D are open on public holidays.

READING PASSAGE 2

You should spend about 20 minutes on ***Questions 15–27****, which are based on Reading Passage 2 below.*

Sleeping

Sleep medicine is a relatively young field in the UK, with only a couple of centres until the 1980s. In the last decade a number of centres have sprouted, often led by chest physicians and ENT surgeons with an interest in obstructive sleep apnoea, forcing neurologists and neurophysiologists to wake up and contribute to the non-respiratory aspect of this neglected subject.

Within sleep, two states are recognised—non-rapid eye movement (NREM) and rapid eye movement (REM). These alternate cyclically through the night with cycle time of 90 minutes (50–60 minutes in the newborn). NREM sleep is divided into four stages: stages 1 and 2 (considered light sleep), and stages 3 and 4 (deep sleep with high arousal threshold).

REM is ontogenically primitive with EEG activity closer to wake state, intermittent bursts of REMs and muscle atonia interrupted by phasic bursts producing asynchronous twitching. The atonia of REM sleep prevents acting out of dreams and is lost in REM behaviour disorder when dreams content becomes violent and patients act out their dream, often resulting in injury. REM behaviour disorder can be a precursor of neurodegenerative disease including Parkinsons. Dream content (pleasant/unpleasant) will be remembered on waking from REM sleep but there is often little memory of the preceding mental activity on arousals from NREM sleep, even when associated with complex behaviours and autonomic disturbance as occurs in night terrors or sleep walking.

In the newborn 50 per cent of total sleep time is occupied by REM sleep, progressively shrinking to 25 per cent in the adult, the first block of REM sleep occurring about 90 minutes after sleep onset. Abrupt withdrawal of alcohol and many centrally acting recreational and non-recreational drugs can cause REM sleep to occur at sleep onset. This can also increase total REM sleep, leading to intense vivid often frightening dreams, similar to that experienced by patients with narcolepsy.

The NREM/REM sleep states are interrupted by brief arousals and transient awakenings. The frequency of the arousals may increase with emotional disturbance or environmental discomfort but also in many intrinsic sleep disorders such as periodic leg movements in sleep, obstructive sleep apnoea and narcolepsy.

A basic rest-activity cycle originates in fetal life. The newborn sleeps an equal amount during the day and night, the sleep-wake cycle organised around three-to-four-hourly feeds. By the second month favouring of sleep towards night-time occurs and by six months the baby will have about 12 hours of sleep at night in addition to a couple of daytime naps. In general, children born prematurely have a tendency to be awake more at night in the first year and breast-fed babies wake more frequently, but the difference disappears by the second year. Persistent night awakenings in infants and toddlers usually reflect the child's inability to self-soothe back to sleep without parental attention and will respond to a well supported behavioural programme.

The establishment of a consolidated night sleep pattern in children reflects brain maturation and may be disrupted in children with developmental problems. Even in this group success is possible by persisting with behavioural work, though many paediatricians prescribe melatonin for these children with some success. But as the long-term safety of melatonin remains unknown it should be used as a last resort. There are now good studies looking at short-term use of melatonin in sleep-wake cycle disorders such as delayed sleep phase syndrome. Its use as a hypnotic should be discouraged, especially in the developing child as there is uncertainty on other cycles, such as menstrual.

In addition to the NREM/REM cycles, there is a circadian (24 hours) sleep/wake cycle entrained by intrinsic rhythms (melatonin and body temperature) and extrinsic factors (light and social cues such as mealtimes, school/work times). The pineal hormone melatonin plays a role in entraining the sleep-wake cycle to the light-dark cycle. Melatonin secretion is high in darkness and low in daylight hours, the process beginning in the retina with the suprachiasmatic nucleus playing a major role as a sleep regulator via melatonin. Blind people may lose this entrainment and develop a free running sleep/wake cycle with progressive advancement of sleep onset time.

Polymorphism of the circadian clock gene has now been identified with the population divided between morning types (larks) and evening types (owls). Those predisposed to later sleep onset time (evening types) are susceptible to developing delayed sleep phase syndrome especially during adolescence when sleep requirement increases and there is a tendency towards later time for sleeping and waking. In delayed sleep phase syndrome, sleep onset is delayed to the early hours of the morning with consequent difficulty in waking in time for school/work. Once established, advancing sleep onset time is difficult and requires treatment with appropriately timed melatonin or bright light therapy—advancing sleep onset progressively forwards until the desired sleep time is reached.

In contrast the elderly who are more susceptible to perturbation in their sleep-wake schedule can develop advanced sleep phase syndrome with sleep onset occurring early in the evening. Shift workers often struggle to cope with shift patterns as they grow older due to difficulty in re-adjusting their circadian clock. In general, morning bright light exposure is a more powerful synchroniser of the circadian rhythm than melatonin.

Questions 15–17

Choose the correct letter, ***A****,* ***B****,* ***C*** *or* ***D****.*

Write the correct letter in boxes 15–17 on your answer sheet.

15 According to the passage,

A the growing concern on sleep medicine from physicians and ENT surgeons contributed to the boom of this domain.

B neurologists and neurophysiologists have neglected the study of obstructive sleep apnoea.

C the infants have the cycle of NREM and REM every 90 minutes.

D NREM and REM alternate periodically in four stages.

16 About the REM and NREM sleep,

A people cannot recall the dream content when they are waking from REM sleep.

B the atonia remains when the content of dream is violent.

C REM is accompanied by the EEG activity.

D the REM will make people act out their dream content.

17 According to the passage,

A the infants have to sleep three to four hours during the daytime.

B babies would rather sleep during the daytime in the second month.

C the newborn sleeps a dozen of hours during the day.

D the difference between prematured and breast-fed babies will cease to exist in the second year.

Questions 18–21

Complete the sentences below.

Choose ***NO MORE THAN TWO WORDS*** *from the passage for each answer.*

Write your answers in boxes 18–21 on your answer sheet.

18 REM behaviour disorder is thought as one kind of predecessor of ....

19 People almost have no .... of what they dreamed when they wake up from NREM sleep even though they have undergone night terrors or sleep walking.

20 The dreams those patients with narcolepsy have are vivid even ....

21 How often the .... happen depends on the many factors involving emotional and environmental effects and intrinsic sleep disorders.

Questions 22–27

Complete the summary below.

Choose ***NO MORE THAN THREE WORDS*** *for each answer.*

Write your answers in boxes 22–27 on your answer sheet.

The use of melatonin

Some developmental problems could influence the sleeping pattern of children negatively and accordingly **22**.................. is prescribed by doctors to children though the behavioural practice works better. The use of melatonin is just suggested as the last resort not as a **23**.................. for it may have harm to some **24**.................. of the developing child. There is an important cycle called the sleep-wake cycle in people, in which with the participation of melatonin secretion the **25**.................. is regulated. People are categorised into two groups, larks and owls. The owl type develops easily the delayed sleep phase syndrome, in which the **26**.................. will be postponed but melatonin and more natural treatment like **27**.................. can be used to reach the desired sleep time.

READING PASSAGE 3

*You should spend about 20 minutes on **Questions 28–40**, which are based on Reading Passage 3 below.*

A A new type of tourism, coined "ecotourism", has recently emerged and is quickly gaining in popularity as a leisure activity. Ecotourism, a type of "getting-back-to-nature" excursion, brings people into environmentally sensitive areas to view exotic and, more often, endangered plants and animals. Proponents of this type of travel such as John Whiteman, a partner in a tourism and community development consulting firm, and Stefan Gossling from the Human Ecology Division of Lund University, view ecotourism as not only beneficial but essential to both the environment and economies of these often-depressed regions. Through such an ecological experience the traveler is supposedly changed or "spiritually renewed", and gains a new-found respect and sensitivity for nature. This, in turn, is expected to promote more environmentally responsible decisions in daily life. Whiteman states, "While there, tourists enjoy a sense of spiritual renewal. And they leave behind an intact ecosystem and increased wealth for the local community". Furthermore, the governments and citizens of the areas in question are, presumably, encouraged to take steps to preserve these tourist sights in order to continue to reap the benefits of the tourist dollar.

B Unfortunately, when popular sites of ecotourism such as Uganda and the Galapagos Islands are carefully examined, it becomes apparent that ecotourism does not provide the benefits so readily claimed by its proponents. The economies of these regions see little benefit. The local people remain impoverished, and offer no protection to the environment: in fact, they are often angered enough to lash out against these fragile ecosystems. The environment is harmed directly by the physical presence of tourists; it is simply not possible to bring people into an area where few humans would otherwise exist without altering or harming the very environment which we seek to preserve. From ostensibly small effects such as crushing plant life underfoot and soil erosion, to larger effects such as altered animal behaviour, it is highly probable that the ecological footprint left by tourists will not go unnoticed. As Heather Lindsay observes in *Ecotourism: The Promise and Perils of Environmentally-Oriented Travel,* "even harmless-sounding activity like a nature hike can be destructive, as hikers can contribute to soil erosion and damage plant roots". Upon examination, the ecological dangers of ecotourism are readily apparent.

C In both Uganda's Bwindi Impenetrable National Park (BINP) and the Galapagos Islands, altered animal behaviour is a significant concern. Studies have shown that, when in the presence of tourists, animals abandon their nesting and feeding sites. Perhaps worse, when animals become accustomed to the presence of tourists, they lose the instinct to flee thus leaving them vulnerable to poachers. In BINP, habituation of the gorillas is fundamental to ecotourism so that they may be safely observed by tourists. Unfortunately, this purposeful habituation may have led to the gorillas losing the instinct to flee from poachers or soldiers. In looking at this problem, Hamilton tells us that "initial indications are not encouraging". What then, will become of these animals if they lose the instinct to flee from danger in their environment? Surely the outlook is not promising. Losing their survival skills places these animals at risk for extinction.

D In the Galapagos, habituation of the wildlife is not intended; however, it has been noted that, "Scientists began noticing behavioural changes in the animals such as iguanas waiting for tourists to give them bananas". It has also been observed that the normally docile male sea lions of the Galapagos have recently become more aggressive. In her work, *Ecotourism and Sustainable Development: Who Owns Paradise?* Martha Honey states that, at present, it is unclear if this aggression can be attributed to an increase in tourism or an increase in sea lion population. Some scientists believe that the impact of tourism on other mammals and birds is minimal but that the system is becoming weak in particular areas. It is important to note that a particular area of the Galapagos is now closed because turtle nests and vegetation were so badly trampled by tourists that these species were threatened with imminent extinction.

E Beyond the issues of altered animal behaviour and trampled vegetation is the problem of newly introduced organisms to these visited ecosystems. When tourists arrive, they present the threat that they carry with them, on their person or in their mode of transportation, bacteria, disease, animals and insects foreign to the environment. This is one of the biggest issues the Galapagos Islands are currently facing. Honey states, "At the top of the agenda of many scientists and park officials is tracking and eliminating the introduced species plants, animals, insects, fungi, bacteria that are brought in by boat or plane by tourists, new immigrants, and illegal fishing operations". The problem with this is that many of these foreign organisms are capable of "out-competing" the unique indigenous species of the Galapagos. Since the native species of the Galapagos evolved without the threat of such organisms, they may be driven to extinction, leaving the ecosystem irreparably changed. For example, black rats introduced to Pinzon Island kill tortoises as they hatch. Pigs on Santiago Island eat the eggs of sea turtles, thereby reducing their survival rate from eighty percent to a mere three percent while introduced aphids are killing native plants. In a related article by Martha Honey and Ann Littlejohn, *Paying the Price of Ecotourism*, Tom Fritts, a biologist with the National Biological Survey, calls this "a critical time" for the ecosystems of the Galapagos Islands, and speaks of its current state as being pushed "towards the brink of disaster". The stakes are high. Ecosystems are forever changed by the consequences of tourism. Fritts tells us that we are dangerously near the "precipice of irretrievable damage". Simply, certain damages cannot be undone. There is no remedy for extinction.

F Adams and Whiteman argue that the revenue from ecotourism is no less than essential to the survival of these protected areas since money is needed for maintenance and protection and to encourage locals and their governments to take an interest in conservation. However, economic benefits for local communities are not what they should be, and this often fosters a sense of ill will, encouraging such things as poaching and violent acts against the ecosystem. Moreover, it seems to be a paradoxical issue, because if the environment is destroyed, what has been accomplished by ecotourism? Guidelines for successful ecotourism are offered by many proponents and critics alike, yet these guidelines lack a reasonable ecological position when applied to such sensitive areas as the Galapagos and the BINP. There is no compromise possible where such fragile environments and unique species are concerned. Guidelines cannot render our presence harmless nor can they let us off the hook for the ensuing damage.

Questions 28–35

Look at the following statements (Questions 28–35) and the list of people below.

*Match each statement with the correct people, **A–F**.*

Write the correct letter, A–F, in boxes 28–35 on your answer sheet.

NB *You may use any letter more than once.*

28 The native plants are confronting threats from foreign organisms resulting from ecotourism.

29 The states should play a role in keeping the sights so as to satisfy the demand of ecotourism.

30 It is easy to find that ecotourism is harmful for the soil and plants.

31 Sufficient funds are necessary to stimulate local government to conserve ecotourism sight.

32 The initial problem for some scientists is to remove introduced species brought by alien visitors.

33 Animals are deprived of their nature.

34 It is lack of evidence to prove that tourism improvement brings about changes of animals temper.

35 We are about to be in a danger of damage from ecotourism.

A	Heather Lindsay
B	Hamilton
C	Tom Fritts
D	Adams and Whiteman
E	John Whiteman
F	Martha Honey

Questions 36–39

Complete the summary below.

*Choose **NO MORE THAN THREE WORDS** from the passage for each answer.*

Write your answers in boxes 36–39 on your answer sheet.

Ecotourism is called and defined as a style of **36** .... process which leads people to view the natural places environmentally friendly. However, after the careful examination about tourism in Uganda and the Galapagos Islands, it is found that ecotourism is of **37** .... to local economy. And it is worth noticing that ecotourism triggers many negative effects like **38** .... in small side and **39** .... in large aspect.

Question 40

*Choose the correct letters, **A**, **B**, **C** or **D**.*

Write it in box 40 on your answer sheet.

Which of the following is the most suitable title for the passage?

A The Nature of Ecotourism

B Ecotourism: the Damage for the Animals and Plants

C Ecotourism: Behind the Green Curtain

D Ecotourism and Its Long-term Effects

Test 6 答案速查 Key

READING PASSAGE 1

1. U	**2.** J	**3.** W	**4.** E	**5.** S
6. K	**7.** D	**8.** G	**9.** O	**10.** C
11. B	**12.** B	**13.** A	**14.** B	

READING PASSAGE 2

15. A
16. C
17. D
18. neurodegenerative disease/Parkinsons
19. memory
20. frightening
21. arousals
22. melatonin
23. hypnotic
24. cycles
25. sleep
26. sleep onset
27. bright light therapy

READING PASSAGE 3

28. F	**29.** E	**30.** A	**31.** D
32. F	**33.** B	**34.** F	**35.** C

36. getting-back-to-nature
37. little benefit
38. crushing plant-life underfoot/soil erosion
39. altered animal behaviour
40. C

Test 6 考题精解 Detailed Explanation

READING PASSAGE 1

Questions 1–9

题型：摘要填空题 (SUMMARY COMPLETION)

◆ 解析

1. U

由空白处后的depending on personal requirements, budget, and location可以定位到原文

第二段最后一句话The amount spent on food, recreation, and entertainment expenses will vary according to requirements, budget, and location，此处需要填一个动词，主语为复数形式，所以填原形vary，故本题答案为U。

2. J

本题填写一个名词。根据题干关键词Owning a car可定位到原文第四段的倒数第二句It is not advisable for a student to own a car unless it is absolutely necessary，所以此空应该填写necessary的名词形式necessity，故本题的答案为J。

3. W

由空白处后面的by public transport可知本题填写一个动词过去分词形式。根据题干关键词public transport可定位到原文第五段的第二句The university and college campuses within the major cities are well served by public buses，题干的public transport与原文的public buses对应，所以本空填写well served，故本题答案为W。

4. E

本空填写一个副词。根据题干关键词summer vacation和budget定位到原文第六段的第二句Expenses for this period must be carefully estimated and added to costs for the academic year in order to give a realistic total figure for the calendar year，题干中的budget和原文中的estimated为同义转换，所以本题填写carefully，故本题答案为E。

5. S

6. K

第5题填写一个名词，第6题也填写一个名词。根据题干关键词Present immigration和work up to可以定位到原文第七段的第一句Under present immigration regulations, international students are allowed to work up to 20 hours weekly during term time and full-time during vacation，很明显第5题应填写regulations，第6题应填写20 hours，故两题分别选择S和K。

7. D

本空填写一个动词分词形式。根据题干关键词clothing可以定位到原文第八段的第二句Students should bring as much clothing from home as possible, especially if funds are limited，原文的主动句在题干中转为被动句，money is in short supply与原文的funds are limited对应，所以本题填写brought，故本题答案为D。

8. G

本题填写一个表示时间的名词。根据题干关键词warm clothes可以定位到原文第八段的第一句Warm clothes are necessary in the southern States during winter months, as night temperatures can drop to less than 10 degrees Celsius，所以可知这里填写winter，故本题选择G。

9. O

本空填写一个动词的分词形式或者形容词。根据题干关键词automobile teller machines可定位到最后一段，由easy to overspend可以定位到最后一句While prices often compare favourably with prices overseas, because Australia is a large and exciting country, it is very easy to overspend, especially if on a tight budget，可知应填写tight来说明budget，但是选项中没有tight，只好选它的同义词restricted，故本题的答案为O。

Questions 10–14

题型：选择题 (MULTIPLE CHOICE)

◆ 解析

10. C

根据题干关键词Sharing accommodation定位到原文第三段的第一句Those who are prepared to live in shared accommodation, which may not be suitable for all, might manage on A$10,000 per year，答案来自which may not be suitable for all，原文说并不是所有人都适合与人合住，所以C项“不适合某些学生们”为正确选项。D项中的most属于过度推理。

11. B

根据题干关键词summer vacation可定位到原文的第六段，由第一、二句The summer vacation requires special financial planning. Expenses for this period must be carefully estimated and added to costs for the academic year in order to give a realistic total figure for the calendar year，可知在暑假，需要多花钱，本段的最后一句也表达了同样的意思，故本题的正确答案为B。由本段中间的University eating facilities, and some university and college housing facilities, close during this time可知A项和C项是错误的。

12. B

根据题干关键词Regular part-time work定位到原文第七段，由本段第一句Under present immigration regulations, international students are allowed to work up to 20 hours weekly during term time and full-time during vacation，可知留学生在上学期间每周工作最多20小时，假期允许全天工作，与选项D“在全职假期可以工作20小时”不相符，所以D项错误。由本段第二句It is impossible for students to expect to earn sufficient funds working part-time to pay for tuition fees and living costs，可知选项C是错误的。由第三句While some students are able to supplement their funds with money from part-time and/or vacation work, such work is not always regular even when available, and this can contribute to anxiety and study problems，可知兼职工作也不是一直都有的，故本题的正确答案为B。

13. A

根据题干关键词Courses和practical可以定位到原文倒数第三段，原文说，总的来说，那些以实践为主的课程一般附加费用更高。虽然说在购买书、文具和仪器上的花费大有不同，但是应该做好每年花费大约500到1 000澳元的准备，B项与第一句的内容相反，所以B项错误；第二句说明500–1 000澳元是附加的书、文具和仪器上的花费，并不是课程的费用，所以C项错误；D项中的difficult信息原文未提及，所以D项错误；而第四段最后一句说道Some courses require specialised equipment which can be quite costly, and it is wise to check any additional costs involved with the course of your choice即additional costs指的是specialised equipment的费用，所以A项正确。

14. B

根据题干关键词Credit unions可定位到原文最后两段。由倒数第二段的最后一句In addition to normal banking and financial services (with no transaction charges), credit unions usually provide special services for international students可知B项正确，同时说明选项C是错误的。原文说：with no transaction charges，而选项C是deduct fees for normal transactions；原文最后一段的第一句Money may be deposited or withdrawn from branches of the credit unions and banks during business hours from Monday to Friday (but not on public holidays) or 24 hours a day from the many on-campus automatic teller machines说自动取款机是24小时可用，而没说是credit union，所以A项错误；由最后一段的第二句Business hours for financial institutions vary, but credit unions are usually open from 9 am to 5 pm weekdays可知信用社只在工作日开放，所以D项错误。故本题的正确答案为B。

◎ 参考译文

生活成本——留学生生活指南

20世纪90年代中期，一个单独居住的学生在其求学期间每年的生活费用大概要12 000澳元，当然，这项费用会随着时间的推移而增加。

刚到学校时，学生们花的钱比平时多，因为要交书本费以及一些安顿费用，例如房租押金和设施使用费。学生在饮食、消遣和娱乐方面的花销是不同的，这主要看他们的需求、预算和所处位置有何不同。

对于那些打算与人合住的学生，其每年的花费大概要10 000澳元，但并不是所有人都适合与人合住。它比较适合需要练习英语的海外留学生，因为他们可以利用与当地人一起生活的便利，与他们随时进行交流。然而，在最开始的时候与容易交流的朋友合住才是更明智的选择。

以上的这些数字并不包含一些费用很高的非必需支出，如购买一些家用设备或汽车。

在澳大利亚，购买和保养一辆机动车的费用十分昂贵。保险是必须要上的而且费用很贵，在校园内外停车也需要额外的费用。对于学生来说，拥有一部车并不明智，除非你确实需要它。买一辆不错的二手车需要4 000多澳元。

几乎所有的学校都有可靠的公共交通可以到达。在一些大城市，大学和学院都有公共汽车可到达。另外，在一些更大的城市拥有广泛的轨道运输系统，如，在悉尼，从火车站到达大多数大学仅需10分钟或20分钟。

在暑假，学生需要有专门的财务计划，在这个时期的花费需要仔细估算，需要加到学年费用中，以得到一个一整年的实际花销数目。这笔花销不计入前面说的10 000澳元到12 000澳元的估算内。大学里的食堂和一些住房在此期间是关闭的。总的来说，留学生在暑假的花费至少会与学期每个月的花费持平。

根据目前的移民制度，留学生可在上学期间每周工作最多20个小时，假期允许全天工作。对于学生来说通过兼职赚到足够的钱以缴纳学费和生活费是不太可能的。尽管一些学生能够在兼职或者假期工作当中增加自己的资金，但是即使能找到工作，也不是一直都有活干的，这就增加了学生的焦虑和学习方面的问题。总之，在带着“奇迹会出现的”这种想法而资金却不足的情况下想开始新的学习，是不切实际的。学生们应该意识到这几年的假期工作是越来越难找了，但是感兴趣的人可以和联保就业服务中心或者学校的学生会联系。

在一些南部地区，冬天里，晚间的气温会降到10摄氏度以下，所以有必要准备一些保暖的衣服。学生们应尽可能从家里多带些衣服，尤其是那些资金有限的同学。在大多数大学里，国际学生中心会告诉你在哪儿能买到便宜的衣服。

不要急于去买一些昂贵的教科书。明智可取的做法是：要等到第一节课结束后，去问老师哪些是需要买的然后再购买。校园里通常有一个二手书书店，教职工通知栏里也会刊登旧课本的广告。

学生会会协调各大学校园里的众多廉价商店，使一些文具、学习设备能够维持在一个合理的价格上。一些课程需要的专用的设备可能非常昂贵，所以最好提前确认所选的课程涉及的任何附加花费。

总的来说，那些以实践为主的课程一般附加费用更高。虽然说在购买书、文具和仪器上的花费大有不同，但是应该做好每年花费大约500到1 000澳元的准备。

大多数学校的校园内有银行和信用社。银行主要发行汇票，旅游支票或者是外国流通的货币，接受电报或者航空邮件业务。在一些大学里的信用社是学校自设的。它们除了提供正常的银行和金融方面的服务（没有相关的手续费）外，信用社经常为留学生提供专门的服务。

你可以在每周一至周五的上班期间（不包含法定节假日）从银行或信用社分支点或者

是在校园里24小时服务的自动存取款机上存取钱。这些金融机构的工作时间不是统一的，但是信用社一般是在每个工作日的早上九点至下午五点营业，而总的来说，银行是从早上九点半至下午四点上班（每周五工作到下午五点）。有些服务在周六早上可以到指定的区域办理。虽然在价格上，澳大利亚与其他国家相比是有优势的，但是因为澳大利亚地域广阔、魅力无限，所以学生很容易超支，特别是在预算紧张的情况下。

READING PASSAGE 2

Questions 15–17

题型：选择题 (MULTIPLE CHOICE)

◆ 解析

15. A

本题题干并无明显的关键词，可从下面的选项中提取关键词，四个选项中A和B项说的是第一段的内容，C和D项是第二段的内容。根据A项中的关键词ENT surgeons可定位到原文第一段的第二句In the last decade a number of centres have sprouted, often led by chest physicians and ENT surgeons with an interest in obstructive sleep apnoea, forcing neurologists and neurophysiologists to wake up and contribute to the non-respiratory aspect of this neglected subject，故选项A为该句的正确推理，选项中的contributed to 与文中的led by为同义转换。

16. C

根据题干关键词REM和选项关键词 EEG activity可定位到原文第三段的第一句REM is ontogenically primitive with EEG activity closer to wake state, intermittent bursts of REMs and muscle atonia interrupted by phasic bursts producing asynchronous twitching。原文中的primitive with转述为选项中的accompanied by，故答案为C。

17. D

根据选项关键词 prematured and breast-fed babies 可定位到原文第六段第三句 In general, children born prematurely have a tendency to be awake more at night in the first year and breast-fed babies wake more frequently, but the difference disappears by the second year，它和选项D意思相同，difference disappears与cease to exist为同义转换。所以答案选D。

Questions 18–21

题型：句子填空题 (SENTENCE COMPLETION)

◆ 解析

完成句子题属于纯粹的填空题，答案均为原文原词。

18. neurodegenerative disease/Parkinsons

根据题干关键词REM behaviour disorder可定位到原文第三段的第三句REM behaviour disorder can be a precursor of neurodegenerative disease including Parkinsons，文中该句话中的precursor对应题干中的predecessor，故答案为neurodegenerative disease/Parkinsons。

19. memory

根据题干关键词night terrors, sleep walking 可定位到原文第三段的最后一句Dream content (pleasant/unpleasant) will be remembered on waking from REM sleep but there is often little memory of the preceding mental activity on arousals from NREM sleep, even when associated with complex behaviours and autonomic disturbance as occurs in night terrors or sleep walking，题干中的no对应该句中的little，故答案为memory。

20. frightening

根据题干关键词narcolepsy, vivid可定位到原文第四段的第三句This can also increase total REM sleep, leading to intense vivid often frightening dreams (hypnogogic—sleep onset/hypnopompic or, on waking, hallucinations), similar to that experienced by patients with narcolepsy。显然要找到一个和vivid所对应的词。文中信息只有frightening满足要求，故答案为frightening。

21. arousals

根据题干关键词emotional, environmental effects, intrinsic sleep disorders可定位到原文第五段的第二句The frequency of the arousals may increase with emotional disturbance or environmental discomfort but also in many intrinsic sleep disorders such as periodic leg movements in sleep, obstructive sleep apnoea and narcolepsy，文中的frequency 是题干中的how often 的对应词，故答案为arousals。

Questions 22–27

题型：摘要填空题 (SUMMARY COMPLETION)

◆ 解析

22. melatonin

根据题干中的关键词prescribed 可定位到原文第七段的第二句Even in this group success is possible by persisting with behavioural work, though many paediatricians prescribe melatonin for these children with some success，该句中的prescribe和题干中的prescribed明显对应，paediatricians与doctors 对应，题干将原文中的主动句改为了被动句，答案为 melatonin。

23. hypnotic

根据题干关键词resort 可定位到原文第七段最后一句Its use as a hypnotic should be

discouraged, especially in the developing child as there is uncertainty on other cycles, such as menstrual，use与resort对应，last与should be discouraged对应，答案为hypnotic。

24. cycles

根据题干关键词developing child 可定位到原文第七段最后一句Its use as a hypnotic should be discouraged, especially in the developing child as there is uncertainty on other cycles, such as menstrual，题干中的the developing child为原词重现，as there is...与for it may have harm...对应，故答案为cycles。

25. sleep

根据题干关键词 regulated 可定位到原文第八段的第三句Melatonin secretion is high in darkness and low in daylight hours, the process beginning in the retina with the supra chiasmatic nucleus playing a major role as a sleep regulator via melatonin，题干中的regulated与句中的regulator对应，所以答案为sleep。

26. sleep onset

根据题干中的关键词 postponed 可定位到原文倒数第二段的倒数第二句In delayed sleep phase syndrome, sleep onset is delayed to the early hours of the morning with consequent difficulty in waking in time for school/work，文中的delayed对应题干中的 postponed，所以答案是sleep onset。

27. bright light therapy

根据题干中的关键词natural treatment, reach可定位到原文倒数第二段的最后一句Once established, advancing sleep onset time is difficult and requires treatment with appropriately timed melatonin or bright light therapy—advancing sleep onset progressively forwards until the desired sleep time is reached，题干的提示是一种天然的治疗方法，故对应bright light therapy，因此答案是bright light therapy。

◎ 参考译文

睡眠

睡眠医学在英国还是一个相对较新的领域，20世纪80年代时全国才只有几家睡眠研究中心。近十年来，一些由对障碍性睡眠呼吸暂停症感兴趣的胸外科医生和耳鼻喉科医生创办的研究中心陆续出现，一些神经病学家和神经生理学家也由此得到启发，投身到这项被忽视的课题的有关非呼吸方面的研究中。

睡眠大致可分为两种状态：慢相睡眠和快相睡眠。这两种状态在夜间每隔90分钟就会交替出现（婴儿则是每隔50到60分钟就会交替出现）。慢相睡眠可分为四个阶段，其中第一和第二阶段是轻度睡眠，而第三和第四阶段则被认为是兴奋值较高的深度睡眠。

快相睡眠是睡眠的原始状态，它的脑电波活动接近清醒状态。在这一阶段，会出现间歇性的眼球快速转动、肌肉张力缺失，会伴有阶段性的抽搐。快相睡眠阶段肌肉反应迟缓，这使得我们无法进入梦境。快相睡眠行为异常时，肌肉迟缓就会消失，这时人们的梦境就会变得格外清晰强烈，此时病人做梦的话就经常会受伤。快相睡眠行为异常有可能导致帕金森综合症等神经退化性疾病。快相睡眠时做的梦——无论是快乐的还是悲伤的——醒后都会记起，而在慢相睡眠阶段做的梦，即便在夜惊或梦游时进行了复杂的活动和自主神经紊乱，醒后也多会被遗忘。

婴儿睡眠的50%都是快相睡眠，成年人的睡眠则会逐渐减少到25%，快相睡眠第一阶段会在入睡的90分钟后出现。突然忌酒和停用消遣性、非消遣性中枢作用的药品会在入睡伊始就进入快相睡眠阶段，此种状态下快相睡眠总量会增加，从而会做一些极其逼真的噩梦，其征兆与患有嗜眠症病人的十分相似。

慢相睡眠或快相睡眠都会被短暂的惊醒和暂时的清醒打断。其发生频率可能因情绪的波动或环境不适而有所加快，在很多内因性睡眠障碍的病例中，诸如睡眠时腿部的周期性运动和障碍性睡眠呼吸暂停和嗜睡症中，睡眠也会时常被打断。

基本休息与活动周期始于胎儿时期。婴儿在白天和夜里睡得一样久，此时的睡醒周期使得婴儿大概每三到四个小时就要喂一次奶。两个月大时，婴儿开始喜欢在夜里睡觉，到了六个月大时，婴儿大概能在夜里睡12个小时，白天只会打几个盹。通常来说，早产的婴儿在第一年的夜里醒来的次数比较多，母乳喂养的孩子平时醒来的次数会比较多，但这种情况在第二年会消失。婴幼儿和初学走路的孩子如果晚上总不能入睡，这表明他们不具备在没有父母关照下自己独立安睡的能力，应该对他们提供有针对性的行为培训计划。

夜间睡眠习惯的养成表明了儿童大脑的成熟，这一过程也有可能被诸多成长问题打断。碰到这样问题的孩子通过持久的行为矫正也可以成功地养成正常的睡眠习惯。有的儿科医生给孩子服用褪黑素，并且已见成效，但是长期使用褪黑素的安全性仍有待验证，所以医生只有在不得已的时候方可使用。尽管现在对在延迟睡眠综合症等睡醒周期异常中短期使用褪黑素的研究已经相当成熟。但若将之作为安眠药使用还应慎之又慎，尤其是不能给尚在发育阶段的儿童使用，因为这可能影响到他们的生理周期，比如月经。

除了慢相/快相睡眠周期外，睡醒周期的生理节奏也受人体内部节奏的影响（褪黑素和体温）和外部因素（光线以及诸如吃饭、学习和工作时间等方面的社会暗示）的影响。松果体激素褪黑素在从睡醒周期向光暗周期转化的过程中发挥了作用。褪黑素在夜间分泌得多，白天分泌得少，这一进程开始于视网膜的前视交叉核，它起到了通过分泌褪黑素来调整睡眠的重要作用。盲人可能会失去这种调节作用，但会逐渐发展出另一种自行调节的睡醒周期，在睡眠伊始时促进睡眠。

生物钟基因的多态性在人群中的表现可分为两种，一种是早睡早起（百灵鸟）型，一种是晚睡晚起型（夜猫子型）。那些习惯于晚睡的人更易患延迟性睡眠综合症，尤其需要更多睡眠的习惯晚睡晚起的青春期人群。患延迟睡眠综合症的人将睡眠时间延迟到了凌晨，结果他们常常很难按时起床上学或上班。习惯一旦养成，就很难再早睡，需要定时使用适量的褪黑素来治疗或者进行强光疗法——逐渐提前睡觉时间直到达到要求的入睡时间。

相反，对那些睡醒计划容易受外界干扰的老人而言，他们会把提前的睡眠综合症提前到晚上睡眠伊始之时。长期倒班的人随着年龄的增长需费力处理睡眠倒班模式，因为他们很难调回他们的生物钟。一般而言，与褪黑素相比，晨光普照是一个更有力的生物节奏指示。

READING PASSAGE 3

Questions 28–35

题型：配对题 (MATCHING)

◆ 解析

28. F

根据题干关键词native plants, threats from foreign organisms可定位到原文E段，本段中间部分提到玛莎·哈尼对于本土物种及外来物种的关系的观点，故该题答案为F。

29. E

根据题干关键词states, play a role, satisfy the demand of ecotourism 可定位到原文A段，由本段最后两句可知约翰·惠特曼提到了政府及居民对于旅游点应给予的关注及原因，故该题答案为E。

30. A

根据题干关键词ecotourism, harmful, soil and plants可定位到原文B段，本段倒数第二句的引号里显示赫瑟尔·林德塞认为生态旅游给土壤和植物带来的后果是极具破坏性的，故该题答案为A。

31. D

根据题干关键词funds, local government, conserve可定位到原文F段，该段开头部分提到了亚当斯和惠特曼对于生态旅游所带来收入要用于做什么的问题的观点，这其中就包括用奖金鼓励政府及民众来保护生态景点，故答案为D。

32. F

根据题干关键词initial problem, introduced species可定位到原文E段，在本段中间部分显示玛莎·哈尼认为科学家处理引入物种问题的方法是消灭，故该题答案为F。

33. B

根据题干关键词deprived of their nature可定位到原文C段，本段的倒数第二及第三句话显示哈密尔顿认为动物被人为地失去他们的本能，故该题答案为B。

34. F

根据题干关键词lack of evidence, changes of animals temper 可定位到原文D段，在本段中间部分显示玛莎·哈尼在她的著作中说海狮的好斗性的成因尚不明确，故该题答案为F。

35. C

根据题干关键词in a danger of damage可定为到原文E段，在本段末尾部分显示弗里茨认为我们正站在“不可挽回的破坏的悬崖”边上，故该题答案为C。

Questions 36–39

题型：摘要填空题 (SUMMARY COMPLETION)

◆ 解析

36. getting-back-to-nature

根据题干关键词called and defined as a style of 可定位到原文A段，在本段第二句给出了生态旅游的定义，是一种“回归自然的”旅行，故该题答案为getting-back-to-nature。

37. little benefit

根据题干关键词Uganda and the Galapagos Islands, economy可定位到原文B段，在该段第二句有提到The economies of these regions see little benefit，题干空白处位于be of 后, to前，应该是一个名词，故该题答案为little benefit。

38. crushing plant-life underfoot/soil erosion

根据题干关键词negative effects, in small side可定位到原文B段，本段中间部分举出了作者认为生态旅游的负面影响，small effects包括crushing plant-life underfoot和soil erosion，故此空两者填一。

39. altered animal behaviour

根据题干关键词negative effects, in large aspect可定位到原文B段，本段中间部分举出了作者认为的生态旅游的负面影响，to larger effects方面包括altered animal behaviour等，故此空填altered animal behaviour。

Question 40

题型：选择题 (MULTIPLE CHOICE)

◆ 解析

40. C

通读全文可知该文章第一段在谈论生态旅游的优势发展情况，然而从文章第二段开头作者话锋一转(unfortunately)，就把整个第一段全部否定掉；在后面的第三、四、五段作者通过不同的例子向读者说明生态旅游会给当地人民、自然界和动物等带来各种负面影响。文章最后一段又列举两个专家的例子，进一步阐述自己的观点，表明他对Ecotourism的反对意见，纵观全篇，文章有些揭内幕的意味，故答案选择C。

◎ 参考译文

A 最近，出现了一种叫做“生态旅游”的新型旅游方式，它作为一种娱乐活动迅速得到普及。所谓生态旅游，是指一种“回归自然”的旅游方式，它将人们带到一些环境敏感区域，去参观一些珍奇的，特别是濒临灭绝的动植物。这种旅游方式的支持者，如约翰·惠特曼，一家旅游及社区发展咨询公司的股东，还有来自伦德大学的人类生态学系的斯蒂芬·戈斯林，认为，在那些经常处于低迷境地的区域，生态旅游对其环境及经济发展不仅是有益的，而且是必要的。希望通过这一生态体验，旅游者能够有所改变或在精神风貌上焕然一新，对自然有全新的认识和感受，从而借此提高人们在日常生活中的环境责任感。惠特曼说：“在那里，旅游者可以享受到精神升华的快感，他们在为当地社会增加财富的同时也保留了完整的生态系统。”并且，这些地区的政府及民众也会因此受到激励，采取措施来保护这些旅游景点，以期借此在旅游方面获取收益。

B 然而不幸的是，仔细观察一些著名的生态旅游景点，如乌干达及加拉帕哥斯群岛，我们就会发现生态旅游似乎并不像其支持者所说的那样可以很轻易地带来利润。这些地区几乎没有获得任何经济利益。当地的居民依然很贫困，他们也并没有去保护环境。实际上，他们还总是被激怒，然后将怒气发泄到这些脆弱的生态系统上。环境直接受到旅游者的破坏。将人们带到只有通过改变或破坏所谓的我们要保护的环境才能生存的地区简直是不可能的。然而毋庸置疑，旅游者到此一游的生态足迹也不应被忽视，从小的方面看，他们在踩伤花花草草这类弱小植物的生命的同时还会破坏土壤，从大的方面看，他们有可能改变动物的生活习性。正如赫瑟尔·林德塞在《生态旅游：环保旅行是希望还是陷阱》一书中说道“即使是诸如大自然徒步旅行这类听起来没有任何伤害的活动都可能是极具破坏性的，因为徒步旅行者会造成土壤腐蚀而且会破坏植物的根”。调查表明，生态旅游的危害是显而易见的。

C 在乌干达的比温蒂禁猎区国家公园和加拉帕哥斯群岛的动物习性的改变引起了广泛关注。研究表明，游客的涌现致使动物放弃巢穴和觅食场所。更糟糕的是：可能一旦动物习惯了这种游客涌现的状况，他们就会失去逃跑的本能从而使得他们更易受到偷猎者的攻击。在比温蒂禁猎区国家公园，驯化大猩猩对于生态旅游十分重要，只有这样游客才能安全地观察大猩猩。不幸的是，这种有目的的驯化导致大猩猩躲避偷袭者及士兵的本能的遗失。意识到这种问题，哈密尔顿告诉我们："最初的指示（这里指驯化）是不受鼓励的。"如果连逃离险境的本能都丢失了，这些动物将如何生存呢？显然，前景不容乐观。失去生存技能令它们面临灭种的危机。

D 而在加拉帕哥斯群岛，野生动物的驯化不是有意而为的；尽管如此，还是有这样的事发生，"科学家开始注意到动物的习性已有所改变，例如鬣蜥（一种产于南美洲和西印度群岛的大蜥蜴）总是在等待游客喂它们香蕉。"加拉帕哥斯群岛的公海狮，通常是很温顺的，最近却变得极具攻击性。玛莎·哈尼在她的著作《生态旅行和可持续发展：谁会拥有天堂》中提到："目前还无法确定海狮的这种好斗性是应归咎于旅游者数量的增加还是应归因于海狮数量的增加"。一些科学家认为：旅游对于其他哺乳动物和鸟类的影响很小，除非特定地区的生态系统变得很脆弱。人们应该注意到加拉帕哥斯群岛的某些区域已经不再对旅游者开放，那是因为他们严重破坏了海龟的巢穴和（这些区域的）植被，致使这些物种濒临灭绝。

E 除了上述的动物习性改变和植被破坏的问题之外，被参观的生态系统经常还面临着外来生物的引入问题。游客到来的同时也带来了威胁，这些威胁或是由他们自身携带的或是通过交通工具携带的，如本不属于这一环境的细菌、疾病、动物和昆虫等。这是加拉帕哥斯群岛目前所面临的最大问题之一。哈尼说："被很多科学家及公园官员提到重要日程的问题是跟踪及消灭由游客以及新的移民和非法垂钓活动通过船只或飞机所引进的物种，如动物、植物、昆虫、真菌及细菌等。"原因在于这些外来生物能使加拉帕哥斯群岛的本土物种"出局"。由于加拉帕哥斯群岛本土的物种在（起初的）进化的过程中并没有受到这些外来生物的威胁，因此它们（指加拉帕哥斯群岛本土的物种）可能被迫灭绝，从而使得生态系统不可避免地改变。例如：引入到平松岛的黑鼠会消灭孵化中的乌龟；圣地亚哥岛的猪吃掉了海龟的卵，从而导致了海龟的存活率从80%下降到只有3%；还有流入的蚜虫也正在扼杀着当地的植物。在一篇由玛莎·哈尼和安·小约翰所写的叫做《生态旅游的代价》的文章中，国家生物调查局的生物学家汤姆·弗里茨，称此为加拉帕哥斯群岛生态系统的"危急时刻"，他认为目前的状态已被推到"灾难的边缘"。（生态旅游的）代价太高了。旅游使得生态系统被永远地改变了。弗里茨告诉我们，我们正站在"不可挽回的破坏的悬崖"边上。简言之，某些损失已经是覆水难收了。物种一旦灭绝就无法弥补。

F 亚当斯与惠特曼认为生态旅游所得的收入只不过是这些被保护区域的生存之本，对区域的维护以及激励当地政府和民众来保护区域都是需要经费支持的。然而，当地团体获取经济利益本不应该是生态旅游的目的所在，这（指经济利益）总是会滋生一些恶意，（那就是）鼓励诸如偷猎或使用暴力等破坏生态系统的行为的发生。此外，这似乎是一个很矛盾的问题，因为如果环境被破坏了，那么生态旅游到底带来了什么呢？一些支持者和批评家提供了看似有效的生态旅游方针，然而当把这些方针运用于诸如加拉帕哥斯群岛和比温蒂禁猎区国家公园这些敏感区域时，从生态角度讲，缺乏合理的立场。考虑到这些脆弱的环境和特殊的物种，我们就不该有任何妥协让步。这些方针既不能让我们不带任何伤害性的出现在上述地区，也不能使我们避免随之而来的损失。

Test 6 核心词汇 Core Vocabulary

READING PASSAGE 1

establishment *n.* 安顿；建立
recreation *n.* 休闲，消遣
compulsory *adj.* 强制性的，义务的
academic year （大学的）学年（在美国通常从9月开始至第二年6月结束）
calendar year 一整年的时间（如自今年5月6日至明年5月6日）
immigration *n.* 移民
supplement *vt.* 补充
stationery *n.* 文具
deposit *vt.* 存款
withdraw *vt.* 取款

READING PASSAGE 2

sprout *vt.&vi.* （使）萌芽
surgeon *n.* 外科医生
apnoea *n.* 呼吸暂停
neurologist *n.* 神经学者
alternate *vt.&vi.* （使）交替
intermittent *adj.* 间歇的
disorder *n.* 混乱
disturbance *n.* 骚动，动乱
shrink *vt.&vi.* （使）收缩
transient *adj.* 短暂的，瞬时的
frequency *n.* 频率
narcolepsy *n.* 嗜眠发作；嗜睡症
toddler *n.* 初学走路的孩子
maturation *n.* 成熟
paediatrician *n.* 儿科医师
menstrual *adj.* 月经的
secretion *n.* 分泌
retina *n.* 视网膜
syndrome *n.* 综合病症
adolescence *n.* 青春期（一般指成年以前13至15岁的发育期）
therapy *n.* 治疗

READING PASSAGE 3

ecotourism *n.* 生态旅游

emerge *vi.* 出现

excursion *n.* 远足，短途旅行

exotic *adj.* 奇异的；从外国引进的

proponent *n.*（某事业、理论的）支持者，拥护者

renew *vt.&vi.*（使）复原；（使）更新

intact *adj.* 完整无缺的，未经触动的

impoverished *adj.* 穷困的；无力的

lash out 大肆挥霍；猛烈抨击

fragile *adj.* 虚弱的，脆弱的

ostensibly *adv.* 表面上

crushing *adj.* 支离破碎的

impenetrable *adj.* 不能通过的，不能穿过的

instinct *n.* 本能

poacher *n.* 偷猎者，侵入者

habituation *n.* 适应

fundamental *adj.* 根本的，基本的

docile *adj.* 驯服的，容易教的

aggressive *adj.* 好争斗的，挑衅的，侵略性的

trample *vt.&vi.* 践踏，蹂躏；侵犯

imminent *adj.* 即将发生的，逼近的

indigenous *adj.* 土生土长的，生来的，固有的

irreparably *adv.* 不能挽回地，不能恢复地

brink *n.*（悬崖峭壁的）边缘；（危险的）边缘

precipice *n.* 悬崖，峭壁

irretrievable *adj.* 不能挽回的，不能复原的

paradoxical *adj.* 事与愿违的，出乎意料的，自相矛盾的

compromise *n.* 妥协，折中方法

ensuing *adj.* 继而发生的

TEST 7

Candidate Number

Candidate Name ______________________

INTERNATIONAL ENGLISH LANGUAGE TESTING SYSTEM

ACADEMIC READING

TIME 1 hour

INSTRUCTIONS TO CANDIDATES

Do not open this booklet until you are told to do so.

Write your name and candidate number in the spaces at the top of this page.

Start at the beginning of the test and work through it.

You should answer **all** questions.

If you cannot do a particular question, leave it and go on to the next. You can return to it later.

All answers must be written on the answer sheet.

Do not remove this booklet from the examination room.

INFORMATION FOR CANDIDATES

There are **40** questions on this question paper.

The test is divided as follows:

Reading Passage 1	Questions 1–14
Reading Passage 2	Questions 15–27
Reading Passage 3	Questions 28–40

Reading Answer Sheet

Are you: Female? ▭ Male? ▭

Your first language code:

0	1	2	3	4	5	6	7	8	9
0	1	2	3	4	5	6	7	8	9
0	1	2	3	4	5	6	7	8	9

IELTS Reading Answer Sheet

Module taken **(shade one box):** Academic ▭ General Training ▭

		✓ ✗			✓ ✗
1		1	**21**		21
2		2	**22**		22
3		3	**23**		23
4		4	**24**		24
5		5	**25**		25
6		6	**26**		26
7		7	**27**		27
8		8	**28**		28
9		9	**29**		29
10		10	**30**		30
11		11	**31**		31
12		12	**32**		32
13		13	**33**		33
14		14	**34**		34
15		15	**35**		35
16		16	**36**		36
17		17	**37**		37
18		18	**38**		38
19		19	**39**		39
20		20	**40**		40

Checker's Initials		Marker's Initials		Band Score		Reading Total	

READING PASSAGE 1

*You should spend about 20 minutes on **Questions 1–14**, which are based on Reading Passage 1 below.*

Of Ducks and Duck Eggs

For people who like to keep poultry, ducks offer certain advantages over hens. Ducks are immune to some common diseases found in hens and are less vulnerable to others. Some breeds of duck produce bigger eggs than hens. In addition, ducks lay eggs over a longer season than hens do.

Poultry keepers with gardens have less to worry about if they keep ducks rather than hens because the former are less apt to dig up plants and destroy roots. While both hens and ducks benefit the garden by eating pests, hens are known to damage herb and grass beds. Ducks, on the other hand, will search for insects and snails more carefully. Only very delicate plants are at risk from the broad, webbed feet of ducks.

Like all waterbirds, ducks need access to water, and duck keepers typically provide this by building a pond. Something this large is not absolutely necessary, however, ducks need only to be able to dip their heads in the water to keep their nostrils clean. If a pond is provided though it is important to keep ducklings away from it until they are old enough to withstand the cool temperature of the water—about eight weeks.

When keeping ducks, one has to consider just how many the land will support. Generally the rule is 100 ducks per half hectare. If more than this proportion is introduced, there is a risk of compacting the soil, which can lead to muddy conditions for long periods as the rain is not easily absorbed into the ground.

While ducks offer many advantages over hens, they must be given greater quantity of food, especially if regular eggs are desired. An adult duck will eat between 170 to 200 grams of food a day. If the ducks have access to grass and a pond, they will be able to find for themselves approximately 70% of their daily dietary, requirements in warmer months but less than half that in colder times. Therefore, it is important that they are fed enough food, such as grain, every day.

Experienced duck keepers raise ducklings every three years or so because it is after this period of time that ducks' egg-laying powers begin to seriously weaken. If the aim is to hatch duckling, keepers should be aware that not all ducks make good mothers, and that certain breeds of duck appear to be worse than others. The poor mothers abandon their eggs a few days after laying them. A sure way of making sure the rejected eggs hatch is to place them next to chicken eggs under a hen.

The eggs of ducks as food for humans have a mixed reputation. This is because of a number of cases of salmonella food poisoning in Europe in the 1970s. Although it was never conclusively shown that duck eggs were to blame, the egg-eating public stopped buying and many duck egg producers went bankrupt. Indeed, there is a risk of salmonella poisoning when ducks lay their eggs in damp conditions, such as on ground that is constantly wet but the same can be said for the eggs of hens. And commercial duck egg production in France and England, where the out-breaks of salmonella poisoning took place, followed the same standards as those used in the hen egg industry, which experienced no salmonella problems. (Storage of eggs, whether those of hen or duck, can also be a factor in contamination. Studies have found that bacterial growth reaches potentially dangerous levels at storage temperatures of 5°C or greater.)

The salmonella scare was over by the early 1980s, but, at least in smaller markets like Australia and New Zealand, few producers wished to risk investment in ducks for fear of problems. No large-scale commercial duck egg production exists in these countries. It has thus been left to small producers, and, more commonly, home duck keepers.

Questions 1–8

Classify the characteristics listed below as belonging to

D *Ducks*

H *Hens*

B *Both ducks and hens*

NI *If there is no information in the reading passage*

Write the appropriate letters in boxes 1–8 on your answer sheet.

1 lengthier laying period

2 better mothers

3 less likely to uproot plants

4 dangerous to grass

5 more eggs per week

6 eat more grain

7 beneficial to garden by eliminating pests

8 more vulnerable to illness

Questions 9–12

Complete the summary below.

Choose ***NO MORE THAN TWO WORDS*** *from the passage for each answer.*

Write your answers in boxes 9–12 on your answer sheet.

To prevent their **9** .... from getting dirty, ducks should have access to water. This may be provided by building a pond, but ducklings under **10** .... of age should be prevented from entering it because of the **11** .... of the water. If too many ducks are kept on a plot of land, the soil may eventually become **12** .... as a result of compaction. For this reason, it is advised that one should limit the number of ducks per half hectare of land to 100.

Questions 13 and 14

Choose the correct letter, ***A***, ***B***, ***C*** *or* ***D***.

Write the correct letter in boxes 13 and 14 on your answer sheet.

13 Salmonella food poisoning

A resulted from consumption of duck eggs.

B created difficulties for the duck egg business.

C occurred all over Europe.

D was found in both duck and hen eggs.

14 Duck eggs

A have been produced in large quantities in New Zealand since the early 1980s.

B are more at risk of salmonella contamination than hen eggs.

C may be contaminated when laid in wet conditions.

D should be kept at 5℃ to prevent contamination.

READING PASSAGE 2

*You should spend about 20 minutes on **Questions 15–27**, which are based on Reading Passage 2 on the following pages.*

Questions 15–19

Reading Passage 2 has six paragraphs, **A–F**.

*Choose the correct heading for paragraphs **B–F** from the list of headings below.*

*Write the correct number, **i–ix**, in boxes 15–19 on your answer sheet.*

List of Headings

- **i** Responsibilities of responding police officers
- **ii** Perceived advantages of rapid response
- **iii** Police response to public satisfaction
- **iv** Communicating response time to people requesting help
- **v** When rapid response is and is not necessary
- **vi** Role of technology in improving police response
- **vii** Rapid response time and success of rapid response
- **viii** Public demand for catching criminals
- **ix** Not quickly contacting the police

Example	***Answer***
Paragraph **A**	vi

15 Paragraph **B**

16 Paragraph **C**

17 Paragraph **D**

18 Paragraph **E**

19 Paragraph **F**

Rapid Police Response

A Police departments in the United States and Canada see it as central to their role that they respond to calls for help as quickly as possible. This ability to react fast has been greatly improved with the aid of technology. The telephone and police radio, already long in use, assist greatly in the reduction of police response time. In more recent times there has been the introduction of the "911" emergency system, which allows the public easier and faster contact with police, and the use of police computer systems, which assist police in planning patrols and assigning emergency requests to the police officers nearest to the scene of the emergency.

B An important part of police strategy, rapid police response is seen by police officers and the public alike as offering tremendous benefits. The more obvious ones are the ability of police to apply first-aid lifesaving techniques quickly and the greater likelihood of arresting people who may have participated in a crime. It aids in identifying those who witnessed an emergency or crime, as well as in collecting evidence. The overall reputation of a police department, too, is enhanced if rapid response is consistent, and this in itself promotes the prevention of crime. Needless to say, rapid response offers the public some degree of satisfaction in its police force.

C While these may be the desired consequences of rapid police response, actual research has not shown it to be so beneficial. For example, it has been demonstrated that rapid response leads to a greater likelihood of arrest only if responses are in the order of 1–2 minutes after a call is received by the police. When response times increase to 3–4 minutes—still quite a rapid response—the likelihood of an arrest is substantially reduced. Similarly, in identifying witnesses to emergencies or crimes, police are far more likely to be successful if they arrive at the scene no more than four minutes on average, after receiving a call for help. Yet both police officers and the public define "rapid response" as responding up to 10–12 minutes after calling the police for help.

D Should police assume all the responsibility for ensuring a rapid response? Studies have shown that people tend to delay after an incident occurs before contacting the police. A crime victim may be injured and thus unable to call for help, for example, or no telephone may be available at the scene of the incident. Often, however, there is no such physical barrier to calling the police. Indeed, it is very common for crime victims to call their parents, their minister, or even their insurance company first. When the police are finally called in such cases the effectiveness of even the most rapid of responses is greatly diminished.

E The effectiveness of rapid response also needs to be seen in light of the nature of the crime. For example, when someone rings the police after discovering their television set has been stolen from their home, there is little point, in terms of identifying those responsible for the crime, in ensuring a very rapid response. It is common in such burglary or theft cases that the victim discovers the crime hours, days, even weeks after it has occurred. When the victim is directly involved in the crime, however, as in the case of a robbery, rapid response, provided the victim was quickly able to contact the police, is more likely to be advantageous. Based on statistics comparing crimes that are discovered and those in which the victim is directly involved, Spelman and Brown (1981) suggest that three in four calls to police need not be met with rapid response.

F It becomes clear that the importance of response time in collecting evidence or catching criminals after a crime must be weighed against a variety of factors. Yet because police department officials assume the public strongly demands rapid response, they believe that every call to the police should be met with it. Studies have shown, however, that while the public wants quick response, more important is the information given by the police to the person asking for help. If a caller is told the police will arrive in five minutes but in fact it takes ten minutes or more. Waiting the extra time can be extremely frustrating. But if a caller is told he or she will have to wait 10 minutes and the police indeed arrive within that time, the caller is normally satisfied. Thus, rather than emphasising rapid response, the focus of energies should be on establishing realistic expectations in the caller and making every attempt to meet them.

Questions 20 and 21

What are the **TWO LATEST** technological developments that reduce police response time?

*Use **NO MORE THAN THREE WORDS** for each answer.*

Write your answers in boxes 20 and 21 on your answer sheet.

20 ....

21 ....

Questions 22–27

Do the following statements agree with the claims of the writer in Reading Passage 2?

In boxes 22–27 on your answer sheet, write

YES	*if the statement agrees with the claims of the writer*
NO	*if the statement contradicts the claims of the writer*
NOT GIVEN	*if it is impossible to say what the writer thinks about this*

22 Police believe there is a better chance of finding witnesses to a crime if response is rapid.

23 A response delay of 1–2 minutes may have substantial influence on whether or not a suspected criminal is caught.

24 The public and the police generally agree on the amount of time normally taken for a rapid response.

25 Physical barriers are the greatest cause of delay in contacting police.

26 Rapid response is considered desirable in handling cases of burglary.

27 Research shows that some 75% of crimes are discovered by victims after they have been committed.

READING PASSAGE 3

*You should spend about 20 minutes on **Questions 28–40**, which are based on Reading Passage 3 below.*

Doesn't That Sound Terribly Yellow to You?

"I can't say. I'm colour blind", was my flat-mate's response. And that was that for another twenty odd years, when by chance I came across an article in a newspaper on research into synaesthesia at a London hospital. At last, I understood my interpretation of the world through colour.

Synaesthesia is the subjective sensation of a sense other than the one being stimulated. For example, the sight of a word may evoke sensations of colour or the sound of music may also have a similar effect, as my taste. Or, to put it simply, synaesthetes, i.e. people with synaesthesia, have their senses held together, so that they experience several senses simultaneously.

To those not already aware of it, synaesthesia seems a new phenomenon. Yet, it is far from new. In 1690, John Locke, the philosopher, wrote of a blind man with synaesthetic capabilities. The first reference in the medical field was in 1710, by Thomas Woodhouse, an English ophthalmologist. In his *Theory of Colour*, the German writer, Goethe, talked about colour and the senses. The poet, Arthur Rimbaud, wrote about synaesthesia in his 1871 poem *Voyelles*, as did another French poet Baudelaire, in *Correspondence*. So, synaesthesia has a respectable history.

Synaesthesia is understandably met with a certain degree of scepticism, since it is something beyond the comprehension of the vast majority of people. Son et lumiere shows in the 19th century were an attempt at combining the senses in a public display, but such displays were not capable of conveying the sensations experienced by involuntary synaesthesia, as the ability which a synaesthete's experience is called. There has been a number of well-documented synaesthetes. Alexander Scriabin, the Russian composer(1871–1915), tried to express his own synaesthetic abilities in his symphony *Prometheus, the Poem of Fire*(1992). And another Russian, Rimsky-Korsakov, noted the colour associations musical keys possessed. For example, Scriabin saw C major as red, while to Rimsky-Korsakov it was white. Arthur Bliss, an English composer, based his *A*

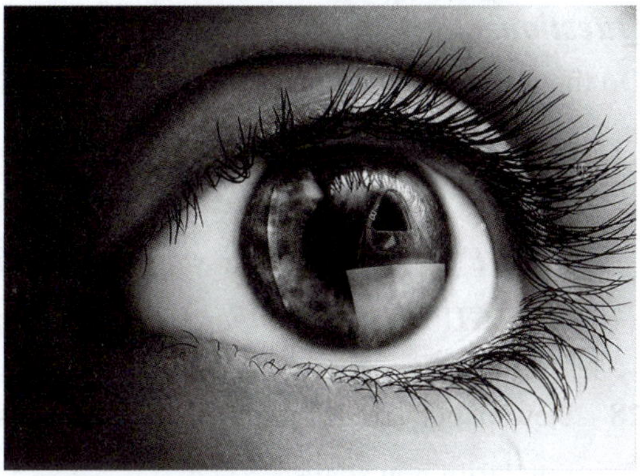

Colour Symphony in 1922 on the concept of synaesthesia. He did not claim to be a synaesthete; his colour choices were arbitrary and the project was an intellectual exercise.

In the field of the visual arts, probably the best-known artist with synaesthetic capabilities is the Russian artist, Wassily Kandinsky (1866–1944), credited with being the founder of abstract painting. It is said he experienced "sensory fusion" at a performance of *Wagner's Lohengrin*, with the music producing colours before his eyes. He did not see colours solely in terms of objects, but associated them with sounds. He even composed an opera, *Der Gelbe Klang* (*The Yellow Sound*), which was a mixture of colour, light, dance and sound.

For many people with synaesthesia, knowing that what they have been experiencing has both a name and a history and that they are among a number of notable sufferers is a revelation. Initially, they often feel that there is something wrong psychologically or mentally, or that everyone feels that way. Then they realise with a thud that other people do not. Suppression is an option, but unwittingly some people have managed to make use of the ability to their advantage. While the condition of synaesthesia may hamper many people because of its disorienting effects, it can also open up a range of new skills. It is not unusual for people who have synaesthesia to be creative and imaginative. As many studies have shown, memory is based to some extent on association. Synaesthetes find they are able to remember certain things with great ease. The person who associates the shape is able to remember a longer sequence of words; and the same goes for other areas where memory needs to be used.

But this condition like all gifts, has its drawbacks. Some people see words as colours; others even individual letters and syllables, so that a word becomes a kaleidoscope of colour. Beautiful though such a reading experience may be, synaesthesia can cause problems with both reading and writing. Reading can take longer, because one has to wade through all the colours, as well as the words! And, because the colour sequences as well as the words have to fit together, writing is then equally difficult.

Questions 28–32

Do the following statements agree with the information given in the Reading Passage 3?

In boxes 28–32 on your answer sheet, write

TRUE	*if the statement agrees with the information*
FALSE	*if the statement contradicts the information*
NOT GIVEN	*if there is no information on this*

28 Newspaper articles and TV news reports about synaesthesia are appearing with monotonous regularity nowadays.

29 Synaesthetes experience several senses at the same time.

30 Synaesthesia is a new phenomenon.

31 Early description of synaesthesia can be traced back to the 17th century.

32 It is strange that many people are sceptical about synaesthesia.

Questions 33–36

Choose the correct letter, ***A, B, C*** *or* ***D****.*

Write the correct letter in boxes 33–36 on your answer sheet.

33 Son et lumiere shows

A attempted to combine public senses.

B were frequent in the 19th century.

C were both public and involuntary.

D did not reproduce the experiences of synaesthetes'.

34 Both Alexander Scriabin and Rimsky-Korsakov

A wanted to have synaesthetic abilities.

B created a lot of documents.

C linked music to colour.

D agreed with Bliss in 1922.

35 The Russian artist, Wassily Kandinsky

A performed Wagner's Lohengrin.

B found many abstract paintings.

C also composed music.

D saw objects.

36 At first, "sufferers" of synaesthesia believe that

A there is something wrong with them.

B they are revelation.

C they are psychologically or mentally superior.

D they are unique.

Questions 37–40

Choose **FOUR** *letters,* ***A–G****.*

Write the correct letters in boxes 37–40 on your answer sheet.

NB *Your answers may be given in any order.*

Below are listed some statements about synaesthetes.

Which **FOUR** of these statements are true about synaesthetes?

A Some synaesthetes are disoriented by their abilities.

B Unusually, some synaesthetes have great creativity.

C Memory may be heightened by synaesthesia.

D Synaesthesia has more advantages than drawbacks.

E Some synaesthetes use their ability to help themselves.

F Their ability can be an obstacle to them.

G Some synaesthetes write in colour.

Test 7 答案速查 Key

READING PASSAGE 1

1. D	**2.** H	**3.** D	**4.** H
5. NI	**6.** NI	**7.** B	**8.** H
9. nostrils	**10.** eight weeks	**11.** cool temperature	**12.** muddy
13. B	**14.** C		

READING PASSAGE 2

15. ii	**16.** vii	**17.** ix
18. v	**19.** iv	**20.** "911" emergency system
21. police computer systems	**22.** YES	**23.** YES
24. YES	**25.** NOT GIVEN	**26.** NO
27. YES		

READING PASSAGE 3

28. NOT GIVEN	**29.** TRUE	**30.** FALSE
31. TRUE	**32.** FALSE	**33.** D
34. C	**35.** C	**36.** A
37. A	**38.** C	**39.** E
40. F		

Test 7 考题精解 Detailed Explanation

READING PASSAGE 1

Questions 1–8

题型：配对题 (MATCHING)

◆ 解析

本题要求将题目中列出的特征与选项进行相应的匹配，题目意义如下：

1. 产蛋期更长

2. 更好的母亲

3. 不太可能将植物连根拔起

4. 对草有威胁

5. 每周（产）更多的蛋

6. 吃更多的谷物

7. 消灭害虫，对花园有好处

8. 更容易得病

读懂了题目要求后，快速阅读文章，注意duck和hen出现的句子。

1. D

根据关键词laying period定位到原文第一段的最后一句In addition, ducks lay eggs over a longer season than hens do，可知母鸭的产蛋期比母鸡的长，故可确定答案为D。

2. H

根据关键词mothers定位到原文第六段最后两句The poor mothers abandon their eggs a few days after laying them. A sure way of making sure the rejected eggs hatch is to place them next to chicken eggs under a hen，可知母鸡是更好的母亲，可确定答案为H。

3. D

根据关键词uproot plants定位到原文第二段的第一句Poultry keepers with gardens have less to worry about if they keep ducks rather than hens because the former are less apt to dig up plants and destroy roots，可知家禽养殖者如果有花园，那么养殖母鸭比养殖母鸡更让人省心，因为母鸭不大可能将植物连根拔起并毁坏根部，uproot plants是原文dig up plants and destroy roots的同义转换，故可确定答案为D。

4. H

根据关键词grass定位到原文第二段第二句While both hens and ducks benefit the garden by eating pests, hens are known to damage herb and grass beds，可知母鸡对草有威胁，故确定本题答案为H。

5. NI

原文中第一段和倒数第三段提到产蛋的内容，但原文中没有明确提到鸭和鸡每周产蛋量的多少，无从比较，故可确定答案为NI。

6. NI

本题较难，容易误选D。有的同学可能会从第五段的最后一句Therefore, it is important that they are fed enough food, such as grain, every day，推出第6题的答案为D。原文说，“因此，每天给它们喂足食物（如谷物）是很重要的。”“如谷物”不能说一定是谷物。而且，从第五段的内容我们可以看出，母鸭是吃得多，但可以靠自己找到很多吃的东西，所以无从比较母鸭和母鸡哪个吃更多的谷物，故第6题的答案为NI。

7. B

根据关键词garden定位到原文第二段中的第二句While both hens and ducks benefit the garden by eating pests, hens are known to damage herb and grass beds，可知两者都吃害虫，对花园有利，可确定答案为B。

8. H

根据关键词illness定位到第一段的第二句Ducks are immune to some common diseases found in hens and are less vulnerable to others，可知母鸭对一些母鸡常得的疾病更有免疫力，也更加不易患上其他疾病，从而确定答案为H。

Questions 9–12

题型：摘要填空题 (SUMMARY COMPLETION)

◆ 解析

★ 注意：此类题目一般需要先进行特殊词定位，以框定考查的段落范围，还要特别注意题目要求，本题要求从原文中选词，答案不超过两个词。仔细读摘要的第一句话，与原文第三段话的第一句相对应：Like all waterbirds, ducks need access to water, and duck keepers typically provide this by building a pond，因此应从这里开始找答案。

9. nostrils

先读题干，然后从原文第三段开始阅读，寻找答案。对应到原文第三段第二句Something this large is not absolutely necessary, however, ducks need only to be able to dip their heads in the water to keep their nostrils clean，题干中的prevent…from getting dirty与原文中的keep…clean为同义转换，可知答案为nostrils。

10. eight weeks

11. cool temperature

先读题干，然后从原文第9题的答案处开始阅读，寻找答案。对应到原文第三段的最后一句If a pond is provided though it is important to keep ducklings away from it until they are old enough to withstand the cool temperature of the water—about eight weeks，由age可得出第10题答案为eight weeks，keep...away from和prevented from为同义转换，第11题答案为cool temperature。

12. muddy

先读题干，然后从原文第10题的答案处开始阅读，寻找答案。对应到原文第四段中的句子If more than this proportion is introduced, there is a risk of compacting the soil, which can lead to muddy conditions for long periods as the rain is not easily absorbed into the ground，此处填一个形容词说明soil，所以可得出此处填 muddy。

Questions 13 and 14

题型：选择题 (MULTIPLE CHOICE)

◆ 解析

这两个四选一与目前考试的形式很接近，选项的干扰性很大。

13. B

先读题干，注意题干中有特殊词Salmonella，依据它很容易找到原文倒数第二段。仔细阅读相关句子，注意该段的第三句Although it was never conclusively shown that duck eggs were to blame, the egg-eating public stopped buying and many duck egg producers went bankrupt.，可知沙门氏菌食物中毒导致鸭蛋产业的困难，因此可确定答案为B。

14. C

先读题干，然后从原文第13题的答案处开始阅读，寻找答案。对应倒数第二段的第四句Indeed, there is a risk of salmonella poisoning when ducks lay their eggs in damp conditions, such as on ground that is constantly wet...可知如果在潮湿的环境中，鸭蛋可能会受污染，所以答案为C。

◎ 参考译文

母鸭和鸭蛋的那些事儿

对于喜欢饲养家禽的人来说，养母鸭确实比养母鸡有优势。母鸭对在母鸡身上发现的一些常见病有免疫力，并且相比而言，母鸭不容易得其他病。某些品种的母鸭可以比母鸡下的蛋更大。另外，母鸭的产蛋期要比母鸡的长。

家禽饲养者如果饲养的是母鸭而不是母鸡的话，就不必担心母鸭会挖掘花园的植物，毁坏其根部。虽然母鸡和母鸭都可以为花园除去害虫，但我们知道母鸡会破坏草本植物和草皮，而母鸭会更仔细地寻找昆虫和蜗牛。只有非常脆弱的植物在面对母鸭宽大的脚蹼时才会有危险。

像所有的水鸟一样，鸭子也需要水，母鸭的饲养者通常会建一个水塘以供母鸭游水，但这个装水的地方并不需要像水塘那么大，因为母鸭仅需要把头伸进水里来保持它们鼻孔清洁。如果有水塘的话，也要注意保持雏鸭与它的距离，这很重要，因为雏鸭长到足够大——八个星期后——才可以经受住冷水。

在饲养母鸭的时候，饲养者只需要考虑某块地可供饲养的数量。通常来讲，每100只母鸭需要半公顷土地。如果大于上述比例，将面临土地被压实的风险，土地一旦被压实就会导致长时期的泥泞，因为土地不能轻易地吸收雨水。

虽然与母鸡相比，母鸭有很多优势，但饲养者必须给母鸭提供更多的食物，尤其需要保证常规鸭蛋产量的时候。一只成年鸭每天会吃170克到200克食物。如果母鸭在草地和水塘里，它们就会每天为自己解决约70%的食物。但上述情况要在温暖的季节里，在寒冷的季节，母鸭自己每天只能解决不到一半的食物。因此，每天给它们喂足食物（如谷物）是很重要的。

有经验的养鸭者每三年左右饲养一批雏鸭，那是因为在这个时期之后母鸭的产蛋能力开始严重下降。如果目标是孵幼鸭，饲养者应该意识到不是所有的母鸭都是好母亲，有些品种相比而言更加糟糕，它们在产下蛋后的几天内会丢弃它们的蛋。确保这些被丢弃的蛋能被孵化的有效方法是把这些鸭蛋和鸡蛋放在一起让母鸡孵化。

就鸭蛋作为人类的食物而言，褒贬参半。这是因为在20世纪70年代欧洲有许多沙门氏菌食物中毒的案例发生。尽管最后没有表明是鸭蛋的原因，但是食蛋一族停止了购买鸭蛋，许多鸭蛋厂关门倒闭。的确，当母鸭在潮湿的环境中生蛋时，是存在着沙门氏菌中毒的风险，例如，长期在潮湿的地面上，但是在这一点上鸡蛋也是一样的。沙门氏菌中毒事件爆发的法国和英国的鸭蛋产业遵循和鸡蛋产业同样的标准，但鸡蛋就没有发生沙门氏菌中毒的问题。（不论是鸡蛋还是鸭蛋，蛋类的储存也可能成为造成污染的一个因素。研究表明，当储存温度达到5摄氏度或者更高时，细菌增长就存在潜在危险。）

沙门氏菌的恐惧在20世纪80年代早期就已经过去了，但是，至少在澳大利亚和新西兰这样较小的市场中，由于怕出问题，几乎没有商家愿意冒风险投资鸭蛋养殖。在这些国家中，已经不存在大规模的鸭蛋生产，只剩下一些小生产商，且更常见的是家庭鸭子养殖。

READING PASSAGE 2

Questions 15–19

题型：段落标题配对题 (LIST OF HEADINGS)

◆ 解析

15. ii

通读Paragraph B，本段讲述了警察快速反应会带来的好处，包括：帮助受害者、抓住嫌疑犯、找到证人、提高警察的声望和预防犯罪等。第一句为段落主题句：An important part of police strategy, rapid police response is seen by police officers and the public alike as offering tremendous benefits，对应选项ii Perceived advantages of rapid response，其中，perceived对应原文的seen，advantages对应原文的benefits。

16. vii

Paragraph C的第一句While these may be the desired consequences of rapid police response, actual research has not shown it to be so beneficial起承上启下的作用。意为虽然这些是警察迅速反应的理想结果，但是实际的研究表明它没有如此有用。接下来的内容主要是关于反应

时间和反应成功之间的关系，即：如果快速反应的时间短，快速反应就会成功，否则，快速反应成功的可能性就不大，故选vii Rapid response time and success of rapid response。

17. ix

Paragraph D的第一句是一个问句，意为警方应该对确保一个迅速反应承担所有的责任吗？第二句Studies have shown that people tend to delay after an incident occurs before contacting the police是主题句，意为研究表明人们在事件发生之后一般会延迟一会儿再联系警方。接下来进行举例论证人们不及时报警导致警察快速反应的效率降低，而段落的最后一句与主题句相互呼应，故正确答案为ix Not quickly contacting the police。

18. v

Paragraph E的第二句是个举例子的句子，所以主题句肯定是该段的第一句The effectiveness of rapid response also needs to be seen in light of the nature of the crime，意为我们也应该看到，迅速反应是否有效还和罪行的性质有关。如果只依据此句，还不能最终确定答案，通读全段，就会发现：对于抢劫等罪行，快速反应是有效的，而对于偷窃等罪行，快速反应是没有什么效果的，即快速反应何时需要，何时不需要，故正确答案为v When rapid response is and is not necessary。

19. iv

Paragraph F段的第一句：Studies have shown, however, that while the public wants quick response, more important is the information given by the police to the person asking for help，意为然而，研究表明，虽然公众需要迅速反应，但是更重要的是警察传递给求助人的信息。根据前面我们讲的解题步骤，这句话肯定是主题句，show后面的从句是重点，它是正确选项的改写，故答案为iv Communicating response time to people requesting help。

Questions 20 and 21

题型：简答题 (SHORT ANSWER QUESTIONS)

◆ 解析

20. "911" emergency system

21. police computer systems

从文章开始快速阅读，在A段中先找到The telephone and police radio，容易错误回答为这两个答案，但注意题目中黑体大写的**TWO LATEST**，The telephone and police radio是already long in use的，所以需要继续往后阅读。在下一句中In more recent times there has been the introduction... 可知答案为"911" emergency system和police computer systems。原文在这两个短语后面都有一个解释说明它们的定语从句。

Questions 22–27

题型：判断题 (YES/NO/NOT GIVEN)

◆ 解析

22. YES

根据题干关键词witness定位到原文B段的It aids in identifying those who witnessed an emergency or crime, as well as in collecting evidence，题干是对原文的改写，答案为YES。

23. YES

根据题干关键词1–2 minutes定位到原文C段中的For example, it has been demonstrated that rapid response leads to a greater likelihood of arrest only if responses are in the order of 1–2 minutes after a call is received by the police. When response times increase to 3–4 minutes—still quite a rapid response—the likelihood of an arrest is substantially reduced，可知反应慢了1–2分钟对于是否能抓捕罪犯可能产生很大的影响，故答案为YES。

24. YES

根据题干关键词The public and the police和the amount of time可定位到原文C段最后一句Yet both police officers and the public define "rapid response" as responding up to 10–12 minutes after calling the police for help，可知公众和警方对于一个正常的快速反应的时间有一个普遍的共识，故答案为YES。

25. NOT GIVEN

此题比较难。根据题干关键词Physical barriers定位到原文D段中的句子Often, however, there is no such physical barrier to calling the police，意为通常，没有这种导致无法报警的身体上的障碍。也就是说有这种身体障碍的概率是非常小的。而题目的意思是身体上的障碍是最大的原因，但实际上小概率事件也可能是最大概率事件，所以答案为NOT GIVEN。

26. NO

根据题干关键词burglary定位到原文E段中的句子It is common in such burglary or theft cases that the victim discovers the crime hours, days, even weeks after it has occurred，但要结合前一句：For example, when someone rings the police after discovering their television set has been stolen from their home, there is little point, in terms of identifying those responsible for the crime, in ensuring a very rapid response，原文中的there is little point和题目中的desirable 意思相反，答案为NO。

27. YES

题干中有特殊词75%，但原文中没有这个词，说明原文中的75%有可能采用的是英文形式（three in four），由此可定位到原文E段中最后一句：Based on statistics comparing crimes that are discovered and those in which the victim is directly involved, Spelman and Brown (1981) suggest that three in four calls to police need not be met with rapid response. 原文说对比的是后

来被发现的案件和受害者在现场的案件的数据，结果表明3/4的求助电话不需做出迅速回应，说明这3/4的案件是受害者发现的，所以答案为YES。

◎ 参考译文

警察快速反应

A 美国和加拿大的警方认为对求助做出及时反应是他们工作的重中之重。由于有了现代科技的帮助，这种快速反应的能力已经大大提高了。应用很久的电话和警方无线通讯设备在很大程度上协助警方减少了反应时间。最近，“911”紧急系统的引入让公众能更容易更迅速地与警方取得联系，同时警方电脑系统的运用有助于警察安排巡逻，并且把紧急事件请求分配给离案发现场最近的警员。

B 警方迅速反应是警察（发展）策略中一个重要的部分，警方和公众认为它可以带来很多好处。较显著的好处是，警方快速应用急救技术救助生命的能力得到提高，并且抓捕犯罪嫌疑人员的可能性增大。快速反应有助于找到突发事件或犯罪活动的目击者，也有助于搜集证据。如果能长期保持反应迅速，那么警察部门的声誉就能整体提高，而且它本身也能起预防犯罪的作用。不用说，迅速反应能使公众对警察在某种程度上满意。

C 虽然这些也许是警方迅速反应的理想结果，但是实际的研究表明它没有那么有用。例如，事实证明，只有警方在接到电话1–2分钟后就做出回应，抓住（嫌疑犯）的可能性才很大。当反应时间增加到3–4分钟时——仍然是迅速反应——抓住的可能性就会大大降低。同样，警方在接到求助电话之后，倘若能在平均4分钟内到达现场，才更有可能成功找到突发事件和犯罪的目击者。但是，警方和公众都定义的“迅速反应”是指在拨打求助电话之后不超过10–12分钟的警方反应。

D 警方应该对确保一个迅速反应承担所有的责任吗？研究表明人们在发生事故之后一般会延迟一会儿再联系警方。例如，一个受害者也许会因为受伤而没有能力去求助，或者也许在事故现场没有电话。然而，通常受害者是不存在这种无法打求助电话的身体障碍。事实上常见的是，受害者首先给家人、代理人员甚或是他们的保险公司求助。当警察最终接到电话时，即使反应再快，效率也已经极大地削减了。

E 我们也应该看到，迅速反应是否有效还和犯罪的性质有关。例如，当某人发现他们家的电视机被盗之后，打电话给警察，那么就确定嫌疑犯而言，一个迅速的反应是没有什么意义的。一般来讲，在入室抢劫或者偷窃案件中，受害者一般在案件发生后的几小时、几天、或者几星期才被发现。然而，当受害者直接卷入一宗像抢劫这样的犯罪案件中时，如果受害者能快速与警方联系，快速反应也许会更有好处。斯贝尔曼和布朗（1981）对比后来发现的犯罪和那些受害人直接被卷入的犯罪，统计结果表明3/4的求助电话不需要做出迅速反应。

F 现在我们清楚了：对于搜集证据或者抓捕罪犯的反应时间的重要性必须结合很多因

素来综合考虑。但是，因为警方认为公众是强烈要求迅速反应的，所以他们认为每一个求助电话都应该得到满足。然而，研究表明，虽然公众需要迅速反应，但是更重要的是警察传递给求助人的信息。如果求助者被告知警方将会在5分钟内到达，但事实上警察到达现场花费了10分钟或者更多，那么多余的等待时间一定会令求助者沮丧。但如果求助者被告知他将需等待10分钟而警方确实在指定的时间内到达的话，那么求助人一般会满意。因此，与其强调迅速反应，不如将重点放在在求助人心里建立能被实现的期望并且尽全力来满足他们上面。

READING PASSAGE 3

Questions 28–32

题型：判断题 (TRUE/FALSE/NOT GIVEN)

◆ 解析

28. NOT GIVEN

本题的关键词是monotonous regularity, 原文中只在第一段提到作者偶然在报纸上看到一篇伦敦一家医院关于通感的研究文章，目的是为了引出下文，文章中没有出现关于monotonous regularity的说明，故答案是NOT GIVEN。

29. TRUE

定位到原文第二段最后一句Or, to put it simply, synaesthetes, i.e. people with synaesthesia, have their senses held together, so that they experience several senses simultaneously，意为：或者，简言之，有通感的人，他们的感官是集中在一起的，他们能同时体验不同的感觉。题干中的at the same time同义替换原句中的simultaneously，答案为TRUE。

30. FALSE

本题的关键词为new phenomenon，关键词出现在文章第三段开头部分To those not already aware of it, synaesthesia seems a new phenomenon，这句话本身就已经涵盖否定的意味了，接下来说Yet, it is far from new，并进行举例说明In 1690, John Locke, the philosopher, wrote of a blind man with synaesthetic capabilities. The first reference in the medical field was in 1710, by Thomas Woodhouse, an English ophthalmologist. In his *Theory of Colour*, ..., in *Correspondence*，最后得出结论：So, synaesthesia has a respectable history，即通感并不是新鲜事物，所以原文和题干意思相反，答案为FALSE。

31. TRUE

原文第三段有第31题的关键词重现In 1690, John Locke, the philosopher, wrote of a blind man with synaesthetic capabilities，可知早在1690年约翰·洛克就曾写过一个具有通感能力的盲人，题干说对于通感的描述最早可追溯到17世纪，1690年属于17世纪，所以答案为TRUE。

32. FALSE

定位到原文第四段第一句Synaesthesia is understandably met with a certain degree of scepticism, since it is something beyond the comprehension of the vast majority of people，可知人们对通感有某种程度的怀疑也是可以理解的，就是说这种怀疑并不足为奇，所以本题答案为FALSE。

Questions 33–36

题型：选择题 (MULTIPLE CHOICE)

◆ 解析

33. D

根据题干关键词Son et lumiere shows定位到文章第四段第二句Son et lumiere shows in the 19th century were an attempt at combining the senses in a public display, but such displays were not capable of conveying the sensations experienced by involuntary synaesthesia, as the ability which a synaesthete's experience is called，原文说"19世纪的声光演出就试图将各种感觉融合展示给公众，但是这样的展示不能传递本能地产生通感的感觉"，故答案为D。

34. C

根据人名定位到原文第四段Alexander Scriabin, the Russian composer (1871–1915), tried to express his own synaesthetic abilities in his symphony *Prometheus, the Poem of Fire* (1992). And another Russian, Rimsky-Korsakov, noted the colour associations musical keys possessed. For example, Scriabin saw C major as red, while to Rimsky-Korsakov it was white. Arthur Bliss, an English composer, based his *A Colour Symphony* in 1922 on the concept of synaesthesia. He did not claim to be a synaesthete; his colour choices were arbitrary and the project was an intellectual exercise，原文说亚历山大·斯克里亚宾和里姆斯基–柯萨科夫在音乐作品中表达他们的通感能力，答案为C。

35. C

根据人名定位到原文第五段In the field of the visual arts, probably the best-known artist with synaesthetic capabilities is the Russian artist, Wassily Kandinsky (1866–1944), credited with being the founder of abstract painting. It is said he experienced "sensory fusion" at a performance of Wagner's *Lohengrin*, with the music producing colours before his eyes. He did not see colours solely in terms of objects, but associated them with sounds. He even composed an opera, *Der Gelbe Klang* (*The Yellow Sound*), which was a mixture of colour, light, dance and sound，原文说瓦斯里·康定斯基是抽象画派的鼻祖，在一次华格纳的音乐会上经历了感觉的融合，音乐带来了不同的颜色，第五段最后一句指出他也创作音乐，他创作的歌剧是色

彩、灯光和音乐的结合，故答案为C。

36. A

根据题干关键词sufferers定位到原文第六段Initially, they often feel that there is something wrong psychologically or mentally, or that everyone feels that way，起初，那些人认为自己心理或者精神上有问题，……，原文的initially就是题干中At first的重现。本题答案为A。

Questions 37–40

题型：多选题 (MULTIPLE CHOICE)

◆ 解析

37–40　A　C　E　F

由关键词disoriented定位到原文第六段的While the condition of synaesthesia may hamper many people because of its disorienting effects, it can also open up a range of new skills，可知A一些通感者被他们的能力弄得不知所措正确。

由关键词creativity定位到原文第六段的It is not unusual for people who have synaesthesia to be creative and imaginative，可知通感者有很强的创造力和想象力很常见，所以B错误。

由关键词Memory定位到原文第六段的Synaesthetes find they are able to remember certain things with great ease，可知通感能增强记忆力，memory与to remember certain things为同义转换，故C正确。

由关键词drawbacks定位到原文最后一段第一句的But this condition like all gifts, has its drawbacks，可知通感这种能力有优点也有缺点，但没有明确的比较，应该因人而异，而且题干是对于通感者的描述，本句话严格而言是对于通感的描述，故D错误。

由关键词use their ability to help themselves定位到原文第六段的but unwittingly some people have managed to make use of the ability to their advantage，可知有的通感者会利用这种能力让它成为一种优势，这里make use of the ability to their advantage与use their ability to help themselves为同义转换，故E正确。

同样根据第六段的While the condition of synaesthesia may hamper many people because of its disorienting effects可知通感的能力有可能成为一种障碍，故F正确。

由关键词write可定位到最后一段，可知有通感能力的人写作时需要克服一些困难，因为要克服单词和颜色的问题，但并非用颜色写作，故G项错误。

◎ 参考译文

对你来说那听起来不是非常黄色吗？

“我说不上来，我是色盲”这是我室友曾经的回答。此后的20多年依旧如此，直到有一天，我偶然在报纸上读到一篇有关伦敦一家医院研究通感的文章。最终，我对于通过颜色认知世界有了自己的诠释。

通感是一种主观的感觉，而不是通过外部刺激产生的。比如，看到一个单词，可能会唤起你对颜色的感觉，或者，听音乐也会有同样的效果，就同我的品味一样。或者，简言之，有通感的人，他们的感官是集中在一起的，因此他们能同时体验不同的感觉。

对于那些还没有意识到通感的人来说，通感似乎是一种全新的现象。不过，其实通感远不是什么新鲜事物了。在1690年，哲学家约翰·洛克描写了一个具备通感能力的盲人。通感在医学领域第一次出现是在1710年，由英国眼科医生托马斯·伍德豪斯提出。德国作家歌德在他的《颜色论》中谈论了颜色和各种感觉。诗人阿尔图尔·兰波在1871年写的诗《元音》中提到了通感，另外一位法国诗人波德莱尔也有诗《感应》为证。因此，通感有着久远而庄重的历史。

通感遭到了一定程度的怀疑是可以理解的，因为通感超出了绝大多数人的认知。19世纪的声光演出就试图将各种感觉融合展示给公众，但是这样的展示不能传递那种本能地产生通感的感觉，也就是经历通感的能力。记录在册的有通感的人很多。俄国作曲家亚历山大·斯克里亚宾（1871–1915）曾试图在交响乐《普罗米修斯“火之诗”》（1992）中表达他的通感能力，另一位俄国人里姆斯基-柯萨科夫注意到琴键与颜色有关。例如，斯克里亚宾认为C大调是红色，然而里姆斯基-柯萨科夫则认为它是白色。英国作曲家阿瑟·布利斯1922年的《颜色交响曲》就是在通感为理念的基础上创作的，他认为自己没有通感，他选择颜色都是随意的，并且整个过程是理智的。

在视觉艺术领域，可能最具有通感才能的艺术家就是俄国艺术大师瓦西里·康定斯基（1866–1944），他被认为是抽象画派的先驱。据说他在华格纳歌剧《罗安格林》的演奏中体验了感觉的融合，他感觉音乐产生的颜色就在他眼前萦绕。他没有单纯地从物质角度来看待产生的颜色，而是把它们和音乐联系到一起。他甚至写了一个歌剧，名叫《黄色声音》，该歌剧将色、光、舞蹈和声音结合在一起。

对于很多具有通感的人来说，他们知道他们正在经历的东西是有名字有历史的，而且知道很多名人也和他们一样有类似的感觉。起初，那些人认为自己心理或者精神上有问题，或者所有人都这样认为，之后他们突然意识到别人不是这样的。压抑是一种选择，但是一些人勉强地利用这种能力，让它成为他们的优势。尽管通感的状况对很多人来说是一种阻碍——因为通感容易使他们迷失，但它也能开拓一系列新的技能。对于有通感的人来说，富有创造性和想象力并非难事，正如很多调查所显示的，记忆在一定程度上跟联想有关。有通感的人发现他们能够很容易记住一些事。一个能够联系图形的人能记住更长一串文字，且他们在需要记忆的其他领域同样如此。

但是通感同所有的天赋一样也有它的缺点。一些人会把单词看成颜色，有些甚至看到的是独立的字母和音节，因此一个词就变成了多彩的万花筒。也许这样的阅读看似美好，但它会给阅读和写作带来问题。由于要费尽力气透过所有的色彩来阅读或认字，所以花的时间会加长。同时，由于要结合色彩顺序和单词，所以写作也变得很困难。

Test 7 核心词汇 Core Vocabulary

READING PASSAGE 1

immune *adj.* 有免疫力的
vulnerable *adj.* 易受伤的，脆弱的
poultry *n.* 家禽
insect *n.* 昆虫
snail *n.* 蜗牛
delicate *adj.* 娇弱的
nostril *n.* 鼻孔
withstand *vt.* 经受得住
compact *vt.* 压缩
absorb *vt.* 吸收
salmonella *n.* 沙门氏菌

READING PASSAGE 2

patrol *n.* 巡逻,侦察
assign *vt.* 分配
tremendous *adj.* 巨大的，极大的
arrest *vt.&n.* 逮捕
participate *vi.* 参与
identify *vt.* 确认
enhance *vt.* 改进
consequence *n.* 结果，后果
demonstrate *vt.* 展示
substantially *adv.* 相当多地，大大地
delay *vi.* 延迟
incident *n.* 意外
diminish *vt.* 降低，减少
in light of 根据，按照
burglary *n.* 破门盗窃；抢劫
frustrating *adj.* 沮丧的

READING PASSAGE 3

odd *adj.* 【口】（用在数字后）有零数的，……以上的
synaesthesia *n.* 通感
interpretation *n.* 诠释
stimulate *vt.* 刺激
evoke *vt.* 引起
simultaneously *adv.* 同时地
ophthalmologist *n.* 眼科医师
scepticism *n.* 怀疑
convey *vt.* 传递，传达
involuntary *adj.* 本能的，不知不觉的
arbitrary *adj.* 随意的
abstract *adj.* 抽象的
compose *vt.* 编写，作曲
revelation *n.* 出乎意料的事；揭露；显示
unwittingly *adv.* 不经意地；不知不觉地
hamper *vt.* 阻碍
disorienting *adj.* 迷惑的，分解的
drawback *n.* 缺点

TEST 8

Candidate Number

Candidate Name ______________________

INTERNATIONAL ENGLISH LANGUAGE TESTING SYSTEM

ACADEMIC READING

TIME 1 hour

INSTRUCTIONS TO CANDIDATES

Do not open this booklet until you are told to do so.

Write your name and candidate number in the spaces at the top of this page.

Start at the beginning of the test and work through it.

You should answer **all** questions.

If you cannot do a particular question, leave it and go on to the next. You can return to it later.

All answers must be written on the answer sheet.

Do not remove this booklet from the examination room.

INFORMATION FOR CANDIDATES

There are **40** questions on this question paper.

The test is divided as follows:

Reading Passage 1	Questions 1–12
Reading Passage 2	Questions 13–27
Reading Passage 3	Questions 28–40

Reading Answer Sheet

Are you: Female? Male?

Your first language code:

0 1 2 3 4 5 6 7 8 9
0 1 2 3 4 5 6 7 8 9
0 1 2 3 4 5 6 7 8 9

IELTS Reading Answer Sheet

Module taken (shade one box): Academic General Training

1		✓ 1 ✗	21		✓ 21 ✗
2		2	22		22
3		3	23		23
4		4	24		24
5		5	25		25
6		6	26		26
7		7	27		27
8		8	28		28
9		9	29		29
10		10	30		30
11		11	31		31
12		12	32		32
13		13	33		33
14		14	34		34
15		15	35		35
16		16	36		36
17		17	37		37
18		18	38		38
19		19	39		39
20		20	40		40

Checker's Initials		Marker's Initials		Band Score		Reading Total	

READING PASSAGE 1

*You should spend about 20 minutes on **Questions 1–12**, which are based on Reading Passage 1 below.*

Wrap up Your Visit With the Perfect Gift

• Section A

"It is better to give than to receive"; "Never look a gift horse in the mouth"; "Beware of Greeks (ancient, of course) bearing gifts". Gifts are a fundamental element of culture and our lives as social creatures. They are also an important part of our business relationships.

There are occasions when giving a gift surpasses spoken communication, since the message it offers can cut through barriers of language and cultural diversity. Present a simple gift to your host in a foreign country and chances are he or she will understand you perfectly, though you may not understand a single word of each other's languages. It can convey a wealth of meaning about your appreciation of their hospitality and the importance you place upon the relationship. Combine the act of giving with some knowledge of and sensitivity to the culture of the recipient and you have an invaluable chance to earn respect and lay the foundations of a durable and mutually beneficial business relationship.

For all countries, take account of climate, especially in regard to clothing. Some gifts can be ruined by extremely hot or humid climate, possibly causing their receiver considerable anguish. Consider the kinds of products that are abundant in the country concerned and try for something that is uncommon there. Think about the level of language skills: a book with hundreds of pages of English text may be at best useless, at worst embarrassing, to a person with limited English. Inform yourself as much as possible about local customs, rules and etiquette, especially to do with wrapping, presenting, superstitions, taboos and, importantly, customs and quarantine regulations. The following is a brief account of the etiquette of gift-giving in some countries of Asia and the Middle East.

Section B

Hong Kong Chinese greatly appreciate simple greeting cards, though obviously they will not refuse small tokens of friendship in the form of gifts.

Books with plenty of illustrations are most appreciated in Indonesia. Inappropriate items: alcohol,

products made from pigs, warm clothing. Ties and cuff links are not commonly worn.

In Iran, short-sleeved shirts and any visual representation of naked or partially dressed people, male or female, are highly inappropriate. Don't bother with ties, videos or records. As in all Islamic countries, there is a strict taboo on any pork products.

Respecting the Arab tradition, gifts should endeavour to praise the recipient in Iraq and should never be of an order that cannot reasonably be reciprocated.

Avoid certain colour combinations: red, white and black (colours of the Nazi flag); and red, green and black (the Palestinian flag) in Israel.

Gifts are normally exchanged at the beginning of meetings with Japanese and should be given and received with both hands. It is seen as impolite to give an unwrapped gift. The emphasis should be on high quality, though not necessarily expensive, items.

When in Jordan, it is preferable, but not vital, to avoid green in packaging. Normal Arab customs apply, so no alcohol, pork, women's clothing etc. Arabs generally do not greatly appreciate handcrafts in wood, fabric or pottery. Gifts should ideally appear valuable.

Again, the exchange should be made with both hands in Korea. Also, similar to Japan, is the emphasis on presentation. Do not use red ink to write the names of the recipients. It is worth remembering that it is customary for a gift given to a company to be shared out around the office concerned, so items that lend themselves to this practice—like a bottle of good whisky—are very well received.

Laos has virtually no cultural taboo items. It would be difficult to offend with virtually any gift.

Business contacts in the People's Republic of China are keen recipients of good Scotch whisky and American cigarettes, to the point where it is almost obligatory to take some along when you go there. Or, if not obligatory, it certainly helps to warm relations.

Do not open gifts in the presence of the giver in the Philippines. Not recommended are items alluding to religion. Many people are Catholic and many others Moslems. This also means literature and art with any possible suggestions of lewdness or racism are to be strictly avoided.

For Thailand, gifts should not be wrapped or packaged in black. Modest gifts, like ties, scarves and key rings, are much appreciated. Traditionally, sharp objects like knives or even letter openers are not given as gifts.

No special gift-giving customs in Vietnam, but the Vietnamese are enthusiastic gift givers and like very much to receive them as well. Liquor and wine can be problematic, for reasons pertaining to Vietnamese tastes rather than morality or religion.

Questions 1–4

Complete the sentences below.

*Choose **ONE WORD ONLY** from the passage for each answer.*

Write your answers in boxes 1–4 on your answer sheet.

1 Differences in culture and .... can be overcome by gifts.

2 You are advised to give gifts to your .... when you are overseas.

3 .... should be considered when giving gifts with thick clothing.

4 To present gift of chocolates in a tropical country might create ....

Questions 5–7

Do the following statements agree with the claims of the writer in Reading Passage 1?

In boxes 5–7 on your answer sheet, write

YES	*if the statement agrees with the claims of the writer*
NO	*if the statement contradicts the claims of the writer*
NOT GIVEN	*if it is impossible to say what the writer thinks about this*

5 An Israeli business manager would undoubtedly appreciate the gift of a black, green and red striped tie.

6 It is recommended to give wine to Vietnamese.

7 An inexpensive pigskin wallet would probably be appreciated in Japan, Vietnam and Laos.

Questions 8–12

Complete the summary below.

Choose ***ONE WORD ONLY*** *for each answer.*

Write your answers in boxes 8–12 on your answer sheet.

There are important details to consider when **8** .... Some cultures have prohibitions on animal products such as those from **9** .... Others have political aversions to specific **10** .... because of their use on certain countries' flags. Similarly, Thais do not like gifts with **11** .... wrappings, and in Korea it is suggested that name tags written in red should be avoided. But presentation is not only restricted to what wrappings or pen you use. In Japan care should also be taken in selecting gifts that are of good **12** ....

READING PASSAGE 2

*You should spend about 20 minutes on **Questions 13–27**, which are based on Reading Passage 2 on the following pages.*

Questions 13–17

Reading Passage 2, has six sections, **A–F**.

*Choose the correct heading for sections **B–F** from the list of headings below.*

*Write the correct number, **i–xi**, in boxes 13–17 on your answer sheet.*

List of Headings

i	The presumptions of policy makers
ii	Need for more equitable parenting policies
iii	The impact of dual employment
iv	Comparison of employed and non-employed mothers
v	The benefits of balanced responsibility
vi	The unchanged role of the female parent
vii	The effect of stress on the female parent
viii	Disadvantages of parental equality
ix	The experts' view of the male parent's role
x	Commitment of mothers to their paid jobs
xi	Origins of anxiety in working mothers

Example	***Answer***
Section **A**	**ii**

13 Section **B**

14 Section **C**

15 Section **D**

16 Section **E**

17 Section **F**

Parenting and Responsibility

Section A

There are still significant gaps between women and men in terms of their involvement in family life, the tasks they perform and the responsibilities they take. Yet, at least in developed Western countries, both women and men express a desire for greater equality in family life. It is evident that in terms of attitudes and beliefs, the problem cannot simply be thought of in terms of women wanting men to share more equally and men being reluctant to do so. The challenge now is to develop policies and practices based on a presumption of shared responsibility between men and women, and a presumption that there are potential benefits for men and women, as well as for families and the community, if there is greater gender equality in the responsibilities and pleasures of family life. These are becoming key concerns of researchers, policy makers, community workers and, more importantly, family members themselves.

Section B

Despite the significant increase in the number of women with dependent children who are in the paid workforce, Australian research studies over the last 15 years are consistent in showing that divisions of labour for family work are very rigid indeed (Watson 1991). In terms of time, women perform approximately 90 per cent of child care tasks and 70 per cent of all family work, and only 14 per cent of fathers are highly participant in terms of time spent on family work (Russell 1983). Demo and Acock (1993), in a recent US study, also found that women continue to perform a constant and major proportion of household labour (68 per cent to 95 per cent) across all family types (first marriage, divorced, step-family or never married), regardless of whether they are employed or non-employed in paid work.

Section C

Divisions of labour for family work are particularly problematic in families in which both parents are employed outside the home (dual-worker families). Employed mothers adjust their jobs and personal lives to accommodate family commitments more than employed fathers do. Mothers are less likely to work overtime and are more likely to take time off work to attend to children's needs (Vanden Heuvel 1993). Mothers spend less time on personal leisure activities than their partners, a factor that often leads to resentment (Demo and Acock 1993).

Section D

The parental role is central to the stress-related anxiety reported by employed mothers, and a major contributor to such stress is their taking a greater role in child care (Vanden Heuvel 1993). Edgar and Glezer (1992) found that close to 90 per cent of both husbands and wives agreed that the man should share equally in child care, yet 55 per cent of husbands and wives claimed that the men actually did this. (These claims are despite the findings mentioned earlier that point to a much lower participation rate by fathers.) A mother's wanting her partner to do more housework and child care is a better predictor of poor family adjustment than the actual time spent by fathers in these tasks (Demo and Acock 1993). It is this desire, together with its lack of fulfillment in most families, that bring about stress in the female parent.

Section E

Family therapists and social work researchers are increasingly defining family problems in terms of a lack of involvement and support from fathers and are concerned with difficulties involved in having fathers take responsibility for the solution of family and child behaviour problems (Edgar and Glezer 1986). Yet, a father accepting responsibility for behaviour problems is linked with positive outcomes.

Section F

Research studies lend strong support to the argument that there are benefits for families considering a change to a fairer or more equitable division of the pleasures and pains of family life. Greater equality in the performance of family work is associated with lower levels of family stress and higher self-esteem, better health, and higher marital satisfaction for mothers. There is also higher marital satisfaction for fathers, especially when they take more responsibility for the needs of their children-fathers are happier when they are more involved (Russell 1984).

Questions 18–26

*Look at the following statements (**Questions 18–26**) and the list of researchers below.*

*Match each statement with the correct researcher(s), **A–E**.*

*Write the correct letter, **A–E**, in boxes 18–26 on your answer sheet.*

NB *You may use any letter more than once.*

18 The number of hours a father spends doing child care is not the best indicator of how well the family is adjusted.

19 The vast majority of fathers do not take part to any great extent in family work.

20 Women do the majority of housework whether they are married or not.

21 With regard to the issue of equal responsibility for child care, there is a discrepancy between the wishes and the claims of parent couples.

22 Both mothers and fathers are happier where the father assumes some responsibility for issues relating to the behaviour of the children.

23 Researchers now link family problems to fathers' lack of involvement in rearing children.

24 In terms of dealing with family issues, employed fathers make fewer sacrifices in their jobs than working women do.

25 Anxiety results from the mother being the primary care giver.

26 There has been little recent change in the housework and child care roles of mothers and fathers.

List of Researchers

A Demo and Acock

B Edgar and Glezer

C Russell

D Vanden Heuvel

E Watson

Question 27

*Choose the correct letter, **A**, **B**, **C** or **D**.*

Write the correct letter in box 27 on your answer sheet.

In "Parenting and Responsibility", the writer's main aim is to

A argue that a division of labour in parenting is equitable.

B argue for increased participation in parenting by working men and women.

C discuss the differences in the contributions of men and women to the job of parenting.

D describe the composition of modern families.

READING PASSAGE 3

*You should spend about 20 minutes on **Questions 28–40**, which are based on Reading Passage 3 below.*

Fermented Foods for Babies

Malnutrition during weaning age—when breast milk is being replaced by semi-solid foods—is highly prevalent in children of poor households in many developing countries. While the etiology is complex and multifactorial, the immediate causes are recognized as feeding at less than adequate levels for children's growth and development, and recurrent infections, including diarrhoea, resulting mainly from ingestion of contaminated foods. As a result, many young children, particularly between six months to two years of age, experience weight loss and impaired growth and development.

Studies by investigators in various countries have concentrated on traditional food preparation methods and have resulted in offering cheap and practical answers to these problems based on familiar, indigenous and culturally acceptable home processing practices.

Two such answers have arisen. Firstly, cereal fermentation is used for reducing the risk of contamination under the existing inappropriate conditions for food preparation and storage in many households. Secondly, a tiny amount of sprouted grains flour is used in preparation of weaning foods as a magic way to lessen the viscosity without decreasing energy density.

A method to eliminate pathogenic bacteria and inhibit their growth during storage of weaning preparations can benefit nutrition and health in young children considerably. Use of fermented foods for feeding children of weaning age appears to be an effective solution. Fermented foods have lower levels of diarrhoeal germ contamination, they are suitable for child feeding, and can be safely stored for much longer periods of time than fresh foods. The practice has been a traditional way of food preservation in many parts of the world. The anti-microbial properties of fermented foods and their relative higher safety—documented since the early 1900's—have been indicated in a number of studies.

In Ghana, it is common to ferment maize dough before cooking it as porridge. In Kenya, cereal-based porridge and milk are traditionally fermented. Preserving milk in the form of yoghurt has been known to many households living in hot climates.

What are the underlying mechanisms by which fermentation processes help to prevent or reduce contamination? A possible answer suggests that during the fermentation process foods become more acid. This explains why diarrhoea-causing bacteria are not able to grow in fermented foods as rapidly as in unfermented ones. It is also hypothesised that some of the germs present in the foods are killed or inhibited from growing through the action of anti-microbial substances produced during fermentation (Dialogue on Diarrhoea, 1990). The fermented foods can, therefore, be kept for a longer time compared to fresh ones. It has been shown that while contamination levels in cooked unfermented foods increase with storage time, fermented foods remain less contaminated.

Whatever the underlying mechanisms, the fact is that the exercise reduces contamination without adding to the household cost both in terms of time and money. Its preparation is easy. The cereal flour is mixed with water to form a dough which is left to be fermented; addition of yeast, or mixing with a small portion of previously fermented dough is sometimes needed. The dough can then be cooked into porridge for feeding to the child.

Although beneficial, unfortunately the practice is going out of fashion, partly because of current emphasis on the use of fresh foods, particularly for children. For example, a study on the use of fermented foods for young children in Kenya (Dialogue on Diarrhoea, 1990), demonstrated that while foods are still frequently fermented at home for child feeding, their use is becoming less popular, particularly in urban areas where commercial products are more available. Clearly they now need to be promoted.

Questions 28–34

*Complete the summary with the list of words **A–N** below.*

Write your answers in boxes 28–34 on your answer sheet.

Malnutrition and the resulting impaired growth and development in children of weaning age in developing countries result not only from **28** .... but also from infections caused by **29** ....

Studies have addressed the problem of inadequate intake by using sprouted grains in food preparation. Contamination has been tackled with **30** .... Both of these methods are, or were, used traditionally and are practical and inexpensive.

Fermented foods have higher **31** ...., and also have anti-microbial qualities. This means that contamination is decreased and that their **32** .... is increased. Fermentation occurs when

33 .... is left to stand, occasionally with simple additives. There is, however, a trend away from this 34 .... to commercial products.

A	porridge	**H**	storage life
B	malnutrition	**I**	sprouted grains
C	fermentation	**J**	inadequate food intake
D	new technology	**K**	acidity
E	contaminated food	**L**	unfermented food
F	diarrhoeal germs	**M**	weaning
G	traditional food	**N**	dough

Questions 35–39

Do the following statements agree with the information given in Reading Passage 3?

In boxes 35–39 on your answer sheet, write

TRUE *if the statement agrees with the information*
FALSE *if the statement contradicts the information*
NOT GIVEN *if there is no information on this*

35 Fermented foods are free of contamination.

36 It can be beneficial to ferment breast milk before feeding to young children.

37 Cooked foods can be stored longer than fresh foods.

38 Cereals can be fermented by adding water and letting the dough stand.

39 Traditional fermented foods are being replaced by commercial products in some locations.

Question 40

Choose the correct letter, ***A***, ***B***, ***C*** *or* ***D***.

Write the correct letter in box 40 on your answer sheet.

Why is the fermentation of foods being investigated?

A It not only improves the nutritional value of food, but also is a process which is cheap and easy.

B It is a traditional method of food preparation which is becoming less popular.

C It both inhibits food contamination and enhances storability.

D It is done using maize flour which is used everywhere as food for infants between 6 months and 2 years of age.

Test 8 答案速查 Key

READING PASSAGE 1

1. language	**2.** host	**3.** Climate	**4.** anguish
5. NO	**6.** NO	**7.** NOT GIVEN	**8.** gift-giving
9. pigs	**10.** colours	**11.** black	**12.** quality

READING PASSAGE 2

13. vi	**14.** iii	**15.** xi	**16.** ix	**17.** v
18. A	**19.** C	**20.** A	**21.** B	**22.** C
23. B	**24.** D	**25.** D	**26.** E	**27.** C

READING PASSAGE 3

28. J	**29.** E	**30.** C	**31.** K
32. H	**33.** N	**34.** G	**35.** FALSE
36. NOT GIVEN	**37.** NOT GIVEN	**38.** TRUE	**39.** TRUE
40. C			

Test 8 考题精解 Detailed Explanation

READING PASSAGE 1

Questions 1–4

题型：句子填空题 (SENTENCE COMPLETION)

◆ 解析

1. language

先读题干，然后从文章开始处找答案。定位到原文Section A第二段的第一句There are occasions when giving a gift surpasses spoken communication, since the message it offers can cut through barriers of language and cultural diversity。原文中的cut through对应题干中的overcome，原文中的diversity对应题干中的differences，所以答案为language。

2. host

先读题干，然后从原文第1题的答案处开始阅读，寻找答案。定位到原文Section A第二段的第二句Present a simple gift to your host in a foreign country and the chances are he or she will understand you perfectly, though you may not understand a single word of each other's languages。原文中的Present对应于题干中的give，故答案为host。

3. Climate

先读题干，然后从原文第2题的答案处开始阅读，寻找答案。根据关键词clothing定位到原文Section A第三段的第一句For all countries, take account of climate, especially in regard to clothing。原文中的take account of 对应题干中的be considered，故答案为Climate。

4. anguish

先读题干，然后从原文第3题的答案处开始阅读，寻找答案。定位到原文Section A第三段的第二句Some gifts can be ruined by extremely hot or humid climates, possibly causing their receiver considerable anguish。原文中的hot or humid climates对应题干中的a tropical country，原文中的possibly causing对应于题干中might create。

Questions 5–7

题型：判断题 (YES/NO/NOT GIVEN)

◆ 解析

5. NO

先读题干，根据题干中的关键词Israeli很容易定位到原文Section B的第五段Avoid certain colour combinations: red, white and black (colours of the Nazi flag); and red, green and black (the Palestinian flag) in Israel。原文所表达的意思是：在以色列送礼物时应避免红、绿、黑三种颜色，而题干中所表达的意思恰恰违背了原文的意思，所以答案为NO。

6. NO

先读题干，根据题干中的关键词Vietnamese很容易定位到原文Section B的最后一段中的句子Liquor and wine can be problematic, for reasons pertaining to Vietnamese tastes rather than morality or religion。根据原文中的Liquor and wine can be problematic可知，在越南送酒会引发问题，所以并不建议送酒，所以答案为NO。

7. NOT GIVEN

先读题干，根据题干中的关键词Japan, Vietnam and Laos很容易分别定位到原文Section B的第六段、第九段和最后一段。三段内容均未提及三个国家对与猪有关的礼物的喜好，所以无法推断出题目所给出的结论。

这几个题目都没有顺序性，但由于每个题目中都包含关键词，非常容易定位，所以都很简单。做这类题，我们提倡的原则是："宁要关键词，也不要顺序性。"

Questions 8–12

题型：摘要填空题 (SUMMARY COMPLETION)

◆ 解析

8. gift-giving

先读题干，对应原文Section A的最后一句The following is a brief account of the etiquette of gift-giving in some countries of Asia and the Middle East，值得注意的是动宾短语give gift，如果用连字符连接，以动名词gift-giving的形式出现，可以算作一个单词。

9. pigs

先读题干，注意空格前后的一些词，此题的关键词为animal products，对应原文Section B的第二段中的句子Inappropriate items: alcohol, products made from pigs, warm clothing，所以为pigs。

10. colours

先读题干，注意空格前后的一些词，此题的关键词为political aversions和countries' flags，对应原文Section B的第五段，所以答案为colours。

11. black

先读题干，题干中有特殊词Thais，依据它很容易在原文Section B的倒数第二段中的第一句找到对应的内容For Thailand, gifts should not be wrapped or packaged in black. 考生应该能够看出原文中的被动语态be wrapped or packaged，在题目中被转化成了名词wrappings，可知答案为black。

12. quality

先读题干，题干中有特殊词Japan，依据它很容易对应到原文Section B的第六段中的最后一句The emphasis should be on high quality, though not necessarily expensive, items，所以答案为quality。

◎ 参考译文

用完美的礼物“包装”你的到访

A部分

“给予比获得更有福”；“不要过于挑剔别人送的礼物”，“警惕希腊人（当然是古代的）带来的木马”。因为人类是社会型动物，所以礼物是我们生活和文化的基本要素。在商业关系中，礼物同样也扮演着重要的角色。

在有些场合，赠送礼物好过语言交流，因为礼物所传达的信息可以克服言语障碍和文化差异。在异国他乡，送一个简单的小礼物给你寄宿的房屋主人，就可能让他或她完全地理解你的意思，尽管你们可能彼此说的话一个字都听不懂。礼物可以充分地传达出你对他们招待的感激之情以及你对与他们的这份关系的重视程度。如果能把赠送的方式与你对收礼人文化背景的了解和敏感度结合起来，你将获得一个宝贵的赢得尊重的机会，这时你已经为你们之间建立持久的互惠互利的商业关系打下了根基。

在任何国家，你都要考虑气候问题，特别是涉及服装。一些礼物可能会被极端炎热或潮湿的气候毁掉，这也许会使收礼物的人相当苦恼。细想你所关注的国家盛产哪些东西，争取找一些在那里比较少见的物品。仔细考虑外语水平：送一个英语能力非常有限的人一本上千页的英语书，往好了说这是没有用处，往差了说这就会使人尴尬。尽可能多地用当地的风俗、规矩和礼节来充实你自己，特别是在包装材料、赠与方式、迷信忌讳等方面，同样重要的还有习俗和检疫条例。下面简单说明一下在一些亚洲和中东国家的送礼之道。

B部分

虽然中国香港人不拒绝以礼物形式赠送的友情小礼券，但他们也很喜欢收到简单的贺卡。

满是插画的书在印度尼西亚是最受欢迎的了。对印度尼西亚人而言，不适宜的物品有：酒精、与猪相关的产品、暖和的衣物。领带以及袖扣通常也很少用到。

在伊朗，短袖衬衫以及穿着裸露或衣着不整的人，不论男女，都是非常不得体的。别考虑带领带、录像带和唱片了。同样，在所有的伊斯兰教国家里，一切猪肉产品都有着严格的禁忌。

尊重阿拉伯传统，在伊拉克，礼物应该力图赞扬接受者，而且绝不要让它成为一个命令，因为那命令将永远都得不到回应。

避免某些颜色的组合，如：红、白、黑（纳粹军旗的颜色）；而在以色列，则要避免红、绿、黑三个颜色（巴基斯坦的国旗颜色）。

与日本人交流，一般都在见面的开始互换礼物，并且要用双手送出或接受礼物。赠送一件没有包装的礼物是非常不礼貌的。礼物不一定要很昂贵，关键在于高品质。

在约旦，最好避免使用绿色的外包装，但那也不是必须的。考虑到阿拉伯通常的习俗，不要赠送酒精、猪肉、女士服装等等。通常阿拉伯人都不太喜欢木制、织物或陶制的手工艺品。送出的礼物应该能够给人带来贵重的感觉。

同样在韩国，互赠礼物时也应该用双手递接。与日本相同的，还有他们对送礼方式的重视程度。不要用红色墨水书写受赠人的姓名。值得牢记的是，送给公司的礼物被周围其他办公室共同享用也是个习俗，所以能够体现这一用途的东西——例如一瓶威士忌佳酿——是非常受韩国人青睐的。

老挝几乎不存在有文化禁忌的礼物，任何礼物都很难找到其冒犯之处。

中国的商业人士都热衷于收到上好的苏格兰威士忌和美国香烟，要想做到顺应潮流，你去中国时不妨带一些。或者，如果不能顺应它，赠送这些东西也无疑会使你们的关系升温。

在菲律宾，不要当着送礼人的面打开礼物。同样不推荐的还有暗示宗教信仰的物品。

那里很多人是天主教徒，也有很多人是穆斯林教徒，这也意味着我们应该严格避免任何带有淫秽信息和种族歧视色彩的文学艺术作品。

在泰国，礼物不可以用黑色的材料包裹或包装。朴素的礼物，如领带、围巾和钥匙扣，都是很受欢迎的。传统上，像刀子或者哪怕是拆信刀这种尖锐的物品都不会被当做礼物来赠与。

在越南没有什么特殊的送礼习俗，但是越南人对于赠送礼物非常热衷，同样也很喜欢接受礼物。送烈酒和葡萄酒可能会引发问题，其原因更多在于其是否适合越南人的口味，而不是在于有道德或宗教信仰问题。

READING PASSAGE 2

Questions 13–17

题型：段落标题配对题 (LIST OF HEADINGS)

◆ 解析

13. vi

Section B，主题句是该段的第一句Despite the significant increase..., Australian research studies over the last 15 years are consistent in showing that divisions of labour for family work are very rigid indeed (Watson 1991)。这句话比较长，但重点在于主句部分中showing that后的宾语从句divisions of labour for family work are very rigid indeed。根据句意可知，家务劳动的分配没有发生变化，换言之就是女性在家庭中的角色没有发生变化，所以选vi。

14. iii

Section C，该段的第一句Divisions of labour for family work are particularly problematic in families in which both parents are employed outside the home (dual-worker families)，大致概括了全段的意思，由此可知本段主要阐述了双职工家庭在分配家务方面存在的问题，所以选iii。

15. xi

Section D，主题句是该段的第一句The parental role is central to the stress-related anxiety reported by employed mothers, and a major contributor to such stress is their taking a greater role in child care (VandenHeuvel 1993)，此题是这五道题中最难的，如果没有搞清意思的话，很容易误选vii（压力对母亲所产生的影响），而实际上本段说的是压力产生的原因。

16. ix

Section E，主题句是该段的第一句Family therapists and social work researchers are increasingly defining family problems in terms of a lack of involvement and support from fathers and are concerned with difficulties involved in having fathers take responsibility for the solution of family and child behaviour problems (Edgar and Glezer 1986)。本句结构复杂，不好理解。

但如果抓住句首的Family therapists and social work researchers以及后面谈的都是有关父亲的事，不难看出该段讲的是专家们对于父亲角色作用的观点。

17. v

Section F，根据本段首句中there are benefits for families considering a change to a fairer or more equitable division of the pleasures and pains of family life可以择取几个关键词分别是benefits，fairer和equitable division，选项v中的benefits，balanced responsibility为原文的同义转化。

上述各段话的主题句均为该段话的第一句。

Questions 18–26

题型：配对题 (MATCHING)

◆ 解析

本题为作者及其观点的搭配题，属于本题无顺序性的细节题。先在原文中将作者及其观点用线划出，然后看题目，一道题一道题地做。

18. A

题干的中文意思父亲们在照顾孩子上花费的时间不能充分地体现家庭配合的效果。对应原文中Section D的第三个观点A mother's wanting her partner...actual time spent by fathers in these tasks (Demo and Acock 1993)。原文提出的观点是妻子要求丈夫多做家务、多照看孩子的需求比丈夫在这些事务上真正花费的时间能更有效地表明家庭配合的糟糕程度。

对应关系：

原文	题目
predictor	indicator
family adjustment	family is adjusted

19. C

题干的中文意思大多数的父亲没有大量参与到家庭工作中。对应原文中Section B的第二个观点...only 14 per cent of fathers are highly participant in terms of time spent on family work (Russell 1983)。原文提出的观点是只有14%的男人能够经常干家务活。

对应关系：

原文	题目
only 14 per cent of fathers	vast majority of fathers do not
highly	great extent
participant	take part

20. A

题干的中文意思无论女人们婚否，她们都承担着大部分的家务工作。对应原文中Section B的第三个观点women continue to perform a constant and major proportion of household labour…。原文提出的观点是妇女一直承担着家务工作的重头比例，原文中的各种婚姻类型（首婚、离婚、再婚、未婚）既是对题干中whether they are married or not的同义转述。

对应关系：

原文	题目
major proportion	majority
family type	married or not

21. B

题干的中文意思：在照顾孩子的平等责任的问题上，父母双方的愿望和表述之间并不一致。对应原文Section D的第二个观点：接近90%的夫妻都认同男方应该平等地承担照顾孩子的责任，但只有55%的夫妻表示男方真正做到了这点。由此不难看出，题目所阐述的观点是对原文的推断性归纳。

22. C

题干的中文意思：如果父亲承担一些涉及子女行为问题的责任，父亲和母亲都会更高兴。对应原文Section F中的观点：在家务工作上的更加平等，会使母亲对婚姻更加满足，父亲也会对婚姻更加满意，特别是当他们担负起更多的责任来满足孩子的需求时——因为父亲们融入家庭生活越多，他们就会越快乐。

23. B

题干的中文意思：研究者们现在把家庭问题和父亲们缺乏参与照顾孩子联系起来。对应原文：Section E中的观点：家庭治疗专家和社会工作研究者越来越多地把家庭问题定义为父亲参与和支持的缺失。

24. D

题干的中文意思：就处理家庭事务而言，职场父亲所做出的牺牲要少于职场母亲所做出的牺牲。对应原文Section C的第二个观点：Employed mothers adjust their jobs and personal lives to...more than employed fathers do。原文提出的观点是母亲会比父亲更多地调节自己的工作和个人生活，以适应承担家务的义务。

25. D

题干的中文意思：焦虑的产生是因为母亲承担了照顾孩子的主要任务。对应原文Section D的第一个观点The parental role is central to the stress-related anxiety reported by employed others, and a major contributor to such stress is their taking a greater role in child care。原文所提出的观点是：已为人母的职场女性在报告中称，父母的角色与压力导致的焦虑存在着很重要的关系，而

产生这种压力的主要原因是她们在照顾孩子时承担着更重要的角色。

对应关系：

原文	题目
contributor to	result from
greater role	primary

26. E

题干的中文意思母亲和父亲在家务工作和照顾孩子上的作用几乎没有改变。

对应原文Section B的第一个观点澳大利亚一项长达15年的研究表明，家务劳动的分工事实上一直都没有改变。题干是对原文的同义转述。

对应关系：

原文	题目
divisions of labour	roles of mothers and fathers
family work	housework and child care
rigid	little change

Question 27

题型：选择题 (MULTIPLE CHOICE)

◆ 解析

27. C

本题为选择题中的主旨题。通读各段，了解各段大意，本文主要讨论了男性与女性在家务工作中的分工差异，故此题答案为C。A、B两个选项为强干扰项，A项中的argue意为"证明"，而本文并不是在证明家务劳动的分工是平等的；B项意为"赞成职场男女更多地参与到家务劳动中"，也不符合作者的写作初衷；D项与文章无关。

◎ 参考译文

家务工作和责任

A段

从男女方照顾家庭、完成的工作以及承担的责任来看，男女间的差异仍然明显。然而，至少在西方发达国家，无论男女，他们都渴望更平等的家庭生活。显然，从态度和信念来讲，问题不能简单地从女性想要男性分担更多而男性不愿服从的角度来考虑。基于如果男性和女性在家庭生活中责任更平等且同样快乐，那么男女双方就会共同承担责任，且会给男女以及家庭乃至社会都带来潜在好处的假设制定出相应的政策和措施是我们现在所面临的挑战，这也成为了研究人员、政策制定者、社区工作者甚至家庭成员自己的关注核心。

B段

尽管奔波于孩子与工作之间的女性数量明显上升，但是澳大利亚的一项长达15年的研究表明，家务劳动的分工事实上一直都没有改变（Watson 1991）。从时间上来看，女性承担了大约90%的照顾孩子的工作以及70%的家务活，而只有14%的男人能够经常干家务活（Russell 1983）。Demo&Acock（1993）在美国最近的一项研究中也表明，不管女性是否受雇于有偿劳动她们仍然在各种家庭类型（包括首婚、离婚、再婚或未婚家庭）中承担了大部分的家务劳力（68%–95%）。

C段

对于那些父母都在外工作的家庭（双职工家庭）来说，家务劳力的分配就尤其成问题。与父亲相比，母亲更需要调节自己的工作和个人生活以承担家务工作。母亲不太可能加班，而且很可能放弃工作来满足照顾孩子的需要（Vanden Heuvel 1993）。母亲在个人休闲活动上所花的时间总是比父亲少，这也是经常导致不满的一个因素（Demo&Acock 1993）。

D段

已为人母的职场女性在报告中称，父母的角色与压力导致的焦虑存在着很重要的关系，而产生这种压力的主要原因是她们在照顾孩子时承担着更重要的角色（Vanden Heuvel 1993）。Edgar&Glezer（1992）发现，接近90%的夫妻都认同男方应该平等地承担照顾孩子的责任，但只有55%的夫妻表示男方真正做到了这点。（这个结果和以前的研究是不一致的，以前的研究表明父亲在家庭生活中的参与率要低得更多）。妻子要求丈夫多做家务、多照看孩子的需求比丈夫在这些事务上真正花费的时间能更有效地表明家庭配合的糟糕程度（Demo&Acock1993），也正是这种需求以及在大多数家庭中得不到实现给女方带来了压力。

E段

家庭治疗专家和社会工作研究者越来越多地把家庭问题定义为父亲参与家庭工作和养家方面的缺失，而且他们还担忧让父亲承担起解决家庭和孩子问题所面临的困难（Edgar&Glezer 1986）。但是，父亲承担起解决这一问题的责任可以产生积极的效果。

F段

众多研究结果都为这一论点提供了强大的论据：对于家庭来讲，更公平、更平等地分担家庭生活的苦与乐是大有裨益的。在家务活上的更加平等会使母亲的家庭压力变小、自尊心更强、身心更健康、对婚姻更加满足。父亲也会对婚姻更加满意，尤其是他们担负起更多的责任来满足孩子的需求时——因为父亲们融入家庭生活越多，他们就会越快乐（Russell 1984）。

READING PASSAGE 3

Questions 28–34

题型：摘要填空题 (SUMMARY COMPLETION)

◆ 解析

28. J

空前的not only及空后的but also提示所填词应与空后的infections并列，均为对Malnutrition and the resulting impaired growth原因的说明。根据题目中的Malnutrition可将答案定位在原文第一段。根据原文中说明的feeding at less than adequate levels是儿童营养不良的一个主要原因，J选项inadequate food intake是对原文的同义转述，所以此题答案为J。

29. E

题干中的关键词infections caused by提示，此处是说患传染病的原因，根据原文第一段第二句中的infection...resulting mainly from ingestion of contaminated foods可知，引发传染病的原因主要是食用了有污染的食物，故此题答案为E。

30. C

根据题干中的关键词Contamination及tackled可将答案出处定位到第三段。第三段提出了两个解决方法，其中对于食品污染的解决方法是cereal fermentation，由此可知答案为C。

31. K

根据题干中的关键词Fermented foods可将答案定位到第六段。该段第二句提到，during the fermentation process foods become more acid，由此不难发现，题干中的higher对应了原文中的more，选项中的K项acidity则是原文中acid的同义再现，所以此题答案为K。

32. H

题干中的This means提示，本题是对上一句的继续说明，由此可将答案定位到第六段第五句。根据原文中的therefore可知，发酵了的食品可以被保存得更久，换言之就是发酵可以延长食物的保存期，故此题答案为H。

33. N

此处是说发酵产生的条件，根据题干中的additives可将答案出处定位到文章的第七段。该段介绍了发酵的准备工作，将谷物面粉与水混合，形成留待发酵的面团（dough），由此可知此题答案为N。

34. G

根据题干中的however，trend可将答案出处定位到文章的最后一段。题目中是说某个事物目前逐渐衰落的趋势，而原文说将食物发酵这种做法日渐失宠，与此题相符的只有G项traditional food。此处是把发酵食品看作了一种传统方法制作出来的食品。

Questions 35–39

题型：判断题 (TRUE/FALSE/NOT GIVEN)

◆ 解析

35. FALSE

原文第三段提到，谷物发酵有助于降低受污染的风险，第四段说发酵食品的腹泻病菌污染率较低，文章中是说reduce和have lower levels of diarrhoeal germ contamination，而题目中的free of contamination过于绝对，所以该题答案为FALSE。

36. NOT GIVEN

原文中并未提及将母乳发酵，所以该题答案为NOT GIVEN。

37. NOT GIVEN

文章第七段提到了cooked food，但并不是与fresh food进行比较，所以该题答案为NOT GIVEN。

38. TRUE

第七段提到了谷物面粉发酵的方法（The cereal flour is mixed with water...or mixing with a small portion of previously fermented dough is sometimes needed.），与本题意思一致，所以该题答案为TRUE。

39. TRUE

文章最后一段提到，食品发酵日趋失宠，尤其是在那些商品随处可见的城市地区，本题的意思与原文吻合，所以答案为TRUE。

Question 40

题型：选择题 (MULTIPLE CHOICE)

◆ 解析

40. C

问题是关于对食物发酵进行研究的原因。文章第六段提出设问："发酵的过程有助于防止或减少污染，而这其中的基本原理又是什么呢"，随后阐述了两点结论，一是与新鲜食品相比，发酵食品的保存时间更长，二是发酵食品保持着较低的受污染度，选项C中的 inhibits food contamination and enhances storability 是对这两点结论的概括，故答案为 C。

◎ 参考译文

给宝宝吃发酵食品

在许多发展中国家，贫困家庭中很多处在断奶期的孩子普遍有营养不良（因为母乳被半固态食物所代替）的问题。虽然病因复杂多样，但是人们认为直接原因是不能充分保证孩子成长和发育的食物供给以及由于摄入污染的食物而引起的包括腹泻在内的很多周期性传染病。因此，许多儿童，尤其是处在6个月至2岁年龄段的儿童，都有体重减轻的问题，影响了他们的生长和发育。

很多国家都将调查研究的重点放在传统食品的制作方法上，且基于人们熟知的、固有的和传统的家庭处理方法，找到廉价又实用的办法来解决这一问题。

由此出现了这样两种方法。首先，很多家庭现有的条件都不适宜制作并储存食物，而利用谷物发酵可以降低污染的风险。其次，少量发芽谷物面粉可以作为一种奇方，用于制作断奶食品，既降低了黏度，又保证了能量密度。

在为断奶做准备的储备期，消除致病菌并抑制其生长，对幼儿的营养和健康大有好处。给断奶年龄的孩子喂发酵的食品似乎是一个有效的解决办法。发酵食品的腹泻病菌污染率较低，它们适用于喂幼儿，而且其安全存放的期限超过了新鲜食品。这种做法在世界许多地区一直是一种传统的食品保存方法。其实发酵食品所具有的抗微生物的特性及其相对较高的安全性——有记载始于20世纪初——已经在很多研究中有所证实。

在加纳，人们通常在煮粥前先要发酵玉米面团。在肯尼亚，用谷物熬的粥和牛奶在传统上讲都属于发酵食品。生活在炎热地区的家庭已经对以酸奶形式保存牛奶这个方法很熟悉了。

发酵的过程有助于防止或减少污染，而这其中的基本原理又是什么呢？一种可能的回答是，在发酵过程中，食物会变得更酸。这就解释了腹泻致病菌在发酵食品中的生长速度不像在未发酵食品中那么快的原因。由此设想，随着在发酵过程中产生的抗菌物质的不断活动，食物中的一些细菌被杀死或被抑制（《关于腹泻的意见》，1990）。因此，与新鲜食品相比，发酵食品的保存时间更长。也已证实，随着存放时间的延长，未发酵熟食的受污染程度有所增加，而发酵食品则保持着较低的受污染度。

无论这其中的原理是什么，这个方法确实能减少污染，这是事实，而且这不增加家庭在时间和金钱两方面的成本。其准备工作也非常简单：谷类面粉与水混合形成的面团是留着待发酵的，有时需要加点酵母，或混合少量先前发酵好的面团。这样面团就可以煮成粥喂孩子了。

虽然发酵有益，但遗憾的是这种做法快要过时了，一部分原因在于人们现在看重吃新鲜的食品，尤其是对孩子来说。例如，一项针对肯尼亚幼儿食用发酵食品的研究表明（《关于腹泻的意见》，1990），虽然人们在家中仍然把食物发酵后再喂给孩子，但它们越来越不受欢迎，尤其是在那些商品随处可见的城市地区。显然，发酵食品目前需要推广。

Test 8 核心词汇 Core Vocabulary

READING PASSAGE 1

surpass *vt.* 超越；胜过，优于
diversity *n.* 多样性；差异
hospitality *n.* 热情好客
durable *adj.* 持久的
anguish *n.* 痛苦，苦恼
etiquette *n.* 礼节；规矩
superstition *n.* 迷信
illustration *n.* 插图，图解
endeavour (to) *vi.* 竭力，尽力
reciprocate *vt.* 报答，酬答；互换
preferable *adj.* 更好的，更可取的
fabric *n.* 织物
obligatory *adj.* 义务的；义不容辞的
allude (to) *vi.* 暗指，暗示，影射
lewdness *n.* 邪恶；淫荡；下流
pertain (to) *vi.* 与……相关，关于

READING PASSAGE 2

presumption *n.* 假定，推测
rigid *adj.* 稳固的，一成不变的
proportion *n.* 比例，部分
regardless of 无论
accommodate *vt.* 调整，（使）适应
commitment *n.* 献身，奉献，投入
leisure *n.* 休闲，闲暇
resentment *n.* 不满，怨恨
therapist *n.* 治疗专家
self-esteem *n.* 自尊，自尊心

READING PASSAGE 3

weaning *adj.* 断奶的
etiology *n.* 致病源
multifactorial *adj.* 多因子的
recurrent *adj.* 复发的，周期性的
ingestion *n.* 摄取，摄入
impaired *adj.* 受损的
indigenous *adj.* 固有的，本土的
fermentation *n.* 发酵
contamination *n.* 污染
viscosity *n.* 黏性，黏度
pathogenic *adj.* 致病的，病源的
germ *n.* 细菌
maize *n.* 玉米
porridge *n.* 粥，糊
underlying *adj.* 基本的，潜在的
mechanism *n.* 原理，机制
acid *adj.* 酸的 *n.* 酸
hypothesise *vt.&vi.* 假设，假定
anti-microbial *adj.* 抗菌的；抗微生物的
dough *n.* 生面团
yeast *n.* 酵母
commercial *adj.* 商业的

TEST 9

Candidate Number

Candidate Name ________________

INTERNATIONAL ENGLISH LANGUAGE TESTING SYSTEM

ACADEMIC READING

TIME 1 hour

INSTRUCTIONS TO CANDIDATES

Do not open this booklet until you are told to do so.

Write your name and candidate number in the spaces at the top of this page.

Start at the beginning of the test and work through it.

You should answer **all** questions.

If you cannot do a particular question, leave it and go on to the next. You can return to it later.

All answers must be written on the answer sheet.

Do not remove this booklet from the examination room.

INFORMATION FOR CANDIDATES

There are **40** questions on this question paper.

The test is divided as follows:

Reading Passage 1	Questions 1–15
Reading Passage 2	Questions 16–27
Reading Passage 3	Questions 28–40

Reading Answer Sheet

Are you: Female? ▭ Male? ▭

Your first language code:

0	1	2	3	4	5	6	7	8	9
0	1	2	3	4	5	6	7	8	9
0	1	2	3	4	5	6	7	8	9

IELTS Reading Answer Sheet

Module taken (shade one box): Academic ▭ General Training ▭

		✓	✗			✓	✗
1		1		**21**		21	
2		2		**22**		22	
3		3		**23**		23	
4		4		**24**		24	
5		5		**25**		25	
6		6		**26**		26	
7		7		**27**		27	
8		8		**28**		28	
9		9		**29**		29	
10		10		**30**		30	
11		11		**31**		31	
12		12		**32**		32	
13		13		**33**		33	
14		14		**34**		34	
15		15		**35**		35	
16		16		**36**		36	
17		17		**37**		37	
18		18		**38**		38	
19		19		**39**		39	
20		20		**40**		40	

Checker's Initials		Marker's Initials		Band Score		Reading Total	

READING PASSAGE 1

*You should spend about 20 minutes on **Questions 1–15**, which are based on Reading Passage 1 below.*

The Research on Self-esteem

A Self-esteem is generally considered the evaluative component of the self-concept, a broader representation of the self that includes cognitive and behavioural aspects as well as evaluative or affective ones. While the construct is most often used to refer to a global sense of self-worth, narrower concepts such as self-confidence or body-esteem are used to imply a sense of self-esteem in more specific domains. It is also widely assumed that self-esteem functions as a trait, that is, it is stable across time within individuals.

B Self-esteem is an extremely popular construct within psychology, and has been related to virtually every other psychological concept or domain, including personality (e.g., shyness), behavioural (e.g., task performance), cognitive (e.g., attributional bias), and clinical concepts (e.g., anxiety and depression). While some researchers have been particularly concerned with understanding the nuances of the self-esteem construct, others have focused on the adaptive and self-protective functions of self-esteem. Self-esteem has been related both to socioeconomic status and to various aspects of health and health-related behaviours, as has a related construct, self-efficacy. Self-efficacy, a term associated with the work of Bandura, refers to an individual's sense of competence or ability in general or in particular domains.

C Low self-esteem is the universal common denominator literally among all people suffering from addictions to any and all mind altering substances such as alcohol—not genes. In the book *Alcoholism: A False Stigma: Low Self-Esteem the True Disease* (1996), Candito reports, "Those who have identified themselves as 'recovered alcoholics' indicate that low self-esteem is the most significant problem in their lives. Low self-esteem is the true problem and the true disease. Alcohol is but a symptom of an alcoholic's disease." Studies have found that 18-year olds who used drugs frequently were using them as early as age seven, already more psychologically troubled than their peers. They were already anxious and unhappy, alienated from their family and peers, and overly impulsive. Low self-esteem, lack of conformity, poor academic achievement and poor parental-child relationships are also indicators of young children likely to end up using drugs.

D Candito comes to the conclusion that low self-esteem is the underlying origin of all problematic behaviours, and the true disease that plagues the world, resulting in alcohol abuse, drug abuse, and all other obsessive behaviors including criminal behaviour. This conclusion is also shared by Andrew Keegan (1987) who maintains that low self-esteem either causes or contributes to neurosis, anxiety, defensiveness, and ultimately alcohol and drug abuse. The reason why some become alcoholic while others do not is dependent upon their ability to contend with low self-esteem.

E However, many of the positive outcomes attributed to high self-esteem are not substantiated by research, according to Brown psychologist Krueger. Krueger, associate professor of psychology and faculty member from three other universities, formed that conclusion after reviewing more than two decades of objective research studies on self-esteem at the invitation of the American Psychological Society. Their report appears in this month's issue of *Psychological Science in the Public Interest*, a supplement to *Psychological Science*. "Across most measures—school and job performance, violence and crime, and health—there were few consistent links between the level of self-esteem and the quality of outcomes," said Krueger. High self-esteem does not prevent children from smoking, drinking, taking drugs or engaging in early sex, the task force reported. If anything, high self-esteem fosters experimentation, which may increase early sexual activity or drinking. The exception was a connection between high self-esteem and reduced chances of the eating disorder bulimia in females. In adults, according to the task force, occupational success may boost self-esteem rather than the reverse. And neither high nor low self-esteem is a direct cause of violence.

F In fact, pleasant feelings and enhanced initiative were the two benefits of high self-esteem found by the task force. High self-esteem has a strong relationship to happiness and low self-esteem is more likely than high to lead to depression under some circumstances. Those with high self-esteem were also found to exhibit more persistence at tasks. Yet the task force also noted that there are basically two types of high self-esteem—that which is realistic, and that which is out of touch with reality. People who fall into the former category accept their good qualities. Those in the latter are characterised as narcissistic, defensive or conceited individuals. In some studies, narcissism led to some negative qualities such as increased aggression in retaliation for wounded pride.

G The self-esteem movement began in California during the 1980s with the idea that many of society's problems were related to low self-esteem. The California legislature financed a task force to increase self-esteem in an effort to reduce welfare dependency, unwanted pregnancy, school failure, crime, drug addiction and other problems, with the goal of saving taxpayer dollars, according to the task force. Since then, there has been a nationwide proliferation of techniques to raise self-esteem—particularly in schools—and a proliferation of books marketed to people helping themselves. Yet, "after a quarter of a century of research, the high hopes of the self-esteem movement have not been realised, and customers of the self-help industry should not look to heightened self-esteem as a panacea," said Krueger.

Questions 1–5

Reading Passage 1 has seven paragraphs, **A–G**.

Which paragraph contains the following information?

Write the correct letter, ***A–G****, in boxes 1–5 on your answer sheet.*

1 Researchers focused their studies on varied aspects of self-esteem.

2 Some researchers related problematic drink behaviours to self-esteem.

3 The reason of violence seems not related to the quality of self-esteem.

4 Andrew Keegan agreed that low self-esteem is the underlying origin of all problematic behaviours.

5 Many inventions of methods are stimulated to increase the self-esteem.

Questions 6–10

Complete the summary below.

Choose ***NO MORE THAN TWO WORDS*** *from the passage for each answer.*

Write your answers in boxes 6–10 on your answer sheet.

The conception of self-esteem includes broader sense and **6** .... one in certain field. In addition, it is regarded as a **7** .... of each individual. Some researchers have been specifically concerned with studying the slight differences of the self-esteem construct, while others have concentrated on the **8** .... and **9** .... functions of self-esteem. As self-efficacy, self-esteem has been related both to **10** .... and to issues involving health.

Questions 11–15

Do the following statements agree with the information given in Reading Passage 1?

In boxes 11–15 on your answer sheet, write

TRUE	*if the statement agrees with the information*
FALSE	*if the statement contradicts the information*
NOT GIVEN	*if there is no information on this*

11 Studies showed that 18-year olds having used drugs are troubled more from psychological depression than their same olds.

12 High self-esteem is less likely to incur depression under some conditions.

13 Any type of high self-esteem will have good qualities.

14 The self-esteem campaign started in California in 1996.

15 Krueger believed self-esteem would have been improved to cure all kinds of difficulties.

READING PASSAGE 2

*You should spend about 20 minutes on **Questions 16–27**, which are based on the Reading Passage 2 on the following pages.*

Questions 16–21

Reading passage 2 has eight paragraphs, **A–H**.

*Choose the correct heading for paragraphs **B–D** and **F–H** from the list of headings below.*

*Write the correct number, **i–x**, in boxes16–21 on your answer sheet.*

List of Headings

i Compromise between two extreme styles

ii An opposite standpoint from a new angle

iii Factors that influence the change of gender role

iv Stereotyped activities in a family

v Conventional family pattern

vi Primary child care-giver

vii Three different types of household labour division

viii Effects of personality on division adoption

ix An even distribution of domestic tasks

x Definition of domestic division of labour

Example	***Answer***
Paragraph **A**	**x**

16 Paragraph **B**

17 Paragraph **C**

18 Paragraph **D**

Example	***Answer***
Paragraph **E**	**i**

19 Paragraph **F**

20 Paragraph **G**

21 Paragraph **H**

Domestic Division of Labour

A Domestic division of labour refers to the division of tasks, roles and duties, within the household. With the increased entry of married women into formal employment, sociologists began to look more closely at the processes that linked home and workplace, including the question of whether or not women's increased involvement in paid labour led to a renegotiation of the "traditional" domestic roles and organisation of domestic labour. A huge empirical and theoretical literature was then generated in a relatively short time.

B Work within the family context takes a variety of forms. In many Western households in the 1990s, it may include tasks such as caring for members of the family, contributing to the household finances, maintaining the house, interacting with kin and establishing and sustaining community relationships. As a way of fostering domestic harmony and creating a manageable routine, some couples choose one of three different styles of household role division: traditional, egalitarian or collaborative.

C Most people who fit the traditional pattern are characteristically men and women who are conventionally married, or have been living together as a couple for some time. The men and women have totally separate spheres of influence and responsibility. For instance, the husband or male partner is usually the chief decision maker and the major financial provider. He brings in the bulk of money and has the final say over major household purchases and important financial transactions. The wife or female partner engages in child care and household management, of which the latter also includes maintaining contact with relatives and family members who may not live under the same roof.

D In ideal situations, an egalitarian style is typified by an equal interchange in household tasks: for example, one partner does the dishes for one week, while the other cooks. Then, the roles are reversed for the next week. As an alternative, individual jobs may be divided equally, so that one partner handles half of the household tasks and the other partner takes on the remaining equal proportion. However, this 50/50 scenario does not usually result in a permanent arrangement some specialisation does tend to creep in. Human beings are not machines to be switched on and off at precise moments, nor is society organised in such a way as to allow a man to do exactly half the breadwinning and a woman to do exactly half the child rearing.

E The collaborative style is a compromise between the two extremes of the traditional and the egalitarian. In these families, partners can specialise in household activities and the inclination is towards doing what one is expert at or prefers. Typically, a woman may do all the cleaning while a man may do all the cooking because they choose to do so. It does not follow patriarchal prescription where a father always has foremost family authority and where the mother's domain is centred around the children and the household. It is guided by personal interest rather than social convention. As such, decisions may be deferred to the one who is the specialist in the particular area. In some cases, couples may reverse their selected roles and the woman may become the main breadwinner, while the man may in turn be the primary child care-giver.

F Traditional, egalitarian and collaborative styles are viewed by some as being dependent on female and male gender-role attitudes, both of self and partner. In other words, personality differences are said to determine whether men and women adopt one division of labour style in preference to another. Femininity or female gender-role stereotypes are commonly associated with the emotional, nurturing qualities usually ascribed to a woman, while masculinity or a male gender-role stereotype is seen in the context of risk-taking, assertiveness and independence—usually attributed to men.

G An opposing view sees the three family divisions of labour styles as a reflection of the progressive changes couples make in response to changing life situations, rather than being an aspect of personality. Essentially, adult women and men modify their behaviour within the context of family life, in accordance with current situations. It is these life situations, rather than people, that should be categorised as typically feminine or masculine. For example, when a couple, attends to a baby or cares for a sick relative, it is the feminine qualities that are foremost. In contrast, competition and the degree of aggressiveness often required an outside employment, are associated with stereotypical masculine qualities.

H So, depending upon demands in life situations, men and women assign what they believe are the appropriate masculine and feminine characteristics to particular contexts. Moreover, depending upon how stereotyped the activities are that they are involved in, gender-roles may alter.

Questions 22–27

Do the following statements agree with the claims of the writer in the Reading Passage 2?

In boxes 22–27 on your answer sheet, write

YES	*if the statement agrees with the claims of the writer*
NO	*if the statement contradicts the claims of the writer*
NOT GIVEN	*if it is impossible to say what the writer thinks about this*

22 There was no labour division in Western households in the 1990s.

23 Decisions and power within marriage are associated with the sense of responsibility.

24 In traditional families, females are expected to keep contact with relatives.

25 Society does not wish a man to handle half of the household tasks as a woman.

26 Work division in a collaborative style is guided by social convention.

27 Social scientists are divided in their views on the different patterns of domestic division of labour.

READING PASSAGE 3

*You should spend about 20 minutes on **Questions 28–40**, which are based on Reading Passage 3 below.*

Worms Put New Life Into Derelict Site

Poisoned soil at an old steelworks is being cleansed by thousands of worms

A Thousands of deep-burrowing earthworms are to help turn the long-derelict site of a steelworks into woodland and a renewable energy park.

B As part of a pioneering low-cost plan to reclaim the site of the former Hallside Steelworks at Cambuslang near Glasgow, worms are being used to accelerate the process of soil regeneration and to transform the land, over time, into an attractive and financially productive site.

C Hallside's closure in 1979 put an end to more than 100 years of steel production. The surrounding land had become heavily compacted and was too contaminated with heavy metals such as chromium, cadmium and lead to support any kind of brick and mortar development.

D The site's 30 hectares were left abandoned until 1990, when a rescue plan put together by local landscaping and earthmoving company, HL Banks, and the regional developer, Scottish Greenbelt, was approved by local authorities.

E Now the site has been covered by a two-metre layer of partially treated sewage material which has been mixed with colliery waste. This will be converted into usable soil by about 21, 000 Lubricus territories (garden lobworms) and Aporrectodea longa (black headed worms) that have been let loose on the site.

F The specially raised hermaphrodites, which are self-impregnation, will spend the next five to ten years chewing their way through the topping layer to create a soil structure able to sustain long-term plant growth. Without them, the process could take up to 60 years.

G Researchers at Bell College of Technology in nearby Hamilton examined the use of earthworms in land regarding, and found that even in the hostile mixture of coal-tip waste and partially treated sewage, earthworms were able to speed up the process of soil recomposition.

H They selected different varieties of deeper burrowing earthworm species, whose bulk feeding and casting actions, as well as their ability to improve the mineral content of soil, would increase the rate of reformulation much faster than the natural processes.

I Sean Ince, of Bell's department of biology, says, "The idea is that earthworms will contribute in a cumulative way to further soil binding, and that they will aerate and add nitrogen to the soil covering the Hallside site."

J At the same time, Scottish Greenbelt has begun planting the area with 250,000 trees including willow and alder specially selected for their ability to grow on degraded land.

K These will have the dual function of extracting contaminants from the soil through their root systems, and burning or chipboard manufacture.

L By using the cash raised from wood harvesting, David Craven, director of Scottish Greenbelt, says he expects Hallside to be self-financing.

M "The first tranche of trees was planted in April and they are now over six feet tall, despite dry weather through the summer," he says. The fields are being planted on a four-year rotation basis and will be used to help us meet our costs.

N Craven says the cost of land bio-remediation—the labour intensive process of removing soil for chemical and bacterial cleansing—could have been more than £30m.

O At Bell College, Ince says "There's a whole legacy of toxic soil contamination going back many years. There is physical degradation of the soil as well as contamination from metals, including lead, chromium and arsenic."

P Sampling of the soil at regular intervals over the next few years will give an indication of the level of contaminants. Within less than 20 years the land could be re-integrated into the community.

Q Hopes of a successful outcome at Hallside have paved the way for similar regeneration plans for the nearby Gartoosh steelworks and at Glengarnock in Ayrshire.

Questions 28–32

*Choose the correct letter, **A**,**B**,**C** or **D**.*

Write the correct letter in boxes28–32 on your answer sheet.

28 The Hallside site has been

A turned into a steelworks from a woodland and an energy park.

B in use as an energy park.

C disused for a long period of time.

D out of use for a short period of time.

29 After more than one hundred years of steel production at Hallside,

A the land could not be used for anything.

B it was impossible to use the land to build on.

C the land could then be built on.

D the land could be used for any purpose.

30 The plan to reclaim Hallside was proposed by

A Scottish Greenbelt and the regional developer.

B local authorities and Scottish Greenbelt.

C a local landscaping company and authorities.

D Scottish Greenbelt and HL Banks.

31 In the conversion of the soil at the Hallside site,

A two types of worms are being used.

B three types of worms are being used.

C many types of worms are being used.

D thousands of different types of worms are being used.

32 The soil regeneration at the Hallside site will take

A 60 years.

B between 5 and 10 years.

C over 60 years.

D less than five years.

Questions 33–36

Choose ***NO MORE THAN THREE WORDS*** *from Reading Passage 3 for each answer.*

Write your answers in boxes 33–36 on your answer sheet.

33 In the research of Bell College, worms were used to quicken ....

34 The Bell researchers chose worms that would convert contaminated soil more rapidly than the ....

35 The soil at Hallside will be enriched by adding air and ....

36 Contaminants will be removed from the soil by ....

Questions 37–40

*Choose **ONE** phrase from the list of phrases A–H below to complete each of the following sentences 37–40.*

Write the appropriate letters in boxes 37–40 on your answer sheet.

37 The Hallside site is expected to ....

38 Bio-remediation at Hallside could ....

39 Within 20 years, the land at Hallside could ....

40 Similar regeneration plans may ....

A	be contaminated
B	be in use again by the community
C	work everywhere
D	take place at other steelworks
E	have cost millions of pounds
F	have been proved intensive
G	pay for itself
H	cost more than bio-remediation

Test 9 答案速查 Key

READING PASSAGE 1

1. B	**2.** C	**3.** E
4. D	**5.** G	**6.** narrower
7. trait	**8.** adaptive	**9.** self-protective
10. socioeconomic status	**11.** TRUE	**12.** TRUE
13. FALSE	**14.** FALSE	**15.** TRUE

READING PASSAGE 2

16. vii	**17.** v	**18.** ix	**19.** viii
20. ii	**21.** iii	**22.** NOT GIVEN	**23.** NO
24. YES	**25.** NOT GIVEN	**26.** NO	**27.** YES

READING PASSAGE 3

28. C	**29.** B	**30.** D
31. A	**32.** B	**33.** soil recomposition
34. natural processes	**35.** nitrogen	**36.** tree root system
37. G	**38.** E	**39.** B
40. D		

Test 9 考题精解 Detailed Explanation

READING PASSAGE 1

Questions 1–5

题型：配对题 (MATCHING)

◆ 解析

1. B

根据题干中的关键词varied aspects of self-esteem可定位到B段的第二句，该句提到一些研究人员特别关注的是了解自尊心理的细微差别，而另一些研究人员关注的是自尊心理的适应性和自我保护功能，可见研究者关注的是自尊心的多个方面，与题干表述一致，故选B。

2. C

根据题干中的关键词problematic drink behaviours可定位到C段首句，该句提到了降低自尊与酒精成瘾的关系，故选C。

3. E

根据题干中的关键词violence和quality of self-esteem可定位到E段尾句And neither high nor low self-esteem is a direct cause of violence，该句提到自尊心的强弱都不是导致暴力的直接原因，由此说明自尊心的强弱与产生暴力的原因无关，与题干表述完全一致，故选E。

4. D

根据题干中的关键词Andrew Keegan可定位到D段，该段提到了两个专家。第一个专家坎迪托提出结论说低自尊是所有问题行为的潜在根源，也是困扰全世界的病症，这最终会导致酗酒、吸毒及其他的包括犯罪的过激行为，第二个专家安德鲁·基根对这一结论表示认同，故答案选D。

5. G

根据题干中的关键词inventions of methods, stimulated和increase the self esteem可定位到G段的倒数第二句，该句提到在全国范围内出现许多提高自尊心的方法——特别是在学校——和大量上市的书籍，供人们自助使用，该句信息与题干表述完全一致，故答案选G。

Questions 6–10

题型：摘要填空题 (SUMMARY COMPLETION)

◆ 解析

6. narrower

根据题干中的关键词broader sense和并列连词and，可定位到A段的第二句While the construct is most often used to refer to a global sense of self-worth, narrower concepts such as...，该句中提到的global sense对应题干中的broader sense，接着说道narrower concepts，故此处填narrower。

7. trait

根据题干中的关键词In addition和each individual，可对应到A段的尾句It is also widely assumed that self-esteem functions as a trait, that is, it is stable across time within individuals，题干中的In addition对应句中的also，each individual对应句中的individuals，故答案为trait。

8. adaptive

9. self-protective

根据题干中的关键词functions of self-esteem，可定位到B段第二句While some researchers have been particularly concerned with understanding the nuances of the self-esteem construct, others have focused on the adaptive and self-protective functions of self-esteem，其中该句的nuances与题干中的slight differences相对应，focused与题干中的concentrated对应，由此可知第3题的答案是adaptive，第4题的答案是self-protective。

10. socioeconomic status

根据题干中的关键词self-efficacy和health，可定位到B段倒数第二句Self-esteem has been related both to socioeconomic status and to various aspects of health and health-related behaviours, as has a related construct, self-efficacy，根据句意可知，此处是将self-esteem与self-efficacy进行对比，来说明self-esteem的特性，句中的issues involving health与题干中的various aspects of health and health-related behaviours对应，故此处应填socioeconomic status。

Questions 11–15

题型：判断题 (TRUE/FALSE/NOT GIVEN)

◆ 解析

11. TRUE

根据题干中的关键词18-year olds, used drugs和psychological depression可定位到C段，该段提到研究发现18岁的长期吸毒者早在7岁时就开始吸毒了，他们比同龄人更多地受到心理问题的困扰，题干表述与原文一致，故答案为TRUE。

12. TRUE

根据题干中的关键词unlikely，depression和under some conditions可定位到F段第二句，该句中的low self-esteem is more likely than high to lead to depression under some circumstances，与题干的表述一致，故答案为TRUE。

13. FALSE

根据题干中的关键词any，type和good qualities可定位到F段倒数第二句，由该句可知属于第一类的人接受自己的好品质，而属于第二类的人却有自恋、自卫、自负的性格特点，由此可知并不是所有类型的自尊心都有好品质，故答案为FALSE。

14. FALSE

根据题干中的关键词campaign, California和1996可定位到G段首句，从该句可知自尊运动于20世纪80年代始于加利福尼亚州，其中明确提到运动的发起时间为1980s，而题干中的1996年明显与原文不符，故答案为FALSE。

15. TRUE

根据题干中的关键词Krueger, would have和cure all kinds of panacea可定位到原文G段尾句，由该句可知克鲁格的态度非常明确，他认为self-esteem并没有达到可以当万灵药的高度。题干中用了虚拟语气，表示克鲁格认为self-esteem的高度是应该达到而没有达到。所以，题干表述与原文一致，答案为TRUE。

◎ 参考译文

关于自尊心的研究

A 自尊心一般被视为自我概念的重要组成部分，它代表了更广泛意义的自我概念，这种自我概念包括评估方面、情感方面，以及认知方面或行为方面。虽然这种说法经常指的是广泛的自我价值，但是狭义的概念中，如自信或躯体自信经常被用来暗指在某些特定领域的那种自尊感。人们还普遍认为自尊是一种品质，这种品质在一个人的内心中长期稳定存在。

B 自尊心在心理学当中是一种极为流行的说法，而且人们一直认为自尊心实际上与其他的心理概念或领域有一定联系，这些概念或领域包括性格（如害羞）、行为（如任务完成能力）、认知（如归因偏差）和临床概念（如焦虑和沮丧）。一些研究人员特别关注的是了解自尊心理的细微差别，而另一些研究人员关注的是自尊心理的适应性和自我保护功能。自尊不仅与人的社会经济地位有关而且也与人的健康及与健康相关的行为有关，如另一种相关的心理，自我效能。自我效能这个词来自于班杜拉的著作中，它指的是一种个人对一般事物或特殊领域所具有的操控感或能力感。

C 低自尊是一种每一个对任何一种或所有对头脑有刺激性物质的成瘾的人都会有的普遍感受，比如酒精（非基因）。在1996年出版的《酒精中毒：假象：低自尊真正的病痛》一书中，坎迪托提出“那些自认为是‘痊愈的酗酒者’指出低自尊才是他们生活中最大的问题。低自尊是真正的问题和症结所在。”酒精仅仅是酗酒症的表象。研究发现18岁的长期吸毒者早在7岁时就开始吸毒了，他们要比同龄人受到更多心理问题的困扰。他们容易焦虑痛苦，远离家人朋友，而且易冲动。低自尊、不合群、学习成绩差，与父母关系紧张都是孩子们可能吸毒的信号。

D 坎迪托最后得出的结论是，低自尊是所有问题行为的潜在根源，也是困扰全世界的病症，这最终会导致酗酒、吸毒及其他的包括犯罪在内的过激行为。1987年安德鲁·基根对这一结论表示认同，他认为低自尊会引起或诱发精神疾病、焦虑、逆反，最终导致酗酒或吸毒。人们是否酗酒取决于他们与低自尊抗争的能力。

E 但是，美国布朗大学的心理学家克鲁格认为，很多由高自尊产生的积极作用并不能被研究所证实。心理学副教授克鲁格和另外三所大学的研究人员应美国心理学会之邀，在回顾了过去20多年针对自尊的客观调查研究后得出了他们的结论。他们的报告刊登在这个月的《大众心理科学杂志》（《心理科学》杂志的增刊）中。克鲁格说：“在大部分针对学习与工作表现、暴力与犯罪及健康的调查中，自尊水平与结果之间几乎没有一致的联系”。报告中还提到，高自尊并没有阻止孩子吸烟、喝酒、吸毒或提早过上性生活。高自尊甚至会有可能增加过早性行为或饮酒。高自尊和降低女性贪食症之间的联系是个例外。研究发现，对于成人来说，事业的成功会提高自尊水平，而不是高自尊促进人们事业的成功。高自尊和低自尊都不是导致暴力的直接原因。

F 研究发现，事实上，愉悦的心情和增强的主动性是高自尊的两大好处。高自尊与幸福感有很大的关系，而低自尊在有些情况下比高自尊更易产生沮丧的心情。那些拥有较高自尊的人在工作方面更有毅力，而研究小组还指出基本上有两类高自尊的人——现实的和脱离现实的。属于第一类的人接受自己的好品质，而属于第二类的人有自恋、自卫、自负的性格特点。在一些研究中发现，自恋会导致一些消极的品质，诸如为报复受挫的自豪感而增加具有攻击性的行为。

G 自尊运动于20世纪80年代始于加利福尼亚州，当时的想法是许多的社会问题与低自尊有关。加州立法机构资助了一个专项小组，力图通过提高自尊来减少依赖福利、意外怀孕、教育失败、犯罪、吸毒及其他问题。据专项小组的工作人员称，其目标是节省纳税人的钱。自那时起，已在全国范围内出现提高自尊的方法——特别是在学校——和大量上市的书籍，供人们自助使用。然而，“经过25年的研究，寄予厚望的自尊运动并没有实现，自助行业的顾客不应该把提高自尊当做医治一切的灵丹妙药，” 克鲁格如是说。

READING PASSAGE 2

Questions 16–21

题型：段落标题配对题 (LIST OF HEADINGS)

◆ 解析

16. vii

通读B段，该段的主题句为尾句...some couples choose one of three different styles of household role division: traditional, egalitarian or collaborative，由该句可知家庭角色划分具有三种不同的类型：传统型、平等主义型和协作型，故对应选项为vii。

17. v

通读C段，该段的主题句为首句Most people who fit the traditional pattern are characteristically men and women who are conventionally married, or have been living together as a couple for some time，主要讲述了上文最后一句总结的家务分工方法中的第一种：传统方式。句中的traditional pattern与选项v 中的Conventional相对应，故选v。

18. ix

通读D段，该段的主题句为首句In ideal situations, an egalitarian style is typified by an equal interchange in household tasks...，主要讲述了第二种家务分工方法：平均分配法。句中的egalitarian与选项ix中的even distribution相对应，故选ix。

19. viii

通读F段，该段的主题句为首句Traditional, egalitarian and collaborative styles are viewed by some as being dependent on female and male gender-role attitudes, both of self and partner，主要讲述了家务分工还受男女性别态度影响，第二句则更清楚地诠释了主题句的意思，即家务分工直接受男女性格差异的影响，故答案为viii。

20. ii

通读G段，该段的主题句为首句An opposing view sees the three family divisions of labour styles as a reflection of the progressive changes couples make in response to changing life situations, rather than being an aspect of personality，主要讲述了有一种观点认为分工并非性格差异的结果，而是夫妻随着生状况的改变做出的一种变化，故答案可以概括为与opposing view对应的选项ii。

21. iii

通读H段，该段主要说的是男女在家庭中扮演的角色受生活状况的约束，进而阐明性别角色的改变取决于夫妻双方所固有的生活模式，因此大意可概述为影响角色改变的某些因素，故答案选iii。

Questions 22–27

题型：判断题 (YES/NO/NOT GIVEN)

◆ 解析

22. NOT GIVEN

根据题干关键词no labour division和in the 1990s可定位到原文B段第二句In many Western households in the 1990s, it may include tasks such as caring for members of the family, contributing to the household finances, maintaining the house, interacting with kin and establishing and sustaining community relationships，句中只交待了家务的种类，并未提到西方是否将家务的种类进行分工，因而答案为NOT GIVEN。此题关键在于理解题意。

23. NO

根据题干关键词decisions and power和the sense of responsibility可定位到原文C段第四句He brings in the bulk of money and has the final say over major household purchases and important financial transactions，题干中的decisions and power 与句中的the final say相对应，由该句可知丈夫具有家庭事务的决定权是因为他是家庭收入的主要来源，而并非题干中所说的因为责任感，故答案为NO。此题为判断题中常见的细节替换。

24. YES

由题干关键词traditional families，females和expected to keep contact with relatives可定位到C段尾句The wife or female partner engages in child care and household management, of which the latter also includes maintaining contact with relatives...，从该句可知妻子有义务维持亲戚间的关系，与题干表述一致，因而答案为YES。

25. NOT GIVEN

根据题干关键词a man to handle half of the household tasks可定位到D段尾句...nor is society organised in such a way as to allow a man to do exactly half the breadwinning and a woman to do exactly half the child rearing，该句提到社会不可能完全平衡，不可能让男人正好承担一半的养家任务，让女人承担正好一半的育儿任务，但并没有提到社会是否希望男人做一半家务，因此答案为NOT GIVEN。

26. NO

根据题干关键词collaborative style, guided by social convention可定位到E段第二句...partners can specialise in household activities and the inclination is towards doing what one is expert at or prefers，可知协作分工的本质是由夫妻双方自愿选择工作方式，而不是源于题干中的“社会习俗”，因而答案为NO。

27. YES

根据题干关键词social scientists可定位到G段首句An opposing view sees the three family divisions of labour styles as...，由该句可知社会学家对家务分工有着不同的看法。题干中的divided in their views与文中opposing view相对应，因而答案为YES。

◎ 参考译文

论家务分工

A 家庭劳动分工是指家庭中的家务、角色和职责的分工。随着越来越多的已婚妇女步入职场，社会学家开始密切关注家庭和工作场所之间的联系，他们想知道有更多的女性活跃在职场这一事实会不会促使人们对传统的家庭角色及家务分工重新进行评判。此话题在短时期内引发了大量的实证性和理论研究。

B 家庭范围内的工作具有多种多样的形式。在20世纪90年代的许多西方家庭里，这种工作可能包括照料家人、增加家庭财力、打理房屋、与亲属沟通以及建立和维持社区关系等。家庭角色划分具有三种不同的类型：传统型、平等主义型和协作型。为了促进家庭和谐并形成一种易于实施的常规，有些夫妻会选择其中一种类型进行家庭角色划分。

C 传统型角色划分的特点是，大多数人都是传统意义上的夫妻，或者像夫妻一样在一起生活了一段时间。男人和女人都有各自的能力范围和责任范围。例如，丈夫或男性伴侣通常是家中主要的决策者和经济供给者。他是家中的经济支柱，对于家中需要购买的大件物品以及重要的财务往来，最后要由他来掌控。妻子或女性伴侣负责育儿和理家的工作，其中理家还包括与众亲戚以及不住在一起的家属保持联系。

D 在理想的情况下，平等主义型的典型特征是家务劳动的平等互换。例如，一方在一星期里负责洗餐具，另一方则负责做饭。等到下一个星期，双方再交换角色。作为一种选择，各自的工作可能会被平均分开，于是一方负责一半的家务劳动，另一方则承担余下的另一半。然而，这种一半一半的方案并不是到哪里都能行得通。人和机器不一样，不能被定时定点地开启或关闭；同样的道理，社会的组织方式也不可能让男人正好承担一半的养家任务，让女人承担正好一半的育儿任务。

E 协作型是传统型和平等主义型这两个极端的折中办法。在这种家庭中，伴侣可以在家务上各有所长，而且他们倾向于做自己擅长或更愿意做的事。在通常情况下，女人可能包揽所有的打扫工作，男人可能承担所有的烹饪工作，因为他们愿意这样做。该类型并不遵循父权制所规定的，父亲总是最重要的家庭权威，母亲总是以孩子和家庭为中心。该类型受个人兴趣的影响，而不为社会习俗所左右。就这点而言，在做决定的时候，就可能会遵从在这方面有特长的人的意见。在有些时候，夫妻双方可能会交换一下他们已经选定的角色，于是女方就成了养家的主力，而男方则承担了照看孩子的责任。

F 有人认为传统型、平等主义型和协作型受女性和男性的性别态度影响。换言之，有人说是性格差异决定了男人和女人选择家庭分工的类型。传统上总是把女性气质和女性形象与多愁善感和家庭主妇联系起来，而男性气质和男性形象则总被与冒险、武断和独立联系起来。

G 与其相反的观点认为家庭分工类型的选择不是因为男女性格的不同，而是他们因为生活状况的变化而做出的积极转变。总的说来，成年男女是根据当前情况的变化而改变了他们的行为方式，是这些生活上的变化决定了其男人和女人的角色而不是人的性别本身。例如，他们中谁照顾婴儿或者是照料生病的亲戚，那么他（她）这时显现的主要是女性特质。相反，参加竞争及在外工作显现一定的野心时则表现出男性特质。

H 所以，男人和女人是依据生活状况的需要，把他们认为适宜的男子特质和女子特质分派在特殊的情景之中。而且，他们还会依据自己参与的这些活动的模式化程度来决定是否变换性别角色。

READING PASSAGE 3

Questions 28–32

题型：选择题 (MULTIPLE CHOICE)

◆ 解析

28. C

根据题干关键词Hallside site可定位到原文C和D段，C段中说霍尔赛德钢厂于1979年关闭，D段说它被废弃直到1990年，结合两个时间点可知霍尔赛德长期处于荒废状态，故C项的长期不被使用与该意相符，为正确选项。

29. B

根据题干中的关键词one hundred years, steel production可定位到C段，该段描述了在经过100年的钢铁生产后，工厂周围的土地已经严重结块，而且受到了一些如铬、镉及铅等重金属的严重污染，以致于不能支撑任何砖块和混凝土建筑，由此可知B项的土地不能做建筑用地的表述正确，而与之意思相悖的C和D项为错误选项，而A项的土地不能做任何使用在本段中并未提及，故答案为B。

30. D

根据题干关键词reclaim, proposed可定位到原文D段...when a rescue plan put together by local landscaping and earthmoving company, HL Banks, and the regional developer, Scottish Greenbelt, was approved by local authorities，该段明确提到了提出改造计划的是HL银行和苏格兰格林贝尔特，所以正确答案为D，注意题干中问的是谁提议的，而非由谁支持的。

31. A

根据题干关键词conversion, Hallside site可定位到E段第二句，该句提到21 000多只沙蚕和黑头虫散放在这块地上，它们可以把这块土地转换成可用的土壤，由此可知用的是两种类型的蠕虫，所以正确答案为A。

32. B

根据题干中的关键词regeneration，Hallside site可定位到F段，该段说沙蚕和黑头虫在未来的5到10年将会通过咀嚼表层的泥土创造一个能够支持植物长期生长的土壤结构。没有它们，这一过程要花费近60年的时间，由此可知土地再生需要5到10年的时间，故答案为B。注意该题容易误选A，在F段作者只是提出了一种假设，假设没有使用沙蚕和黑头虫，可能会用近60年的时间完成土地再生。

Questions 33–36

题型：句子填空题 (SENTENCE COMPLETION)

◆ 解析

33. soil recomposition

根据题干关键词research, Bell College和quickened可定位到原文G段，该段主要说的是研究发现即使是在不利生长的煤矿废渣和经过部分处理的污水混合物中，蚯蚓也能加速土壤分解。题干关键词Bell College在G段首句重现，关键词quickened与该段最后一句中的speed up为同义词转换，所以答案为soil recomposition。

34. natural processes

根据题干关键词Bell, chose worms, convert和more rapidly than可定位到H段，该段说到选择某种worm后，可增reformulation的速度，而这比natural processes快。此题最主要的突破点为题干中的比较级more...than...，而它在H段结尾也明显重现，故答案是natural processes。

35. nitrogen

根据题干关键词enriched 和adding air可定位到I段最后一句...they will aerate and add nitrogen to the soil covering the Hallside site，该句说蚯蚓能够给土壤透气，给覆盖在霍尔赛

德钢厂上的土壤带去氮元素，故答案为nitrogen。

36. tree root system

根据题干关键词Contaminants和be removed可定位到原文K段These will have the dual function of extracting contaminants from the soil through their root systems...，该段说它们会起到双重功效——根部系统可以吸收contaminants...。而题干关键词contaminants和soil同时出现在原文中，be moved与原文中的extract属于同义词转换，故答案为tree root system。

Questions 37–40

题型：配对题 (MATCHING)

◆ 解析

37. G

根据题干中的关键词Hallside和expected可定位到原文L段... David Craven, director of Scottish Greenbelt, says he expects Hallside to be self-financing，句中提到苏格兰格林贝尔特的主管大卫·克雷文说他希望霍尔赛德钢厂能够通过木材赚来的钱来维持经费自给，故答案选G。

38. E

根据题干中的关键词bio-remediation可定位到原文N段的尾句Craven says the cost of land bio-remediation—the labour intensive process of removing soil for chemical and bacterial cleansing—could have been more than £30m，该句提到花费为£30 million，这与E项的表述一致，故E为正确选项。

39. B

根据题干中的关键词20 years可定位到原文P段，该段结尾说不到20年的时间里，这块土地就会重新成为一个生物群落的一部分，故答案选B。

40. D

根据题干中的关键词similar regeneration plans可定位到原文Q段，该句说霍尔赛德的成功为其他钢厂的土地再生计划铺平了道路，由此可知同样的计划也可以用在其他工厂。题干关键词regeneration在原文中重现，故答案选D。

◎ 参考译文

蚯蚓给废地带来生机

（成千上万只蚯蚓正在清理一家旧钢厂里的有毒土壤）

A 成千上万条钻入深土的蚯蚓正将一个长期废弃的钢厂恢复成林地和生态公园。

B 原霍尔赛德钢厂位于格拉斯哥附近的坎巴斯兰，重新开垦这里的土地是一项史无前例的、低成本计划的一部分。本计划中蚯蚓被用于加速土壤再生的过程，并随着时间的推移，使土地变成能创造财富的良田。

C　　1979年霍尔赛德钢厂关闭，结束了它100多年的钢铁生产历史。钢厂周围的土地已经严重结块，而且受到了一些如铬、镉及铅等重金属的严重污染，以致于不能支撑任何砖块和混凝土建筑。

D　　这块占地30公顷的土地一直被废弃，直至1990年，由当地的美化园林和掘土开发公司、HL银行协同区域开发机构苏格兰格林贝尔特共同提出一项整治计划，并最终被当地政府批准。

E　　如今这块土地已经被煤矿废物与经过部分处理的污水物质混在一起的物质所覆盖，其厚度有两米。21 000多只沙蚕和黑头虫被散放在这块土地上，它们可以把这块土地转换成可用的土壤。

F　　这些经过专门喂养的雌雄同体的生物是自我受精的。它们在未来的5到10年将会通过咀嚼表层的泥土创造一个能够支持植物长期生长的土壤结构。没有它们，这一过程要花费近60年的时间。

G　　贝尔科技大学位于汉密尔顿附近，这所大学的研究员针对蚯蚓的使用进行了调查，并发现即使是在不利生长的煤矿废渣和经过部分处理的污水混合物中，蚯蚓也能加速土壤分解。

H　　研究员挑选了能够钻入深土的不同类别的蚯蚓。这些蚯蚓进食多，排土量大，提高土地矿物质含量的能力强，都会加快土地改良，而这一速度比大自然的进程要快得多。

I　　贝尔大学生物系的肖恩·英斯说：“我们认为蚯蚓能够逐步帮助土壤进一步粘合，并能为土壤透气，给覆盖在霍尔赛德钢厂上的土壤带去氮元素。”

J　　同时，苏格兰格林贝尔特已经开始在这块土地上种了柳树和桤木，共计25万棵。这些树因其在劣质土地上的顽强生命力而被精心挑选出来。

K　　它们会起到双重功效——根部系统可以吸收土壤中的污染物，也可用作燃木或制造纸板。

L　　苏格兰格林贝尔特的主管大卫·克雷文说他希望霍尔赛德钢厂能够通过木材赚来的钱维持经费自给。

M　　他说：“第一批树是四月份种的，尽管夏日天气干燥，这些树如今已经长到6英尺多高了。”这块土地实行四年轮作制，它将帮助我们处理开销。

N　　克雷文说如果用人力去清除土壤中的化学物质和细菌，成本会高于3 000万英镑。

O　　英斯在贝尔大学说道：“有毒土壤的污染历史可以追溯到很多年以前。这包括土壤本身的退化和来自铅、铬、砷等金属的污染。”

P　　未来几年里对土壤的定期取样能说明污染的程度。不到20年的时间里，这块土地就会重新成为一个生物群落。

Q　　霍尔赛德有希望取得成功，这也为附近艾尔郡格兰格诺克的加特图什钢厂类似的土地再生计划铺平了道路。

Test 9 核心词汇 Core Vocabulary

READING PASSAGE 1

domain *n.* 领域，产业
nuance *n.* 细微差别
denominator *n.* 起源；命名者；分母
alienate *vt.* 使疏远；离间
plague *vt.* 折磨，使苦恼
obsessive *adj.* 强迫性的，分神的
substantiate *vt.* 证明，证实
bulimia *n.* 贪食症
narcissistic *adj.* 自恋的，自赏的
retaliation *n.* 反击，回敬
proliferation *n.* 激增
panacea *n.* 治百病的药

READING PASSAGE 2

household *n.* 家庭，一户
empirical *adj.* 实证的；以经验为依据的
theoretical *adj.* 理论上的
kin *n.* 亲戚，家族，亲属关系
foster *vt.* 鼓励，促进
harmony *n.* 和睦，融洽
egalitarian *adj.* 主张平等的，平等主义的
bulk *n.* 大部分，一大半
transaction *n.* 交易
reverse *vt.&vi.*（使）反转；（使）颠倒
alternative *n.* 抉择，可供选择的事物
scenario *n.*（行动的）方案，纲要
creep *vi.* 逐渐开始发生（或影响）
breadwinning *n.* 养家糊口
compromise *n.* 妥协，折中方法
femininity *n.* 妇女特质，柔弱性，温柔
masculinity *n.* 男性气概，男子气
stereotype *n.* 陈规，老套，固定的形象
assertiveness *n.* 武断
ascribe *vt.* 把……归于

READING PASSAGE 3

derelict *adj.* 被遗弃的
chromium *n.*【化】铬
cadmium *n.*【化】镉
sewage *n.* 污物，垃圾
territory *n.* 领土
hermaphrodite *n.*【动】雌雄同体；【植】雌雄同株
impregnation *n.*【动】授孕，怀孕，受精
hostile *adj.* 敌方的，仇敌的；怀敌意的；敌对的(to)
aerate *vt.* 使空气进入
chipboard *n.* 硬纸板，纸板
tranche *n.* 部分，份额
arsenic *n.*【化】砷(33号元素，符号As)；砒霜，三氧化二砷
remediation *n.* 补救

TEST 10

Candidate Number

Candidate Name ______________________

INTERNATIONAL ENGLISH LANGUAGE TESTING SYSTEM

ACADEMIC READING

TIME 1 hour

INSTRUCTIONS TO CANDIDATES

Do not open this booklet until you are told to do so.

Write your name and candidate number in the spaces at the top of this page.

Start at the beginning of the test and work through it.

You should answer **all** questions.

If you cannot do a particular question, leave it and go on to the next. You can return to it later.

All answers must be written on the answer sheet.

Do not remove this booklet from the examination room.

INFORMATION FOR CANDIDATES

There are **40** questions on this question paper.

The test is divided as follows:

Reading Passage 1	Questions 1–13
Reading Passage 2	Questions 14–26
Reading Passage 3	Questions 27–40

Reading Answer Sheet

Are you: Female? ▭ Male? ▭

Your first language code:

0	1	2	3	4	5	6	7	8	9
0	1	2	3	4	5	6	7	8	9
0	1	2	3	4	5	6	7	8	9

IELTS Reading Answer Sheet

Module taken (shade one box): Academic ▭ General Training ▭

		✓ ✗			✓ ✗
1		1	**21**		21
2		2	**22**		22
3		3	**23**		23
4		4	**24**		24
5		5	**25**		25
6		6	**26**		26
7		7	**27**		27
8		8	**28**		28
9		9	**29**		29
10		10	**30**		30
11		11	**31**		31
12		12	**32**		32
13		13	**33**		33
14		14	**34**		34
15		15	**35**		35
16		16	**36**		36
17		17	**37**		37
18		18	**38**		38
19		19	**39**		39
20		20	**40**		40

Checker's Initials		Marker's Initials		Band Score		Reading Total	

READING PASSAGE 1

You should spend about 20 minutes on ***Questions 1–13****, which are based on Reading Passage 1 below.*

The Ant Society

Described as a "six-legged lliad", Wilson's *Anthill* draws parallels between human and ant societies. Though there are no ant symphony orchestras, secret police, or schools of philosophy, both ants and men conduct wars, divide into specialized castes of workers, build cities, maintain infant nurseries and cemeteries, take slaves, practice agriculture, and indulge in occasional cannibalism, though ant societies are more energetic, altruistic, and efficient than human ones. (*The New York Review of Books*)

A "Go to the ant, thou sluggard" says *the Bible*. "Consider her ways, and be wise." The book of *Proverbs*, chapter six, says that the industrious legions of ants, which have now colonized every continent on earth, except Antarctica, have "no guide, overseer, or ruler".

B In fact, the good book got ants all wrong. Ant societies are rigidly stratified and usually ruled by queens. The little creatures are constantly guided by their scent trails and other chemical signals, not to mention their genes. Nobody has done more to reveal the true nature of the "superorganisms" that ant societies comprise than Edward Wilson, a Harvard biologist, campaigning green, two-time Pulitzer prize-winning author, pioneer of sociobiology, and now, at the age of 80, also a debut novelist.

C One part of *Anthill*, by the world's leading myrmecologist, demonstrates that in Mr. Wilson ants have found not only their Darwin but also their Homer. Midway through the novel, and comprising a fifth of the whole, is a self-contained novella, "The Anthill Chronicles", which purports to be an undergraduate biology thesis by the protagonist of *Anthill*, about the rise and fall of four ant colonies in a tract of forest in southern Alabama. Happily for the reader, these chronicles bear no resemblance to student reports, though most of the details of life among the six-legged will be familiar to fans of Mr. Wilson's entomological writings. The "thesis", we are told, has been lightly edited by two professors to present the story "as near as possible to the way ants see such events themselves".

D The success of this novella-within-a-novel derives from the fact that Mr. Wilson has no need to resort to the Hollywood method of anthropomorphizing his ants, as two popular animated features—*Antz* and *A Bug's Life*—did in 1998. There are no individual perspectives in *The Anthill Chronicles*: no lovers, no personalities, no neuroses, and no selves. The only heroes are the ant colonies themselves, and they are as engaging and at least as memorable as most two legged Hollywood creations.

E Mr. Wilson's mini-epic begins with the demise of the queen of the Trailhead Colony, whose death is not at first noticed by her daughter-followers. While her body rots encased in its external skeleton, her lingering scent misleadingly tells the colony that all is still well.

F The neighbouring Streamside Colony wipes out the Trailheaders, and then itself falls victim to a "supercolony", comprising millions of workers and thousands of queens, which rose to power thanks to a single-gene mutation that weakens their sensitivity to queen-odors, and thus permits them to tolerate multiple simultaneous queens. Growing out of control, the supercolony in effect eats up its own territory and is exterminated by "the moving tree trunks, the ant gods"—i.e., humans spraying insecticide. This leaves room for the tiny Woodland Colony to expand its territory and thrive, and so the epic struggle continues, as it has for thousands of years.

G The tale within a tale is an astonishing literary achievement; nobody but Mr. Wilson could have written it, and those who read it will tread lightly in the forest, at least for a while. Yet Mr. Wilson wants his audience to do more than that. The novel as a whole is mainly about people, and an author's prologue—echoing the theme of some of Mr. Wilson's earlier work—warns of further disaster if this wayward species does not start to take better care of its biosphere, the planet.

H The hero of *Anthill* is Raff Cody, an Alabaman youngster who follows up his biology studies with a stint at Harvard law school, with the express purpose of returning equipped to save his beloved patch of forest from rapacious property developers. This character owes something to Mr. Wilson's own background, and so does the story's narrator, Raff's biology professor. It's one of the few defects in the novel that Mr. Wilson hasn't quite decided which of the pair is him.

I Raff's early adventures in the swamps owe something to Huck Finn's; and the novel's denouement, with a monstrously eccentric woodsman and some implausible Fundamentalist villains, recalls the Florida black comedies of Carl Hiaasen, only without the laughs. One can't help rooting for the ants. Thanks to the depth of Mr. Wilson's understanding of them, his evocation of their ways is a more powerful tool for raising ecological awareness than any Disneyfication is likely to be.

Questions 1–6

Reading Passage 1 has nine paragraphs, **A–I**.

Which paragraph contains the following information?

*Write the correct letter, **A–I**, in boxes 1–6 on your answer sheet.*

1 fierce struggle of the ant world

2 comparison of the book with biology paper

3 the real theme of the novel

4 the hierarchical system of the ant society

5 the weakness that existed in the book

6 particular feature of *Anthill* in contrasted with Hollywood products

Questions 7–12

Complete the summary below.

*Choose **NO MORE THAN TWO WORDS** from the passage for each answer.*

Write your answers in boxes 7–12 on your answer sheet.

The main character of the novel is **7** ………………, who fought against greedy **8** ……………… for the saving of the forest. This protagonist has something in common with the author himself, as well as the **9** ……………… of the book. But it is one of the **10** ……………… within the novel since it seems hard for the writer to have **11** ……………… which person mentioned above was the representative of himself. In spite of this, the writer still has a profound understanding of the ant's society as he intends to increase people's **12** ……………….

Question 13

*Choose the correct letter, **A**, **B**, **C** or **D**.*

Write the correct letter in box 13 on your answer sheet.

The author of *Anthill* mainly talks about the ……………… in the book.

A importance of ecological awareness

B fascinating story of insects

C secret life of ants

D intelligence of ants

READING PASSAGE 2

*You should spend about 20 minutes on **Questions14–26**, which are based on Reading Passage 2 below.*

The History of Women's Suffrage

A In the early nineteenth century, women were considered second-class citizens whose existence was limited to the interior life of the home and care of the children. Women were considered sub-sets of their husbands, and after marriage they did not have the right to own property, maintain their wages, or sign a contract, much less vote. It was expected that women be obedient wives, never to hold a thought or opinion independent of their husbands. It was considered improper for women to travel alone or to speak in public.

With the belief that intense physical or intellectual activity would be injurious to the delicate female biology and reproductive system, women were taught to refrain from pursuing any serious education. Silently perched in their birdcages, women were considered merely objects of beauty, and were looked upon as intellectually and physically inferior to men. This belief in women's inferiority to men was further reinforced by organised religion which preached strict and well-defined sex roles.

B **The Seneca Falls Convention**

The women's suffrage movement was formally set into motion in 1848 with the first Women's Rights Convention in Seneca Falls, New York.

The catalyst for this gathering was the World Anti-Slavery Convention held in 1840 in London and attended by an American delegation which included a number of women. In attendance were Lucretia Mott and Elizabeth Cady Stanton, who were forced to sit in the galleries as observers because they were women. This poor treatment did not rest well with these women of progressive thoughts, and it was decided that they would hold their own convention to "discuss the social, civil and religious rights of women".

Using *The Declaration of Independence* as a guideline, Stanton presented her *Declaration of Principles* in her hometown chapel and brought to light women's subordinate status and made recommendations for change.

Resolution 9 requesting the right to vote was perhaps the most important in that it expressed the demand for sexual equality. Subsequent to the Seneca Falls Convention, the demand for the vote became the centerpiece of the women's rights movement.

C Suffrage During the Civil War

During the Civil War, women's suffrage was eclipsed by the war effort and movement for the abolition of slavery. While annual conventions were held on a regular basis, there was much discussion but little action. Activists such as slave-born Sojourner Truth, Elizabeth Stanton, and Susan B. Anthony lectured and petitioned the government for the emancipation of slaves with the belief that, once the war was over, women and slaves alike would be granted the same rights as the white men. At the end of the war, however, the government saw the suffrage of women and that of the negro as two separate issues and it was decided that the negro vote could produce the immediate political gain, particularly in the South, that the women's vote could not. Abraham Lincoln declared, "This hour belongs to the negro."

D Women Unite

With the side-stepping of women's rights, women activists became enraged, and the American Equal Rights Association was established by Stanton and her colleagues in 1866 in effort to organise in the fight for women's rights. In 1868, the ratification of *the Fourteenth Amendment* proved an affront to the women's movement, as it defined "citizenship" and "voters" as "male", and raised the question as to whether women were considered citizens of the United States at all. The exclusion of women was further reinforced with the ratification of *the Fifteenth Amendment* in 1870, which enfranchised black men. In a disagreement over these Amendments, the women's movement split into two factions. In New York, Stanton and Anthony established the radical National Woman Suffrage Association (NWSA). Lucy Stone, Julia Ward Howe, and Henry Blackwell organised the more conservative American Woman Suffrage Association (AWSA) in Boston. These two groups later merged in 1890 to form the National American Woman Suffrage Association (NAWSA) under the leadership of Elizabeth Cady Stanton.

E Winning the Vote

Susan B. Anthony was arrested for attempting to vote for Ulysses S. Grant in the 1872 presidential election. Six years later, in 1878, a *Women's Suffrage Amendment* was introduced to U.S. Congress. With the formation of numerous groups, such as the Women's Christian Temperance Union (WCTU), the National Council of Jewish Women (NCJW), the National Association of Coloured Women (NACW) and, the Women's Trade Union League, the women's movement gained a full head of steam during the 1890's and early 1900's. The U.S. involvement in World War I in 1918 slowed down the suffrage campaign as women pitched in for the war effort. However, in 1919, after years of petitioning, picketing, and protest parades, *the Nineteenth Amendment* was passed by both houses of Congress and in 1920 it became ratified under the presidency of Woodrow Wilson.

F Amendment xix

1. The right of citizens of the United States to vote shall not be denied or abridged by the United States or by any State on account of sex.
2. Congress shall have power to enforce this Article by appropriate legislation. (Ratified August 26, 1920)

G Equal Rights Amendment

Upon this victory of the vote, the NAWSA disbanded as an organisation, giving birth to the League of Women Voters. The vote was not enough to secure women's equal rights according to Alice Paul, founder of the National Woman's Party (NWP), who moved to take women's rights one step further by proposing the *Equal Rights Amendment* (E.R.A.) to Congress in 1923. This demand to eliminate discrimination on the basis of gender failed to pass.

The push for the E.R.A. continued on a state-by-state basis, until the newly formed National Organisation for Women (NOW) launched a national campaign during the 1960's. Despite many heated debates and protests, the E.R.A., while passed by Congress in 1972, has never been ratified.

Questions 14–19

Do the following statements agree with the information given in Reading Passage 2?

In boxes 14–19 on your answer sheet, write

TRUE *if the statement agrees with the information*

FALSE *if the statement contradicts the information*

NOT GIVEN *if there is no information on this*

14 In the early nineteenth century it was generally believed that men and women performed different roles in society.

15 The World Anti-Slavery Convention preceded the first Women's Right Convention.

16 During the American Civil War, the Women's suffrage movement flourished.

17 Men were not allowed to join the National Woman Suffrage Association.

18 The National Woman Suffrage Association (NWSA) was less radical than the American Woman Suffrage Association (AWSA).

19 Abraham Lincoln was not sympathetic to the women's movement.

Questions 20–23

Complete the table below.

Write ***NO MORE THAN FOUR WORDS*** *for each answer.*

Write your answers in boxes 20–23 on your answer sheet.

Date	Person or Organisation	Activity
1840	Elizabeth Cady Stanton, Lucretia Mott	Attending World Anti-Slavery Convention
1848	Women's Rights Convention	Requesting **20** ....
21	Susan B. Anthony	Being arrested for voting
1890	**22**	Becoming the leader of NAWSA
1919	**23**	Passing *Nineteenth Amendment*

Questions 24–26

Answer the questions below.

Write ***NO MORE THAN THREE WORDS*** *for each answer.*

Write your answers in boxes 24–26 on your answer sheet.

24 What demand did *Resolution 9* express in requesting the women's suffrage?

25 In which year did NWSA and AWSA merge to form the NAWSA?

26 What did Alice Paul propose to Congress in 1923?

READING PASSAGE 3

*You should spend about 20 minutes on **Questions 27–40**, which are based on Reading Passage3 on the following pages.*

Questions 27–33

Reading Passage 3 has nine paragraphs, **A–I**.

*Choose the correct headings for paragraphs **A–G** from the list of headings below.*

*Write the correct number, **i–x**, in boxes 27–33 on your answer sheet.*

List of Headings

i	The opportunities are equally extraordinary.
ii	Clever programmes allow computers to recognize handwriting or turn photographs into cartoons.
iii	Old assumptions about innovation in the developed countries are also being challenged.
iv	In some cases the traditional global trend is even being reversed.
v	Japan became the world's leading carmaker for business innovations.
vi	The emerging world is making a growing contribution to innovations.
vii	The emerging world is undergoing changes at home and abroad.
viii	The multinationals neglect the emerging markets.
ix	Western multinationals are investing more R&D in emerging markets.
x	It is really not easy for Westerners to prosper in these booming markets.

27 Paragraph **A**

28 Paragraph **B**

29 Paragraph **C**

30 Paragraph **D**

31 Paragraph **E**

32 Paragraph **F**

33 Paragraph **G**

Example	***Answer***
Paragraph **H**	**v**

The World Turned Upside Down

A Developing countries, the emerging world, are becoming hotbeds of business innovation. They are coming up with new products and services that are dramatically cheaper than their Western equivalents: \$3,000 cars, \$300 computers and \$30 mobile phones. They are reinventing systems of production and distribution, and they are experimenting with entirely new business models. All the elements of modern business, from supply-chain management to recruitment, are being reinvented in this emerging market. Emerging market champions have not only proved highly competitive in their own backyards, they are also going global themselves.

B Western multinationals now regard these emerging developing countries as sources of economic growth and high-quality brainpower, both of which they desperately need. Multinationals expect about 70% of the world's growth over the next few years to come from emerging markets. They have also noted that China have been pouring resources into education over the past couple of decades. China produces 75,000 people with higher degrees in engineering or computer science every year. The world's biggest multinationals are becoming increasingly happy to do their research and development in emerging markets. Companies in the Fortune 500 list have 98 R&D facilities in China and 63 in India. Some have more than one. Knowledge-intensive companies such as IT specialists and consultancies have hugely stepped up the number of people they employ in developing countries.

C Both Western and emerging-country companies have also realised that they need to try harder if they are to prosper in these markets. That means rethinking everything from products to distribution systems. Anil Gupta, of the University of Maryland at College Park, points out that these markets are among the toughest in the world. Distribution systems can be hopeless. Income streams can be unpredictable. Pollution can be lung searing. Governments sometimes failed to provide basic services. Pirating can squeeze profit margins. And poverty is ubiquitous. The islands of success are surrounded by a sea of problems, which have defeated some doughty companies.

D However, the potential market is huge. The populations are already much bigger than in the developed world and growing much faster, and in both China and India hundreds of millions of people will enter the middle class in the coming decades. The economies are set to grow faster too. Brainpower is relatively cheap and abundant: in China over 5m people graduate every year and in India about 3m, respectively four times and three times the numbers a decade ago. No visitor to the emerging world can fail to be struck by its prevailing optimism. Large majorities in China and India say their country's current economic situation is good and think their children will be better off than they are. This is a region that, to echo Churchill's phrase, sees opportunities in every difficulty rather than difficulties in every opportunity.

E Until now it had been widely assumed that globalisation was driven by the West and imposed on the rest. Bosses in New York, London and Paris would control the process from their glass towers, and Western consumers would reap most of the benefits. This is changing fast. Embraer buys many of its component parts from the West and does the assembly work in Brazil. The emerging-market brainy ones are taking over office work. Consumers in developing countries are getting richer faster than their equivalents in the West.

F People in the West like to believe that their companies cook up new ideas in their laboratories at home and then export them to the developing world, which makes it easier to accept job losses in manufacturing. But this is proving less true by the day. Western companies are embracing "polycentric innovation" as they spread their R&D centres around the world. And non-Western companies are becoming powerhouses of innovation in everything from telecoms to computers.

G The very nature of innovation has to be rethought. Most people in the West equate it with technological breakthroughs, embodied in revolutionary new products that are taken up by the elites and eventually trickle down to the masses. The emerging developing countries are offering us many breakthrough innovations. For instance, it has already leapfrogged ahead of the West in areas such as mobile money (using mobile phones to make payments) and online games. Microsoft's research laboratory in Beijing has produced clever programmes that allow computers to recognise handwriting or turn photographs into cartoons. But the most exciting innovations are of the Wal-Mart and Dell variety: smarter ways of designing products and organising processes to reach the billions of consumers who are just entering the global market.

H In the past, emerging economic giants have tended to embrace new management systems as they tried to consolidate their progress. America adopted Henry Ford's production line in the 1960s. In 1980 American car executives were so shaken to find that Japan had replaced the United States as the world's leading carmaker that they began to visit Japan to find out what was going on. The visitors discovered that the answer was not industrial policy or state subsidies, as they had expected, but business innovation.

I The Japanese had invented a new system of making things that was quickly dubbed "lean manufacturing", which almost destroyed the American car and electronics industries. Now the emerging markets are developing their own distinctive management ideas, and Western companies will increasingly find themselves learning from their rivals. People who used to think of the emerging world as a source of cheap labour must now recognize that it can be a source of disruptive innovation as well.

Questions 34–36

Do the following statements agree with the claims of the writer in Reading Passage 3?

In boxes 34–36 on your answer sheet, write

YES	*if the statement agrees with the claims of the writer*
NO	*if the statement contradicts the claims of the writer*
NOT GIVEN	*if it is impossible to say what the writer thinks about this*

34 The emerging markets and their populations are growing much faster.

35 The Western countries are focusing on many breakthrough innovations.

36 The emerging world, a source of cheap labour before, now rivals the rich countries for business innovation.

Questions 37–40

Complete the summary below.

Choose ***NO MORE THAN TWO WORDS*** *from the passage for each answer.*

Write your answers in boxes 37–40 on your answer sheet.

In 1960s, the **37** .... invented by Henry Ford became popular in United States. In the auto industrial history, the US manufacturers were once surpassed by their Japanese counterparts. Later they figured it out and realized that their Japanese rivals applied a novel management approach known as **38** .... It is gradually accepted that the emerging world are the origins of both **39** .... and **40** ....

Test 10 答案速查 Key

READING PASSAGE 1

1. F **2.** C **3.** G
4. B **5.** H **6.** D
7. Raff Cody **8.** property developers **9.** narrator
10. few defects **11.** decided **12.** ecological awareness
13. C

READING PASSAGE 2

14. TRUE **15.** TRUE **16.** FALSE
17. NOT GIVEN **18.** FALSE **19.** NOT GIVEN
20. the right to vote **21.** 1872 **22.** Elizabeth Cady Stanton
23. Both houses of Congress **24.** sexual equality **25.** 1890
26. Equal Rights Amendment

READING PASSAGE 3

27. vii **28.** ix **29.** x
30. i **31.** iv **32.** iii
33. vi **34.** YES **35.** NOT GIVEN
36. YES **37.** production line **38.** lean manufacturing
39. cheap labour **40.** disruptive innovation

Test 10 考题精解 Detailed Explanation

READING PASSAGE 1

Questions 1–6

题型：配对题 (MATCHING)

◆ 解析

1. F

根据题干关键词fierce struggle 可定位到原文F段，该段首句The neighbouring Streamside Colony wipes out the Trailheaders...为主题句,可知本段主要介绍蚂蚁间的激烈战争，wipes out

与此题干中的fierce struggle对应，因此答案为F。

2. C

根据题干关键词comparison, with biology paper可定位到原文C段第二句，该句提到生物专业论文，最后一句重复提到thesis，与题干paper对应，因此答案为C。

3. G

根据题干关键词 the real theme 可定位到原文G段，此段是对蚂蚁世界进行描述之后的结论，由yet转折引出作者真正想告诉读者的主题，Yet Mr. Wilson wants his audience to do more than that. The novel as a whole is mainly about people...，作者实际想谈论的是人类世界，与题干the real theme对应，因此答案为G。

4. B

根据题干关键词 hierarchical system可定位到原文B段，此段第二句Ant societies are rigidly stratified and usually ruled by queens中的关键词stratified意为“分层”，与题干hierarchical system意思相对应，因此答案为B。

5. H

根据题干关键词weakness 可定位到原文H段，此段最后一句提到...one of the few defects in the novel...，意为小说败笔之处，这里defects与题干中的weakness对应，因此答案为H。

6. D

根据题干关键词feature of *Anthill* in contrasted with Hollywood products可定位到原文D段，此段第一句出现Hollywood method，与题干信息Hollywood对应，说明《蚁山》这部作品与好莱坞作品的不同之处，因此答案为D。

Questions 7–12

题型：摘要填空题 (SUMMARY COMPLETION)

◆ 解析

7. Raff Cody

根据题干关键词main character可定位到原文H段首句The hero of *Anthill* is Raff Cody, an Alabaman youngster who follows up his biology studies with a stint at Harvard law school...，文中hero与题干main character对应，故此题的答案为Raff Cody。

8. property developers

根据题干关键词fought against, saving of the forest可定位到原文H段，首先根据第一句可知主人公的研究目的是returning equipped to save his beloved patch of forest from rapacious property developers，意即从房产商手中夺取森林，其次根据空前greedy（贪婪的）可知此处应该填指某类人的名词，而且greedy与原文中的rapacious为同义转换，故此题的答案为property developers。

9. narrator

根据题干关键词in common with author himself, as well as可定位到原文H段，通过审题得知此题要求找出与作品人物性格对应的除作者之外的因素，根据此段第二句...owes something to Mr. Wilson's own background, and so does the story's narrator，可知本小说的主人公与威尔逊的个人经历极为相似，也和本故事的讲述者有关系。故此题的答案为narrator。

10. few defects

11. decided

根据题干关键词which person mentioned above was the representative of himself 可定位到原文H段，此题与下一题较难，是对H段最后一句的高度归纳。根据最后一句It's one of the few defects in the novel that Mr. Wilson hasn't quite decided which of the pair is him，可知11题和12题的答案分别是few defects和decided。

12. ecological awareness

根据题干关键词profound understanding可定位到原文I段，最后一段的总结中很容易找到对应句...the depth of Mr Wilson's understanding...，depth与题中profound对应，故此题的答案为ecological awareness。

Question 13

题型：选择题 (MULTIPLE CHOICE)

◆ 解析

13. C

通读全文可知本文主要描写的是蚂蚁的生活，故此题答案为C。A选项为标准陷阱，只是文中提到的《蚁山》作品的一个侧面内容，B和D项均与文章无关。

◎ 参考译文

蚂蚁世界

威尔逊在其作品《蚁山》中把蚂蚁描述为一个“六腿伊利亚特”，他在书中描绘了人类与蚂蚁世界的相似之处。蚂蚁世界虽然没有交响乐团，秘密警察或哲学流派，但蚂蚁和人类都在发动战争。它们对成员进行分工管理，建造城邦，看管托儿所和墓地，使用奴隶，发展农业，偶尔还会自相残杀。只不过相比于人类，蚂蚁世界更具活力，更无私，更有效率。（摘自《纽约书评》）

A 《圣经》上说：“懒惰的人呐，你去察看蚂蚁的动作，就可得智慧”。《圣经·旧约·箴言篇》第六章还说：“勤奋的蚂蚁群没有元帅，没有长官也没有君王”。可如今，蚂蚁却已将其殖民地拓展到了地球上除南极以外的每个大陆。

B 事实上，这部《圣经》对蚂蚁的认识是完全错误的。蚂蚁社会等级十分森严，且通常由蚁后统治。蚁后通过自身的气味、化学信息，乃至基因引导蚁群中的其他成员。在对蚁群组成的研究中，还没有人能像爱德华·威尔逊这样对蚁群这么庞大的群居昆虫进行如此深入的研究。爱德华·威尔逊是哈佛大学的生物学家，倡导绿色环保，曾经两次获得普利策奖，生物社会学的领军人物，在其80岁高龄时，出版了他的第一部小说。

C 世界著名蚁学家认为，《蚁山》中的部分内容表明威尔逊的蚁群世界中不仅有它们的"达尔文"，也有它们的"荷马"。小说中段，也就是第五章"蚁山变迁"，是一个独立章节，全章以《蚁山》主人公想要写一篇生物专业论文展开，描述了阿拉巴马州南部森林中四个蚁族部落的兴衰起落。尽管有关蚁族具体生活的素材均选自威尔逊的相关昆虫学著述，但这章一点都不像学生报告。据说经过两位教授的妙笔改编，"论文"以近乎逼真的形式呈现了蚁族世界。

D 这部在长篇小说中独立成篇的中篇小说之所以获得成功，是因为威尔逊并没有利用好莱坞的拟人化手法描写蚁群，没有借助于像1998年上映的两部广受喜爱的动画片《小蚁雄兵》和《虫虫危机》那样的手法。在"蚁山变迁"里没有个人元素：没有情人爱侣、没有风云人物、没有意乱情迷、没有利欲熏心。整篇故事的主人公是蚁群部落自己，他们贯穿整篇故事，如同好莱坞中创造的卡通人物一样，给人们留下深刻的印象。

E 威尔逊的微型蚁群史始于特尔汉德蚁族蚁后的死亡，蚁后死亡之初，蚁后的追随者并没有发现蚁后的逝去。尽管肉体已经在躯壳中腐烂了，但她的久久未能散去的气味让整个蚁群误以为一切正常。

F 特尔汉德的邻族——斯特姆塞得，此时灭掉了特尔汉德蚁族，随后斯特姆塞德蚁族又成了"超级蚁群"的口下亡魂。"超级蚁群"由数百万只工蚁和数千只蚁后组成。该群落之所以能够威力强劲，所向披靡，皆源于一次单基因突变，这使得蚁群对蚁后气味的敏感度下降，从而导致了多蚁后的同时存在。然而，该蚁族蚂蚁数量急剧膨胀，渐失控制，超级蚁群最终吃光了领地内的所有食物，它们也最终被"移动树干，蚂蚁诛神"（意即使用杀虫剂的人类）所灭。然而，它们的灭亡却为弱小的伍德兰德蚁群拓展疆土，繁衍生息留下了机会。这史诗般的生存斗争持续进行着，就像已持续了数千年的那样。

G 故事中蕴含故事的写法在文学史上是一个创举。只有威尔逊能够创作出如此逼真的作品。读完这本书的读者在行经森林时，会时时放轻脚步。然而，威尔逊想启发的远不止这些，就小说整体而言，这还是一本给人类的书。正如威尔逊早期作品中一再强调的那样，作者借此书再次重申：如果人类继续刚愎自用，我行我素，全然不顾我们的生态环境，我们的星球，那么，更大的灾难就会到来。

H 《蚁山》的主人公拉夫·科迪是一位阿拉巴马青年，就读于哈佛法学院，他学习了一些生物课程，科迪的主要目的是用这些知识武装自己，以便去拯救他所钟情的却被贪婪的开发商掠夺去的森林绿地。这部小说主人公的一些特点与威尔逊的个人经历极为相似，本故事的讲述者，拉夫的生物学教授身上，也留存了威尔逊自己的影子。本小说不多的败笔之一就是威尔逊没有弄明白，到底这两个角色哪一个是他自己。

I 拉夫早期在沼泽中的探险与哈克·费恩的探险极为相似。小说在怪异的森林居住者和一群恶棍的登场中画上句号。这一结局让人们回忆起了佛罗里达州的卡尔·海森的黑色幽默剧。整个故事使得人们不得不对蚁群的生存环境担忧，同时为他们的未来呼吁社会。与任何一部迪斯尼电影相比，威尔逊对蚁群生活习性的深度剖析和生动描述成为提高人们生态意识的更强有力的工具。

READING PASSAGE 2

Questions 14–19

题型：判断题 (TRUE/FALSE/NOT GIVEN)

◆ 解析

14. TRUE

根据题干关键词early nineteenth century, men and women, different roles可定位到原文A部分第一段的首句，该句说“女人是二等公民”，且“只能待在家里做家务或照顾孩子”，此句充分证明男女在社会中角色不同，因而答案为TRUE。

15. TRUE

根据题干关键词The World Anti-Slavery Convention (ASC)和first Women's Right Convention (WRC)可定位到B部分的第一段和第二段的第一句，由此可知ASC发生在1840年，而WRC发生在1848年，很明显ASC早于WRC，因而答案为TRUE。

16. FALSE

根据题干关键词American Civil War和flourished可定位到原文C部分首句During the Civil War, women's suffrage was eclipsed by the war effort and movement for the abolition of slavery，由该句可知在内战时期，由于战争和废奴运动，女性的选举权运动受到影响。而题干说的是美国内战期间，女性选举权运动蓬勃发展起来，与原文表述不一致，因而答案是FALSE。

17. NOT GIVEN

根据题干关键词National Woman Suffrage Association可定位到原文D部分尾句，该句只是说斯坦顿和安东尼在纽约建立了全国妇女选举协会但并没有提到男性是否可以加入这个组织，因而答案是NOT GIVEN。

18. FALSE

根据题干关键词National Woman Suffrage Association (NWSA), less radical和American Woman Suffrage Association (AWSA)可定位到D部分倒数第一、二句，在这两句中作者在提到NWSA时用到了radical一词，而提到AWSA时用了more conservative（更加保守），因而通过这两个信息可知答案应该是FALSE。

19. NOT GIVEN

根据题干关键词Abraham Lincoln和not sympathetic可定位到原文C段尾句（此题违反顺序原则），该句只提到了林肯对黑人所说的一句话，而且未出现他对女权运动的态度描写，因而答案是NOT GIVEN。

Questions 20–23

题型：表格填空题 (TABLE COMPLETION)

◆ 解析

20. the right to vote

根据题干关键词1848和Women's Rights Convention可先定位到原文B部分第一段，由于第一段中只是说随着第一届女权大会的召开，女权运动于1848年正式启动，而真正需要的信息点在该段中并未出现，接着再根据题干另一关键词requesting定位到B部分第四段首句*Resolution 9* requesting the right to vote was perhaps the most important in that it expressed the demand for sexual equality，该句说宣言中的第九项即要求拥有选举权是其中最重要的部分，由此可知答案为 the right to vote。

21. 1872

根据题干关键词Susan B. Anthony和arrested可定位到原文E段首句Susan B. Anthony was arrested for attempting to vote for Ulysses S. Grant in the 1872 presidential election，由该句可知Susan被逮捕的时间是1872。

22. Elizabeth Cady Stanton

根据题干关键词1890和leader of NAWSA可定位到原文D部分尾句These two groups later merged in 1890 to form the National American Woman Suffrage Association (NAWSA) under the leadership of Elizabeth Cady Stanton，由此可知组织的领导人是Elizabeth Cady Stanton。

23. Both houses of Congress

根据题干关键词1919和*Nineteenth Amendment*可定位到原文E部分尾句However, in 1919, after years of petitioning, picketing, and protest parades, *the Nineteenth Amendment* was passed by both houses of Congress，从该句可知答案是Both houses of Congress。

Questions 24–26

题型：简答题 (SHORT ANSWER QUESTIONS)

◆ 解析

24. sexual equality

根据题干关键词*Resolution 9*可定位到原文B部分的第四段第一句*Resolution 9* requesting the right to vote was perhaps the most important in that it expressed the demand for sexual equality，由该句可知*Resolution 9*提出的要求是sexual equality。

25. 1890

根据题干关键词NWSA, AWSA和NAWSA可定位到原文D部分，再根据疑问词In which year寻找对应的时间，该部分共提到了三个时间点1866，1870和1890，仔细阅读三个时间所在的句子，发现只有1890所在的句子提到了后来两个组织在斯坦顿的领导下合并成全美妇女选举权协会(NAWSA)，所以答案为1890。

26. Equal Rights Amendment

根据题干关键词Alice Paul, Congress和1923可定位到原文G部分第一段的第二句...Alice Paul, founder of the National Woman's Party (NWP), who moved to take women's rights one step further by proposing the *Equal Rights Amendment* (E.R.A.) to Congress in 1923，由该句可知Alice Paul于1923年提出的议案为Equal Rights Amendment。

◎ 参考译文

女性选举权的历史

A 19世纪早期，女性被视为二等公民。她们的工作只是局限于干家务活和照顾孩子。女性被视为丈夫的附属品。婚后，她们没有权利拥有财产、获取收入或者签署合同，更不用说是选举。人们那时希望女性成为顺从的妻子，要一直与丈夫的思想或观点保持一致。女性单独外出或在公共场合讲话也被认为是不合适的。

人们一直认为高强度的体力劳动和脑力运动会伤害到女性脆弱的生理系统和生育系统，这就抑制了女性去接受任何正式的教育。女性默默地被困在“鸟笼”中，并且只是被视为美丽的物品，被认为体力和智力都不如男性。那些鼓吹严格划分性别角色的宗教组织使女性劣于男性的这一观念进一步加深了。

B 赛尼卡福尔斯会议

随着第一届女权大会在纽约州的赛尼卡福尔斯召开，女权运动于1848年正式启动。

1840年在伦敦召开的世界废奴大会是此次集会的催化剂，而且出席大会的美国代表团中有很多是女性，其中包括鲁克瑞莎·莫特和伊丽莎白·凯蒂·斯坦顿，她们女性的身份使得她们被迫以旁听者的身份坐在旁听席上。这种无理的待遇让这些有着进步思想的女性难以接受，她们决定召开属于她们自己的大会去“讨论女性的社会权利、公民权利及宗教权利”。

以《独立宣言》为指导方针，斯坦顿在她家乡的小礼拜堂陈述了她的《原则宣言》，指出了女性的从属地位并提议去改变现状。

宣言中的第九项即要求拥有选举权是其中最重要的部分，它表达了女性对性别平等的要求。在赛尼卡福尔斯大会之后，要求获得选举权成为了女权运动的核心。

C 内战时期的选举权

在内战时期，由于战争和废奴运动，女性的选举权运动受到影响。虽然每年都会定期召开大会，但是讨论太多而行动太少。一些女权运动中的积极分子，像奴隶出身的索贞纳 · 特鲁斯、伊丽莎白 · 斯坦顿和苏珊 · B · 安东尼等，通过演讲和向政府请愿力图使奴隶获得解放。她们坚信，一旦战争结束，女性和奴隶们都应像白人一样享有同等的权利。然而战争快结束时，政府将女性的选举权和黑人的选举权区别对待，认定黑人的选举权能产生立竿见影的政治效果，尤其是在南方地区，然而女性选举权就不能。亚伯拉罕 · 林肯宣告，“这一时刻属于黑人。”

D 女性联合

由于对女性权利漠视，女性激进主义分子被激怒了，1866年斯坦顿和她的同事建立了美国平等权利协会，致力于争取女性的权利。1868年，《第十四条修正案》的通过是对女性运动的公开蔑视，因为它将公民和选举人定义为男性，并质疑是否要将女性视为美国公民。1870年，《第十五条修正案》的通过进一步加剧了对女性的排斥，而在此修正案中黑人获得了选举权。由于对这些修正案的意见不一致，使得女性运动最终分为两个组织：在纽约，斯坦顿和安东尼建立了激进的全国妇女选举权协会（NWSA）；露西 · 斯通、朱莉亚 · 沃德 · 豪和亨利 · 布莱克威尔在波士顿组建了比较保守的美国女性选举权协会（AWSA），后来两个组织在伊丽莎白 · 斯坦顿的领导下于1890年合并成全美妇女选举权协会（NAWSA）。

E 赢得选举权

1872年的总统竞选中，苏珊 · B · 安东尼因试图投票支持尤利西斯 · S · 戈兰特而被捕。六年之后，也就是1878年，《妇女选举修正案》被引入美国国会。随着各种组织的形成，如基督教妇女禁酒联合会（WCTU），犹太妇女全国委员会（NCJW）和全国有色妇女协会（NACM），妇女运动在19世纪90年代和20世纪初发展迅猛。1918年，美国卷入第一次世界大战，而妇女也努力投入到战争中，由此减缓了女权运动的发展。然而，经过数年的请愿、示威和游行，美国国会参众两院终于在1919年通过了《第十九条修正案》，并于1920年在威尔逊总统的任期内被批准。

F 《第十九条修正案》

1. 合众国或任何一州不得因性别而否认或剥夺合众国公民的选举权。
2. 国会有权通过适当立法来实施本条规定。（批准于1920年8月26日）

G 《平等权利修正案》

全国妇女选举协会在成功获得选举权后被解散，由此产生了妇女投票者联盟。国家妇女政党的创始人爱丽丝 · 保罗，认为投票不足以确保女性的平等权利，于是她于1923年向国会提出《平等权利修正案》，从而将女性的权利又向前推进了一步。此修正案要求消除性别歧视，但最终未能通过。

《平等权利修正案》不断从一个州推向另一个州，直到20世纪60年代，新成立的全国妇女组织发动了一次全国性的运动。尽管遇到了强烈的争议和反对，《平等权利修正案》于1972年在国会获得通过，但未获批准。

READING PASSAGE 3

Questions 27–33

题型：段落标题配对题 (LIST OF HEADINGS)

◆ 解析

27. vii

通读A段，从该段首句可知发展中国家正在变成商业创新的温床。再从该段尾句…not only proved highly competitive...are also going global themselves可知，新兴市场的这一举动不仅证明了他们在自己的国家的高度竞争力，也证明他们正在走向国际化，由此说明新兴市场无论在国内还是国外都在发生着变化，与vii项表述一致。

28. ix

通读B段，该段主题句为首句Western multinationals now regard these emerging developing countries as sources of economic growth and high-quality brainpower...是在说西方跨国公司把这些新兴发展中国家看作是经济增长的源泉和高质量人才的人才库，再根据该段中间的The world's biggest multinationals are becoming increasingly happy to do their research and development in emerging markets...得到信息说跨国公司越来越乐于在新兴市场上搞研发。而且后面又列举了世界财富500强中的企业在中国和印度建立研发机构的具体数字来说明这一点，所以选ix。

29. x

通读C段，可知此段从开始就提到they need to try harder if they are to prosper 即进入新兴市场的外国公司需要做出更加艰苦的努力；之后在第三句又通过these markets are among the toughest in the world来说明在这个新兴市场发展是很艰难的，所以选x。

30. i

通读D段, 通过该段首句...the potential market is huge可知这是一个巨大的市场。此段中间又说The economies are set to grow faster. Brainpower is relatively cheap and abundant...经济发展很快，而且人才资源也相对廉价和丰富，由此说明市场潜力巨大，所以选i。

31. iv

通读E段，从该段首句globalisation was driven by the West and imposed on the rest可以看出原来是西方影响东方，但是后来又提到This is changing fast，情况现在开始反过来了，由此可知传统的全球趋势正在反转，所以选iv。

32. iii

通读F段，从该段首句的People in the West like to believe that their companies cook up new ideas in their laboratories at home and…看出以前西方公司是主要的技术发明者，但是在后来的叙述和尾句可以看出新兴市场已经成了技术创新的发源地，所以选择iii。注意：new ideas对应innovation。

33. vi

通读G段，主题句为该段第三句The emerging developing countries are offering us many breakthrough innovations，由该句可知新兴市场提供了很多突破性的创新，这与vi的表述一致。

Questions 34–36

题型：判断题 (YES/NO/NOT GIVEN)

◆ 解析

34. YES

根据题干关键词populations, growing和faster可定位到原文D段第二句和第三句The populations are already much bigger than in the developed world and growing much faster...economies are set to grow faster too，由该句可知人口和经济都在增加，与题干表述一致，故答案为YES。

35. NOT GIVEN

根据题干关键词breakthrough innovations可定位到原文F段和G段，文章在该两段均提到新兴的市场正在做出许多技术性突破，但是并没有提到西方国家在做什么，所以该题答案为NOT GIVEN。

36. YES

根据题干关键词cheap labour, rivals和business innovation可定位到原文H段和I段，文章在I段的最后一句，提到了把新兴市场看作是廉价劳动力的来源（a source of cheap labour），这一点与本题中的“a source of cheap labour before”论点吻合。再从H段最后一句话和I段最后半句话可知，本题干中的now rivals the rich countries for business innovation也是对的，所以该题答案为YES。

Questions 37–40

题型：摘要填空题 (SUMMARY COMPLETION)

◆ 解析

37. production line

根据题干关键词1960s和Henry Ford可定位到原文H段的第二句America adopted Henry Ford's production line in the 1960s，可知美国在20世纪60年代采用了Henry Ford的生产线，所以应填production line。

38. lean manufacturing

根据题干关键词 Japanese, management approach known as可定位到原文I段首句The Japanese had invented a new system of making things that was quickly dubbed “lean manufacturing” ...，由该句可知日本人发明了被称为“简约制造”的新生产系统，所以答案是lean manufacturing。

39. cheap labour

40. disruptive innovation

根据题干关键词gradually accepted, origines, both, and可定位到原文I段，由于39题和40

题是并列结构，所以考生在文章中也要寻找相应的并列结构，在I段的最后有as well这个词，这是并列结构的明显特征。通过分析不难发现39和40这两个空应是名词结构，所以会看出比较重要又符合并列关系结构的两个名词是cheap labour和disruptive innovation。

◎ 参考译文

颠倒的世界

A 一些发展中国家，即所谓的新兴世界，正在成为企业创新的温床。他们生产新的产品，提供新的服务，其价格要比西方的同行便宜得多：3 000美元的汽车，300美元的电脑和30美元的移动电话。他们正在革新生产和分配系统，尝试全新的商业模式。所有现代企业的元素，从供应链管理到人才招聘，正在这个新兴的市场重新亮相。该市场中的佼佼者不仅证明了他们在自己的国家高度的竞争力，也证明了他们正走向国际化。

B 西方跨国公司现在把这些新兴的发展中国家看作是经济增长的源泉和高质量人才的人才库，而这两点也正是他们迫切需要的。跨国公司预计未来几年内全球70%左右的经济增长将来自于新兴市场。他们也已注意到中国在过去几十年中在教育上投入了巨大的资源。中国每年可造就75 000名工程和计算机方面的高学历人才。一些世界上最大的跨国公司越来越愿意在这个新兴市场做研发工作。世界财富500强的公司在中国和印度分别设有98家和63家研发机构。有些公司在这两个国家有不止一家研发机构。像IT公司和咨询公司这样的知识密集型企业已经大幅增加了他们在发展中国家的雇员人数。

C 西方企业与新兴国家企业也意识到，如果他们要想在这些市场中取得成功，他们需要付出更加艰苦的努力。这意味着要重新思考从生产到运销的一整套体系。马里兰大学帕克分校的阿尼尔·古普塔指出，这些是世界上最棘手的市场。分配系统根本指望不上，资金流无法预估，污染足以令人窒息。政府有时连基本的服务都不能提供，盗版使利润空间被压缩到最低，贫穷普遍存在。问题和困难多似海洋，困住了许多坚定的企业，使其无法获得最终的成功。

D 不过潜在的市场是巨大的。这个市场的人口已经远远多于发达国家，并且还在快速增长，在中国和印度，数以亿计的人都将会在随后的几十年中步入中产阶层。经济也将快速增长。人才也相对廉价和丰富：在中国每年有超过500万的大学生毕业，是十年前的四倍；在印度这个数字大约是300万，是十年前的三倍。来访者会对新兴市场普遍存在的乐观所打动。在中国和印度大多数人认为他们国家的当前经济状况不错，并且认为他们的下一代会比他们这一代过得更好。借用丘吉尔的一句话，这片土地上，人们在每个困难中都看到机遇，而不是在每个机遇中看到困难。

E 直到现在很多人认为全球化是由西方推动，然后推及其他地区。身在纽约、伦敦和巴黎的老板们在他们的摩天大楼里控制着整个世界，西方消费者则坐收渔利。这一点正在迅速转变。巴西航空工业公司从西方公司购买许多零件，然后在巴西组装。新兴市场的精英们逐渐接管办公室的管理工作。发展中国家的消费者正以比西方消费者更快的速度富裕起来。

F 西方人总愿意相信他们的公司在他们本土的实验室酝酿出新的创意，然后输出到发展中国家，这使人们更容易接受本国制造业职位减少的现实。然而，今天这一想法也日益变得不符合事实。西方公司正在接受“多中心创新”的观点，他们正在全世界扩展它们的研发中心。非西方公司正在变成从电信到计算机的每个领域创新的输出中心。

G 创新的本质需要重新审视。大部分西方人将其等同为那些体现在革命性新产品中的技术突破，它们由知识精英们率先采用，最终推广到大众。新兴的发展中国家提供给我们很多突破性的创新。比如它们已经在诸如移动支付（即使用手机支付账单）和在线游戏等方面超越了西方同行。北京的微软研究实验室开发了一款智能程序，能使计算机识别笔迹或把照片转变成动画效果。但最激动人心的创新来自沃尔玛公司和戴尔：产品设计更加灵活，组织更加有序，拥有了几十亿的消费者份额，而这些消费者才刚刚涉入全球市场。

H 在过去，新兴经济体倾向于采用新的管理系统，试图巩固所取得的成果。美国在20世纪60年代采用亨利·福特的生产线。1980年美国汽车行业的经理们惊讶地发现日本已取代美国成为世界汽车界的领袖，这促使他们开始访问日本，想弄清楚原因究竟是什么。出乎意料的是参观者发现答案不是产业政策或政府资助，而是业务创新。

I 日本人发明了被称为“简约制造”的新生产系统，这几乎摧毁了美国的汽车和电子产业。现在，新兴市场正在开发独特的管理理念，西方公司也会渐渐发现自己正在向对手学习。那些把新兴国家看作是廉价劳动力市场的人现在应意识到新兴市场也会成为无坚不摧的创新的源泉。

Test 10 核心词汇 *Core Vocabulary*

READING PASSAGE 1

altruistic *adj.* 利他的，无私心的
stratify *vt.* 划分阶层
purport *vt.* 声称是……
tract *n.* 大片土地
entomological *adj.* 昆虫学的
anthropomorphize *vt.&vi.* 拟人化
rot *vt.&vi.* 使腐烂
linger *vi.* 逗留，徘徊
mutation *n.* 变异
insecticide *n.* 杀虫剂
prologue *n.* 序言
wayward *adj.* 任性的
denouement *n.* （戏剧、小说等的）结局
evocation *n.* 唤出，唤起

READING PASSAGE 2

suffrage *n.* 选举权，参政
refrain *vi.* 制止，避免
preach *vt&vi.* 鼓吹
catalyst *n.* 催化剂
chapel *n.* 小礼拜，小教堂
subordinate *adj.* 次级的，从属的
subsequent *adj.* 后来的
centerpiece *n.* 核心部分
eclipse *vt.* 使蒙上阴影
abolition *n.* 废除，废止
petition *vt.* 祈求
emancipation *n.* 解放，释放
enraged *adj.* 暴怒的
ratification *n.* 批准，认可
affront *n.* 公开侮辱，有意冒犯
enfranchise *vt.* 授予选举权
abridge *vt.* 删节，缩短
disband *vt&vi.* 解散
discrimination *n.* 鄙视

READING PASSAGE 3

emerge *vi.* 出现，暴露
hotbed *n.* （坏事、暴力等的）温床
innovation *n.* 改革，创新
dramatically *adv.* 引人注目地，显著地
equivalent *n.* 相等的东西
reinvent *vt.* 重复发明
distribution *n.* 分发，分配
recruitment *n.* 征募
brainpower *n.* 智囊团
desperately *adv.* 极度地
consultancy *n.* 咨询公司
prosper *vi.* 成功；兴旺
unpredictable *adj.* 不可预测的
sear *vt.* 烧焦
pirate *vt.* 剽窃，非法翻印
squeeze *vt.* 挤压
margin *n.* 边缘
ubiquitous *adj.* 普遍存在的，无所不在的
doughty *adj.* 刚强的，勇敢的
respectively *adv.* 分别地，各自地
impose *vt.* 把……强加于
reap *vt.* 收割，收获
component *n.* 元件
assembly *n.* 装配，组装
take over 接管
polycentric *adj.* 多中心的
equate *vt.* 使相等，视为平等
embody *vt.* 表现，象征；包括
elite *n.* 社会精英
trickle *vt.&vi.* 慢慢地移动
leapfrog *vt.&vi.* 交替前进，跃过
consolidate *vt.&vi.* 巩固，使固定
dub *vt.* 授予称号
lean *adj.* 瘦的；贫乏的
distinctive *adj.* 有特色的，与众不同的
disruptive *adj.* 破坏性的

TEST 11

Candidate Number

Candidate Name ____________________

INTERNATIONAL ENGLISH LANGUAGE TESTING SYSTEM

ACADEMIC READING

TIME 1 hour

INSTRUCTIONS TO CANDIDATES

Do not open this booklet until you are told to do so.

Write your name and candidate number in the spaces at the top of this page.

Start at the beginning of the test and work through it.

You should answer **all** questions.

If you cannot do a particular question, leave it and go on to the next. You can return to it later.

All answers must be written on the answer sheet.

Do not remove this booklet from the examination room.

INFORMATION FOR CANDIDATES

There are **40** questions on this question paper.

The test is divided as follows:

Reading Passage 1	Questions 1–13
Reading Passage 2	Questions 14–26
Reading Passage 3	Questions 27–40

Reading Answer Sheet

Are you: Female? Male?

Your first language code: 0 1 2 3 4 5 6 7 8 9 / 0 1 2 3 4 5 6 7 8 9 / 0 1 2 3 4 5 6 7 8 9

IELTS Reading Answer Sheet

Module taken (shade one box): Academic General Training

		✓ ✗			✓ ✗
1		1	21		21
2		2	22		22
3		3	23		23
4		4	24		24
5		5	25		25
6		6	26		26
7		7	27		27
8		8	28		28
9		9	29		29
10		10	30		30
11		11	31		31
12		12	32		32
13		13	33		33
14		14	34		34
15		15	35		35
16		16	36		36
17		17	37		37
18		18	38		38
19		19	39		39
20		20	40		40

Checker's Initials		Marker's Initials		Band Score		Reading Total	

READING PASSAGE 1

*You should spend about 20 minutes on **Questions 1–13**, which are based on Reading Passage 1 below.*

Implementing the Cycle of Success: a Case Study

Within Australia, Australian Hotels Inc (AHI) operates nine hotels and employs over 2, 000 permanent full-time staff, 300 permanent part-time employees and 100 casual staff. One of its latest ventures, the Sydney Airport hotel (SAH), opened in March 1995. The hotel is the closest to Sydney Airport and is designed to provide the best available accommodation, food and beverage and meeting facilities in Sydney's southern suburbs. Similar to many international hotel chains, however, AHI has experienced difficulties in Australia in providing long-term profits for hotel owners, as a result of the country's high labour-cost structure. In order to develop an economically viable hotel organization model, AHI decided to implement some new policies and practices at SAH.

The first of the initiatives was an organizational structure with only three levels of management—compared to the traditional seven. Partly as a result of this change, there are 25 per cent fewer management positions, enabling a significant saving. This change also has other implications. Communication, both up and down the organization, has greatly improved. Decision-making has been forced down in many cases to front-line employees. As a result, guest requests are usually met without reference to a supervisor, improving both customer and employee satisfaction.

The hotel also recognized that it would need a different approach to selecting employees who would fit in with its new policies. In its advertisements, the hotel stated a preference for people with some "service" experience in order to minimize traditional work practices being introduced into the hotel. Over 7, 000 applicants filled in application forms for the 120 jobs initially offered at SAH. The balance of the positions at the hotel (30 management and 40 shifts leader positions) was predominantly filled by transfers from other AHI properties.

A series of tests and interviews were conducted with potential employees, which eventually left 280 applicants competing for the 120 advertised positions. After the final interview, potential recruits were divided into three categories. Category A was for applicants exhibiting strong leadership qualities, Category C was for applicants perceived to be followers, and Category B was for applicants with both leader and follower qualities. Department heads and shift leaders then composed prospective teams using a combination of people from all three categories. Once suitable teams were formed, offers of employment were made to team members.

Another major initiative by SAH was to adopt a totally multi-skilled workforce. Although there may be some limitations with highly technical jobs such as cooking or maintenance, wherever possible, employees at SAH are able to work in a wide variety of positions. A multi-skilled workforce provides far greater management flexibility during peak and quiet times to transfer employees to needed positions. For example, when office staff is away on holidays during quiet periods of the year, employees in either food or beverage or housekeeping departments can temporarily fill in.

The most crucial way, however, of improving the labour cost structure at SAH was to find better, more productive ways of providing customer service. SAH management concluded this would first require a process of "benchmarking". The prime objective of the benchmarking process was to compare a range of service delivery processes across a range of criteria using teams made up of employees from different departments within the hotel which interacted with each other. This process resulted in performance measures that greatly enhanced SAH's ability to improve productivity and quality.

The front office team discovered through this project that a high proportion of AHI Club member reservations were incomplete. As a result, the service provided to these guests was below the standard promised to them as part of their membership agreement. Reducing the number of incomplete reservations greatly improved guest perceptions of service.

In addition, a programme modeled on an earlier project called "Take Charge" was implemented. Essentially, Take Charge provides an effective feedback loop from both customers and employees. Customer comments, both positive and negative, are recorded by staff. These are collated regularly to identify opportunities for improvement. Just as importantly, employees are requested to note down their own suggestions for improvement. (AHI has set an expectation that employees will submit at least three suggestions for every one they receive from a customer.) Employee feedback is reviewed daily and suggestions are implemented within 48 hours, if possible, or a valid reason is given for non-implementation. If suggestions require analysis or data collection, the Take Charge team has 30 days in which to address the issue and come up with recommendations.

Although quantitative evidence of AHI's initiatives at SAH is limited at present, anecdotal evidence clearly suggests that these practices are working. Indeed AHI is progressively rolling out these initiatives in other hotels in Australia, whilst numerous overseas visitors have come to see how the programme works.

Questions 1–5

*Choose the correct letter **A**, **B**, **C** or **D**.*

Write the correct letter in boxes 1–5 on your answer sheet.

1 The high costs of running AHI' s hotels are related to their

A management. B size. C staff. D policies.

2 SAH's new organizational structure requires

A 75% of the old management's positions.

B 25% of the old management positions.

C 25% more management positions.

D 5% fewer management positions.

3 The SAH's approach to organizational structure required changing practices in

A industrial relations. B firing staff.

C hiring staff. D marketing.

4 The total number of jobs advertised at the SAH was

A 70. B 120. C 170. D 280.

5 Categories A, B and C were used to select

A front office staff. B new teams.

C department heads. D new managers.

Questions 6–13

Complete the summary below.

Choose ***NO MORE THAN TWO WORDS*** *from the passage for each answer.*

Write your answers in boxes 6–13 on your answer sheet.

What They Did at SAH

Teams of employees were selected from different hotel departments to participate in a **6**.............. exercise. The information collected was used to compare **7**...................... processes which, in turn, led to the development of **8**................ that would be used to increase the hotel's capacity to improve **9**................ as well as quality.

Also, an older programme known as **10**................. was introduced at SAH. In this programme, **11**.................... is sought from customers and staff. Wherever possible **12**.................... suggestions are implemented within 48 hours. Other suggestions are investigated for their feasibility for a period of up to **13**...................

READING PASSAGE 2

You should spend about 20 minutes on ***Questions 14–26****, which are based on Reading Passage 2 below.*

The discovery that language can be a barrier to communications is quickly made by all who travel, study, govern or sell. Whether the activity is tourism, research, government, policing, business, or data dissemination, the lack of a common language can severely impede progress or can halt it altogether. "Common language" here usually means a foreign language, but the same point applies in principle to any encounter with unfamiliar dialects or styles within a single language. "They don't talk the same language" has a major metaphorical meaning alongside its literal one.

Although communication problems of this kind must happen thousands of times each day, very few become public knowledge. Publicity comes only when a failure to communicate has major consequences, such as strikes, lost orders, legal problems, or fatal accidents—even, at times, war. One reported instance of communication failure took place in 1970, when several Americans ate a species of poisonous mushroom. No remedy was known, and two of the people died within days. A radio report of the case was heard by a chemist who knew of a treatment that had been successfully used in 1959 and published in 1963. Why had the American doctors not heard of it seven years later? Presumably because the report of the treatment had been published only in journals written in European languages other than English.

Several comparable cases have been reported. But isolated examples do not give an impression of the size of the problem—something that can come only from studies of the use or avoidance of foreign-language materials and contacts in different communicative situations. In the English-speaking scientific world, for example, surveys of books and documents consulted in libraries and other information agencies have shown that very little foreign-language material is ever consulted. Library requests in the field of science and technology showed that only 13 per cent were for foreign language periodicals. Studies of the sources cited in publications lead to a similar conclusion: the use of foreign-language sources is often found to be as low as 10 per cent.

The language barrier presents itself in stark form to firms who wish to market their products in other countries. British industry, in particular, has in recent decades often been criticized for its linguistic insularity—for its assumption that foreign buyers will be happy to communicate in English, and that awareness of other languages is not therefore a priority. In the 1960s, over two-thirds of British firms dealing with non-English-speaking customers were using English for outgoing correspondence; many had their sales literature only in English; and as many as 40 per cent employed no-one able to communicate in the customers' languages. A similar problem was identified in other English-speaking countries, notably the USA, Australia and New Zealand. And non-English-speaking countries were by no means exempt—although the widespread use of English as an alternative language made them less open to the charge of insularity.

The criticism and publicity given to this problem since the 1960s seems to have greatly improved the situation. Industrial training schemes have promoted an increase in linguistic and cultural awareness. Many firms now have their own translation services; to take just one example in Britain, Rowntree Mackintosh now publish their documents in six languages (English, French, German, Dutch, Italian and Xhosa). Some firms run part-time language courses in the languages of the countries with which they are most involved; some produce their own technical glossaries, to ensure consistency when material is being translated. It is now much more readily appreciated that marketing efforts can be delayed, damaged, or disrupted by a failure to take account of linguistic needs of the customer.

The changes in awareness have been most marked in English-speaking countries, where the realization has gradually dawned that by no means everyone in the world knows English well enough to negotiate in it. This is especially a problem when English is not an official language of public administration, as in most parts of the Far East, Russia, Eastern Europe, the Arab world, Latin America and French-speaking Africa. Even in cases where foreign customers can speak English quite well, it is often forgotten that they may not be able to understand it to the required level—bearing in mind the regional and social variation which permeates speech and which can cause major problems of listening comprehension. In securing understanding, how "we" speak to "them" is just as important, it appears, as how "they" speak to "us".

Questions 14–17

Complete the sentences below.

Choose ***NO MORE THAN THREE WORDS*** *from the passage for each answer.*

Write your answers in boxes 14–17 on your answer sheet.

14 Language problems may come to the attention of the public when they have .... such as fatal accidents or social problems.

15 Evidence of the extent of the language barrier has been gained from .... of materials used by scientists such as books and periodicals.

16 An example of British linguistic insularity is the use of English for materials such as ....

17 An example of a part of the world where people may have difficulty in negotiating in English is ....

Questions 18–22

*Choose the correct letter **A**, **B**, **C** or **D**.*

Write the correct letter in boxes 18–22 on your answer sheet.

18 According to the passage, "They don't talk the same language" (Paragraph 1), can refer to problems in

A understanding metaphor.

B learning foreign languages.

C understanding dialect or style.

D dealing with technological change.

19 The case of the poisonous mushrooms (paragraph 2) suggests that American doctors

A should pay more attention to radio reports.

B only read medical articles published in English.

C are sometimes unwilling to try foreign treatments.

D do not always communicate effectively with their patients.

20 According to the writer, the linguistic insularity of British businesses

A later spread to other countries.

B had a negative effect on their business.

C exsisted as a problem in 1960s.

D made non-English-speaking companies turn to other markets.

21 According to the writer, English-speaking people need to be aware that

A some foreigners have never met an English-speaking person.

B many foreigners have no desire to learn English.

C foreign languages may pose a greater problem in the future.

D English-speaking foreigners may have difficulty in understanding English.

22 A suitable title for this passage would be

A Overcoming the Language Barrier.

B How to Survive in an English-speaking World.

C Global Understanding—the Key to Personal Progress.

D The Need for a Common Language.

Questions 23–26

*List the **FOUR** main ways in which British companies have tried to solve the problem of the language barrier since the 1960s.*

*Write **NO MORE THAN THREE WORDS** for each answer.*

Write your answers in boxes 23–26 on your answer sheet.

23 ……………………………………

24 ……………………………………

25 ……………………………………

26 ……………………………………

READING PASSAGE 3

*You should spend about 20 minutes on **Questions 27–40**, which are based on Reading Passage 3 below.*

Cleaning up the Thames

A The River Thames, which was biologically "dead" as recently as the 1960s, is now the cleanest metropolitan river in the world, according to the Thames Water Company. The company says that thanks to major investment in better sewage treatment in London and the Thames Valley, the river that flows through the United Kingdom capital and the Thames Estuary into the North Sea is cleaner now than it has been for 130 years. The Fisheries Department, who are responsible for monitoring fish levels in the River Thames, has reported that the river has again become the home to 115 species of fish including sea bass, flounder, salmon, smelt, and shad. Recently, a porpoise was spotted cavorting in the river near central London.

B But things were not always so rosy. In the 1950s, sewer outflows and industrial effluent had killed the river. It was starved of oxygen and could no longer support aquatic life. Until the early 1970s, if you fell into the Thames you would have had to be rushed to hospital to get your stomach pumped. A clean-up operation began in the 1960s. Several Parliamentary Committees and Royal Commissions were set up, and, over time, legislation has been introduced that put the onus on polluters—effluent-producing premises and businesses—to dispose of waste responsibly. In 1964 the Greater London Council (GLC) began work on greatly enlarged sewage works, which were completed in 1974.

C The Thames clean up is not over though. It is still going on, and it involves many disparate arms of government and a wide range of non-government stakeholder groups, all representing a necessary aspect of the task. In London's case, the urban and non-urban London boroughs that flank the river's course each has its own reasons for keeping "their" river nice. And if their own reasons do not hold out a sufficiently attractive carrot, the government also wields a compelling stick. The 2,000 Local Government Act requires each local borough to "prepare a community strategy for promoting or improving the economic, social and environmental well-being of their area". And if your area includes a stretch of river, that means a sustainable river development strategy.

D Further legislation aimed at improving and sustaining the river's viability has been proposed. There is now legislation that protects the River Thames, either specifically or as part of a general environmental clause, in the Local Government Act, the London Acts, and the law that created the post of the mayor of London. And these are only the tip of an iceberg that includes industrial, public health and environmental protection regulations. The result is a wide range of bodies officially charged, in one way or another, with maintaining the Thames as a public amenity. For example, Transport for London—the agency responsible for transport in the capital—plays a role in regulating river use and river users. They now are responsible for controlling the effluents and rubbish coming from craft using the Thames. This is done by officers on official vessels regularly inspect fling craft and doing spot checks. Another example is how Thames Water (TW) has now been charged to reduce the amount of litter that finds its way into the tidal river and its tributaries. TW's environment and quality manager, Dr. Peter Spillett, said: "This project will build on our investment which has dramatically improved the water quality of the river. London should not be spoiled by litter which belongs in the bin not the river." Thousands of tons of rubbish end up in the river each year, from badly stored waste, people throwing litter off boats, and rubbish in the street being blown or washed into the river. Once litter hits the water it becomes too heavy to be blown away again and therefore the rivers act as a sink in the system. While the Port of London already collects up to 3,000 tons of solid waste from the tideway every year, Thames Water now plans to introduce a new device to capture more rubbish floating down the river. It consists of a huge cage that sits in the flow of water and gathers the passing rubbish. Moored just offshore in front of the Royal Naval College at Greenwich, south-east London, the device is expected to capture up to 20 tons of floating litter each year. If washed out to sea, this rubbish can kill marine mammals, fish and birds. This machine, known as the Rubbish Muncher, is hoped to be the first of many, as the TW is now looking for sponsors to pay for more cages elsewhere along the Thames.

E Monitoring of the cleanliness of the River Thames in the past was the responsibility of a welter of agencies—British Waterways, Port of London Authority, the Environment

Agency, the Health and Safety Commission, Thames Water—as well as academic departments and national and local environment groups. If something was not right, someone was bound to call foul and hold somebody to account, whether it was the local authority, an individual polluter or any of the many public and private sector bodies that bore a share of the responsibility for maintaining the River Thames as a public amenity. Although they will all still have their part to play, there is now a central department in the Environment Agency, which has the remit of monitoring the Thames. This centralisation of accountability will, it is hoped, lead to more efficient control and enforcement.

Questions 27–32

Look at the following actions and the names of the agencies (Questions 27–32) below.

Match each action with the agency responsible for doing it.

*Write the appropriate letters, **A–G**, in boxes 27–32 on your answer sheet.*

Actions to Clean up the River Thames

A Operating the Rubbish Muncher

B Creating community strategies

C Monitoring the cleanliness of the River Thames

D Monitoring fish levels

E Collecting solid waste from the tideway

F Creating enlarged sewage works

G Controlling the River Thames' traffic

Example	***Answer***
The Fisheries Department	**D**

27 The Environment Agency

28 Transport for London

29 The Greater London Council

30 Thames Water

31 Port of London

32 Local Boroughs

Questions 33–40

Do the following statements agree with the claims of the writer in Reading Passage 3?

In boxes 33–40 on your answer sheet, write

YES	*if the statement agrees with the claims of the writer*
NO	*if the statement contradicts the claims of the writer*
NOT GIVEN	*if it is impossible to say what the writer thinks about this*

33 The Thames is now cleaner than it was in 1900.

34 Swimming in the Thames now poses no health hazards.

35 It is now mainly the responsibility of those who pollute the Thames to clean their waste up.

36 All local London boroughs are now partly responsible for keeping the Thames clean.

37 Transport for London now employs a type of River Police to enforce control of their regulations.

38 Rubbish Munchers are now situated at various locations on the Thames.

39 Previously no one department had overall responsibility or control for monitoring the cleanliness of the Thames.

40 British Waterways will no longer have any part in keeping the Thames clean.

Test 11 答案速查 Key

READING PASSAGE 1

1. C	**2.** A	**3.** C
4. B	**5.** B	**6.** benchmarking
7. service delivery	**8.** performance measures	**9.** productivity
10. Take Charge	**11.** feedback	**12.** employee
13. 30 days		

READING PASSAGE 2

14. major consequences **15.** studies/surveys

16. outgoing correspondence/sales literature

17. Far East/Russia/Eastern Europe/the Arab world/Latin America/French-speaking Africa

18. C	**19.** B	**20.** C
21. D	**22.** A	**23.** (industrial) training (schemes)
24. translation services	**25.** (part-time) language courses	**26.** (technical) glossaries

READING PASSAGE 3

27. C	**28.** G	**29.** F	**30.** A
31. E	**32.** B	**33.** YES	**34.** NOT GIVEN
35. NOT GIVEN	**36.** YES	**37.** YES	**38.** NO
39. YES	**40.** NO		

Test 11 考题精解 Detailed Explanation

READING PASSAGE 1

Questions 1–5

题型：选择题（MULTIPLE CHOICE）

◆ 解析

1. C

根据题干关键词high costs of running AHI’ s hotels可定位到原文第一段倒数第二句...as a result of the country’s high labour-cost structure，由该句可知AHI酒店的高成本与员工有关，

所以本题答案为C。

2. A

根据题干关键词new organizational structure和选项中的百分比可定位到原文第二段第二句...there are 25 per cent fewer management positions，由该句可知有25%的员工被裁掉，那就是要保留75%的老员工，所以本题答案为A。

3. C

根据题干关键词approach to organizational structure和changing practices可定位到原文第三段第一句The hotel also recognized that it would need a different approach to selecting employees who would fit in with its new policies，由该句可知SAH要想实现新型组织结构就需要在雇佣员工方面做出改变，所以本题答案为C。

4. B

根据题干关键词jobs advertised和选项中的数字可定位到原文第四段第一句A series of tests and interviews were conducted with potential employees, which eventually left 280 applicants competing for the 120 advertised positions，由该句可知有280位应聘人员竞争120个空缺职位，SAH广告招聘的职位共有120个，所以本题答案为B。

5. B

根据题干关键词Categories A, B and C可定位到原文第四段最后一句Once suitable teams were formed, offers of employment were made to team members，由该句可知分成A, B, C三类是为了选出new teams，所以本题的答案为B。

Questions 6–13

题型：摘要填空题 (SUMMARY COMPLETION)

◆ 解析

6. benchmarking

由题干关键词Teams of employees were selected from hotel departments可定位到原文第六段倒数第二句话的...made up of employees from different departments within the hotel，由此可知本题答案可在该句附近找。由该段第三句SAH management concluded this would first require a process of “benchmarking”可知组内的员工从酒店各个部门选出来后去参加一个benchmarking活动，所以本题填benchmarketing。

7. service delivery

由题干关键词used to compare可定位到原文第六段第四句The prime objective of the benchmarking process was to compare a range of service delivery processes ... 本题空白处后面为processes，所以本题填写service delivery。

8. performance measures

由题干关键词led to the development可定位到原文第六段最后一句This process resulted in performance measures that greatly enhanced SAH's ability to improve productivity and quality，其中led to和resulted in 为同义转换，所以本题答案为resulted in后面的performance measures。

9. productivity

由题干关键词improve和as well as quality可定位到原文第六段最后一句This process resulted in performance measures that greatly enhanced SAH's ability to improve productivity and quality，题干中的as well as和句中的and为同义转换，所以答案应为and前面的productivity。

10. Take Charge

由题干关键词an older programme可定位到原文第八段第一句...a programme modeled on an earlier project called "Take Charge" was implemented，题干问的是这个早期项目的名称，所以应填Take Charge。

11. feedback

本题继续说这个过去的programme，根据关键词from customers and staff 可定位到第八段第二句...Take Charge provides an effective feedback loop from both customers and employees，由该句可知从顾客和员工那里搜集来了feedback。

12. employee

由题干关键词48 hours可定位到原文第八段第七句Employee feedback is reviewed daily and suggestions are implemented within 48 hours, if possible, or a valid reason is given for non-implementation，题干空白处前后分别为possible和suggestions，由此可知需填写说明suggestions的单词，虽然原文suggestions前没有单词，但是实质上指的就是前面限定feedback的employee，故本题应填employee。

13. 30 days

由题干关键词a period of up to可知该空白处应填写数字，并以此定位到原文第八段第八句If suggestions require analysis or data collection, the Take Charge team has 30 days in which to address the issue and come up with recommendations，可知应填写30 days。

◎ 参考译文

使成功的循环生效：一项案例研究

在澳洲本土，澳大利亚酒店公司（AHI）共经营九家酒店，雇佣了2 000多名固定的全职员工、300多名固定兼职员工和100多名临时工作人员。其中最新建立的企业之一——悉尼机场酒店 (SAH)于1995年3月开业，它是最接近悉尼机场的一家酒店，旨在为悉尼南郊地区提供最佳的住宿、餐饮以及会议设施。类似于许多国际酒店连锁集团，AHI也曾因为澳洲劳动力成本过高，在为酒店业主提供长期利益方面遇到困难。为了发展经济可行的酒店组织模式，AHI决定在SAH实施新政策和新措施。

首要举措便是采取只有三级管理的组织结构——与传统的7级管理机构形成鲜明对比。源于这一改进的部分效果如下：管理岗位减少了25%，节约了大量成本。这一改进还具备其他意义：上下级之间的沟通大大改善了。在许多情况下决策权已经被迫交由一线员工来进行抉择。因此，客人的要求通常不需要再提交给主管进行解决，提高了客人和员工的满意度。

酒店也意识到它需要一种截然不同的方法来选择适合其新政策的员工。酒店在其招聘广告中指出，为减少传统工作经验引入到酒店中，酒店更青睐于聘用拥有一些“服务业”经验的员工。7 000多名申请人填写了SAH最初提供的120个工作岗位的就业申请表格。酒店的其他职位空缺（30名管理层人士和40名轮班领导位置）主要从其他AHI下属公司来调动人员进行填补。

SAH对有潜质的求职者进行了一系列的笔试和面试，留下了280名求职者参与最终面试并竞争招聘广告中提及的120个职位。最终面试之后，SAH把这些潜在的新员工分成三类：A类求职者表现出很强的领导素质，C类求职者则被认为是忠实的随从人员，而B类求职者兼具领导者和追随者的素质。然后部门经理和生产领班就会从这三类求职者中进行选拔来组成未来的团队。一旦形成了合适的小组，就会向这个小组的组员发放录取通知书。

SAH采取的另一项重要举措是雇佣多技能的员工。虽然他们在一些需要高技能的工作上会有所不足，诸如烹饪或维修，但是无论在什么情况下，SAH的雇员总是能够适应各个工作岗位。对于一名拥有多技能的员工，可获得较大的弹性管理空间，酒店可以根据对工作岗位的实际需求在高峰期和低谷期调动员工。例如，办公室的工作人员将在每年的生意低谷期间休假，可以由工作在餐饮或家务部门的员工来临时代替。

然而，SAH改善人工成本结构所采取的至关重要的方法是找到更好、更有效地为客户提供服务的方式。SAH 管理部门总结说这将首先需要一个“基准评价”的过程。基准评价的主要目标是通过酒店内部互相影响的各个部门的员工来组成小组，进而对比这些小组在一系列准则下提供服务的过程。结果，此过程对功能执行进行了评定，极大地提高了SAH的工作效率和服务质量。

前厅部通过这一项目发现了AHI俱乐部会员的大部分预订并未完善。结果，为这些客人所提供的服务低于在会员协议中所承诺的标准。减少未完善的预订数量可极大地提高客人对服务质量的感知。

此外，SAH还执行了新项目，该项目是以早些时候名为“负责”的项目为模型。从本质上讲，“负责”在顾客与员工之间提供了有效的反馈循环。无论是肯定的还是否定的顾客意见，工作人员必须予以记录，并且需要定期核对，以发现改进的机会。同样重要的是，员工也需要记下自己的改进建议。（AHI设定了一个期望：每名员工将提交至少三条来自客户的建议。）员工的反馈每天都会进行审查，并且如果可行的话其建议必须在48个小时之内执行；或者如果不能得以执行也要给出正当的理由。如果建议需要分析和数据采集，“负责”小组有30天的时间来解决这一问题和推荐解决方案。

尽管目前一些证据表明AHI在SAH的倡议具备一定的局限性，仍有轶事证据明显表明这些措施是有效的。事实上，AHI在澳洲其他的酒店中正逐步推行这些举措，与此同时，许多海外游客也来到这里观看这一项目是如何运作的。

READING PASSAGE 2

Questions 14–17

题型：句子填空题 (SENTENCE COMPLETION)

◆ 解析

14. major consequences

根据题干关键词come to, the attention of public 和fatal accidents可定位到原文第二段的第二句Publicity comes only when a failure to communicate has major consequences, such as strikes, lost orders, legal problems, or fatal accidents...,其中the attention of public与publicity为同义转换，而fatal accidents为原词再现，题干问语言问题只有在什么时候才能引起公众的注意，由该句可知只有当沟通失败产生重大影响时才能引发公众的关注，由此可知该题填major consequences。

15. studies/ surveys

根据题干关键词the extent of the language barrier可定位到原文第三段第二句But isolated examples do not give an impression of the size of the problem—something that can come only from studies of the use or avoidance of foreign-language materials and contacts in different communicative situations，其中的“size of the problem”就是指问题的严重程度，即题干中的“extent of the language barrier”。可见“研究”外语材料的使用情况可以帮助了解语言障碍问题的程度。由此，答案可以是“studies”；接着再看第三句In the English-speaking scientific world, for example, surveys of books and documents consulted in libraries and other information agencies have shown that very little foreign-language material is ever consulted 。该句指出调查信息机构中书和文件的查阅情况可以知道对外语材料的查阅很少。可见“调查”这些材料的查阅情况可以获得证据。由此，答案也可以是“surveys” 。

16. outgoing correspondence/sales literature

先根据题干关键词linguistic insularity和the use of English 定位到原文第四段的第二句British industry, in particular, has in recent decades often been criticized for its linguistic insularity...，该句主要是说英国工业界因其在与国外买家做生意时存在的语言褊狭而频繁受

到指责，注意题干中的另外一个关键词 materials, 在本句中并未提到；接着看第三句In the 1960s, over two-thirds of British firms dealing with non-English-speaking customers were using English for out going correspondence; many had their sales literature only in English，由该句可知他们用英语来写往来函件、销售宣传这样的一些材料。由于题干只要求写出一个例子，所以答案可以是“sales literature”或者“outgoing correspondence”。

17. Far East/Russia/Eastern Europe/the Arab world/Latin America /French-speaking Africa

根据题干关键词negotiating in English 可定位到原文第六段的第一句...where the realization has gradually dawned that by no means everyone in the world knows English well enough to negotiate in it，该句主要说的是人们逐渐认识到并不是世界上的所有人都能很好地用英语进行沟通洽谈，接下来作者指出尤其是在英语为非官方语言的国家中，如Far East, Russia, Eastern Europe, the Arab world, Latin America and French-speaking Africa，由于题干只要求给出一个例子，所以只要写出以上一个国家或地区即可。

Questions 18–22

题型：选择题 (MULTIPLE CHOICE)

◆ 解析

18. C

根据题干关键词They don't talk the same language可定位到原文第一段最后一句“They don't talk the same language” has a major metaphorical meaning alongside its literal one，由于该句话是出现在段落的结尾，所以应该是对前面所述内容的总结概括，可仔细阅读前面内容，看是什么问题令作者做出如此阐述，倒数第二句“Common language” here usually means a foreign language, but the same point applies in principle to any encounter with unfamiliar dialects or styles within a single language，该句先是说通常情况下，共同语言指的是一门外语，接着话锋一转(but)说同一语言下的不熟悉的方言或文体内也会有类似的问题，由此可知 “They don't talk the same language”也指在理解dialects or styles上存在的问题，所以该题选C。

19. B

毒蘑菇的例子出现在原文的第二段，作者在说完毒蘑菇事件后先是提了一个问题Why had the American doctors not heard of it seven years later? 接着自答Presumably because the report of the treatment had been published only in journals written in European languages other than English，由此可知美国医生之所以在长达七年的时间里都没有掌握治疗方法是因为医疗报告是用欧洲文字写成，而非英语，所以可推知美国医生只读用英语发表的医疗资料，所以该题选B。

20. C

根据题干关键词the linguistic insularity可定位到原文第四段第二句，阅读该处上下文可知该句下一句，即第四段第三句即为描述英国语言狭隘性的事实根据。其他答案在文章中并未提及，故C是正确选项。

21. D

本题可采用排除法，通读全文可知A、B和C项所述内容在原文中都没有出现，另根据最后一段的倒数第二句Even in cases where foreign customers can speak English quite well，it is often forgotten that they may not be able to understand it to the required level-bearing in mind the regional and social variation which permeates speech and which can cause major problems of listening comprehension，可知作者认为无论外国顾客能够多么熟练地使用英语，在理解英语上还是存在许多问题，所以该题答案为D。

22. A

可用排除法做这道题。A的意思是克服语言障碍，B的意思是怎样在说英语的世界中存活下来，C项的意思是个人进步的关键——全球理解，D项的意思是对共同语言的需要。整篇文章都没有提到B、C两项的内容，可排除。D虽然在文章中有提及，但是不能够概括整篇的内容。

Questions 23–26

题型：简答题 (SHORT ANSWER QUESTION)

◆ 解析

该题要求列举出英国公司在60年代解决语言障碍问题的四种方法，根据关键词1960s可定位到原文第四段的第三句，不过阅读该句及其前后内容可知并没有提到相关的解决办法，可略过。1960s在第五段的首句也有出现，仔细阅读第四段可知解决语言障碍的四种方法均可在本段中的第二、三和四句中找到。

23. (industrial) training (schemes)

对应第五段第二句Industrial training schemes have promoted an increase in linguistic and cultural awareness。

24. translation services

对应第五段第三句Many firms now have their own translation services...。

25. (part-time) language courses

对应第五段第四句Some firms run part-time language courses in the languages of the countries with which they are most involved...。

26. (technical) glossaries

对应第五段第四句...some produce their own technical glossaries...。

◎ 参考译文

研究发现，在人们旅行、学习、管理或买卖中，语言极可能成为障碍。不管是旅游、研究、政府、治安、商业、或者数字传播，缺乏共同的语言沟通会大大地阻碍其进展或者使其完全停滞。这里的“共同语言”通常指一门外语，但不熟悉的方言或者单一的语言类型也会有类似的问题。“不说同一种语言”除了字面意义之外，还有深层的隐喻意义。

尽管每天定会发生此类交流问题千万次，但它却很少成为公共常识。只有当失败的交流造成重大影响时才会进行宣传，诸如罢工、秩序混乱、法律问题、或者死亡事故——甚至战争。曾对一个交流失败的例子进行报道的事情发生在1970年，当时几个美国人吃了一种毒蘑菇，却无人知晓治疗方法，其中两个人几天内便死去了。一名知道治疗方法的化学家在广播中听到了关于这个案件的报导，他知道的这种治疗方法已于1959年成功应用，并且在1963年正式发布。为什么在七年之后美国医生都没有听说过这种治疗方法呢？大概是因为关于治疗方法的报告以非英语的欧洲语言仅发表在日报上。

人们对于类似案例也进行过报道，但孤立的案例不会令人们对问题的大小加深印象——一些问题只来源于应用学习或避免外语材料，以及在不同交流情境下的接触。例如在以英语为母语的科学世界里，在图书馆和其他信息机构对书籍和文献的查阅情况进行的调查表明外语资料被查阅的次数微乎其微。图书馆在科学技术领域对外语期刊的需求只有13%。出版物中所引用的研究来源导致了相似的结论：通常外语资源的使用率低至10%。

语言障碍明显地体现在那些希望为其产品开拓国外市场的公司中。尤其是英国的工业在最近的几十年里经常因为语言的狭隘性而备受批评——因为它总是假定外国买家乐于用英语交流并且以为其他语言无优先权。在20世纪60年代，超过2/3的英国公司用英语处理非英语客户的往来函件，许多促销资料只采用英语，并且高达40%的员工不能用客户的语言进行交流。类似的问题同样发生在其他以英语为母语的国家，美国、澳大利亚和新西兰尤为显著。非英语国家也不能幸免——虽然英语作为替代语言而被广泛应用，这导致他们很少去公开指控语言的狭隘性。

针对这一问题的批评和宣传自20世纪60年代以来似乎有很大改善。工业培训计划促进了语言和文化意识方面的进步。现在许多公司都具备翻译服务；只举一个发生在英国的案例，Rowntree Mackintosh用六种语言（英语、法语、德语、荷兰、意大利和科萨语）发行他们的文件。一些公司针对与其交流较多的国家的语言会举办业余的语言课程；一些公司制作自己的技术词汇以确保翻译资料时协调一致。现在更加容易意识到营销效果可能会因为未能有效地考虑客户的语言需求而被推迟、破坏或中断。

英语国家在意识上的变化最为显著，绝不是一个人英语足够好就可以去参与洽谈的这种意识已逐渐被大众所接受。尤其是当英语并非是行政管理部门的官方语言时，这也是问题，如远东、俄罗斯、东欧、阿拉伯世界、拉丁美洲和非洲法语国家的大部分地区。即使在某些情况下，外国客户英语能够讲得很好，但常常会忽略对于所要求的语言水平他们有可能无法理解——牢记地域和社会差异，因为这二者经常渗入到谈话中，而且也是造成听力理解的主要问题。确切地理解是，“我们”如何对“他们”讲与“他们”如何对“我们”说同等重要。

READING PASSAGE 3

Questions 27–32

题型：配对题 (MATCHING)

◆ **解析**

27. C

根据题干关键词The Environment Agency可定位到原文E段倒数第二句Although they will all still have their part to play, there is now a central department in the Environment Agency, which has the remit of monitoring the Thames，由该句可知The Environment Agency现在有专门部门负责监督清洁的工作，与此同时该段首句提到Monitoring of the cleanliness of the River Thames，故该题答案为C。

28. G

根据题干关键词Transport for London可定位到原文D段第五句For example, Transport for London—the agency responsible for transport in the capital—plays a role in regulating river use and river users，该句很明确提到该机构负责管理交通工作，同时，在Transport for London一词的后面有明显的插入语the agency responsible for transport in the capital，故答案选G。

29. F

根据题干关键词The Greater London Council可定位到B段最后一句In 1964 the Greater London Council (GLC) began work on greatly enlarged sewage works, which were completed in 1974，说明此机构负责sewage的工作，而sewage一词与F选项形成对应，故答案选F。

30. A

根据题干关键词Thames Water可定位到原文D段倒数第五句...Thames Water now plans to introduce a new device to capture more rubbish floating down the river，由该句可知此机构打算引进一种新设备，而最后一句说这一设备叫作Rubbish Muncher，故答案选A。

31. E

根据题干关键词Port of London可定位到原文D段倒数第五句While the Port of London

already collects up to 3,000 tons of solid waste from the tideway every year...，说此机构负责collects up to 3,000 tons of solid waste的工作，故答案选E。

32. B

根据题干关键词Local Boroughs可定位到原文C段倒数第二句local borough to "prepare a community strategy for promoting or improving the economic, social and environmental well-being of their area"，引号中的话证明此机构负责community strategies的工作，故答案选B。

Questions 33–40

题型：判断题 (YES/NO/NOT GIVEN)

◆ 解析

33. YES

根据题干关键词Thames, cleaner, 1900可定位到原文A段第二句...the Thames Estuary into the North Sea is cleaner now than it has been for 130 years.，由该句可知泰晤士河现在是130年来最干净的，1900包含在距今130年内，故答案为YES。

34. NOT GIVEN

根据题干关键词Swimming, hazards可定位到原文B段第四句Until the early 1970s, if you fell into the Thames you would have had to be rushed to hospital to get your stomach pumped，该句虽然提到了70年代掉进河里应当立即去医院就医，但并没有说现在在泰晤士河里游泳是否有对身体有害，故该题答案很显然为NOT GIVEN。

35. NOT GIVEN

根据题干关键词responsibility, pollute可定位到原文B段倒数第二句...legislation has been introduced that put the onus on polluters—effluent-producing premises and businesses—to dispose of waste responsibly，由该句可知推出让污染者承担责任的法律，但没有提到目前谁负最主要的责任，故该题答案应为NOT GIVEN。

36. YES

根据题干关键词London, boroughs, keeping, clean可定位到原文C段，本段说明所有boroughs都有责任保持河水干净，故答案为YES。

37. YES

根据题干关键词Transport for London, River Police可定位到原文D段，本段中有提到此机构雇佣的警察工作，因为officers on official vessels是type of River Police的同义表达，故答案为YES。

38. NO

根据题干关键词Rubbish Munchers,various locations可定位到原文D段最后一句This machine, known as the Rubbish Muncher, is hoped to be the first of many, as the TW is now looking for sponsors to pay for more cages elsewhere along the Thames，由该句可知目前正在寻找投资人去投放更多的机器，证明不是很多地方有很多机器，且沿着定位词Rubbish Munchers向上看会发现此种机器现在只出现在Royal Naval College at Greenwich附近，故答案为NO。

39. YES

根据题干关键词previously, overall responsibility可定位到原文E段第一句Monitoring of the cleanliness of the River Thames in the past was the responsibility of a welter of agencies—British Waterways, Port of London Authority, the Environment Agency, the Health and Safety Commission...由该句可知有很多的部门一起管，而不是由一个部门主管，故答案然为YES。

40. NO

根据题干关键词British Waterways可定位到原文E段倒数第二句Although they will all still have their part to play, there is now a central department in the Environment Agency, which has the remit of monitoring the Thames，由该句可知以前的部门还参与清洁工作，故答案为NO。

◎ 参考译文

治理泰晤士河

A 据泰晤士水利公司称，泰晤士河在20世纪60年代，从生物学角度讲已经“死亡”，但它现在是世界上最干净的城市河流。该公司说多亏了对伦敦和泰晤士河谷污水治理的大力投资，这条流经英国首都和泰晤士河口到达北海的河流，现在是130年来最干净的。渔业部是负责监控泰晤士河中的鱼量的部门，他们也报告说河中出现了115种鱼类，包括黑鲈、比目鱼、大马哈鱼、胡瓜鱼、西鲱等。最近，还有人看到一只海豚活跃于伦敦中心区附近的水域中。

B 但过去的景致可不总是那么乐观。在20世纪50年代，下水道排出的废物和工业废水严重污染了泰晤士河。水中氧气急缺，已经无法供给水生物的呼吸所需。20世纪70年代早期之前，如果你掉进泰晤士河中，你必须尽快赶到医院洗胃。上世纪60年代，一项治理泰晤士河的工程开始实施，许多议会委员会和皇室委员会也随之建立，后来，针对污染者（包括产生污水的地点和工业）的相关法律条款也被提出，以便能够在处理污水方面各负其责。在1964年，大伦敦区政务会（GLC）开始致力于进一步扩大污水治理厂，并在1974年完成了这项工作。

C　　但是，泰晤士河的治理工作还没有结束，它仍然在继续，而且已经有越来越多的各种政府部门和民间团体加入到治理的队伍中来，所有这些都体现了治理污水的必要性。以伦敦为例，河道的两侧无论是伦敦的城区还是乡村，他们都有自己的理由去保持“他们”的河段干净、美丽。即使这些理由未能给他们提供十分诱人的前景，政府也会采取强制性措施。2000年的当地政府法案要求每一个地方区域都要“准备一个为了促进和发展经济，社会和环境共创美好家园的社区策略”。如果你所在的地区有一段河流，那就意味着你要遵守有关河流可持续性发展的策略。

D　　更多旨在改善和维持河流生机的法规被提了出来。作为专门的条例，或是作为总的环境保护条例中的一部分，当地政府法案，伦敦市法案和伦敦市长职责的法案中都有有关保护泰晤士河的条款。而这些只是有关工业、公共卫生和环境保护等法规的冰山一角。这样一来，越来越多的组织以这种或那种方式承担起了把泰晤士河治理成一个宜人的公众环境的责任。举个例子，负责首都交通的伦敦交通部门（Transport for London）在规范河水使用和河水使用者方面起着重要的作用，这个部门现在负责防控泰晤士河上船只所带来的工业废水和垃圾。公务船上的官员通过定期视察和抽查河面的船只来防控废水和垃圾。另一个例子是，泰晤士水利公司（以下简称TW）怎样通过付费来减少在潮水和支流中丢弃废物的数量。TW的环境质量经理皮特博士说：“这个项目将建立在已经大大改善了河水质量的投资之上。”每年，数千吨的垃圾就这样被扔进了泰晤士河里，有些是存储的坏掉的废物，有些是人们从小船上扔进河里的垃圾，还有些是从城市街道里被风吹到河里或是被雨水冲到河里的垃圾。一旦垃圾沾了水就变得很沉，不能再被吹到其他地方了，因而泰晤士河成了整个水域中的“地漏”。虽然每年伦敦港都会从河中收集3 000多吨的固体垃圾，但是TW公司现在打算引进一种新的设备来打捞沉在河底的垃圾。这个设备是由一个巨大的笼子组成的，把它放进水里它就会套着流过的垃圾。皇家海军学院位于伦敦东南的格林威治，这个装置被固定在学院正前方的河岸上，预计每年能够打捞20吨的漂浮垃圾。如果这些垃圾被冲到海洋中，他们会杀死海里的哺乳动物、鱼和鸟类。TW公司正在寻找赞助商，让他们在泰晤士河中可以投放更多的这种叫做“垃圾克星”的机器。

E　　过去监控泰晤士河水质的是很多代理机构，诸如英国水路部门、伦敦港口主管部门、环境代理公司、健康与安全委员会、TM公司以及学术机构和全国及地方的环保组织。如果出了问题，有人就会被判犯规，而且必须有人为此负责。不论当地政府、污染者个人，还是任何公共或私人团体，都有责任保护泰晤士河及其周边的环境。虽然这些部门仍然起作用，但是现在伦敦的环境代理机构中有了一个专门的部门来集中管理和监控泰晤士河。我们相信这种集中管理的负责制会更加有效地监控和治理泰晤士河的环保。

Test 11 核心词汇 Core Vocabulary

READING PASSAGE 1

accommodation *n.* 膳宿；预订铺位
implement *vt.* 实现，使生效，执行
viable *adj.* 切实可行的；可实施的
initiative *n.* 首创精神，主动权
fit in 装配好；相处融洽，合得来
fill in 填充，填写
predominant *adj.* 占主导地位的，卓越的
exhibit *vt.* 展现，陈列，展览
adopt *vt.* 采用，正式通过
objective *n.* 目的，目标
adj. 客观的，如实的
enhance *vt.* 提高，加强，增加
proportion *n.* 比例，比率，均衡
collate *vt.* 校对，校勘
note down 记下
valid *adj.* 正当的；有确实根据的
numerous *adj.* 许多的，无数的

READING PASSAGE 2

dissemination *n.* 宣传；散播
impede *vt.* 阻碍，妨碍
halt *vt.&vi.* （使）停下来
dialect *n.* 方言
metaphorical *adj.* 含有许多隐喻的
publicity *n.* 宣传，宣扬；公开
poisonous *adj.* 有害的；恶毒的
presumably *adv.* 大概，可能
periodical *n.* 期刊
insularity *n.* (思想，观点的)偏狭
disrupt *vt.* 使混乱，扰乱
dawn *vi.* 开始出现
permeate *vt.&vi.* 渗入；弥漫

READING PASSAGE 3

metropolitan *adj.* 大城市的，大都会的；首府的
monitor *vt.* 监控
cavort *vi.* 跳跃
sewer *n.* 阴沟，污水管，下水道
starve *vt.&vi.* 渴望；饿死
disparate *adj.* （根本）不相同的；（种类）全异的
borough *n.* 区
flank *vt.* 侧面
compelling *adj.* 强制的
amenity *n.* 舒适，便利设施
accountability *n.* 职能
enforcement *n.* 实施，执行

TEST 12

Candidate Number

Candidate Name ______________________

INTERNATIONAL ENGLISH LANGUAGE TESTING SYSTEM

ACADEMIC READING

TIME 1 hour

INSTRUCTIONS TO CANDIDATES

Do not open this booklet until you are told to do so.

Write your name and candidate number in the spaces at the top of this page.

Start at the beginning of the test and work through it.

You should answer **all** questions.

If you cannot do a particular question, leave it and go on to the next. You can return to it later.

All answers must be written on the answer sheet.

Do not remove this booklet from the examination room.

INFORMATION FOR CANDIDATES

There are **40** questions on this question paper.

The test is divided as follows:

Reading Passage 1	Questions 1–13
Reading Passage 2	Questions 14–27
Reading Passage 3	Questions 28–40

Reading Answer Sheet

Are you: Female? ▭ Male? ▭

Your first language code:

0	1	2	3	4	5	6	7	8	9
0	1	2	3	4	5	6	7	8	9
0	1	2	3	4	5	6	7	8	9

IELTS Reading Answer Sheet

Module taken (shade one box): Academic ▭ General Training ▭

		✓	✗			✓	✗
1		1		**21**		21	
2		2		**22**		22	
3		3		**23**		23	
4		4		**24**		24	
5		5		**25**		25	
6		6		**26**		26	
7		7		**27**		27	
8		8		**28**		28	
9		9		**29**		29	
10		10		**30**		30	
11		11		**31**		31	
12		12		**32**		32	
13		13		**33**		33	
14		14		**34**		34	
15		15		**35**		35	
16		16		**36**		36	
17		17		**37**		37	
18		18		**38**		38	
19		19		**39**		39	
20		20		**40**		40	

Checker's Initials		Marker's Initials		Band Score		Reading Total	

READING PASSAGE 1

*You should spend about 20 minutes on **Questions 1–13**, which are based on the Reading Passage1 below.*

Zoo Conservation Programmes

One of London Zoo's recent advertisements caused me some irritation, so patently did it distort reality. Headlined "Without zoos you might as well tell these animals to get stuffed", it was bordered with illustrations of several endangered species and went on to extol the myth that without zoos like London Zoo these animals "will almost certainly disappear forever". With the zoo world's rather mediocre record on conservation, one might be forgiven for being slightly skeptical about such an advertisement.

Zoos were originally created as places of entertainment, and their suggested involvement with conservation didn't seriously arise until about 30 years ago, when the Zoological Society of London held the first formal international meeting on the subject. Eight years later, a series of world conferences took place, entitled "The Breeding of Endangered Species", and from this point onwards conservation became the zoo community's buzzword. This commitment has now been clearly defined in *The World Zoo Conservation Strategy* (WZCS, September 1993), which—although an important and welcome document—does seem to be based on an unrealistic optimism about the nature of the zoo industry.

The WZCS estimates that there are about 10,000 zoos in the world, of which around 1,000 represent a core of quality collections capable of participating in co-coordinated conservation programmes. This is probably the document's first failing, as I believe that 10,000 is a serious underestimate of the total number of places masquerading as zoological establishments. Of course it is difficult to get accurate data but, to put the issue into perspective; I have found that, in a year of working in Eastern Europe, I discover fresh zoos on almost a weekly basis.

The second flaw in the reasoning of the WZCS document is the naive faith it places in its 1,000 core zoos. One would assume that the caliber of these institutions would have been carefully examined, but it appears that the criterion for inclusion on this select list might merely be that the zoo is a member of a zoo federation or association. This might be a good starting point, working on the premise that members must meet certain standards, but again the facts don't support the theory. The greatly respected American Association of Zoological Parks and Aquariums (AAZPA) has had extremely dubious members, and in the UK the Federation of Zoological Gardens of Great Britain and Ireland has occasionally had members that have been roundly censured in the national press. These include Robin Hill Adventure Park on the Isle of Wight, which many considered the most notorious collection of animals in the country. This establishment, which for years was protected by the Isle's local council (which viewed it as a tourist amenity), was finally closed down following a damning report by a veterinary inspector appointed under the terms of *the Zoo Licensing Act 1981*. As it was always a collection of dubious repute, one is obliged to reflect upon the standards that the Zoo Federation sets when granting membership. The situation is even worse in developing countries where little money is available for redevelopment and it is hard to see a way of incorporating collections into the overall scheme of the WZCS.

Even assuming that the WZCS's 1, 000 core zoos are all of a high standard—complete with scientific staff and research facilities, trained and dedicated keepers, accommodation that permits normal or natural behaviour, and a policy of co-operating fully with one another—what might be the potential for conservation?

Colin Tudge, author of *Last Animals at the Zoo* (Oxford University Press, 1992), argues that "if the world's zoos worked together in co-operative breeding programmes, then even without further expansion they could save around 2, 000 species of endangered land vertebrates". This seems an extremely optimistic proposition from a man who must be aware of the failings and weaknesses of the zoo industry—the man who, when a member of the council of London Zoo, had to persuade the zoo to devote more of its activities to conservation. Moreover, where are the facts to support such optimism?

Today approximately 16 species might be said to have been "saved" by captive breeding programmes, although a number of these can hardly be looked upon as resounding successes. Beyond that, about a further 20 species are being seriously considered for zoo conservation programmes. Given that the international conference at London Zoo was held 30 years ago, this is pretty slow progress, and a long way off Tudge's target of 2, 000.

Questions 1–7

Do the following statements agree with the claims of the writer in the Reading Passage 1?

In boxes 1–7 on your answer sheet, write

YES	*if the statement agrees with the claims of the writer*
NO	*if the statement contradicts the claims of the writer*
NOT GIVEN	*if it is impossible to say what the writer thinks about this*

1 One of London Zoo's advertisements is dishonest.

2 Zoos made an insignificant contribution to conservation until 30 years ago.

3 The WZCS document is not known in Eastern Europe.

4 The zoos in the WZCS select list were carefully inspected.

5 No one knew how the animals were being treated at Robin Hill Adventure Park.

6 Colin Tudge was dissatisfied with the treatment of animals at London Zoo.

7 The number of successful zoo conservation programmes is unsatisfactory.

Questions 8–10

Choose the correct letter, ***A, B, C*** *or* ***D****.*

Write the correct letter in boxes 8–10 on your answer sheet.

8 What is the objective of the WZCS document?

A to improve the caliber of zoos worldwide

B to identify zoos suitable for conservation practice

C to provide funds for zoos in underdeveloped countries

D to list the endangered species of the world

9 Why does the writer refer to Robin Hill Adventure Park?

A to support the Isle of Wight local council

B to criticize the *Zoo Licensing Act 1981*

C to illustrate a weakness in the WZCS document

D to exemplify the standards in AAZPA zoos

10 Which word best describes the writer's response to Colin Tudges' prediction on captive breeding programmes?

A disbelieving B impartial C prejudiced D accepting

Questions 11–13

The writer mentions a number of factors which lead him to doubt the value of the WZCS document.

Which ***THREE*** *of the following factors are mentioned?*

Write your answers ***(A–F)*** *in boxes 11–13 on your answer sheet.*

List of Factors

A the number of unregistered zoos in the world

B the lack of money in developing countries

C the actions of the Isle of Wight local council

D the failure of the WZCS to examine the standards of the "core zoos"

E the unrealistic aim of the WZCS in view of the number of species "saved" to date

F the policies of WZCS zoo managers

READING PASSAGE 2

*You should spend about 20 minutes on Questions **14–27**, which are based on Reading Passage 2 below.*

Tidal Power on the Cheap?

A The startup, located on the Orkney Islands, way north of Scotland, has raised £6.2 million to build a working prototype of a floating tidal turbine that it says will be cheaper to install and maintain than others being tested now. The 8-meter-long prototype, ideally, will go into the water at the European Marine Energy Centre (EMEC) Tidal Test Site that sits just down the road from ScotRenewables in 2010. Commercial versions of the turbine will measure up to 40 meters long and weigh 250 tons, but generate 1.2 megawatts of power.

B "That's quite impressive when you compare it to others," said CEO Barry Johnston. "We want to be competitive with offshore wind." Rather than anchor a permanent turbine on the ocean floor, ScotRenewables will build a floating turbine that is slack moored with chains to an anchor on the sea floor. The body of the turbine—a long 40-meter tube of metal with a point at the end—will face directly into the tide. Below, two turbines attached to fins will convert the power of the tides into electricity. Johnston explained "A 1-meter prototype ScotRenewables is experimenting with in the wave tank is built. It looks like a model rocket with two fins with propellers attached to the ends of the fins."

C Tidal is the potentially most predictable, reliable form of renewable energy. With a tide table and computer, ScotRenewables can calculate the power output of a turbine decades in advance. You can't do that with intermittent, variable sources like wind, solar or wave. Unfortunately, harnessing tidal power is quite difficult. Some of the prototypes that have been tested in the decades are quickly destroyed by rushing tides. Pulling those turbines up from the sea bed and taking them into the shop consumes time and money. Taking the ScotRenewables turbine in for repairs should be easy: maintenance workers would just have to take a boat out, unhook it, and put another in its place while the first is being entangled.

D Tidal power is also 50 percent stronger at the surface than at the seabed so these turbines should be capable of generating more power. Other companies have tried to create surface tidal turbines before. The difficulty has been keeping the turbine pointed in the direction of the tide. Some get washed away. Other times, the creators build large superstructures around the turbine, which costs money. ScotRenewables says it will come up with control mechanisms and advanced hydrodynamics (i.e., aerodynamics in water) to keep the turbines pointed in the right direction.

E Scotland is betting heavily on wind and wave power. The notoriously harsh waves and currents of the Pentland Firth, a channel which separates the main body of the U.K. with the Orkneys that is often referred to as the Saudi Arabia of Marine Energy by locals. By 2020, Scotland wants to get half of its power from renewable sources, including large hydroelectric dams. Hydroelectric constitutes about 11 percent of the country's power now and 9 percent comes from wind and other renewables. A large portion of the new renewable sources of power will come from wind, tidal and wave. Marine energy could provide up to 35 terawatt hours of power to the U.K. by 2020 and 84 terawatt hours of power by 2050, according to Edwina Cook, business development officer at EMEC. The U.K. in 2004 consumed 340 terawatt hours of power. The EMEC has created tidal and wave testing centers for companies to build and validate prototypes. (The Pelamis—that sea snake looking wave power device—was tested at EMEC before commercial rollouts in Portugal.) The government has also passed exceptionally large credits for power providers that put tidal and wave power on the grid. (Prototypes participating in the EMEC test beds are actually connected to the grid and selling small amounts of power.) The hope is that the programme will create jobs, exports and green energy. Offshore, the Dublin based Open Hydro Power is already testing a large tidal device that looks like a big rotating fan.

F Talking about the prototype and commercial power production, however, is easier said than done. ScotRenewables did not like the software simulation tools it found when it first set out. Some software focused on tidal changes; others focused on waves. To build an effective surface tidal turbine, Johnston realised that both tidal and wave power should be taken into account. Thus, it had to build its own tools, which cost several thousands. It also built its own wave tank. It was easier than trying to book time at an EMEC wave tank. The company now hopes to lease time on the tank to other wave companies to generate revenue. And, because ships to deploy tidal and wave devices are in short supply, it is contemplating buying or building its own multi-purpose vessel.

Questions 14–18

Complete the summary below.

Choose ***NO MORE THAN TWO WORDS*** *from the passage for each answer.*

Write your answers in boxes 14–18 on your answer sheet.

The experiment ScotRenewables does is taking advantages of tidal power rather than those sources such as **14** ...., solar and wave. The turbine output can be counted by use of **15** .... as well as computer. Upon the past failure, some companies found it hard to keep the turbine pointed to the **16** ...., but ScotRenewables had the confidence to cope with such problems by building up **17** .... and advanced hydrodynamics in water. The EMEC has developed tidal and wave testing centers to validate prototypes. Also, **18** .... are passed by government aiming to put tidal and wave power on the grid.

Questions 19–22

Reading Passage 2 has six sections labelled **A–F**.

Which paragraph contains the following information?

Write the correct letter, ***A–F****, in boxes 19–22 on your answer sheet.*

19 New plan has been made to involve a new factor besides tidal.

20 Damages have happened to the models in the past years.

21 A detailed structure of a model is demonstrated.

22 The immature model is expected to apply at the beginning of the twenty first century after further development.

Questions 23–27

Do the following statements agree with the information given in Reading Passage 2?

In boxes 23–27 on your answer sheet, write

TRUE	*if the statement agrees with the information*
FALSE	*if the statement contradicts the information*
NOT GIVEN	*if there is no information on this*

23 Floating turbine is not good enough because it could not be anchored to the ocean floor forever.

24 Tidal has proved to be forecasted upon the renewable energy.

25 ScotRenewables model is easier to repair because it will take less time to replace.

26 Scientists have enough experience to design and modify the prototype so as to put it into commercial use.

27 Booking time at an EMEC wave tank is more difficult than the ScotRenewables.

READING PASSAGE 3

*You should spend about 20 minutes on **Questions 28–40**, which are based on Reading Passage 3 below.*

The Great Barrier Reef

All along the Queensland coast, inshore coral reefs, smothered by silt and algae, are dying. Some lagoons and reefs, once pristine examples of a tropical paradise, now consist of broken skeletons of dead coral, buried in layers of silt. Even the most remote reefs are at risk of pollution from tourist resorts releasing sewage and ships dumping their rubbish. Tourists are so numerous that at one popular reef, urine from swimmers, and droppings from fish they feed, have increased the nutrient level in the water so much that algal blooms flourish and threaten the very existence of the colourful corals.

Marine experts say about 70% of coral reefs around the world are dead or severely degraded. Australia's Great Barrier Reef, the globe's largest reef system, stretching 2, 300 kilometers and comprising 2, 900 separate reefs, is in better shape than most. But experts warn that it requires concerted effort and diligence to keep it that way and in some places it is already too late.

The Great Barrier Reef is internationally renowned for its spectacular marine life and the tourist and fishing industries are economically important. Reef-based tourism and fishing have a combined economic worth of more than $1 billion a year. Reef tourism is now more valuable than sugar exports and tourist numbers are forecast to quadruple within eight years. The industry depends on protecting a spectacular marine environment that is home to at least 10,000 species of animals (including 400 varieties of coral) and plants. They include such endangered creatures as the dugong, the giant clam and the humpback whale.

It is an environment so little known that thousands more species almost certainly await discovery: during one recent 12 month field study, 200, 000 new biological records, information not previously known to science, were made. Many promising compounds for new medical treatments and other products are being discovered on the reef. Compounds derived from sponges and other reef organisms are being evaluated in the United States for possible use in drugs to fight cancer and AIDS. Through newly developing technology, corals are giving us an extraordinary insight into past weather patterns.

Scientists have discovered that long-lived corals on the Great Barrier Reef are vast storehouses of weather information. Over the centuries, corals have absorbed humid acid from plant material washed into the reef from Mainland Rivers. By examining bands in coral skeletons (analogous to tree rings) under ultraviolet light, scientists have been able to trace rainfall levels back to the 1640s; eventually, they will know what the rainfall was at least 1, 000 years ago.

Sadly, after several years of research, marine experts agree that inshore reefs are being devastated by a vast deluge of sediment and nutrients washed into the sea as a result of development on the mainland. Some claim that outer reefs will eventually meet the same fate. As internationally renowned marine scientist Leon Zann sums it up: "It's not the waste on the beaches we have to worry about, it's what we can't see below the surface".

The reef is being assaulted on other fronts:

- Research suggests that a new invasion of crown-of-thorns starfish, a coral devouring creature, may be imminent. Authorities believe that human activities are implicated in such population explosions.
- Fresh outbreaks of coral bleaching—which occurs when rising temperatures cause polyps to discard the tiny algae that give reefs their colours and which is linked by some scientists to the greenhouse effect, are being recorded.
- Catches of reef fish by commercial and recreational fishermen are falling.
- Ships are illegally discharging oil and dumping garbage; with only one ranger per 5, 200 square kilometers of the Great Barrier Reef Marine Park, it is difficult to stop them.
- In a controversial move, the oil industry—with the government's blessing—plans to explore waters off the reef for petroleum within the next decade.

Australia is regarded internationally as being in the forefront of reef management and research and is providing $2 million worth of advice on marine issues this year to other countries. Australian scientists have advised Ecuador on how to protect the seas around the famed Galapagos Islands and are helping the Association of South-East Asian Nations to monitor their marine environment, where 80% of reefs are ruined and fish stocks are close to collapse. The hope is that the Great Barrier Reef will avoid a similar fate.

Questions 28–31

*Choose the correct letter, **A**, **B**, **C** or **D**.*

Write the correct letter in boxes 28–31 on your answer sheet.

28 The Great Barrier Reef

A has mostly been destroyed.

B could die in the next decade.

C is healthier than most other reef systems.

D is in good condition.

29 Corals are scientifically valued because

A they can be made into medicine.

B they provide shelter for plants.

C fish feed on them.

D climatic change is recorded in them.

30 Dangers to the marine environment include

A warmer water.

B coral skeletons.

C new fish species.

D sponges.

31 Oil exploration

A has provided an income to the Great Barrier Reef Marine Park.

B will continue for 10 years.

C although supported by the government, is not popular.

D can help scientists monitor marine life.

Questions 32–34

Look at the following questions and the list of answers below.

*Match each question with the correct answer, **A–J**.*

Write the correct letter, A–J, in boxes 32–34 on your answer sheet.

32 What causes the most devastation to the coral reefs?

33 Why are scientists still able to make discoveries in the reef system?

34 What is destroying the reefs near the mainland?

A	sediments and nutrients
B	technology
C	there are too few marine scientists
D	fishing
E	fish and swimmers
F	there are so many marine species
G	it is still largely unexplored
H	damage
I	pollution
J	tourists and ships

Questions 35–37

Complete the summary below.

Choose ***ONE WORD ONLY*** *from the passage for each answer.*

Write your answers in boxes 35–37 on your answer sheet.

The Great Barrier Reef, the most extensive reef system in the **35** ……………, is important to weather experts who, by studying the structure of **36** ……………, can learn more about amounts of **37** …………… centuries ago.

Questions 38–40

Answer the questions below.

Choose ***NO MORE THAN TWO WORDS*** *from the passage for each answer.*

Write your answers in boxes 38–40 on your answer sheet.

38 Which marine animal is seriously threatening coral?

39 Whose job is it to protect the reef?

40 Which country has been given a suggestion by Australian scientists on how to protect the seas?

Test 12 答案速查 Key

READING PASSAGE 1

1. YES	**2.** YES	**3.** NOT GIVEN	**4.** NO
5. NO	**6.** NOT GIVEN	**7.** YES	**8.** B
9. C	**10.** A	**11.** A	**12.** D
13. E			

READING PASSAGE 2

14. wind	**15.** tide table	**16.** tide direction
17. control mechanisms	**18.** large credits	**19.** F
20. C	**21.** B	**22.** A
23. FALSE	**24.** FALSE	**25.** FALSE
26. NOT GIVEN	**27.** TRUE	

READING PASSAGE 3

28. C	**29.** D	**30.** A
31. C	**32.** I	**33.** G
34. A	**35.** world	**36.** coral (s)
37. rain /rainfall	**38.** crown-of-thorns starfish	**39.** ranger
40. Ecuador		

Test 12 考题精解 Detailed Explanation

READING PASSAGE 1

Questions 1–7

题型：判断题 (YES/NO/NOT GIVEN)

◆ 解析

1. YES

根据关键词advertisements 将答案定位在原文第一段的第一句One of London Zoo's recent advertisements caused me some irritation, so patently did it distort reality London Zoo's advertisements are dishonest，其意思是伦敦动物园最近的一则广告让我有些愤

怒，因为它明显地歪曲了事实。而题干One of London Zoo's advertisements is dishonest.意思是伦敦动物园的一则广告不符合实际。题干中的dishonest对应原文的distort。因此，答案为YES。

2. YES

根据关键词30 years ago将答案定位在第二段第一句Zoos were originally created as places of entertainment, and their suggested involvement with conservation didn't seriously arise until about 30 years ago, when the Zoological Society of London held the first formal international meeting on the subject，其意思是动物园起初是作为娱乐场所而建立的，并且直到30年前动物园才建议并认真参与到保护动物的计划中，即当时伦敦动物学会针对这一课题首次举行了正式的国际会议。题干中Zoos made an insignificant contribution to conservation until 30 years ago其意思是直到30年前动物园在保护（动物）方面的贡献才突出。题干中的insignificant对应原文的didn't serious arise因此，答案为YES。

3. NOT GIVEN

根据关键词WZCS document和East Europe将答案定位在第三段，该段的意思是WZCS预估世界上约有10 000所动物园，其中大概有1 000所动物园代表了参与合作保护动物项目的质量集合的核心。这可能是此文件的第一个失败之处，因为我相信这10 000的数据严重低估了伪装成动物学机构的总数。当然若想获得精准的数据是非常困难的，但是带着这一问题去观察，在我在东欧工作的一年里，基本上一周左右就会有一些新的动物园出现。而题干的意思是保护世界动物园战略在东欧并不出名。显然原文没有谈到这个问题，因此，答案为NOT GIVEN。

4. NO

根据关键词WZCS select list将答案定位在第四段前两句话The second flaw in the reasoning of the WZCS document is the naive faith it places in its 1, 000 core zoos. One would assume that the caliber of these institutions would have been carefully examined, but it appears that the criterion for inclusion on this select list might merely be that the zoo is a member of a zoo federation or association，其意思是WZCS文件的第二个败笔在于投入到那1 000所核心动物园上的天真理念。人们认为这些机构的水平应该是经过仔细检验的，但是显而易见，包含在选择列表中的标准可能仅仅是这家动物园为动物园联盟或动物园协会的成员而已。虽然题干中的carefully inspected和原文的carefully examined对应，但是整体看来题干中...were carefully inspected是肯定语气，而原文的...would have been carefully examined是虚拟语气，因此答案为NO。

5. NO

根据关键词Robin Hill Adventure Park将答案定位在第四段第八行These include Robin

Hill Adventure Park on the Isle of Wight, which many considered the most notorious collection of animals in the country，这一句意思是包括怀特岛的罗宾冒险公园，许多人认为它是国内最声名狼藉的动物聚集地。而题干的意思是没有人知道在罗宾希尔冒险公园中动物是如何被对待的，显然，答案是NO。

6. NOT GIVEN

根据关键词Colin Tudge将答案定位在第六段的前两句，它的意思是《动物园里最后的动物》（牛津大学出版社，1992年）的作者科林·图什，提出“如果全世界的动物园致力于合作培育计划，即使没有进一步扩充，他们仍然能挽救约2 000种濒危陆生脊椎动物”。这对于必须认识到动物园产业的败笔及弱点的人来说是一种非常乐观的观点——作为一名伦敦动物园协会的成员，就不得不说服动物园投入更多的行动来保护动物。显然这里没有提到他对伦敦动物园对待动物方式的态度。所以，答案是NOT GIVEN。

7. YES

根据关键词successful zoo conservation programmes可将答案定位到文章最后一段，阅读上下文找出能够反映人们态度的两处意群，即a number of these can hardly be looked upon as resounding successes（这些数字很难被认定是成功之作）和this is pretty slow progress, and a long way off Tudge's target of 2, 000（这是一个相当缓慢的进程，图哲计划还有很长的路要走），由此可判断出题干所述“成功的动物园保护项目的数量并不令人满意”是正确的，因此，答案是YES。

Questions 8–10

题型：选择题 (MULTIPLE CHOICE)

◆ 解析

8. B

题干的大致意思：世界动物园保护策略的目的是什么

文章中出现WZCS的部分是第二、三和四段，从第三段的主题句This is probably the document's first failing以及第四段的主题句The second flaw in the reasoning of the WZCS document is...可知这两段分别讲WZCS的两个缺点。因此答案应在第二段，读WZCS周围上下文...onwards conservation became the zoo community's buzzword. This commitment has now been clearly defined in...可知答案选B。A说的是提高动物园的水准，B说的是确定适合保护计划的动物园，C说的是为发展中国家的动物园提供资金，D说的是列出世界濒危物种。

9. C

题干问为什么作者提到Robin Hill Adventure Park。由Robin Hill Adventure Park可将答案

定位在倒数第四段，由该段首句The second flaw in the reasoning of the WZCS document is the naive faith...可知该段主要讲述的是WZCS的不足，而Robin Hill Adventure Park就是其不足的例证之一，所以C举例说明WZCS文件的不足是正确选项。

10. A

题干问哪一个词能最好地形容作者对科林·图哲预测的保护计划的回应。根据关键词Colin Tudges可将答案定位在倒数第二段，纵观整段，只有最后一句话是作者对图哲计划的态度，最后一句反问去哪里找支持这种乐观主义的事实依据呢？由此可见，作者对图哲的预测保护计划是不信的。选项A正确。

Questions 11–13

题型：选择题 (MULTIPLE CHOICE)

◆ 解析

11–13 A, D, E

11–13题干的意思是要考生找出作者提到的三点使他怀疑世界动物园保护计划价值的因素。根据题干的关键词WZCS document可将答案定位在文章的第二段及其以下段落，再由另外一个关键词doubt可将答案缩小在第二、三、四段，因为这个document有缺点和不足才可能使作者对他产生疑问。第二段的最后一句可以选出E项，第三段第三句话可以选出A项。再由第四段的第二句..., but it appears that the criterion for...可选出D选项，而且题干中的standard对应原文criterion，可知D是正确的。其他选项的意思是B发展中国家缺乏资金，C怀特岛委员会的行动，F世界在动物园保护计划里的动物园负责人的政策，这些都是第四段的一些例证但不是使作者怀疑的原因。

◎ 参考译文

动物园保护计划

伦敦动物园最近的一则广告让我有些愤怒，因为它竟如此公然地歪曲事实。广告的标题是“没有动物园你最好还是让这些动物喂饱自己”，广告的边缘还配了几幅濒危动物的插图，该广告不断颂扬这一荒诞的说法——若没有像伦敦动物园这样的动物园，这些动物“基本上会永远消失”。鉴于动物园在保护动物方面的成绩平平，人们稍微质疑一下这样一个广告也情有可原。

动物园起初是作为娱乐场所而建立的，并且直到30年前动物园才建议并认真参与到保护动物的计划中，当时伦敦动物学会针对这一课题首次举行了正式的国际会议。八年之后，又召开了一系列名为“濒危物种繁衍”的世界会议，从此之后保护动物成为动物园组织的口号。这一承诺现在已经被明确定义在《世界动物园保护策略》（简称WZCS，1993

年9月）中——虽然这是一个重要并且受欢迎的文件，但却似乎是建立在对动物园产业不现实的乐观主义之上。

WZCS预估世界上约有10 000所动物园，其中大概有1 000所动物园代表了参与合作保护动物项目的质量集合的核心。这可能是此文件的第一个失败之处，因为我相信这10 000的数据严重低估了伪装成动物学机构的总数。当然若想获得精准的数据是非常困难的，但是带着这一问题去观察，在我在东欧工作的一年里，基本上一周左右就会有一些新的动物园出现。

WZCS文件的第二个败笔在于投入到那1 000所核心动物园上的天真理念。人们认为这些机构的水平本应该是经过仔细检验的，但是显而易见，包含在选择列表中的标准可能仅仅是这家动物园为动物园联盟或动物园协会的成员而已。这也许是一个良好的起点，以成员必须符合一定标准为前提，但事实仍不支持这一理论。备受尊敬的美国动物园和水族馆协会（AAZPA）已经出现一些异常可疑的成员了，在英国，大不列颠和爱尔兰动物园联盟的一些成员偶尔会招致全民责难，包括怀特岛的罗宾希尔冒险公园，许多人认为它是国内最声名狼藉的动物聚集地。这个被该岛的当地政府（作为一处旅游场所）保护多年的机构，最终因为一个由1981年《动物园许可条例》指定的兽医检查员所做出的毁灭性报告而关闭。由于其名声总是被不断质疑，所以人们应该反思动物园联盟会要对准许加入的成员设定标准。对于只有少量资金可以用于再开发的发展中国家，形势更为糟糕，他们很难找到一种合并到WZCS总体方案中的方式。

即使假设WZCS的1 000个核心动物园都具备高标准——即拥有完备的科研人员、研究设施和受过培训的专业管理人员、允许正常或自然行为的栖息场所和一项彼此充分合作的政策——那么什么可能会成为动物保护措施的潜在力量？

《动物园里最后的动物》（牛津大学出版社，1992年）的作者科林·图哲，提出“如果全世界的动物园致力于合作培育计划，即使没有进一步扩充，他们仍然能挽救约2 000种濒危陆生脊椎动物”。这对于必须认识到动物园产业的败笔及弱点的人来说是一种非常乐观的观点——作为一名伦敦动物园协会的成员，就不得不说服动物园采取更多的行动来保护动物。而且，哪里才能找到支持这种乐观主义的事实呢？

如今大概有16个物种被认为是培育计划中的“挽救”对象，尽管这些数字很难被认定是成功之作。除此之外，另有20多个物种将被正式地列入动物园保护计划中。鉴于30年前在伦敦动物园举办的国际会议，要实现图哲提出的挽救2 000种濒危陆生脊椎动物的计划真的是一个非常缓慢的进程，还要走很长的一段路。

READING PASSAGE 2

Questions 14–18

题型：摘要填空题 (SUMMARY COMPLETION)

◆ 解析

14. wind

根据题干关键词experiment, ScotRenewables, solar和wave可定位到原文C段第三句，其中like和such as 是同义表达，因而答案是wind。

15. tide table

根据题干关键词output, use, computer可定位到原文C段，该段第二句中with表使用，and computer和as well as computer，calculate 和count为同义表达，因而答案是tide table。

16. tide direction

根据题干关键词hard, pointing to可定位到原文D段，该段第三句中difficulty和hard为同义表达，因而答案是tide direction。

17. control mechanisms

根据题干关键词ScotRenewables, building up, advanced hydrodynamics可定位到原文D段该段最后一句中come up with 和building up为同义表达，因而答案是control mechanisms。

18. large credits

根据题干关键词EMEC, government, put tidal and wave power on the grid 可定位到原文E段中部，题干用被动将原文的主动表现出来，因而答案是large credits。

Questions 19–22

题型：配对题 (MATCHING)

◆ 解析

19. F

根据题干关键词New plan, a new factor和tidal可定位到原文F段第四句，其中...both tidal and wave power...为并列关系（both...and...），它对应题干中的关键词besides，而定位词tidal在原文中重现，故判断题干中提到的new factor 一定与原文中的wave power有关，因而答案是F。

20. C

根据题干关键词Damages, in the past years可定位到原文C段第五句，句中出现了destroy这个词，和damages为同义转换，而in the decades和 in the past years为同义转换，因而答案是C。

21. B

根据题干关键词detailed structure of model可定位到原文B段，该段详细阐述了模型的构造，最后一句中又有model的重现，因而答案是B。

22. A

根据题干关键词immature model, at the beginning of the twenty first century可定位到原文A段，该段prototype和model为同义转换，2010与at the beginning of the twenty first century 在时间上有所对应，因而答案是A。

Questions 23–27

题型：判断题 (TRUE/FALSE/NOT GIVEN)

◆ 解析

23. FALSE

根据题干关键词Floating turbine, be anchored, forever可定位到原文B段，其中forever与permanent为同义转换，答案定位到B段的第三句话及后面的内容，整句均是对floating turbine持正面评价的，题干中的not good enough与此相悖，因此答案是FALSE。

24. FALSE

根据题干关键词forecasted, renewable energy可定位到原文C段，该段第一句话就出现了关键词forecast的同义表达predictable，但原文讲潮汐能很可能是可预测的能源，而题干则说已经证明了，属于偷换概念，因此答案为FALSE。

25. FALSE

根据题干关键词ScotRenewables model, easier, replace可定位到原文C段最后一句，由该句可知说ScotRenewables turbine维修简单的原因在于其操作流程很简单，而并不是题干所说的因为花费时间少，因此答案为FALSE。

26. NOT GIVEN

根据题干关键词enough experience prototype, commercial use可定位到原文F段，关键词prototype, commercial虽然可以在原文找到，可与题干没有关系,因而答案只能选NOT GIVEN。

27. TRUE

根据题干关键词Booking time, EMEC wave tank, more difficult可定位到原文F段，由本段倒数第三句话可知本题答案为TRUE。

◎ 参考译文

潮汐能源价格低廉?

A 位于苏格兰北部奥克尼群岛的主办方筹集了620万英镑用于建造浮动潮汐涡轮的模

型。据说该模型的安装和维修成本要比目前正在测试的一些其他涡轮的成本都要低。预计，这个八米长的模型将于2010年在欧洲海洋能源中心潮汐试验基地入水，该中心位于ScotRenewables（一家研究潮汐涡轮发电技术公司）的沿路。用于商业的涡轮长仅有40米，重仅有250吨，但能够产生1.2兆瓦特的功率。

B　“与其他涡轮相比，它的确令人印象深刻”，首席执行官巴里·约翰斯顿说：“我们想与离岸风竞争。”ScotRenewables将把一个漂浮的涡轮用链条松弛地固定在海底的锚上，而不是在海底的锚上固定一个永久的涡轮。涡轮的主体——一个带有金属的管，末端很尖，长达40米——将直接朝向潮流。机体下面，两个连在翼展上的涡轮将潮水能量转化成电能。约翰斯顿解释道“一个一米长的模型正在ScotRenewables建的造波水池中试验。它外形像是一个带有一对机翼的火箭模型，在每个机翼的末端都有几个螺旋推进器。”

C　潮汐可能是最易预测的，最可靠的可再生资源。通过潮汐表和电脑显示，ScotRenewables可以提前几十年测算出一个涡轮的功率输出。如果是一些断续的、易变的资源，如太阳能，或波浪，你就无法测算。不幸的是，利用潮汐能源也相当困难。近几十年投入测试的一些模型都是很快地被急流摧毁了。把这些涡轮从海底拉出来再送去商铺维修不仅耗时费力，而且还增加了成本。而把ScotRenewables的涡轮送修则应该很简单：维修工人只需要把一艘船拉出来，解开，在这艘船上的涡轮进行维修时，用另一艘船载好涡轮暂代其放在原有位置即可。

D　海面的潮汐能量要比海底的能量高50%，因此涡轮也应能产生更多功率。之前也有其他公司尝试创造海面潮汐涡轮。如何让涡轮指向潮流的方向一直都是个难题。其中有一些涡轮被冲走了。还有些创造者花费巨资在涡轮周围建立超大型建筑。ScotRenewables将使用调控装置和高级的流体力学（如水中空气动力学）来确保涡轮的正确指向。

E　苏格兰很依赖风能和波浪能。彭特蓝湾，不仅把英联邦主体与被当地人喻为海洋能源的沙特阿拉伯隔开，而且还因其巨浪疾流而闻名。到2020年，苏格兰想要从可再生资源中开发一半的能源，其中包括大型的水力电气大坝。水力电气目前占该国能源的11%，风能和其他能源占9%。很大一部分新的可再生能源将来自风、潮汐和波浪。据欧洲海洋能源中心商业发展官员埃德温娜·库克统计，海洋能源到2020年将给英国提供高达35太瓦时的功率，到2050年达到84太瓦时的功率。英国2004年就消费了340太瓦时的功率。

欧洲海洋能源中心已经为一些公司建立了潮汐和波浪测试中心，并已证实了模型的有用性。（Pelamis——外形酷似海蛇的测试波浪仪器——已在葡萄牙首次商业展出之前通了测试。）政府还为能将潮汐列入电网的能源供应商提供了巨额的贷款。（在

EMEC参加测试的原型事实上都和电网相连接，并出售少量的电。）这个项目的前景在于可以增加就业，促进出口和生产绿色能源。海面上，以都柏林为基础的露天水电厂正在测试一个巨大的潮汐仪器，该仪器看起来像一个旋转式风扇。

F　然而，模型的创建和商业用电的生产等这些课题，说起来容易，做起来难。建设伊始，ScotRenewables根本不喜欢软件模拟工具。这些软件有的关注潮汐变化，有的则关注波浪动向。约翰斯顿意识到，要想建立一个有效的水面潮汐涡轮，就要把潮汐能和波浪都要考虑进去。因此，ScotRenewables不得不花费上万英镑来制造自己的工具。与此同时，它还建立了自己的造波水池。这比在EMEC预定造波水池容易很多。公司现在希望将水池租赁给其他波浪公司，并以此来获得利润。因为缺少配置潮汐设备的船，公司正在考虑是购买还是建造属于自己的多功能船。

READING PASSAGE 3

Questions 28–31

题型：选择题 (MULTIPLE CHOICE)

◆ 解析

28. C

题干关键词是Great Barrier Reef，由于本篇文章主要讲的是Great Barrier Reef，因此该词在文中出现的频率很高，只能一段一段的往下寻找，该词最先出现在原文第二段的第二句Australia's Great Barrier Reef, the globe's largest reef system, stretching 2, 300 kilometers and comprising 2, 900 separate reefs, is in better shape than most，仔细阅读不难得知该句的Australia's Great Barrier Reef...is in better shape than most与选项C是对应的。注意 in shape 意为“健康”，与healthy为同义词转换。

29. D

本题的关键词并不明显，scientifically很容易被替换成其他词性的与科学相关的词。仔细阅读全文，不难发现关于珊瑚的科学价值的讲述集中在第四段和第五段，根据第四段的最后一句Through newly developing technology, corals are giving us an extraordinary insight into past weather patterns和第五段的第一句Scientists have discovered that long-lived corals on the Great Barrier Reef are vast storehouses of weather information，可知科学家们可以通过珊瑚了解天气信息，weather 与climate为同义替换 ，正确答案为D。

30. A

题干问的是对海洋环境的威胁都是什么。定位词为danger在原文倒数第二段（有分类符号的那段）的第二点Fresh outbreaks of coral bleaching—which occurs when rising temperatures cause polyps to discard the tiny algae that give reefs their colors and which is linked by some scientists to the greenhouse effect, are being recorded，其中的when rising temperature

与warmer对应。陷阱答案为C因为前文提到了一个crown-of-thorns starfish，但这是一个物种的爆发而不是一个新物种。

31. C

根据题干关键词oil exploration可定位到原文倒数第二段的尾句In a controversial move, the oil industry—with the government's blessing—plans to explore waters off the reef for petroleum within the next decade，controversial代表有争议，即虽然有政府保护，但是是有争议的，跟原文C的表述相符。陷阱答案是B，文中只提到计划10内年去开采，但没提到会持续多久，所以B项错误。

Questions 32–34

题型：配对题 (MATCHING)

◆ 解析

32. I

根据题干关键词devastation和coral reefs可定位到原文第一段的第三句Even the most remote reefs are at risk of pollution from tourist resorts releasing sewage and ships dumping their rubbish，由此可知给珊瑚礁带来破坏性灾害的是污染。

33. G

根据题干关键词 scientists和discoveries可定位到原文第四段第一句It is an environment so little known that thousands more species almost certainly await discovery: during one recent 12 month field study, 200, 000 new biological records, information not previously known to science, were made，由该句可知有千余多物种有待发现，所以科学家们之所以能够有所发现，是因为还有大量的礁系未被勘探。

34. A

根据题干关键词near the mainland，可定位到原文倒数第三段首句Sadly, after several years of research, marine experts agree that inshore reefs are being devastated by a vast deluge of sediment and nutrients washed into the sea as a result of development on the mainland，由该句可知是sediment and nutrients毁坏了珊瑚礁。

Questions 35–37

题型：摘要填空 (SUMMARY COMPLETION)

◆ 解析

35. world

根据题干关键词The Great Barrier Reef, extensive定位到原文第二段的第二句Great

Barrier Reef, the globe's largest reef system,所以答案是world。

36. coral (s)

关键词wealth，因为第四段整个是在讲珊瑚礁 所以填coral。

37. rainfall

根据题干关键词centuries ago定位到第五段尾句：eventually, they will know what the rainfall was at least 1, 000 years ago，所以填rainfall。

Questions 38–40

题型：简答题 (SHORT ANSWER QUESTIONS)

◆ 解析

38. crown-of-thorns starfish

题干意思是什么珊瑚礁动物严重的干扰了珊瑚礁？

找到倒数第二段的第一点，crown-of-thorns starfish 是惟一出现的动物。

39. ranger

题干意思是谁的工作是保护珊瑚？

找到倒数第二段的第三点：Ships are illegally discharging oil and dumping garbage; with only one ranger per 5, 200 square kilometers of the Great Barrier Reef Marine Park, it is difficult to stop them.

这题比较隐蔽，但是没有干扰的答案，文中提到的科学家的工作是研究，而真正进行保护的应是ranger。

40. Ecuador

题干意思是澳大利亚科学家就如何保护海洋，给哪个国家提供了建议？

由题干关键词Australian scientists和 on how to protect the seas可定位到最后一段第二句，由该句可知澳大利亚科学家提供建议的国家是Ecuador。

◎ 参考译文

大堡礁

沿着昆士兰海岸线，沿海的珊瑚礁覆盖于淤泥和海藻之下，正濒临死亡。某些泻湖和环礁，曾是热带天堂的未受污染的范例，现在却遍布着死珊瑚的残骸，这些残骸被埋在淤泥之下。甚至离岸最远的礁石也冒着被污染的风险，这些污染来源于度假村排放的污水以及船只倾倒的垃圾。对于那些受欢迎的礁石，由于游客太多以至于他们游泳时排泄的小便，以及他们喂食的鱼所排泄的粪便，都大大增加了水域的营养程度导致海藻的茂盛生长，威胁到了丰富多彩的珊瑚们的存活。

海洋专家指出全球大约70%的珊瑚礁已经死亡或者严重退化。澳大利亚的大堡礁，全球最大的礁系，延伸2 300公里同时包含2 900个不同的礁石，正处于最好的状态。然而专家警告要保持大堡礁这种状态需要共同的努力，而实际上有些地方已经太晚了。

大堡礁由于其壮观的海洋生物，以及对经济发展非常重要的旅游业和渔业而闻名国际。以珊瑚礁为基础的旅游和捕鱼一年产生的合计经济价值超过10亿美元。目前礁脉旅游比糖类出口更有价值，而游客数量预计8年内将达到目前的四倍。这个产业取决于对壮丽的海洋环境的保护，这里至少生活着1万种动物（包括400种不同的珊瑚）和植物。其中包括像儒艮，巨蚌以及座头鲸这样濒危的物种。

在最近一个为期12个月的领域研究表明由于这里的环境不为人所知以至于千余多物种正有待发现，这次研究得到了20万个以前不为科学界所知的新的生物学记录和信息。正在对礁石进行的研究可以得到许多有希望用于新的医学治疗的复合物和其他的产物。美国对从海绵体得到的复合物和其他礁石组织器官进行评估，衡量它们在抗癌和治疗艾滋病药物中使用的可能性。通过使用最新开发的技术，珊瑚可以向我们展示对过去天气状况的非凡的洞察力。

科学家已经发现大堡礁中长寿的珊瑚们是巨大的储存天气信息的宝库。几个世纪以来，珊瑚从被内陆河流冲击到礁石的内部的植物中吸收潮湿的酸。通过紫外线光检查珊瑚的骨骼带（类似树的年轮），科学家们可以追溯17世纪40年代的雨量；最终，他们将会知道至少1 000年以前的雨量。

令人难过的是，经过多年研究，海洋专家承认，由于内陆的发展将大量的沉积物和营养物质冲进海里导致近海的礁石正在被毁坏。有些人认为离岸的礁石终将面临相同的命运。正如国际知名海洋科学家利昂·赞恩所总结的：我们要担心的不是海滩上面的垃圾，而是那些我们看不到的表面之下的东西。

礁石受到冲击的其他方面：

- 研究表明以珊瑚为食的棘冠海星的新的侵袭迫在眉睫。权威人士相信该物种的爆发与人类活动有关。
- 新爆发的珊瑚变白——当升高的温度导致水螅弃食那些使礁石富有颜色的微小海藻时，珊瑚开始变白而水螅的行为也被一些科学家与温室效应联系起来并记录在案。
- 商业及休闲娱乐的钓鱼者所捕获的礁石鱼类正在减少。
- 船只在海洋非法卸油以及倾倒垃圾；然而大堡礁海洋公园里每5 200平方公里只有一个巡警队员，很难阻止这些非法行为。

一个有争议的行动是，受政府保护的石油企业，计划在未来十年在礁石周围水域勘探石油。

澳大利亚被国际认为一直处于管理研究礁石的最前线，今年它给其他国家提供的解决海洋事务的建议折算成钱的话几乎价值200万美元。澳大利亚科学家为厄瓜多尔在怎样保护著名的加拉帕克斯海滩周围海域的问题上提供建议，同时帮助东南亚国家联盟监控他们的海洋环境，在那里80%的礁系遭到毁坏而且鱼类的存量接近崩溃。希望大堡礁将免于同样的命运。

Test 12 核心词汇 Core Vocabulary

READING PASSAGE 1

irritation *n.* 激怒；恼怒；生气
patently *adv.* 明白地；公然地
distort *vt.* 歪曲，曲解
extol *vt.* 赞颂，赞扬
skeptical *adj.* 怀疑性的，好怀疑的
onwards *adv.* 向前
buzzword *n.* 流行行话
underestimate *n.* 低估
masquerade *vt.* 假装（是），冒充
perspective *n.* 远景，景；观点，想法
criterion *n.* 标准，准则
federation *n.* 联邦；同盟，联盟
aquarium *n.* 养鱼缸；水族馆
dubious *adj.* 半信半疑的，可疑的
veterinary inspector 兽医检验
dedicated *adj.* 专注的；献身的
resounding *adj.* 鸣响的，回响的，回荡的，响亮的

READING PASSAGE 2

prototype *n.* 原型，雏形，蓝本
turbine *n.* 涡轮机
permanent *adj.* 永久（性）的
slack *adj.* 松弛的
moor *vt.&vi.* 系住，使停泊
fin *n.* （汽车、飞机、炸弹上的）尾翅
propeller *n.* 螺旋桨，推进器
intermittent *adj.* 间歇的，断断续续的
harness *n.* 治理，利用
hydroelectric *adj.* 水力发电的
notoriously *adv.* 臭名昭著地，名声狼藉地
validate *vt.* 证实，确证
rotate *vt.&vi.* 旋转
simulation *n.* 模仿，模拟
lease *n.* 租约，租契
deploy *vt.* 配置
contemplate *vt.&vi.* 思考，细想
vessel *n.* 船，舰

READING PASSAGE 3

inshore *adj.* 近海岸的，内陆的
smother *vt.&vi.*（使）窒息，（使）透不过气
silt *n.* 淤泥，淤滓
lagoon *n.* 泻湖
pristine *adj.* 原始状态的；未受损的
sewage *n.*（下水道里的）污物
urine *n.* 尿
dropping *n.* 兽粪
algal *adj.* 海藻的
diligence *n.* 勤勉，勤奋
spectacular *adj.* 壮观的，雄伟的，引人入胜的
quadruple *adj.* 四倍的
dugong *n.* 儒艮
sponges *n.* 海绵皂
humid *adj.* 潮湿的，湿气重的
imminent *adj.*（通常指不愉快的事）即将发生的，逼近的
implicate *vt.* 牵连，涉及
polyp *n.* 珊瑚虫（水螅型），息肉

APPENDIX

附　录

最新雅思阅读机经

1. 拥挤和密度

◆ **文章大意**

人口密度大是基本事实，而拥挤则是一种心理感受。前面几个是标题配对题，后面的填空可直接回原文定位。填写privacy, males和male prison等。讲拥挤和密度的关系，其实密度是思绪上的想法。又说了以前哪个科学家做的试验，后来又有人拿老鼠做试验，现实社会中，人们对这种感受的处理等等。因为文章略长，答案并不好找。

◆ **题型**

List of Headings; Sentence Completion

2. 水底探测

◆ **文章大意**

这是一篇有关水底深测的文章。一个图，右边的两个填空。是讲海洋船，第二段开始讲船的构造，包括它上面连的线当中的水下传声器（underwater microphone），专业术语叫水听器（hydrophone），又讲了搜集海底信息，然后穿越海时还对气候有影响，还关联到当地的一个习俗。由于本篇文章涉及的题型比较多样，所以第一眼看上去会觉得难，但总体来说，大概浏览全文后，还是能够很容易地找出答案来。

◆ **题型**

Diagram; TRUE/FALSE/NOT GIVEN; Sentence Completion

3. 海象

◆ **文章大意**

先是描述它像海豚，之后又说关于它的进食，大嘴唇上有味蕾，爱吃一种海菜，会连根吃掉，之后会留下明显的痕迹和海菜的残骸。它们的种群不会排斥弱小的个体进食，一般会把一个地方的菜吃光后等菜重新长出来后再来吃。1992年大危机以前海象数量很多，现在很少了，大概需要十年时间恢复，人们用的渔网对其有害，现在已经在想办法保护了。问题点大概是这些，考的比较细找起来不是特别容易，但是真的不难。注意：这样的文章如果最先做肯定会超时的，因为你会缺少时间上的紧迫感，结果给后面文章留下的答题时间就很少了！

◆ **题型**

TRUE/FALSE/NOT GIVEN; Sentence Completion; Short Answer Questions

4. 美国的垃圾处理

◆ **文章大意**

讲美国的垃圾处理和再利用问题。先说美国是垃圾制造大国，日本的垃圾填埋场大多都已经饱和，只有西方国家还有剩余的地方，钢铁回收比开采要便宜，燃烧垃圾破坏环境。之后说西雅图回收垃圾非常成功，因为居民要为不可回收的垃圾多付钱，接着列举拉斯维加斯的反面例子，再是德国的情况，最后说美国的情况虽然不好，但是长期来看是可以解决的，西雅图的情况就远比预想的要好。所有题目都是按顺序出的，基本上20分钟都能做出来。

◆ **题型**

Sentence Completion; TRUE/FALSE/NOT GIVEN; Short Answer Questions

5. 美国人的工作时间

◆ **文章大意**

关于美国人应该减少工作时间。全文一共八段，编号为A–H。

A 通过一个人严重超时工作的例子引入主题。

B 关于美国号召减少工作时间的活动的介绍。

C 美国人现在工作严重超时的数字体现。

D 大部分人认为多挣钱生活才会好。

E 建议工作时间减半，多雇一倍的工人。

F 工作时间长和心情的关系。

G 一项指标信息分析，说明美国人生活质量其实不高，政府高生产高消费的号召不一定有道理。

H 建议借鉴另一个国家的经验。

◆ **题目**

Which paragraph contains the following statement?——各有一个题目来自B–F段，有两个题目来自H段。

Matching People with Opinion——四个人，七个主张，分别来自B–G段。

6. 用风筝建筑金字塔

◆ **文章大意**

讲修建埃及金字塔的一种新理论。一位科学家在埃及看见了一幅画，画上有一个很奇怪的动物，样子有些像鸟。这位科学家由此提出了一种新理论，认为修金字塔时埃及人可能用风筝做搬运工具。

文章结构比较清楚，首先说传统观点认为金字塔是靠很多奴隶的辛勤劳动修建而成，然后介绍了这种新的观点。接着说一个科学家对这种观点很感兴趣，他还和他的学生一起进行了一个实验。然后一个组织就这个观点也进行了实验，最后发现风筝的力量确实很大，很可能在建造金字塔时助了埃及人一臂之力。最后为了支持这个观点，文章又举了一些例子，说埃及的水手很早就懂得利用风的力量，中国很早就发明了风筝。但是，要注意这只是一个理论，文章并没有很确定地说这个理论就是正确的。

◆ **题型及题目**

Multiple Choice; Sentence Completion; TRUE/FALSE/NOT GIVEN

Sentence Completion:

埃及人有木制的滑轮（wooden pulleys），可以提起large pieces of stones... their skill as sailor...experimented in flight ...resemble a modern glider

TRUE/FALSE/NOT GIVEN:

- 人们以前认为金字塔的建造需要很多的人。
- 第一位科学家在壁画中发现了风筝。
- 当高度增加时，风力也会加大。
- 有两位科学家是先做实验的。

7. 收集蚂蚁

◆ **文章大意**

分类学收集蚂蚁的要求和生态学收集蚂蚁的要求。然后讲了四种收集方法：人工收集、诱饵收集、垃圾收集和陷阱收集。

◆ **题型**

TRUE/FALSE/NOT GIVEN; Matching; Picture

Picture: 圆圈代表落叶层（leaf litter），下面的液体是酒精，顶上是保温罩（heat cover），虚线是纱窗（screen）。

8. 蜘蛛丝

◆ **文章大意**

根据蜘蛛吐丝的原理，人们用两种人工材料制丝，并比较了这两种材料的特点。并且科学家正在对另一种新材料进行研究。

9. 厄尔尼诺与海鸟

◆ **文章大意**

海鸟是科学家研究海洋生态最好的实验工具，因为它的捕食能力很强。今年的厄尔尼诺现象特别肆虐。接着讲了海鸟作为实验工具的其他好处。最后说有些人认为阿拉斯加的物种大量死亡是由于厄尔尼诺现象在作祟。但是科学家Hatch认为现在下结论为时过早。最后文章也没有得出明确的结论。

◆ **题目及答案**

Multiple Choice; TRUE/FALSE/NOT GIVEN

Multiple Choice:

- 为什么科学家要研究这种现象？
- 为什么要用海鸟来做研究对象，有什么好处？
- 岛上的生物受到了怎样的影响？
- 在某个季节厄尔尼诺现象的情况怎么样？

TRUE/FALSE/NOT GIVEN:

- 科学家通过海鸟的觅食可以看出当地生物物种的健康状况。
- 海鸟通过发现猎物的特征来觅食。

● 寻找海洋生物可能给科学家造成困难。——TRUE

● 阿拉斯加的动物和阿拉斯加以北的动物习性相似。——NOT GIVEN

● Hatch认为阿拉斯加的物种大量死亡一定是由于厄尔尼诺现象在作祟。——FALSE（如前所述，文章中科学家Hatch认为现在下结论为时过早）

10. 蝴蝶研究

◆ **文章大意**

研究蝴蝶以及同类昆虫的进化。一位科学家讲他认为蝴蝶身上的斑斓色彩是警告标志，告诉别的动物“我有毒，离我远点”。按道理同一地区的蝴蝶身上的图案应当是相同或相近的，但实际上蝴蝶谷的蝴蝶无论是身上的颜色还是图案差异都很大。另一科学家认为蝴蝶的颜色根据天空的高度变化，也就是按照光照的高度变化，但这个理论很快被推翻了，因为同一高度有不同图案的蝴蝶。最后另外一个科学家做了很多次试验，证明蝴蝶喜欢在两个高度飞行。当然这不绝对，蝴蝶也偶尔在它喜欢的高度飞翔。

◆ **题型及题目**

Matching; Multiple Choice; YES/NO/NOT GIVEN

Matching:

● 讲述抓蝴蝶的方法。

● 另一个教授批判蝴蝶飞行高度理论。

● 某教授为什么选择此处研究蝴蝶。

● 厄瓜多尔某森林丰富的昆虫种类。

Multiple Choice:

● 蝴蝶飞行的高度。

● 蝴蝶飞行的方式。

YES/NO/NOT GIVEN:

● 蝴蝶的某种特性被别的昆虫模仿。

● 蝴蝶飞行高度由食物决定。

● 蝴蝶颜色可以警告其他动物“我有毒，离我远点”。

● 以前的很多教授都没有蝴蝶的数据记录。

● 某教授一开始就不相信另一教授关于蝴蝶飞行高度的解释。

11. 昆虫翅膀的进化

◆ **文章大意**

文章是有关昆虫翅膀与其飞行之间关系的研究。

◆ **题型及题目**

List of Headings; TRUE/FALSE/NOT GIVEN; Summary

TRUE/FALSE/NOT GIVEN:

- 科学家是不是忽略了昆虫飞行的问题。
- 有一个教授的试验是不是转折点（turning point）。
- 是不是只有最大的昆虫才有翅膀。
- 动物长翅膀是为了飞行吗？
- 某生物最后灭绝的原因是因为翅膀不能折起。—— TRUE

Summary: 填两个空，答案分别为the stoneflies和bigger。

12. 恐龙灭绝

◆ 文章大意

根据足迹研究恐龙的存在与灭绝。讲到彗星和流星可能将地球撞出一个大洞，导致恐龙灭绝。

◆ 题型及题目

TRUE/FALSE/NOT GIVEN; Summary; Multiple Choice

TRUE/FALSE/NOT GIVEN:

- 书和杂志过分夸大某事。
- 恐龙的爪印比骨骼化石多。
- 恐龙早在侏罗纪时代就出现了。

Summary: 恐龙个头大是因为没有竞争

Multiple Choice: 三个原因

- overlooked by scientists
- ocean flood produced sth.
- misdated

13. 染料和颜料

◆ 文章大意

文章一直在介绍染料，从天然染料（nature dye）开始。先是其特点，接着是不足，然后说该染料作为一种衣服的染料应该达到什么标准，最后由这些总结出其优点。第二部分简单说了颜料（pigment）。

◆ 题型及题目

Matching; Summary

Summary: 染料和颜料的相同点在于给世界增添色彩。

Dyes however ... physically and chemically.

说明天然染料的特点: 容易褪色, 不鲜艳（not attractive）。

使染料发生化学反应的必要条件: quick, non-toxic, strain from other colours。

14. 蝙蝠与雷达

◆ **文章大意**

蝙蝠之所以要在夜间捕食，是因为其已经适应了在夜间环境下活动。然后讲如何能够在夜间看清物体，要能发出可以照亮物体的光，但是这样要消耗很多能量，所以用这种方式发光的动物很少见，只有一种深海鱼是这样。萤火虫（glowworm）发光不是为了看见物体，而是为了吸引异性。

然后讲盲人，说他们的听觉十分发达。接着讲声波技术的军事运用，尤其是二战时，用于反潜艇。最后讲人类使用的声波和蝙蝠使用的声波不同。一位科学家把它们统称为回声定位（echolocation）。

◆ **题型及题目**

Matching; Sentence Completion; Summary

Matching:

- 第一次将蝙蝠的特点应用于军事。
- 新发现加深了人们对蝙蝠的了解。
- 蝙蝠在夜间捕食的原因。
- 动物避免灭绝的古老方法。

Summary：回声定位针对盲人的应用。

15. 日本塔

◆ **文章大意**

日本古建筑宝塔（pagoda）能够抗地震，即使是在现代科技十分发达的日本，类似的技术也是才发明出来。文章将日本古建筑宝塔和日本近现代建筑进行对比。宝塔是从中国传到日本的，日本人根据自身的地理特点进行了改良和本土化。日本建宝塔的技术源自中国，但不同于中国。中国宝塔用于瞭望景物，而日本仅用于艺术欣赏。后讲日本宝塔的屋檐（eaves），顶梁柱（central pillar）与众不同。一位在日本号称“宝塔教授”的教授对日本宝塔进行了研究。

◆ **题目及答案**

TRUE/FALSE/NOT GIVEN; Matching; Multiple Choice

TRUE/FALSE/NOT GIVEN:

- 在1400年间，有两座宝塔塌了。—— TRUE
- 地震毁了日本的某一座宝塔。—— FALSE
- 那座宝塔附近的建筑是30年前建成的。—— NOT GIVEN
- 古代的建筑师能够用自然界的力量对建筑……。—— FALSE

Matching: 匹配国家和宝塔的特点

A in China and Japan

B in China

C in Japan

- 宝塔的起源与宗教有关。——B
- 宝塔很容易上去。——B
- 屋檐上的瓦片。——A
- 屋檐伸出来很多。——C
- 用作瞭望台。——B
- 宝塔是松松垮垮叠上去的。——C

16. 鲑鱼保育

◆ **文章大意**

鲑鱼是通过溯河进行繁殖的鱼类，由于人类的活动，其产量、质量都发生了很大的变化。科学家们对其分布、习性以及海洋环境、气候对它们的影响进行了一系列的研究。

◆ **题型及题目**

Matching; YES/NO/NOT GIVEN; Multiple Choice

Matching: before1970s; in1970s; recent years

YES/NO/NOT GIVEN: 题目涉及整篇文章

Multiple Choice: 研究成果

17. 穹顶建筑

◆ **文章大意**

两种房屋的构造和用途有什么不同之处。有两个图（类似一个半圆球体扣在地上，穹顶dome），两图形状一样，不过第二幅图的球表在构造上与第一幅稍有不同。它由几个三角形构成，优点是节能和节省建筑材料等，缺点是不能任意改变其高度。然后有个教授对该模型进行了改良，自认为改良后的模型很实用，还有两个潜在用途——用于建造太空空间站和节能房屋，尽管改良后的模型可以任意改变形状和边的数量（这样更节能，更节省建筑材料），但增加了数学上的变动性（mathematic flexibility），此外描述了这个模型的曲线及圆底。

很多专家对该改良模型提出批判，说高度上升时会增加底部的承受力，又说没有留出门的位置，还说以前的另一个模型已经解决了该问题。最后教授宣称该模型很好，有几个优点。

然后说要优化计算机，做更多的计算。

◆ **题目及答案**

Matching; Sentence Completion

Matching: 结构或功能是第一幅图

A 表示只描述第一种模型

B 表示只描述第二种模型

C 表示both

- 由六个三角形组成的模型。——A
- 可以任意改变高度的模型。——B
- 节能的模型。——C

Matching: 观点

A 表示作者的观点

B 表示专家的观点

C 表示设计者的观点

- 该模型有数学上的可变性。——A
- 这个结构很好很有实用价值。——C
- 升级计算机系统，再计算，完成一个完美的方案。——C
- 该模型没有门的位置。——B
- 以前的模型已经解决了第一个模型的问题。——A
- 该模型会造成建筑力学方面的问题，高度增高的时候会使底部承受力（bearing）增大。——C

Sentence Completion:（NO MORE THAN THREE WORDS）

答案：Space station construction, energy-saving housing

18. 动物思考和行为

◆ 文章大意

第一段讲的是思考的概念。如果对于一个问题不能马上给出解答，要经过一段时间之后才能找出答案，有这么一个解决问题（problem-solving）的过程就叫思考。有的人可能会对给出的概念不满意，因为他们觉得思考是只属于人类的，人类才是具有科学和艺术天分的天才。但是如果我们考虑到智力的高峰和低谷的话，其实很难分清人与动物智力的界限。下面我们来看看动物的识别能力。

用虫子、昆虫、鸟、狗、猴子和老鼠做实验来研究动物的行为。对虫子来说，是把它们的大脑去掉，看有什么影响。蜜蜂可以通过跳舞定向。但是它们的这种能力似乎是本能的（instinct），而不是学来的。对母鸡来说，是看它们对日夜的反应，结果有的母鸡只有夜里下蛋，有的全天都下蛋，母鸡还可以学会辨认盒子的颜色深浅。哺乳动物的识别能力就更厉害了，如狗和猴子，把一个食物藏在盒子后面，狗盯着看的话就认得，猴子不盯着看也认得。最后一段提到老鼠的实验，看老鼠对路径的反应。老鼠在迷宫里面能找到出路。以上可以看出，人类与动物之间的智力界限并不是稳定而持久的。

◆ 题型

Matching; YES/NO/NOT GIVEN

19. 法国城堡

◆ 文章大意

法国人G买了一座15世纪的城堡，发现此城堡地基下竟然还有一座城堡，于是突发奇想决定再建一座城堡，这是个很幼稚的想法。一位建筑师帮他实现了这个想法，在另外一个地方重新按照古书上记载的建筑方法建了一个比较小的城堡。这个地方是旅游景点，需要接待游客，否则就没有收入。他在十个月内筹集了钱款，购买了建筑材料等。然后，开始讲如何建造。接着讲这个工程耗费十年时间才竣工的原因：工人必须遵守现代工作时间——8小时工作制，现代的工人不是很专业，不会运用古代的建筑方法；还要接待游客。

◆ 题目及答案

Flowchart; Multiple Choice; YES/NO/NOT GIVEN

Flowchart: 城堡修建材料的炼制过程，填空流程图

Masons drill holes, use metal wedges, until rock splits, then used for bricks, then a process heating

Multiple Choice：选择三个导致建筑城堡如此耗时的原因。

- limited by modern policy
- not enough professional workers
- influence of visitors

YES/NO/NOT GIVEN:

- one aim of castle is let history to go public——YES
- short lifespan of workers is due to overdue heating——NO (due to toxic gas)
- the French people would not abandon his idea in favour of realistic one—— NOT GIVEN

20. 微波测量桥梁

◆ 文章大意

用微波（microwave）来测定桥梁的损坏情况。段落很多。主要说的是原来桥梁损坏的检验只能由人工检测来完成。现在科学家们发明了一种微波探测仪来检验。然后介绍了微波探测仪具体的工作过程。有一座大桥由于正好要被政府拆除，便成了这台仪器的实验对象，科学家故意破坏了大桥的某个部位来检验仪器的有效性。最后展望了这台仪器的应用前景。

第一段：微波技术的产生使得科学家们可以不用像以前那样爬到桥上去检测桥梁的损坏情况；第二段：微波技术的运作原理是通过测量两点之间的距离来检测桥梁的承重；第三段：有一个政府已经打算将一座废弃的桥梁作为科学家的实验品；第四段：科学家们开始对此桥梁进行加重（put pressure）；第五段：科学家们用刀子在桥梁的大梁（girder）上切割出长口，直到桥梁底下的凸缘（flange）最后导致桥梁的坍塌；第六段：最初的分析表明，科学家们通常只能在桥面出现裂缝之前检测桥梁的损伤，但微波技术的应用使得科学

家们可以在桥墩底部的凸缘出现损伤时就检测到；第七段：有关微波技术将进一步应用的讲述；第八段：科学家预测该技术在十年后的发展前景。

◆ **题目及答案**

Matching; Picture; Multiple Choice

Matching: 信息和段落匹配

- put pressure 第四段
- apply knife 第五段
- chance of experiment 第三段
- in a decade 最后一段

Picture: 桥梁的图例，将girder，flange，microwave，dish，puncher，span，accelerator等几个词汇填在图上。

Multiple Choice: 问现在大桥的损坏情况是：B由人工检验。

21. 摩天大楼

◆ **文章大意**

过去的建筑；摩天大楼的出现；摩天大楼的意义；环境问题和人们对它的态度。

◆ **题目及答案**

Flowchart; Summary; TRUE/FALSE/NOT GIVEN

Flowchart:

过去的建筑: not much interior space

现在用了: new material & technical advance,摩天大楼成为可能

因为它的practical use 和increased value of property，所以摩天大楼越来越多

TRUE/FALSE/NOT GIVEN:

- 摩天大楼代表名声、威望等。—— TRUE
- 房地产公司过去因为经济原因不愿意建造摩天大楼。
- 摩天大楼可能会对周围环境有影响。—— TRUE

22. 非洲修建公路

◆ **文章大意**

这是非洲的一个工程，解决非洲坦桑尼亚（Tanzania）农村偏远地区的交通困难问题。那条路部分连接了整个地中海区域。首先研究了该国的交通情况，包括人们最常使用的交通工具、路况和地理等。整个工程分为三个阶段来实施，阶段一：勘探；阶段二：制定计划；阶段三：施工。最后还提到了工程的圆满完成是当地的官员和研究人员共同努力的结果。还提到欧洲政府、欧盟对修路的态度，欧盟对一家给修路提供贷款的银行不信任以及那个银行的态度。

◆ **题型**

List of Headings; YES/NO/NOT GIVEN; Multiple Choice

Multiple Choice: 选文章主旨

23. 儿童多动症

◆ **文章大意**

介绍什么是注意力集中困难症，这种病症除用一般药物可以治疗之外，文章还介绍一种叫生物反馈（biofeedback）的方法，也可以治疗这种症状。关于S发明的这种治疗方法，他说，目前这种方法虽然已发明出来有好几十年了，但是还有很多人仍然认为这只是边缘疗法（fringe treatment）。然后介绍了这种方法之前是用于病人控制自己心跳速度的，即把一些线（wire）接到头皮（scalp）上，然后可以通过监视器（monitor）看到自己的情况，并通过这种方法来控制自己的心跳。同样这种方法也可以用于治疗注意力集中困难症，因为病人通过监视器可以了解自己脑电波的跳动情况，长时间训练后，病情会有所改善。P说，这种方法好，不像药物，不但治标还治本。

接着说这种方法的缺点。第一：治疗费用太高；第二：时间太长，很多小孩根本就坚持不下去；第三：很多基本的医疗险种并没包括这一项。

P原来是NASA的研究员。他在研究飞行员玩飞行器模拟机的时候发现并将生物反馈的方法应用到模拟机上，飞行员感觉到新系统很舒适，因而很快就适应了。P还用生物反馈法把PS2的赛车游戏结合到S的设施里面，结果发现赛车速度一提高，心跳速度也跟着提高。

基于此，两个高手强强联合做了个实验，把几十个小孩分成两组，一组用传统方式来治疗，一种用P的改装赛车方法治疗。结果发现，这两组小孩的病都治得差不多，但是P组很少有缺课的。更大的好处是，P的方法降低了医疗成本，S的方法需要单对单，P的方法一个医疗师就可以对付几个小孩了。

最后说生物反馈还需要大量的临床试验来验证。药物和物理治疗两种方法其实各有各的好处，药物见效快、成本低，持续时间短，很多小孩也就上课的时候吃吃；物理治疗周期长，费用高，各位家长可以根据情况自行选择。

◆ **题型**

Multiple Choice; Matching; TRUE/FALSE/NOT GIVEN

24. 英国孩子缺乏身体锻炼

◆ **文章大意**

第一段是介绍小孩不运动，个个只顾着看电视和玩电脑，有关专家担心他们长大后会得病。第二段是对小孩运动的研究，研究表明孩子运动偏少。专家Armstrong说心脏要锻炼才会变强。还说到不运动会导致肥胖（男孩多过女孩：12%的男孩和10%的女孩超重）和小孩胆固醇（cholesterol）偏高。第三段说英国教育中体育课设备不够，时间过短，一周只有一个多小时，其他欧洲国家都有两个小时。专家Armstrong说英国政府之前为了改变小孩不运动的情况提倡团队运动的措施可能不是很好。因为一些学生离开学校后就不再做这些运动了。文章建议做一些一生都会从事的运动，比如游泳和骑自行车等。第四段讲一些为了让小孩动起来的活动，比如跳绳（rope skipping）。第五段讲一个官员说家长要以身作则，多运动。建议家长尽量不要开汽车，制造锻炼的气氛。但是现状是孩子现在不锻炼，长大后也不会锻炼。

◆ **题目及答案**

List of Headings; TRUE/FALSE/NOT GIVEN; Multiple Choice

TRUE/FALSE/NOT GIVEN:

● A教授的评论，第一段出现。

● 文章的目的是什么？是为英国人将来的健康考虑。因为文章说现在关注的是这些行为对将来孩子长大后健康的影响。

● 男孩子的胆固醇比女孩子高。—— NOT GIVEN

● 跳绳已经在英国很流行。—— NOT GIVEN（因为文章中说成立了一个什么组织，发展了多少会员，但没有看到有什么总体评价）

● 家长鼓励他们的孩子多做运动。—— NOT GIVEN

25. 蝴蝶农场

◆ **文章大意**

主要讲述了什么是蝴蝶农场，如何养殖，有什么好处，如何取得经济效益以及失败和成功的原因。

◆ **题目及答案**

Multiple Choice; YES/NO/NOT GIVEN

Multiple Choice:

● 蝴蝶农场失败的原因（7选3）

较少品种可供观赏

引进不合适的品种

没有好的环境

没有专业的喂养

● 美国一位很成功的蝴蝶农场主怎样运送蝴蝶？

——export/post sleeping butterfly

● 一位教授说蝴蝶农场应该注重教育价值。

● 一位教授说反对运输成年蝴蝶。

● 一位教授说他的运输方法是趁蝴蝶睡觉的时候。

● 一位教授评价大多数蝴蝶农场运行良好。

YES/NO/NOT GIVEN:

- 大多数热带国家（tropic country）都养殖蝴蝶。
- farms number stops falling——YES（1980年以后英国养殖农场的数量趋向稳定）
- 他们错误地估算了养殖费用，大家误解养殖蝴蝶最容易赚钱。
- butterfly farms are protected by law（文中说：farms need to be protected）
- rare species are difficult to grow
- green/glasshouses make butterfly reduce lifespan.

26. 美国肥胖问题

◆ 文章大意

美国人肥胖的现象很严重，在40年内增长很多。文章中出现了很多人名、机构名和相应的观点，需要配对。讲到科技发展使得食物的价格降低，人吃得越来越胖。一位教授说到一种和肥胖有关的疾病。美国人花很多钱治疗肥胖，但他们不锻炼，百分之……的人除了上班就不运动了。

◆ 题型及题目

Matching; TRUE/FALSE/NOT GIVEN

Matching: 机构、人名和观点匹配

TRUE/FALSE/NOT GIVEN:

- 得肥胖症的人认为没有必要医治。
- 美国使用糖的人数下降了。
- 某数字过去40年里翻了两番。
- 大公司可以进入学校推销。

27. 英国校园暴力

◆ 文章大意

媒体报道英国学校的高年级学生欺负（bully）低年级学生。校园暴力（school bully）的定义、种类。在英国，调查表明初中（secondary school）的情况比小学（primary）的要好；这对学生的影响是：Extreme example is to commit a suicide，often affect the relationship with others when they grow up.（题目中改写为： affect the relationship in their adulthood）

学校对暴力的态度。有英国的、威尔士的学校，还有挪威的。学校说自己没有暴力的原因是对暴力的研究不够充分以及对解决问题的方法不清楚。后来学校要写一个“AGAINST BULLYING”。对此，有三个解决办法。In Norway，research proved that two years after the campaign，the bullying is halved.

◆ 题型及题目

YES/NO/NOT GIVEN; Summary

Summary:

...In order to solve issue...need to publish written document...also need a school policy in detail to tell teachers how to and what to do with bullying. Teachers need to encourage the potential pupils to be confident to avoid bullying. Training special teacher to identify the bullying and play fighting.

28. 妇女受教育的程度和儿童健康

◆ **文章大意**

调查研究发现母亲受教育程度高，婴儿存活率就高，孩子的健康状况就好。文章提供了该结论的原因分析及数据证明。最后得出结论，因此要对妇女普及教育。

◆ **题型及题目**

YES/NO/NOT GIVEN; Multiple Choice

YES/NO/NOT GIVEN:

- now, women trained by the programme has the lowest child death rate
- at first, women who had received education and women without education have the same child death rate
- women who had received education have the biggest changes
- women still with illiteracy have undernourished their children

Multiple Choice:

- fast effects of maternal literacy
- maternal literacy improve the child heath rate

29. 蚂蚁的智力

◆ **文章大意**

第一段：蚂蚁很聪明。第二段：蚂蚁的交流方式以及和人类交流方式的比较等。第三段：蚂蚁通过基因来遗传，不像人类是通过文化来教育孩子，但是蚂蚁寻找食物或打洞的本领却是后天学来的。后面几段讲蚂蚁的农耕本领。

◆ **题目及答案**

Summary; YES/NO/NOT GIVEN

Summary: 很多蚂蚁不能消化甘蓝，要通过真菌（fungi）来转化。它们interbreeding with neighbours。

YES/NO/NOT GIVEN:

- 是不是蚂蚁和人类一样，也都是用同一种渠道来交流。
- 蚂蚁在城市里是否发展得很快。—— YES
- 蚂蚁造房子的速度是不是比人类造房子还要快。—— NOT GIVEN

（只说了蚂蚁造房子很快，科学家对它们的杰作啧啧称奇，但没有比较到底谁造得更快。）

- 在一个实验室中，蚂蚁可以通过嗅觉（sense of smell）来寻找食物。—— NO

（两位科学家试验蚂蚁是不是可以传递信息（transmit information），所以他们把蚂蚁的嗅觉神经给掩盖了，结果蚂蚁还是通过互相传递信息而直接找到了食物。）

- 在一位女作家的书里，是不是说了关于蚂蚁交流（ant communication）的内容。

—— NOT GIVEN

（文中的这个女人爱蚂蚁如命，即使不做记号也可以认出很多她熟悉的蚂蚁，还在她的书里说人们最好仔细观察家中厨房里的蚂蚁。但是没有提到交流的问题。）

30. 水獭

◆ **文章大意**

水獭（otter）的外部特征、生活习性和对其的保护措施。

◆ **题目及答案**

List of Headings; Matching; TRUE/FALSE/NOT GIVEN; Sentence Completion

- 什么技能没有用处：Swimming speed
- 盐水（salt water）会对水獭（otter）的皮肤（fur）有影响。
- 水獭有时会吃一些小的哺乳动物，比如鼹鼠（moles）。

31. 老年的疾病研究

◆ **文章大意**

美国近年来65岁以上老人患某种疾病的数量在下降（falling），而且这个下降的速率在攀升（rising），得病的年龄也推迟了。这除了跟药物疗效提升有关，还和早期营养（nutrition）的提高有关。研究者发现教育和寿命有一定的联系，受教育程度高的人能多活七年。美国政府花在残疾人身上的资金（funding）比预计的要少很多。

◆ **题型及题目**

Matching; Summary

Summary:

Controlling over life can be helped by treatment; feeling lonely causes _________ rising; doing exercise regularly may _________.

32. 乐观与人类健康

◆ **文章大意**

研究证明乐观的（optimistic）心态和健康有关系。

◆ **题型及题目**

Sentence Completion; Matching; TRUE/FALSE/NOT GIVEN

Sentence Completion:

乐观的人能多活七年（seven years）。

670; lung function; immune system, heart patients

TRUE/FALSE/NOT GIVEN:

- 乐观与健康有联系。
- 乐观的人的社会关系。
- 95岁以上的老人定期地运动。

33. 眼镜蛇毒

◆ 文章大意

关于眼镜蛇（cobra）的研究，以及其毒液对人的影响，研究人员对其进行了进一步的研究，希望找到治疗其他疾病的方法。

一旦人或动物被眼镜蛇咬，会感到疼痛和疲劳（pain and fatigue）。疼痛是众所周知的，这篇文章主要讲的是蛇毒（venom）中的某一种成分会使被咬者感到疲劳，从而丧失反抗能力，只能坐以待毙。接着说蛇毒如何进入被咬者的体内。蛇的毒液通过蛇中空（hollow）得像针尖（needle-like）一样的牙齿射入人畜体内，进入血液（bloodstream），从而发挥作用。

从1960起，人们就对眼镜蛇毒的化学成分有了大致了解。但是对其中一些同时起作用的化学成分的功能依旧不了解。

接下来英国专家开始破解这种成分。他们分离出这种化学物质，发现这是一种消化酶（digestive enzyme），它能够消化肽（peptide）。为了知道这种酶的攻击目标，科学家们就在寻找是哪一种类型的肽受这种化学物质的破坏。他们首先用食物作为受攻击目标，但惊奇地发现蛇毒中的消化酶比一般的酶消化食物的速度要慢得多。

科学家们缩小范围去找到那种肽，他们开始试验神经系统的肽（neuropeptide），并发现此酶对人体中的神经肽的破坏速度非常快。然后，讲述人体中神经肽的作用。第一种作用是能够在人体遭受创伤时减轻人体的疼痛，其作用和毒品中的吗啡（morphia），海洛因（heroin）类似。第二，它是人在遭受危险时由肾上腺（adrenalin glands）分泌的肾上腺素的主要成分。那这样自然而然，当这种酶通过血液进入人体的防御系统（defend system）后便摧毁了人畜的这种使之产生反抗力的神经肽，从而使蛇能够轻松获胜。

同时，还发现这种酶可以溶解于水中，但要使它发生作用必须让它变为晶体结构（crystal）。毒液还有两种化学物质，这两种物质和人体神经上的物质很相似。接着在这两种化学物质的催化下，毒酶具有了晶体形式，可以开始破坏了。专家们也将这两种化学物质分离了出来。

最后总结，通过这项研究人们可以更好地治疗蛇毒伤，并可以研制出能够治疗失落和沮丧情绪的药物。

◆ 题型及答案

Summary; Multiple Choice

Summary: 答案主要集中在文章的前中部分。

Multiple Choice: 答案主要集中在文章的中部，最后选文章题目。

34. 人的寿命

◆ 文章大意

对于寿命的科学研究。主要说人的寿命。任何种群的寿命都是有一种模式（mode）的，到了一定的时间就会死去。不过用科学的方法可以保持人的青春，以至于达到永生（immortality）。不过这种永生对进化是有害的。用一些动物做实验，结果显示：冬眠的动物比不冬眠的动物活得长，因为消耗的能量少。然后又拿老鼠做实验，发现节食的老鼠比不节食的老鼠寿命长。结论就是我们应该多锻炼，控制饮食，这样才能长命百岁。

◆ 题型及答案

List of Headings; Sentence Completion; YES/NO/NOT GIVEN

Sentence Completion: immortality thermodynamics

35. 医生与药品推销

◆ 文章大意

关于医生和药品推销员的事情，一个推销员游说医生说如果用他们公司生产的新药，就送一些东西给他。医生要旅游，由于销售员有权调用的经费有限，最后只给了电影票还有音乐会的票。现在这种现象很普遍，大家只有附送一些东西才能卖出药。此方法有利有弊。有些医生拿东西也不办事。其实不管是送礼给医生还是送药物试验品，成本都是病人出的。

◆ 题型

List of Headings; YES/NO/NOT GIVEN

36. 健康医疗

◆ 文章大意

医疗保健的发展近况，随着经济的增长一些发达国家的医疗需求也随之增长。发达国家和发展中国家在这方面有什么不同。讲到医疗保健和人权，经济体制，富有的国家的态度和花费等等。时间贯穿：1950前，1950–1980年，1980年后。

◆ 题型及题目

List of Headings; Matching; YES/NO/NOT GIVEN

Matching: 年代和现象匹配

A 1945－1950

B 1950－1980

C 1980以后

37. 味觉和嗅觉

◆ 文章大意

文章是关于味觉（taste）和嗅觉（smell）的研究。此篇文章使用的科技术语比较多。

◆ 题型

Summary; Matching; TRUE/FALSE/NOT GIVEN

38. 噪音研究

◆ **文章大意**

关于噪音对人的影响的研究。主要介绍科学家通过实验研究噪音对人们工作表现的影响。

◆ **题目及答案**

Summary; Matching; Multiple Choice

Summary: 主要是介绍两个科学家的实验，讨论在知道会有噪音的情况下以及突然有噪音影响的情况下人们的工作表现。

Different types of noise; performed as well as make more mistakes; unexpected

Matching: 学者和观点的匹配

Multiple Choice:

- 问人们为什么在山上睡不着？是人们习惯一定程度噪音的环境。（文中说人们认为他们会很习惯很安静的地方，但实际上不是，科学家研究表明人们习惯暴露于一定程度的噪音中）
- 噪音对只需完成一项工作的人而言影响并不是很大。

39. 摄影

◆ **文章大意**

全文主要讨论了摄影的发展，以及对艺术，尤其是绘画艺术的冲击。有人认为摄影仅仅是一种图像的记录，而有人则认为摄影是一门艺术。绘画与艺术相互影响，文章举例说明了这种影响。第一段，介绍了摄影的历史。第二段，某艺术家认为摄影只是某种记录手段，而完全谈不上是艺术。第三段，某人支持这种观点。肖像画后来多半被照片代替了，但现在没有完全消失，因为有些有钱人也画肖像画。但是摄影给更多人带来了这种记录自己面容的机会。第四段，对摄影是否是艺术的意见，大家表现出两种态度。一种人认为摄影就像画油画一样会追求某种艺术效果，或者对照片进行再创作。第五段，另一些人则觉得摄影是一种纪实的艺术。和油画相比，摄影的特点在于它能够捕捉瞬间的表情。所以后来印象主义和现实主义画家都受到了艺术的影响。

◆ **题型及题目**

Matching; Summary; TRUE/FALSE/NOT GIVEN

比较两种摄影者拍照时的态度，是受绘画艺术的影响还是直接将其当作艺术。

Summary: compositions, scratched...

TRUE/FALSE/NOT GIVEN: 判断人们对摄影（photography）和绘画（painting）的认识。

40. 生物杀虫A

◆ **文章大意**

杀虫剂（pesticide）导致了环境失衡。杀虫剂使得某些害虫（pest）有了免疫（immune）

功能，有些害虫的基因受到影响，天生免疫杀虫剂。杀虫剂对农业的副作用以60年代美国棉花生产为例，为了提高棉花产量农民逐年增加杀虫剂的使用次数，最后导致棉花减产50%。新的杀虫方式，生物杀虫（bio-control），以虫制虫，有效而且无毒副作用。

◆ **题目及答案**

Multiple Choice; Matching; TRUE/FALSE/NOT GIVEN

Multiple Choice:

化学试剂的使用cause an imbalance in...? (文中为disorder一词，讲40–50年代,美国农民大量使用杀虫剂是因为它使棉花的收成提高很多; 70年代左右,因为害虫的抗药性,人们不得不花费收益的50%来控制害虫。)

Matching: 害虫 / 益虫 / 果树

TRUE/FALSE/NOT GIVEN:

- 传播疾病的昆虫比吃农作物的害虫更容易有抗药性。——NOT GIVEN (文中第二段中只有种类的比较)
- 使用杀虫剂会使某些昆虫一出生就有抗药性。——TRUE (文中的第二、三段中说会bear offspring with resistance of chemicals)
- 使用生物学的方法只有暂时效果。——FALSE (文中倒数第四段说了eternal一词)
- biological ways may be free from danger under certain conditions——TRUE (文中有一段的最后一句说使用这种方法可healthy, with no pollution。)

41. 生物杀虫B

◆ **文章大意**

蚂蚁能杀死害虫，有利于果树成长。一种蚂蚁会对柠檬树、橘子树有好处。当美国第一次在佛罗里达使用昆虫帮助果树成长的时候，中国已经使用这种方法有1 700年了。后来说，西方很多科学家对此很怀疑。这些科学家不相信可以用一种小虫子来防治另外一种小虫子。他们相信一种化学杀虫剂，但是这种杀虫剂并不好用，并不会使产量提高。

◆ **题目及答案**

Multiple Choice; Matching; TRUE/FALSE/NOT GIVEN

Matching: 年份事件匹配

- 公元三百多年：中国一个学者写了一本关于用虫治虫的书。
- 1915年：JS教授在中国学习了这个用蚂蚁治虫的方法。
- 1950年：中国农民抛弃了传统治虫方法，改用了农药。

TRUE/FALSE/NOT GIVEN:

- 中国的害虫种类比别的国家都多。—— TRUE
- 农药价格的变化。—— TRUE (原文将价格提高了)
- JS教授所介绍的这个关于中国的防虫方法令西方学者印象深刻。—— FALSE (原文

讲好多学者都持怀疑态度)

- 有蚂蚁的果树会遭受另一种虫灾。
- 不用蚂蚁的果树会掉叶子。

42. 鸟类定向

◆ 文章大意

鸟类有不可思议的方向感，这一点远胜于人类。为此，人们做过很多实验来测试鸟是怎样认路的。鸟的认路本领分几种。比如凭视觉，以鸽子为例，它能记住空中的俯瞰图，只要是在它熟悉的地方放飞，它都能飞回来。但是有局限性，800公里以外的飞回来就困难了。此外，要是在它的觅食区域以外的地方放，回来的概率也不高。而且，不同年龄段的鸽子认路本领也不一样。

◆ 题型及答案

Summary; Matching

Summary: latitude，migration routes等

Matching: 4个相关的句子匹配段落

43. 脑力训练

◆ 文章大意

脑力训练（Gymnastic of brain）。文章讲某公司一天早晨的头脑训练课程的情况。有个年轻的讲师给员工上课，让他们想象自己正在fill each room and fill the building，from the low key to the top。有个机构叫做Gym of brain，专门开设这种类型的课程，大概有70种不同的课程。它们使用同样的销售理念：follow my way之类的。著名心理学家说，“人的大脑就像身体一样，通过锻炼就能更加发达”。年轻讲师介绍他上课的一些感受。他说有些人自己给自己贴上缺乏创造力的标签，其实他们都没有意识到自己实际上是缺乏一种创造性的技巧。这些技巧通过他们的课程和一些锻炼就可以获得。创造力其实主观性很强，因为很难平衡。某学者说大多数人都是没有得到恰当的训练，才导致创造力低下。还说神经元（nerve cell）的问题，关键是要建立神经元之间的一些联系等等。举例子说，有些人经过意外的事故，损失了原有的一些联系，还提到IQ测试。有学者认为，学校应该花更多的精力培养学生的创造力，而不是用一些事实性的知识填充学生的大脑。

◆ 题目及答案

YES/NO/NOT GIVEN; Matching

YES/NO/NOT GIVEN:

- 脑力训练课程的讲师让员工想象自己是一栋建筑。——NO
- Gym of Brain机构的课程使用相同的营销理念。——YES
- 学者A是Gym of Brain创始人之一。
- 全世界商务领域都在使用这种课程培训自己的员工。——NO

● Gym of Brain机构说他们的课程都有科学根据(scientific background)。——NOT GIVEN

Matching: 学者和观点匹配

● 人的头脑就像身体一样，锻炼就能更发达。
● 人们往往不能认识到自己在创造力方面的潜力。
● 人们缺乏创造方面的技巧。
● 学校应该多花精力培养孩子的创造力。
● 人们得不到科学的创造力训练。
● 人们在开始做一件事情之前，往往不愿意先看清他的状况再动手。
● 人们在失去神经元之间的一些旧联系时，可能得到新的联系。

44. 俄罗斯考古

◆ 文章大意

最近俄罗斯考古有了新发现，其中出土的一些东西帮助人们更了解中世纪人们的生活。中世纪的时候俄罗斯能用来记载的东西很有限，只能用木头和动物皮来记载。往往因为细菌的分解，水腐蚀等原因，现在很难找到有机物的记载了。然而在俄罗斯的某个地方因为地理的特殊原因，使一些有机物的记载保存下来了（一种特殊的土壤使它可以隔绝空气和水，这样就让细菌分解不了了。即使洪水淹没了也不会使这些东西受到影响。俄罗斯的考古学家与历史学家的不同点是，前者关注环境，后者关注人。前后有三次探险，第一次是在19世纪30年代，说的是他们研究些什么，他们以往有过什么重大发现（俄罗斯也生产工艺品，这地方原来是一个手工业制造者的作坊中心，以前认为俄罗斯只出产蜂蜜、蜂蜡（bee wax）等，这个地方的发现一下子让人们了解到原来俄罗斯也有能和其他文明相提并论的繁荣的手工业）。人类科学家从这些文物中分析出人们的实际生活习惯。提到出土了一些手工品，还发现了上百家商店、市场。从这些手工艺品的制作上来看，当时俄罗斯已经从欧洲一些国家进口手工艺品了，而且还模仿了他们的做法，所以说工艺水平达到了和欧洲国家差不多的水平。这些文物的出土对俄罗斯的历史有价值。

◆ 题目及答案

Multiple Choice; YES/NO/NOT GIVEN

多选： C， F

单选：

● 在某城市发现的文物：a plenty of
● 这些文物：include organic materials
● 人类学家最在乎：恢复某特定年代普通人的生活场景
● 怎样测量东西的年代——东西埋的程度
● 重大的经济发现：当地的手工艺品制作

YES/NO/NOT GIVEN:

- 俄罗斯的手工艺水平是否与欧洲的国家不相上下。
- 当地是否加工黄金白银。
- 是否那种特殊的粘土保护了文献。
- 科学家是否已经掌握了当地大部分的历史情况。

45. 电影评论

◆ 文章大意

文章讲一位法国电影艺术家拍的一部反映工业时代的影片，作者觉得寓意很好，不过故事情节一般。影片反映的是工业社会中人们越来越被机械化的现象。影片摄于60年代，讲的是2001年的城市两极分化很严重，工人住在地下，老板住在摩天大楼里。影片中的企业和现在的企业很像；影片中的社会没有政府，全都被大公司操控着；电影的败笔之处就是扯进了爱情。最后提到了导演，说这个导演跟他太太分开了，他太太也是一个导演。

◆ 题目及答案

Multiple Choice; Summary; TRUE/FALSE/NOT GIVEN

Summary:

影片反映了一种社会现象：人们变得越来越像机器，跨国公司只对金钱和权利感兴趣。影片没有直接影射政府，所以作用没有得到完全发挥，影片的表现手法是抽象的。

TRUE/FALSE/NOT GIVEN:

- 导演是因为在纽约遇到一位工业家（industrialist）才有灵感来创作的。
- 影片中的工业家的原型就是导演的一个商业家朋友。
- 导演和他太太离婚了。——NOT GIVEN（文中只提到他们各自在两地工作，都很忙）

46. 美国电影发展

◆ 文章大意

从电影的创造原型以及第一部电影的拍摄开始，讲了人们觉得应该将电影应用到新闻上，因为电影能留住时间且现场化。之后讲电影后来用作表现故事，然后有了很多明星。最后讲了电影的将来。

◆ 题目及答案

Multiple Choice; Matching; TRUE/FALSE/NOT GIVEN

Multiple Choice:

- 电影成本的增加造成了什么?制片商更注重做成功的电影（successful movie）。
- 作者描写火车是为了表明：第一部电影的影响（impact of the first film）。
- T认为电影的特点：流逝的时光（passing time）。
- 文章的标题：Power of Big Screen。

Matching: 信息与段落标号

- 第一个电影院的位置。——A
- 电影发展的速度。——J
- 电影反映人的个性（写star的那段）。

TRUE/FALSE/NOT GIVEN:

- 理解人们对电影的反应很重要。
- 某大导演认为火车的那个镜头是最伟大的场面之一。

47. 智力智商

◆ 文章大意

IQ（intelligence quotient）成为人们评价智力的一种标准，很多儿童因此受到了不好的影响（limited by the line）。一位教授受邀进行智商测试，他宣称做这种测试很困难，因为有时会受很多因素影响。如果年龄比较大的孩子（七到八岁）测定的结果很差，就必须对他们进行特别的帮助。他并没有采用一般阅读技巧或做数学题的传统方法，结果测试表明：有好的文化背景的孩子的成绩较好，家庭富裕的孩子的成绩比贫困家庭的孩子的要好。

教授表示该测试只是一个参考。这种测试方式很流行，学校、公司和军队都拿它对学生、员工和士兵进行测试。

后来文章作者及一些专家提出观点说：测试受很多方面影响（如紧张与否），而且对一个人来说，除了智商以外还有性格等多方面因素影响其成功。

◆ 题型及题目

Matching; Multiple Choice; TRUE/FALSE/NOT GIVEN

Matching:

The passage has eleven paragraphs A–K.

Which paragraph contains the following information?

- IQ is just a single factor of human being just as other characteristics.
- discussion of methodology behind the professor's test
- inadequacy of IQ test

Multiple Choice:

- The purpose of the text is to_________

A discuss the validity of IQ test. **B** ...

C demonstrate the limitation of test. **D** outline the history of the test.

- The professor Binet devise the test to _________

A find those who do not perform satisfied. **B** choose the best one.

C measure the intelligence. **D** establish the standard of intelligence.

- The test is designed according to _________

A math.　　**B** age.　　**C** reading skill.　　**D** ...

TRUE/FALSE/NOT GIVEN:

- To use this IQ test in arm force is not the intension of the professor Binet.
- The test are only intended to be used in Paris school.
- The professor regard measuring intelligent test as impossible.

48. 大学教育

◆ **文章大意**

讲述现在大学中存在的一些不合理的现象，说大学教师把精力放在课题研究上，而忽视了其本来的职能：教育学生，教他们如何解决问题，使学生在毕业后更能适应社会。文章列举了好教师的类型，并展望了今后大学的发展方向和教育改革的方向。

◆ **题型及题目**

TRUE/FALSE/NOT GIVEN; Matching

Matching: 列举了几条有关老师的描述，根据文章内容所提到的好教师的类型（一共有八种，A–H），选择每条描述对应的好教师的类型。

49. 公司的管理

◆ **文章大意**

写给经理们的关于公司管理方面的建议。

◆ **题型**

List of Headings; Multiple Choice

50. 炼金术

◆ **文章大意**

本文主要讲的是炼金术（alchemy）的发展和改进。说有人在南非开金矿公司淘金，后其公司又扩大到美国。炼金术随后应用于实践，申请专利（patent）的波折，最后讲南非受到的影响。

◆ **题目及答案**

Matching; YES/NO/NOT GIVEN

Matching: 年份配对题目

- 1885年，公司搬去美国。
- 1887年，出版了一本著作。
- 1891年，第一次踏足南非的某个地方。

YES/NO/NOT GIVEN:

- 主人公的发明把黄金的提炼率提高了一倍多。——YES（因为文中说一种老办法的提炼率为大约45%左右，后来也谈到新方法把提炼率提升到92–98%，正好一倍以上。）
- 南非矿主们对这种提炼法的热切态度。

● 在南非著名的黄金产地，除黄金外还有银等金属。——NOT GIVEN（文中没有提到黄金以外的东西）

● 南非法庭剥夺主人公专利权的理由是该提炼法不够新，是以前使用过的老方法。——YES（文中提到最后南非政府终于承认了这位科学家的功绩。）

● 这些科学家都是生物化学专家。——NO（文中只提到化学，与生物没有关系。）

● 这种新的黄金提炼法节省了大量费用。——NOT GIVEN（文中没有提到。）

● 这种提炼法对水源供应有污染。——YES（文中最后提到现代发明和使用的最新方法大大减轻了对水和土地的污染。）

51. 移民历史

◆ 文章大意

关于移民的话题。先回顾了人类迁移的历史，然后从二战说起，由于战争造成人口的大量流失，各国战后严重缺少劳动力。以澳洲为例，人口出生比例下降，因此战后大量吸引外来移民，尤其是来自亚洲的移民数量如今已超过欧洲，占据了外国移民的首位。接着把注意力转到欧洲和美国，说西欧（如英国，法国和西德）和美国在战后也是涌入了大批的移民。文章提到发展中国家的移民数量很少，以输出为主。最后说了当今世界的移民情况，以澳洲为例，已经开始去亚洲开设工厂，直接在当地招收雇员，因此移民数量有所下降。

◆ 题型

Matching; YES/NO/NOT GIVEN

Matching: 每个国家对应的一种移民情况

52. 世界旅游业的发展

◆ 文章大意

旅游业与社会经济。

◆ 题目及答案

List of Headings; YES/NO/NOT GIVEN; Sentence Completion

List of Headings:

● A段 Example

● B段 介绍旅游业的发展。

● C段 经济和社会对旅游业的影响。

● D段 difficult in...economic

● E段 旅游业成了国家外贸收入的主要来源。

YES/NO/NOT GIVEN:

● 旅游是许多国家最主要的收入来源。

● 旅游是澳大利亚的主要产业。——YES

● 旅游从1983年到1996年长了6%以上。——NO（文中说12%）

Sentence Completion; 几个百分比，代表不同国家的情况，在文章倒数第二段。

53. 空间与人权力大小的关系

◆ 文章大意

权力与空间（Power and Space）主要分三个部分：第一部分主要讲了管理层（high status）工作的私人空间比较大，楼层高，客户不可以直接进入，需预约。而员工工作的私人空间很小，噪音也很大，和别人共用办公室。大学里文秘类的职员（secretarial）和学术类（academic）的职员工作内容不同，工作时间也不同。现在的一些管理者有时候只通过电话，传真等信息工具进行工作。

第二部分讲到，现在的人地位升高了之后，一般会把旧房子卖掉，然后购置新房子，而且会把房子装修得很现代，并以此向人们炫耀自己的社会地位。

第三部分讲一些大公司喜欢将公司的办公位置选在比较好的地方，然而这样很容易造成交通堵塞，各国金融类的建筑都在市中心，而且很高，睥睨群雄。总之，空间与权力是有关系的。

◆ 题目及答案

Multiple Choice

- 从A–G选出三个地位高（high status）的特点。
- 选出三个地位低（low status）的特点。
- 人们地位提高了会干什么？
- 员工为什么不满管理者在家里办公？
- 问为什么现在西方的大公司都喜欢把楼盖得很高？——权力的象征
- 为文章选标题权力与空间的相互联系（interaction between space and power）

54. 地图发展史

◆ 文章大意

第一段，地图绘制的起源；第二段，19世纪末及20世纪初一些著名的地图；第三段，地图因为加了插页和彩色而为广大人民群众所接受；第四段，过去绘制地图是件非常辛苦的事情，要花6–9个月时间；画地图很费时间，因为每幅地图都是不同的，过去每幅地图都是单独面。第五段，说自从引进了计算机等先进技术，画地图变得容易多了；第六段，虽然计算机工作效率高，但是一些基本的绘图技能和地理知识对一个地图绘制者来说还是必要的。有些学徒工在只有15或16岁时就进入了这个领域，还干得很不错；第七段，很多人不了解世界上还有很多地方没标在地图上，而且很多信息是不准确的，或者是过时的；第八段，现代地图的发展方向，在地图上标注了城市未来的发展规划（city plans）。

◆ 题目及答案

Matching; List of Headings; Short Answer Questions

Matching

- 对于画地图的人来说什么是重要的？——不同的对象画不同的地图

- 为什么A段里那个人的地图册一开始卖得很好？——使用了colour system
- 绘制地图（map-making）什么最重要？——可信的信息（trustworthy information）

List of Headings:

- 第一段：Example
- 第二段：...attractiveness...
- 第三段：...Colour...
- 第四段：...time-consuming process...
- 第五段：...technology...
- 第六段：...need of expertise level...
- 第七段：...data source...
- 第八段：...the new development...

Short Answer Questions：NO MORE THAN FIVE WORDS OR NUMBERS

- 过去画一幅地图要多久时间？——6–9个月
- 图集里新添了什么？——城市规划（city plans）

55. 摩尔代码

◆ 文章大意

文章讲有关摩尔斯（Morse）发明电报（telegraph）的事情。他当时还是一个画家和偶然的发明家（occasional inventor）。他用了12年的时间才从英政府那里获得了财政支持，建立了他的第一条生产线（line）。摩尔斯的助手帮助他进行了一个改进。文章介绍了另一种容易操作的方法但是它需要五个针，而用摩尔斯代码发电报只要一个。接下来群雄奋起发电报，成立了一个协会，不过摩尔斯没参加，最终形成了两种协议。摩尔斯代码（Morse code）在一种新技术中被广泛应用（expanded）。1871年摩尔斯退休之后，摩尔斯代码风靡世界各地。

◆ 题目及答案

List of Headings; TRUE/FALSE/NOT GIVEN

List of Headings:

- 第二段：The invention of Morse code 摩尔斯代码的发明。
- 第三段：Advantages of Morse code 摩尔斯代码的优势。
- 第四段：电（electricity）的发明促进了摩尔斯代码的普及。
- 第五段：Morse code creates many employment opportunities 摩尔斯代码带来许多就业机会。
- 第六段：摩尔斯代码的国际化（internationalise）。
- 第七段：摩尔斯代码虽然不用于电信但是在广播和航海还在运用。

TRUE/FALSE/NOT GIVEN:

- 摩尔斯是不是在发明摩尔斯代码之前就很有名。

- 摩尔斯是不是等了很久才得到大公司的支持。
- 摩尔斯代码是不是很难学。
- 很多大公司是否喜欢聘请农村的员工。
- 摩尔斯是不是因工作太辛劳而死。

56. 科学家欺骗

◆ 文章大意

序言主要是作者对欺诈行为（fraud）的一个总论。正文第一部分讲一个叫W的人，他的老板将他实验快得出的理想结论满世界宣扬。但W发现有一个实验结果是无法得出此结论的，于是他摒弃了这个实验以维护其理想化的结论。第二个例子包括两个人，一个人被认为是发现了癌症（cancer）的病理（mechanism）；另一个人是哈佛大学（Harvard）的初级研究员（junior research），他在哈佛发表的论文数以千计。后来其他科学家发现这两个人在学术研究上均有欺骗行为，两人都因此失去了工作。

正文第二部分主要讲的是名誉撰稿人的问题。有一个叫W的人将自己的一篇论文提交给一个科学家研究组织。后来他在继续整理的时候忽然发现J的论文完全引用了他的观点和论据。于是一怒之下将J和J论文上的名誉撰稿人G告上了法庭。后来调查发现，某名牌大学的高级教授G，也就是J的导师，根本不知道此事。由于G德高望重，导致此事的调查颇为艰难，最后此事终于得以澄清。W也因对科学的厌倦而放弃了科学研究。

正文中第三部分讲到了科学家如何通过申报已经有进展的研究项目来申请研究资金的问题。

◆ 题型及答案

Matching; TRUE/FALSE/NOT GIVEN

Matching: 学术不规范行为方式和欺骗定义。

- 一个人做实验的结果与预期的不符，私自篡改结果，应导师推荐得以发表。
- 有两个论文发表太多，被别人发现。属于太过暴露于公众眼前（exposed by too much publications）。
- 有一个人发现别人剽窃他的东西，去控告（attempted to sue）那两个人，最后还是失去兴趣放弃不干了。属于disillusioned and gave up his job。
- 两个剽窃他人作品的人一个失掉了工作，还有一个是他的导师。属于honorary authorship。

TRUE/FALSE/NOT GIVEN:

- 科学家中大部分是做学术研究（academic research）的。
- 所谓的欺骗是指支持根本不成立的假设。
- 人们认为导师把自己的名字写在学生的研究成果上是诚实的行为。
- 科学家们对错误的行为达成了共识。

- 推动科学家取得成就的是他们的同僚（peers）。
- 通过申报已经有进展的研究项目来申请研究资金是否能为其他科学家所接受。
- 赞助单位已经默许这样的行为。

57. 个人工作和家庭的冲突

◆ 文章大意

在大不列颠，人们需要在家工作（Work in family is needed in Britain），先讲由于严格的工作时间（rigid time of work）和家庭生活（family life）之间的冲突，从而产生了在家工作（work in family）这样的解决方式。澳大利亚的调查报告探讨管理人员与一般人员对家庭关系的看法，文章最后得出结论，讲到一些已经允许员工（employee）在家工作的公司所获得的好处——旷工现象减少，生产力提高了（less absenteeism and more productivity）。

◆ 题型及答案

Sentence Completion; Matching; TRUE/FALSE/NOT GIVEN

Sentence Completion: 4.5%; 3.47%; lack of demand of workers

TRUE/FALSE/NOT GIVEN:

- 澳大利亚的调查是在1992年进行的。
- 调查的内容是人力资源经理（HR manager）对和谐家庭（friendly family）的态度。

58. 古代钱币

◆ 文章大意

有记录的最早的钱币来自古巴比伦。中国从周朝起就有刀、戟等形状的货币，但直到1866年，英国人来了才开始用银币（silver coin）。泰国（Thailand）用老虎做货币，因为很难弄到，后来Tiger tongue bar流行，再后来由于向西方开放商业和没有常规的货币（open commerce to west and no regular currency），那时候也没有西方的钞票，政府就让铸造者造Tiger Bullet。

日本的货币：大部分用银子做的，幕府将军下令把银器具都化了制成钱币，因为它们都是没有用的奢侈品。这种货币叫Japanese tree（日本树）在东亚国家流通，另一个叫做Bon，重1.5斤，是目前发现的最重的货币。有些非洲的货币是用鲸骨做的，以前被认为稀少，所以只给酋长佩戴。狗牙齿货币只给新娘用，做成手镯型，价值很高。有些可以修补，如果一面坏了就立刻变废品了。

◆ 题型及答案

Multiple Choice; Matching; TRUE/FALSE/NOT GIVEN

Multiple Choice:

- 中国19世纪大部分时间用的是：silver sycee（银锭）。
- 为什么制造bullet？没有standard currency（标准货币）。
- 狗牙齿货币给新娘可以使：价值提高。

Matching:

- 巴比伦（Babylon）的Clay货币是最早的货币形式。
- 泰国用老虎身上的东西做的货币现在是收藏品。
- 日本的money tree是用奢侈品做的。
- 用鲸鱼骨做的项链只有部落酋长能佩戴。
- 有一种货币如果其外观改变了就没有价值了。
- 日本的一种货币Bons是世界上最重的货币。
- 津巴布韦的一种货币是把融化的金属倒入模子里铸出来的。

59. 纸币的发展

◆ 文章大意

文章从远古的石头贝壳讲到中国的第一张纸币，造纸法和古埃及的造纸材料。

先讲远古时代是怎样交易的，然后是硬币（coin）的出现，硬币由重到轻，上面刻什么东西。然后是纸币（money paper）的出现。提到中国的造纸术。

接着讲制造纸币的三个要素：油墨的改进；造纸原料的发展；印刷技术的发展（墨、纸和雕刻）。讲墨（ink）提到墨褪色（ink fade），讲到纸币的缺点，有经济问题（economic problem），油墨褪色、造纸花费、外国人。接下来讲怎么制造纸，然后讲刻印（engrave），提到纸币容易被伪造。最后是说纸币将来可能被电子（electrical）货币替代。

◆ 题型

Matching; YES/NO/NOT GIVEN

60. 老年职工

◆ 文章大意

关于老年工人（gray worker）工作的问题。发达国家的知名企业在对待企业中老年人员工（older worker）的不同做法和态度。

学者研究发现了几个公司的现状，并讨论一种在美国开始形成的新型方法，就是让那些年纪接近退休的人尝试一种非全职的过渡工作阶段模式，这样对公司来说新型的安置工作方法既减轻了人力成本开销，又留下了这些年纪较大职员——对公司来说意味着可贵的价值财富。

加拿大的某个公司决定裁减他们的英国籍员工（British employees），因为需要有新鲜血液注入公司。有些人认为年轻人比较有优势，因为他们能灵活地接受新事物。然而另一些人认为年老的人才有优势，因为他们的教育背景要比现在的年轻人好，并且他们具备预测危机事件的能力。

有个德国公司现在的员工平均年龄提高了，并不是因为他们不想裁减老年员工，而是政府有非常严格的政策不允许他们这样做。

IBM成立了一个公司，专门雇佣年纪比较大的自愿雇员，以使他们充分发挥自己的优势。老年人自己开办的公司倒闭几率明显低于年轻人所开办的公司。

◆ 题型及答案

Multiple Choice; TRUE/FALSE/NOT GIVEN

Multiple Choice:

老年雇员的两个优点：

- 能预先知道可能出问题的领域（spot the area from which problem may occur）。
- 适应公司文化，能灵活处理人际关系（relationship）。

年轻员工的缺点：

- 容易跳槽（change work quickly），不值得培训。
- 现在年轻人的受教育程度不如老一辈。

61. 汽车未来发展

◆ 文章大意

文章主要讲了汽车及未来发展，汽车的设计变化以及设计局限可以改变。汽车一直被指燃烧油料，排放废气和二氧化碳，它是导致全球变暖（global warming）的罪魁祸首，但是，另一个类似的污染源航空旅行（air travel）却一直被忽视。文章还提到了汽车外形发展，辅助驾驶系统，政府的计划和人们的观点。

◆ 题目及答案

List of Headings; Summary

List of Headings:

- Paragraph A: Example
- Paragraph B: Variety of design
- Paragraph C: Market strategy
- Paragraph D: Need new fuel
- Paragraph E: Cleaner engineer
- Paragraph F: Driver assistant
- Paragraph G: Joys of car ownership

Summary:

- linked together electronically
- accident avoidance system
- drivers, air travel

62. 计时器

◆ 文章大意

古代，人们根据日光影子随时间变化而变化来计时。由于经纬不同，日晷（sundial）需要有不同设计。还有沙漏，它是用一个瓶子装上水或沙向下漏用来计时；后来用油灯，根据油的高度来计时；现在有的地区还用火绳计时，即在一个凹槽中放一条火绳，点火燃烧来计时。

◆ **题目及答案**

Matching: TRUE/FALSE/NOT GIVEN

Matching: lunar shadow; sundial; portable clock; candle lamp

● 水漏：两个正在滴水的图，两个不滴水的图。不滴水的图马上排除掉。在两幅滴水的图中，向烧杯中滴水的那个图是正确的。

● 测量日光影子的木条：一头竖着一个与底端呈十字型（cross）的木条，像个“丁”字型。

● 火绳：先排除掉两个只有一根棍的图，然后看底座。

63．数字发展

◆ **文章大意**

文章讲人类的数字发展史。数字最早是用来帮助完成农活的，那些人只关心够不够，不关心有多少。接下来讲最早大家开始数数，但是局限于几个，泰什米尔人只有三种数字：一，二和许多。还说了用手势可以帮助理解数字的概念，消除含糊。下一段又说这种局限不足为奇，现在聪明的欧洲人，当时只会数到9！埃及、英国和哥伦比亚把不同的“长物”，“独木舟”等分成七类，不同的类用不同的计数单词。最后说数字和抽象的概念联系起来发展使人们有了真正意义上的sense of number。

◆ **题目及答案**

Multiple Choice; Matching; TRUE/FALSE/NOT GIVEN

TRUE/FALSE/NOT GIVEN:

● 考核公职人员的方法是让他们从一数到十，可见大多数人都不会。—— TRUE

● 身体语言有助于理解数字。—— TRUE

64．日本的数学教育

◆ **文章大意**

第一段比较日本和欧洲的数学教育现状。有很多日本学生取得了很好的成绩，欧洲学生的成绩则不佳。在相同的条件下，为什么会有这么大的差异呢？

然后是日本中学的背景介绍，提到国立学校（state school）和私立学校（private school）。但只有3%的学生念私立学校。然后提到现代学校设计和先进的设施。

接着具体介绍学生是怎样学习的。他们先把作业的答案写在黑板上由老师纠错，然后再讲解教的主题。有时候老师也会因为学生没有学会而额外再留下来教。再讲混合班是帮助差生而设立的。还有从小家长和老师就给孩子这样一个印象，一定要做出题目，不可以落后 。同学之间也会互相帮助。

最后讲到为什么日本的数学会发展得好，有两个关键，其中一个是老师和家长的重视。

◆ **题型及答案**

Matching; Multiple Choice; TRUE/FALSE/NOT GIVEN

Multiple Choice:

- 帮助差生的方式是：put pupils to the mixed class 把小学生放在混合班。
- Japanese teachers introduce a new math will 日本老师介绍一种新的数学意向。
- 日本学生数学书的内容。
- 对日本数学教学现状的态度。

TRUE/FALSE/NOT GIVEN:

- 英国学生比日本学生在数学上获得更好的成绩（greater achievement in math）。—— FALSE
- 大部分孩子都去私立学校（private school）。—— FALSE
- 私立学校要比公立学校时髦。—— NOT GIVEN
- 日本老师给作业打分。—— FALSE

65. 澳洲体育的成功

◆ **文章大意**

澳大利亚在体育方面的成就。澳大利亚用先进的科学实验研究成果来促进运动的发展。具体提到澳大利亚游泳项目的成功，1996年奥运会只有2%的人用了科研成果。文中提到哪些成果是澳洲目前正在使用的，哪些是澳洲运动员和竞争对手都在用的，哪些是澳洲将来会用到的。

◆ **题型及答案**

List of Headings; Matching

Matching: camera; protein test; censor

66. 消费心理学

◆ **文章大意**

文章给流行和时尚（fad）下了一个定义，讲了为什么会出现。一家公司的抗抑郁药普拉唑药怎么流行起来的。然后介绍了三个理论信息瀑布（information cascade），制裁理论（sanction theory）和互动消费（interaction consumption）：健康引导（美国人虽然不知道吸烟的具体坏处，但还是少吸烟了），消费因为群体（看电影不是因为电影好看，而是因为这样能使大家有共同话题），信息传递（有人买了东西后，用着好，就会介绍给朋友，朋友正确选择产品的机会就会多些）。前两个解释为什么会流行；后一个解释时尚。有一个趋势表（trend chart）对比三类市场战略（marketing strategy）中的顾客选择的成功率。

◆ **题型及答案**

Summary; Matching; TRUE/FALSE/NOT GIVEN

Matching: 理论和表现形式匹配

- information cascade 信息瀑布

- sanction theory 制裁理论
- interaction consumption 互动消费

67. 儿童教育

◆ 文章大意

以前父母对自己的孩子很不好，因为那个时候医疗条件不好导致儿童经常夭折，所以父母不投入过多的感情，以免失去孩子的时候太悲伤。还有儿童被当成劳动力。

随着社会经济的发展，出现了中产阶级，中产阶级的父母有为孩子投资的钱，为他们购买玩具和儿童书籍。

欧洲几个思想家开始搞革命，他们有些人提出人的命运不是生来就注定的，而是取决于后天的教育。还有就是把人的儿童阶段单独提出来，指出儿童与成人的不同之处。

其后一些人开始实践理论，有个法国人对一个狼孩（文章里说，这个孩子被发现时候显然和人类社会隔绝了，而且没有受到任何教育）进行训练，但是收效甚微。

P发展了xx的理论，认为学校的教育应该改革。然后又有人对P的理论进行实践，建立一所新型学校，很快在欧洲流行，并于20世纪初在全世界流行。

◆ 题型

List of Headings; Matching

Matching: 事件和时间匹配

68. 城市交通工具发展

◆ 文章大意

讲公交的发展，提到电力机车（tram），公交（bus），火车（railway），地铁（subway），自动人行道（moving pavement）。说以前都是马拉的电力机车，奔驰和戴母勒的motor很成功。

第一段：发动机的飞速发展；讲火车对城市的扩张起到了很大的作用；第二段：原始地铁路的出现，蒸汽机车车头的很多烟让顾客不满意，没发展多久就衰落了；第三段：电力机车的出现给地铁带来了新的生机；第四段：地铁在全世界范围内的飞速发展；第五段：自动人行道的发明；第六段：改进的自动人行道在美国得到很好的应用。

◆ 题型及答案

List of Headings; YES/NO/NOT GIVEN

List of Headings:

- Paragraph A: Example
- Paragraph B: Establishment of buses
- Paragraph C: Pros and cons of underground railway
- Paragraph D: Electricity tram
- Paragraph E: Spread of underground
- Paragraph F: Alternative transport-moving pavement

- Paragraph G: Spread of moving pavement

YES/NO/NOT GIVEN:

- 公交在伦敦一开始就受欢迎。——NO
- 马拉的车被认为很慢。—— NOT GIVEN
- 火车比公交对城市的贡献大。——NOT GIVEN
- 火车一开始就受欢迎。——YES
- 电的出现使一辆地下车出现了。——YES
- 人行道的问题被解决了。——YES

69. 城市交通现状

◆ 文章大意

关于城市交通调查了37个城市。墨尔本的居民原来愿意住在郊区，现在变了。富裕与交通没有必然关系。欧洲许多国家的公共交通系统开始引起世界关注，有个显著特征是车的数量少，举了几个国家的例子，然后说自行车多的城市交通系统也比较优化。又举了几个欧洲国家的例子，同时说一个国家Q花了17% GDP（国内生产总值）的经费，可是交通系统的先进程度还不如中国等三个只花了5% GDP的国家。后来提到国家Q的国力等特征和珀斯（Perth）很类似。文章说许多富裕国家车的拥有量实际上是比较小的，有钱的人趋向去郊区（suburb）居住。曼谷（Bangkok）不是很富有但汽车多，还提到了地铁、轻轨等交通工具。

◆ 题型及答案

Multiple Choice; Matching; TRUE/FALSE/NOT GIVEN

Multiple Choice: 选title

Matching: 城市名字和交通特点匹配，找出一个适合珀斯、奥克兰和波特兰的

- 奥克兰（Auckland）——在山地也能把轻轨（light railway）应用充分。
- 波特兰（Portland）——自行车使国家飞速发展。

70. 新型汽车

◆ 文章大意

文章讲了两个汽车系统（car system）的比较。虽然其他科技都发展很快，但是城市交通的发展却不尽人意，为了改善交通，人们发明了两种由电脑控制的交通工具。一个是Rnt，一个是Ruf。Rnt和Ruf差不多，不过Ruf允许驾驶者自己驾驶一段路，到了真正的路上就要由计算机来控制了，而且普通的车也可以改装成Ruf，所以可能会受汽车生产厂家的欢迎。

◆ 题型

TRUE/FALSE/NOT GIVEN; Multiple Choice; Matching

71. 新型燃料

◆ 文章大意

文章讲一种新型燃料，指出让一些有名望的人推广一下这种燃料是很有必要的。

◆ **题型及答案**

List of Headings; TRUE/FALSE/NOT GIVEN

● 美国汽油的30%是用于加热。

● 发动机（engine）使用汽油达到了最佳的速度。——FALSE（原文讲再怎么用现在也只能达到30%）

72. 美国垃圾处理

◆ **文章大意**

文章提到美国的垃圾被日本购买，西雅图人扔垃圾要交钱，美国一个地方为什么垃圾回收率最高等等。和其他国家如德国相比垃圾回收的区别。

在西雅图，人们很重视环保，他们很自觉地收集垃圾，这是因为如果他们乱扔垃圾会被政府罚（charge）很多钱。但在洛杉矶（L.A.），没有相关的法律来支持环保政策，因为有个市政官员说，洛杉矶附近有很多填埋垃圾的场所，没必要花那么多钱把垃圾收集起来运来运去。文章中提到两种被填埋的主要物质，不过纸张才是被埋掉最多的垃圾。

◆ **题型及答案**

Short Answer; YES/NO/NOT GIVEN

Short Answer:

● 哪种垃圾多？——纸

● 哪个国家购买美国的废金属垃圾？——日本（文中提到日本将美国消耗的废金属垃圾购买回国生产成汽车后再卖给美国）

● 西雅图的垃圾废品回收率是多少？——45%（文中提到全美国平均垃圾回收率是17%，干扰项）

● 美国哪个地方还有很多空间作为垃圾填埋之地？——西部州

● 哪种材料从回收中获得，比重新制造这种材料来得更加划算？——钢材

YES/NO/NOT GIVEN:

● 德国关于回收利用的法律是不是最先进的。

● 美国是不是要更多的燃烧垃圾。

● 德国的垃圾处理法制是不是最完善的。

● 西雅图人回收垃圾是因为扔垃圾要交钱。

● 德国人的垃圾回收法（recycling law）是最先进的。

73. 视觉盲点

◆ **文章大意**

文章开头讲一位教授根据一个场景实验提出他的论点——人们其实看到很多东西，但只选择他们认为重要的东西去记忆。但又有一位教授提出相反的论点，他做的实验是让一组人盯着屏幕看一个画面，然后让画面消失一会儿，再出现有信息缺失的相同画面，但实

验者没有注意到。这说明人们对于非常重要的东西也会看不见的。另外又做的一个实验是打篮球时的录像，一样的道理。然后第三位教授提出人看到什么是根据他的想象得出的。最后一位教授提出看到的东西跟眼睛的运动有关。

◆ **题型**

List of Headings; Multiple Choice; YES/NO/NOT GIVEN

74．运输业的发展

◆ **文章大意**

现代货物航运（包括集装箱）带来的好处，价格和货物本身价值。现在都是成品不像以前都是很重的原材料。新加坡生产电脑配件，日本进口。

文章还介绍了运输的发展及运输如何发展；只要货物做出来，运过去就可以了。但实际上，有的地方劳动力便宜（如中国），而且有的货物要求及时到达（如季节性衣服）。德国、法国、日本等国家的工业和农业产品运输量提升。日本从东南亚进口的电脑光驱比本国制造还便宜。政府关税，美国订立运输标准。国际贸易现在的成本降低了。

◆ **题型**

Summary; Matching; YES/NO/NOT GIVEN

75．市场营销的演变

◆ **文章大意**

广告就要针对顾客针对市场做。美国公司诸如锐步、耐克、可口可乐营销策略的变化——从单一产品到多元成品，到市场细分，广告商的一些做法。

过去美国人不管做什么运动，只能买到一种运动鞋。后来锐步（Reebok）有所变化，生产气垫鞋，耐克也有所改善，还有个牌子设计鞋只注意时尚而不要功能。原来商家就是通过卖得多来降低成本。现在市场变得复杂，商家开始细分市场。特别提到一个公司，它是根据美国行政区（州）来细分市场，而不是以人种来区分。有的公司则针对不同顾客使用不同的广告，但是产品是一样的，如可口可乐公司。最后说公司的资源都是有限的，不可能吸引所有人，所以有的公司把目标定位在特定的消费群上，以求获得最大利润，如：书店就是把高收入者当做主要客户。

◆ **题目及答案**

Matching; YES/NO/NOT GIVEN

Matching: 公司名称和做法

- 耐克（Nike）——use celebrities effect（名人效应）
- 可口可乐（Coca-cola）——market the same product to different groups
- Campel——stressed fashion and appearances more than actual functions
- 一个美国公司——differentiate markets according to regions（22 states of US）
- 高露洁（Colgate）——market to wrong groups of people

● 某书店——定位在高收入人群中

76. 沉船保护

◆ **文章大意**

文章先介绍一艘瑞典海军的古沉船的历史，它被捞上来时像新的一样，这是因为一种物质的存在，但在博物馆里放久了船就开始坏了，因为离开了原来的海水环境。船木里分解几种酸，有腐蚀作用。然后科学家想保护船的办法，但先要把船上的骨架和铁零件拆下来，用一个电缆替代船骨。然后文章说海里还有好多沉船面临着的威胁：虫子、海流和风等等。最后一个组织认为这艘瑞典船在海里没坏是因为那里的海水被污染过，没有氧气和虫子，所以保护沉船的最好办法就是还原当时的水环境，把船留在水里。

◆ **题型**

Multiple Choice; TRUE/FALSE/NOT GIVEN

77. 海底探测船

◆ **文章大意**

比较两种可以探测海底的船。一种是垂直翻转船（flip ship），另一种是铰链船（hinge ship）。

第一段：你可以想象，以后人们可以在一种船里穿T恤，牛仔裤通过楼梯走向海底观看美丽的海底世界吗，这是一种多么美好的想象啊，现在随着科技的发展，出现了一种叫垂直翻转船的就可以做到了。

第二段：说这种船的原理，文章最后有图。一个非盈利性（non-profit）的科研工作组对这种船进行了研究，但是海底并不是随便就可以看的，要交一定费用才行。

第三段：开始说这种船具体怎么工作的。

第四段：说因为垂直翻转船存在一些问题，然后某大学研究出了另外一种船，这种船比它好，叫铰链船。

第五段：说这种铰链船的原理，说到它只能在200米范围内进行科研。

第六段：这种铰链船的缺点是价格贵，如果铰链船的花费可以降低的话，就更好了。后面提到了油箱，说还好这种油轮可以经过改装变成其中一种船。

◆ **题型及答案**

Matching; YES/NO/NOT GIVEN

Matching: 船名和特点

A Flip ship

B Hinge ship

C Both flip ship and hinge ship

D Neither flip ship nor hinge ship

● 不到200米的时候工作。

● 恶劣天气下能工作。

● 谁需要特殊的改装。

● 在测量的时候是垂直的。

● 需要用电梯把人运到实验室里去。

YES/NO/NOT GIVEN

● 造铰链船比垂直翻转船便宜。——NO

78. 英国农业

◆ 文章大意

英国农业有个误区，那就是用不绿色不健康的手段做到产品低成本。这样会带来污染问题，人们的健康水平也会下降。政府应该注意这个问题，帮助农民和消费者实现绿色农业。

首先简要列举了现代农业的种种负面影响，文章一开始就表明了否定的态度。第二段稍稍讲了一些农业的发展历程，人们对科技和机械的投入越来越大。结果是英国环境的改变，田间的小鸟没有了，河流污染了。现在食物的价格是原来的三倍，但这些耗费没有引起经济学家的重视。他们和许多生产者和消费者都看不到这些巨额投入，因为他们认为这是经济循环之外的费用，不影响任何人的经济利益。（文章给了个专业词语来定义这些消耗，并有相关填空题。）有位大学教授算出了这些消耗，他认为这是可以计算的。接着列出了各项以百万英镑计算的花费，包括污染治理和残留农药等问题。这位教授总结说这些消耗应该避免。尤其英国并不是急需食品的国家，可以将消耗降到一定的程度。他建议取消工业化养殖（industrial farming），而且许多农民还无法实施有机养殖（organic farming）。他提出一项计划叫“绿色食物”，这将有助于降低食物的生产成本。

◆ 题型及答案

Matching; Sentence Completion; YES/NO/NOT GIVEN

Matching: 信息与段落标号

● 英国有种鸟消失了。

● 农业发展历程。

● 关于那些消耗的专业词语。

● 水污染。

Sentence Completion:

食物账单超出人们的想象，农民不能适应有机耕作（organic farming），政府应该控制绿色食品标准（greener food standard），这样做对消费者和农民都有益处。

79. 通讯手段的发展

◆ 文章大意

文章讲的是通讯手段的发展。从古代的鼓（drum），烟（smoke），烽火信号（signal fire）到如今的互联网（internet）。人类最早利用（signal）来交流，后来贝尔（Bell）发明电话，海底光缆（cable）的发明，电脑的应用，互联网冲浪（surf），调制解调器（Modem），综合业务数字网（ISDN），英美正在开发的“信息高速公路”，最后的结论是：不管通讯手段如何发展，它最初的目的并没有改变，那就是与人的沟通。

◆ **题型及答案**

List of Headings; Short Answer

Short Answer:

- 年代题。
- 列举一种古代的有声通讯手段——鼓。

80. 手机短信参与电视节目

◆ **文章大意**

电视节目（TV programme）中手机短信取代了电子邮件（e-mail），因为观众可以直接参与，并直接影响比赛的最终结果，这一趋势在中国正风靡（如：中国超级女声），以前用e-mail上网，现在直接用手机发短信给节目就可以对节目进行评论，也可以投票。通信公司以此大赚，它索要的费用比正常的短信高，电视节目制作人（TV programme maker）也分享利益。短信的巨大成功源于一种技术short rode，这种技术以前不行，后来才可以运用到手机上。但是不能用在电视上，因为电视总闪屏。最后说，这并不意味着传统的电视节目（traditional programme）不行了，还有很多一系列的服务需要提供给那些就喜欢躺在沙发上练习拇指的“土豆”们。

◆ **题型**

List of Headings; Multiple Choice; Matching

Matching: 不同机构和观点匹配

81. 移动电话是否对飞机有影响

◆ **文章大意**

文章讲移动电话是否对飞机的飞行有影响，移动电话不允许在飞机上使用，不是因为信号影响，而是为了让人们用飞机上的电话。人们对此有不同意见，并且做了不少实验，给了一些建议。CAC、BOEING等五家公司表明了意见，每家公司的意见其实差不多，都认为手机对飞行的危害不大。

◆ **题型及答案**

Summary; Matching; YES/NO/NOT GIVEN

Summary: navigation; communications; radiation; antenna

Matching: CAC，波音（BOEING）等五家公司的意见匹配

82. 飞行控制

◆ **文章大意**

美国一个控制管制机构的成立、历史和作用。这个控制管制的机构是因为56年前一个事故成立的，旨在控制各种飞机的飞行区域和高度，它规定了在不同天气条件下应该怎么飞以及不同水平的飞机和飞行员应该遵守哪些规定。

◆ 题型

List of Headings; TRUE/FALSE/NOT GIVEN

83. 小班授课的研究

◆ 文章大意

美国人家境富裕，家长受教育程度高，越来越多人考虑小班授课的好处。若干的实验项目由此展开。第一个实验项目采用了很多方式确保实验的公平性。分了两个班，并且请了一批专门的顾问（adviser），咨询者（consultant），助教（assistant）协助，结果证明小班授课好，并且学生在一定时间内都效果明显。有人质疑这个项目的准确性，认为其不完全公平，尤其是在项目运行中考虑到家长的压力，有部分学生从大班调到了小班。第二个试验项目，是选择了部分院校进行，但是加重了本来就有的一个负面因素，即很多院校本来就缺老师，但是为了保证被选中的较发达地区的实验院校能有充足的老师完成小班授课，项目采用了高工资的方式从那些贫困地区聘用老师，结果导致贫困地区老师更加缺乏。第三个实验项目是一个飞行员（pilot）项目。最后比较三个实验项目。其中一个项目提到了不同种族有同样的效果。

◆ 题型

List of Headings; Matching

Matching: 三个实验和相关概念特点匹配

84. 水利发展

◆ 文章大意

第一段：古代的水利设计，以古罗马为例。

第二段：近代灌溉系统的发展满足了不断加大的水利需求。

第三段：很多国家和地区因为供水不足等问题使得健康问题日益严重。

第四段：很多人择水而居，还有建筑堤坝等问题，对环境产生了影响。

第五段：科学家们认为，现在主要的问题不是让有水的人获得更好的供给，而是应当让更多的人能够用上水。

第六段：近年来很多地区对水需求量的增长速度比人们预计的要低。

第七段：以上现象归因于人们比以往更善于利用水资源，一些科学技术使得人们的生活更加省水。

第八段：展望未来，很多地方还需要进行水利方面的基础建设。

◆ 题型

List of Headings; TRUE/FALSE/NOT GIVEN

85. 网上资料

◆ 文章大意

网上资料的储存，一些人建立了互联网档案馆（internet archives），要把网上的东西全部存起来给子孙后代看。还和出版商、美国档案机构合作。

◆ **题型及答案**

Matching; Sentence Completion; Multiple Choice

Matching: 信息与段落匹配

- 互联网与传统媒体形式的相同点（similarities between internet and traditional types of media）——B
- 总结这项工作面临的挑战——A
- 具体储存这些资料的方式——F

Sentence Completion: political; accessible; areas; 1996

86. 男女合校

◆ **文章大意**

讨论男女同校（co-education）好还是男女分校（single-sex）好。讲到澳大利亚莫纳什大学（Monash）。

◆ **题型**

Matching; TRUE/FALSE/NOT GIVEN; Multiple Choice

Multiple Choice: 家长给孩子选学校的时候考虑几个因素：学校的大小、宗教等。

87. 香蕉

◆ **文章大意**

文章讲香蕉，包括香蕉的历史，它是不是历史上最古老的水果。它有了细菌之后还能放很久，而使用杀虫剂来杀虫会使害虫产生抗药性。对于使用基因改良的香蕉，人们接受起来有困难。

香蕉很早以前就在东南亚（Southeast Asia）出现了，但是原来的香蕉果实中含有太多种子（masses of seeds），它们几乎不可食用（uneatable）。然后某一种香蕉逐渐变成了普遍种植的物种。科学家就说，这样种类单一化的情况对香蕉有些不利。现在普遍种植的香蕉甜，但是很容易染上萎蔫病（panama disease），这种病影响土地，并且持续时间很长。在1950年之后那种甜香蕉基本上就没有人种植了。而且这种疾病对杀虫剂产生了耐药性，很难对付。对西方国家来说，香蕉仅仅是一种水果，但对贫困国家的人来说，香蕉就变成了粮食。所以香蕉减产的影响应该值得注意。

◆ **题目及答案**

Sentence Completion; TRUE/FALSE/NOT GIVEN; Matching

Sentence Completion:

- 多少年前香蕉就出现了？——一万年（ten thousand）
- 在哪里出现的？——东南亚（Southeast Asia）
- 以前的香蕉不能作为食物吃是因为？——种子（seeds）

TRUE/FALSE/NOT GIVEN:

- 某公司现在是否还是最大的香蕉供应商。—— NOT GIVEN
- 香蕉在某些国家是当口粮的。
- 香蕉是最古老的作物。
- 香蕉成了很多家庭的食物供应（food supply）。

Matching: 人名和观点匹配

88. 香水

◆ 文章大意

两个人在马达加斯加发现可以从植物和自然中提取香料，后面有一个装置图，填怎样把花里的香味弄出来以及关于香水（perfume）、香料（spice）的寻找。两位科学家在人烟稀少的地方找，这里的香料大多在别处都没有，是这里独有的。人们现在不用动物香料而用植物香料代替，还有松香（resin）。

◆ 题型及题目

TRUE/FALSE/NOT GIVEN; Multiple Choice; Matching

Matching: 信息和段落匹配

- 现在人们不用哪一种香料了。
- 现在人们最喜欢的香料。

89. 龙涎香

◆ 文章大意

龙涎香（ambergris）很久以前就有了，它的用途很广，可以用来制药、香料、香水（perfume）等等。但是人们不知道它是从哪里来的，再就是说在古代，它的价值相当于同样重量的黄金的价值，可见其昂贵。

以前人们一直把龙涎香和琥珀（amber）当作同一种东西。但是有个叫迪克的人写了一本关于二者区别的书。龙涎香通常在海面或者海滨（shore）被发现，但是人们仍然不知道它是从哪里来的。琥珀非常小，与松树（pine）有关。然后讲到琥珀的一些特征：坚硬（hard），透明（transparent）等等，用来做装饰品同样很贵重。

龙涎香与抹香鲸肠道消化某种东西有关。具体描述龙涎香的产生过程。大意是：抹香鲸（sperm whale）呕吐出来某种东西。然后这种东西遇到空气就会变硬（harden），于是就形成了龙涎香，也解释了为什么龙涎香总在海面和海滨被发现。

人们为了获得龙涎香而捕杀抹香鲸，导致其濒临灭绝。给了一个数据说，在20世纪，90%的龙涎香是在杀戮抹香鲸的过程中生产出来的。于是人们就开始采取措施保护抹香鲸，在工业生产中采用了很多龙涎香的替代品，例如香水制造业中就用了某种东西代替了龙涎香。

抹香鲸的数量会有恢复（recover）的那么一天。

◆ **题型及答案**

Matching; Summary; TRUE/FALSE/NOT GIVEN

Matching:

A only ambergris B only amber C both D neither

- very expensive——C
- use in medicine——A
- use as currency——D
- refers to in a book written by Dick——C
- could be seen through——B

Summary：龙涎香的形成步骤

TRUE/FALSE/NOT GIVEN

- in 20th century most ambergris was made in the processing of killing of sperm whale——TRUE
- ambergris's cost increased recently—— NOT GIVEN
- ambergris still remains in the perfume making——TRUE（文中说可以人工来合成某些材料，可是还是有些方面需要使用龙涎香）

90．拥挤与密度

◆ **文章大意**

文章讲拥挤对城市、对人群、对工作地点的影响（effect of crowding on city，on people，on workplace，etc.）。为什么会出现拥挤的现象。文章前一部分讲影响因素，后一部分讲负面影响，人们往往更注重条件，而不是形势等。

◆ **题型及答案**

List of Headings; TRUE/FALSE/NOT GIVEN; Summary

List of Headings:

- 给拥挤和密度下定义，它们的主要特征。
- 然后一个人用鼠（rat）做实验，揭示实验的本质和结果。
- 后面一个大学做实验，这次选择了一个精神病人进行实验。
- 提到足球赛散场以后人们往往觉得特别拥挤，因为大家没有了关注的目标，体现的是拥挤的感觉。
- 你挂几张画就会觉得好些，是对工作条件的建议。

Summary: 人的感觉比起周围的环境更能让人觉得拥挤。（运动员要是把精力集中在比赛上，而不是集中在其他比赛选手身上，就不会觉得那么拥挤了），拥挤的负面效应肯定是男人比女人严重，这就能解释男监狱时常发生暴力事件的原因了。

91. 小提琴

◆ **文章大意**

文章讲小提琴的制作、改良、技术进步、科学制作和手工制作。还陆续提到了科学的方法、小提琴的保护和用老木材来制作小提琴的好处，最后一段提到音乐家们偶尔会用现代的小提琴。

◆ **题型及题目**

List of Headings; TRUE/FALSE/NOT GIVEN

A段：关于价格浮动（changes about prices）

B段：举例（example）

C段：制作技术上的挑战

92. 彗星的形成

◆ **文章大意**

彗星（comet）的形成、结构、变化等。彗星和气候现象的关系。

◆ **题型及题目**

Multiple Choice; Picture

Picture: 彗星从外部到内部的结构

93. 磁

◆ **文章大意**

磁（magnetism）的发现，科学家吉伯（Gilbert）的家庭历史及有成就的文章。

◆ **题型及题目**

List of Headings; TRUE/FALSE/NOT GIVEN; Multiple Choice

List of Headings:

A段：科学界名人

B段：家庭的支持

C段：吉伯先生的早年

D段：他的关注点不变化

E段：他在磁学上的发现

F段：对传统天文学的质疑

G段：他的新方法

94. 手势

◆ **文章大意**

不同地区手势（gesture）的话题。手势用来引起人们的注意，它跟电话铃声很相似，表示愤怒的手势都很强有力，但是如果你不那么用力的话，手势就失去了原来的意义。不同国家同一手势的意义不同，文中举了一个例子，就是把五指捏在一起，在意大利表示什么。除了文化的差异以外，还有个人的差异，即在同一个国家中，由于本身的身体条件（physical condition）不同，所以表示同一个手势（gesture）的方式也稍有差异，有的人因为牙齿不好，可能会抿着嘴，有的人可能就会露出牙齿，这种个人的差异也可以被其他人理解，不会产生歧义。如果两个国家交流频繁，渐渐地就会消除这种手势的差异，慢慢达到统一，不会混淆。

◆ **题型**

TRUE/FALSE/NOT GIVEN; Multiple Choice; Matching

95. 学习方法

◆ **文章大意**

讲传统的阅读模式不好。文章先介绍两种观点，紧接着就有人质疑、反对，中间段落还做了实验研究。最后还总结了一下什么样的方法适当。

◆ **题型**

TRUE/FALSE/NOT GIVEN; Summary

96. 澳大利亚更新能源

◆ **文章大意**

澳大利亚大规模更新能源。

◆ **题型及题目**

Matching; TRUE/FALSE/NOT GIVEN

TRUE/FALSE/NOT GIVEN:

- 澳大利亚的新能源比传统的便宜。
- 澳大利亚是新能源领域的领导者。
- GEOENERGY已经研究了氡气（radon gas）对环境的影响。
- Wavetech的建立是在它的发明人被另一个公司拒绝以后。
- 环境使旅游业不能发展。

97. 中世纪的玩具

◆ **文章大意**

文章讲了中世纪的小孩怎样玩耍，讲到玩具在英国的发展，以及中世纪的父母与小孩的关系是否像现代社会一样。

◆ **题型**

Matching; TRUE/FALSE/NOT GIVEN

98. 口译

◆ **文章大意**

文章讲口译与笔译的各自定义，口译的重点在哪里。以前有一种口译方式，讲话人一说完，口译者也翻译完，这种方式用语不太正式，适合小规模会议。现在这种方式正在被另外一种口译方式所代替。口译会受到诸多因素的影响。正常的口译的速度是100-120个词，如果超过200个词就不行；口译的难点是：口译的时候最怕碰到句子结构不同的语句，如动词放最后等，所以口译要等说话人说完了才能翻译。另外一个影响口译的因素是说话人的速度，速度快了翻译就跟不上。

◆ **题型及题目**

Multiple Choice; Summary

选项式Summary，选项都是数字，如2，3，10，100，120，200等。原文中只要有数字的地方就可能是答案。

99. 外语对商业的影响

◆ **文章大意**

英语被所有企业重视，负责人（director）的英语应更好。商务旅游对英语有不同层次的要求，英语在所有企业中都起明显作用。语言作用于商业的两种方式有直接方式和间接方式两种；它对商务的作用没有引起足够的重视。语言对公司的领导很有用；因为要全球旅行，所以了解不同地方的语言会很方便；跨国企业的领导用不同语言与非本国职员交流。公司职员直接面对不同语言的情况为：电话员和接待员需要懂得客户的语言；一些特殊的领域，比如海运（shipping）一定要懂外语，某年的撞船事故就是因为双方职员不能交流；聘请翻译，特殊情况下需要聘请专门的翻译，尤其是谈判（negotiation）的时候；哪些机构提供类似服务；选择翻译的标准，忠于（loyalty）原文和准确（accuracy）；有时候需要在聘请专业翻译的同时，自己的员工也要懂得这种语言，这样可以监控翻译的准确性。

◆ **题型及答案**

YES/NO/NOT GIVEN; Short Answer

Short Answer:

- 客户服务、销售等部门对外语水平的要求：high level。
- 公司里最先接触客户的员工：接待员（receptionists），电话员（telephonists）。
- 对外语要求很高的行业：shipping。
- 翻译人员最重要的品质是可信性。
- 翻译人员必须准确传达信息。
- 在谈判中请一个懂双方语言的翻译是很有必要的。

100. 英语在科学领域的应用

◆ **文章大意**

文章讲到词汇、语法及拉丁语对英语的影响。然后讲了英国有个提高英语地位的提议（proposal），最后讲工业革命（industrial revolution）提高了英语的地位。

◆ **题型及题目**

Summary; Table; YES/NO/NOT GIVEN

Table: 比较拉丁语和英语的特点

101. 面试技巧

◆ **文章大意**

面试的基本知识，人力资源招聘技巧、面试流程等。

◆ **题型及答案**

Summary; Matching; Multiple Choice

Summary: 美国人的失业是因为____或____，下一个空是____和____，____降低了20%

Multiple Choice: 文章中心思想——C

102. 年龄与外语学习

◆ **文章大意**

影响英语学习能力的因素——年龄。年纪越小，特别是小于3岁的小孩特别容易学习外语，因为有这样的环境。但是年纪越大越不容易掌握外语，因为形势（situation）的改变。如果只掌握了很少的语言，那么很难加入别人的谈话。如果你的语言掌握得很好，那么就可以和别人交流了。不同年龄的人学习外语的目的不同，孩子可能只是为了好玩，成年人可能是为了好的工作。青少年主要是在课堂上学习外语，所以外语与他们所学习的专业有很大的关系，而不像孩子一样。文章比较了孩子、年长的人和年轻的人学习语言的能力和快慢。

◆ **题型及答案**

List of Headings; Summary; Matching

Summary: ability, the same, younger children, situation, older children

103. 语言学习

◆ **文章大意**

某学者写了一本书，他认为学生学习时往往容易记住一些不重要的东西，而重要的东西却记不住。因此他推出了一种教学方法，研究学生的教育心理（educational psyche）。比如在上课的时候让老师在一种柔和的背景音乐中给同学们读文章，然后再用慢语速读，最后放音乐让学生自己读，这样的话学生就很容易记住重要的东西。他的这一理论受到了同学们的欢迎，尽管有些教师刚开始反对，但最终仍然接受了他的方法。

◆ **题型及题目**

Multiple Choice; Sentence Completion; TRUE/FALSE/NOT GIVEN

Multiple Choice: 某学者的书是关于：C suggestion的作用

TRUE/FALSE/NOT GIVEN:

- 学生认为学语言比较吃力。
- 老师认为某学者的方法比传统方法好。

Sentence Completion:

- 不那么直接（less direct）的方法。
- 越来越出名（well-known）。
- 如礼仪（such as ritual）。
- 如安慰的话（just as placebo）。
- 效果普通的（unspectacular）。

104. 语言变迁

◆ 文章大意

语言是人们的工具，它已经成为了交流的必要条件。从一个人的语言能力可以看出他的为人、学习方法、聪明才智以及性格等，因此人们常因为语言使自己受到伤害或伤害别人（hurt or be hurt）。1762年的时候出现了语言规范法，后来某教授说只有描述的语言才是唯一正确的语言。最后人们正式编写了语法。

语言是不断变化的，人们可以知道以前的语言是怎样的，到今天它又有了什么变化。还有一种研究依据叫语音定律。举例：对/b/和/p/的研究。

语言变化的原因之一是语言与语言之间的影响。比如：移民在使用第二语言时，会受到母语的很多影响。但移民的孙辈完全可以掌握第二语言，且不受母语的影响。因为他们整个家族（kin group）脱离了原来的母语环境。原因之二是某类人对语言的掌控。随着时间的推移，如果这种语言不再是他们独有的，他们就会对其进行改变，以保持他们语言独特或专属的特点。人们认为这种语言的独特性将他们从大众中区分开，达到突显其社会地位的目的。例子提到由于经济发展，中产阶级（middle class）地位得以提高，他们的语言就得以传播和改变。原因之三是在孩童语言学习过程中，没有准确地学到父母的语言，这些无意中造成的偏差保留了下来。这种情况也发生在成人身上。

人都有惰性，如果单词不好发音，就会进行更改。比如原先skamt（不确定拼写是否正确）因为m不容易读出来而改成了n。有些字母不再发音，比如：Christmas中的字母t。根据现代的发展，新词temporary因为有重复发音而简化成了tempery。

◆ 题型及答案

Summary; TRUE/FALSE/NOT GIVEN; Matching

Summary: 以英语为例，一种语言影响另一种语言，时尚的作用，大人对小孩的影响，不同字母发音的难易。

TRUE/FALSE/NOT GIVEN:

- it is easy to see the reason of argument about the usage of language
- when people talk about language，they will be irritated
- pre-descriptive language still exists today
- pre-descriptive language is main in European countries

- descriptive language only appears after 18th century
- descriptive language does not care about grammar
- both descriptive language and pre-descriptive language are misrepresented in people's mind

Matching:

A pre-descriptive language

B descriptive language

C grammarian

D non-linguist

- believe there is one right standard in language——A
- think the right standard is the usage used in life——C
- John is represented as an...——B
- in general,...is authority in...——D

105. 儿童语言研究

◆ **文章大意**

从19世纪说起采用的研究方法，以及使用录音机改进研究及存在的问题，在儿童能看见研究者的情况下实验效果如何，在儿童熟悉的环境下实验效果如何等。

◆ **题型及答案**

Matching; Summary; YES/NO/NOT GIVEN

Matching: 信息与段落匹配

- 在儿童说话之前记录的可能性。
- 教育（education）有困难。
- 儿童和成人研究的不同。
- 在儿童熟悉的房间。

Summary: acoustic quality, experimental psychology

YES/NO/NOT GIVEN:

- 19世纪就有人研究自己的孩子。
- 微型录音机的使用是为了记录在不同房间的孩子。
- 孩子喜欢打扰。

106. 英文拼写

◆ **文章大意**

英文拼写的重要性。主要说英语的拼写是社会地位的象征，不能简化英文书写，那样就失去了几百年的历史。

小朋友正在学校里痛苦地学习英文拼写。他们要把那些英文单词的拼写全部记下来。

某公爵给他的儿子写了封信，信的内容说英文拼写是很重要的。这不仅涉及语言交流的问题，更是一个人身份地位以及个人修养的体现。作者认为这个人把英文拼写的作用说得有点夸张了，但是英文拼写真的很重要。然后列举一个美国某次公务员考试的例子，强调有些人没通过就是因为英文拼写太差。

英文拼写在社会中的地位：举了几个例子，比如莎士比亚的英文拼写就很差，但是他仍然是戏剧大师。还举了个别的作家的例子。大意就是英文拼写虽然很重要，但也不代表一切。

有一种思想认为英文拼写并不重要，认为关键是要传达意思而不应过分注重英文拼写本身。一个人可以按照他的意思拼写单词。学校完全不应该花过多精力教孩子们如何拼写，他们应该教孩子们怎样进行创造性写作。

有些人试图进行英文拼写方面的改革，以便使英文的拼写更有规律，便于学习和掌握。

一些人则认为应该完全按照读音来进行英文拼写。现在越来越多的人把英语作为第二语言，如果英语本身更加有规律，那么就更便于普及和学习。但是完全按照读音来拼写也有问题。一些单词具有相同的发音，但是含义完全不一样，例如son和sun，weigh和way。如果采用相同的拼写，就会出现一些问题。此外，拼写还有一些历史的、表意的内涵在里面，如果单纯按照读音来拼写，那么英语文化中的一大部分就会损失殆尽。还提到各个地区的发音也不一样，不知道以谁的为准。

英文拼写的改革在英国总是难以推行。英国人相当重视捍卫历史和传统，因此这种拼写改革得不到大多数人的支持。

◆ **题型及答案**

List of Headings; TRUE/FALSE/NOT GIVEN; Summary

List of Headings:

A 孩子们在学校里学习拼写的情况。

B 一个例子，说拼写上的失误可能导致失去工作。

C 拼写在社会生活中的地位。

E 英文拼写方面的一些改革。

F 一些例子，关于英语中具有相同发音不同含义的词汇。

TRUE/FALSE/NOT GIVEN:

在英国拼写改革是否受欢迎。

Summary:

有些人主张按照读音来拼写单词，以便使英语更容易普及。但是这种做法有两个弊端。其一，单词背后的历史无法表达出来。其二，单词的含义也无法体现。然后说英语拼写改革在英国不受欢迎的原因在于英国人对传统的重视。

Momentum，history，meanings，tradition

107. 植物净水

◆ 文章大意

用植物来净化（purify）水的效果很好，但是这个方法在大城市不适用，因为太慢了。基本原理是植物可以增加水里的含氧量，微生物有充足的氧就可以分解污染物。然后讲了几种效果比较好的植物，植物名都用斜体写的。有两种方法，一种是水平流动，就是水直接从种着植物的池子里流过，另一种是向下流动（downward flow），这种净水池的构造也比较复杂，要一层软泥（sludge），一层沙子（sand），一层砂砾（gravel），水是垂直运动的。每过一段时间池子要休息一下，不然净水能力就变弱了。

两种方法有各自的优势：第一种容易建造，不需要人看管，但效率较低。第二种建造起来麻烦，还得有人看着。植物净水和传统净水的比较：植物净水比较便宜，好建造且具有观赏意义。

◆ 题型及答案

Picture; Summary; TRUE/FALSE/NOT GIVEN

Picture:

图中芦苇（reed）下面由上往下分别是：sludge，sand，gravel。

Summary: 水平流动（horizontal system），向下流动（downflow system）和自然流动（natural system）各自的优缺点。

- horizontal system的优点是更有效率。
- downflow system需要更多的河床（beds），而且建造麻烦、需要有人看着。
- natural system的优点是经济和美观。

108. 农作物

◆ 文章大意

介绍可可（cocoa），竹（bamboo），米（rice），龙舌兰（agaves），芦荟（aloe），马铃薯（potato）。某人把番茄（tomato）带到欧洲，还有其他几种农作物。

◆ 题型

Matching; TRUE/FALSE/NOT GIVEN

Matching: 农作物和特点匹配

109. 自然韵律

◆ 文章大意

讲节奏（rhythm）对生物的影响。第一段讲节奏对人脑的影响，第二段讲节奏对星体的影响。文章提到星球的运动对生物的影响可以从哪些地方看出来，又提到白天（daylight）的长短。要了解四季、白天、黑夜、潮汐和地球、月球、太阳运动的关系。周期性变化对生物的影响，对人的影响。周期性变化是由行星引起的。讲潮汐对鱼类繁殖的影响，季节影响鸟类，然后是光对动物和人的影响，人要调整生物钟以适应周期性变化。讲述自然界的四种周期性变化对生物的影响：高潮和低潮（high and low tides），月球围绕地球和太阳（moon around the earth and sun），地球和太阳（earth and sun），万有引力（gravitation），这些是影响气温、动物休息时间等问题的因素。自然周期对动物生理的影响主要是光及四季的变化，其中应该注意搞清白天和黑夜交替是由地球自转（rotation）引起的，月亮的变化是由月球、地球、太阳的运动引起的，四季是由地球绕太阳公转引起的。

周期性变化影响人类、仓鼠、鱼和其他生物，所以你必须选出影响他们的因素。

◆ **题型及答案**

List of Headings; Short Answer; Matching

List of Headings: B，C，C，D

第一段：周期性变化对生物的影响，对人的影响。（会增加犯罪率）

第二段：周期性变化由行星（planet）引起。

第三段：潮汐对鱼类繁殖的影响。（鱼会回游）

第四段：季节对鸟类的影响。

第五段：光对动物的影响。（人的生物钟）

第六段：人要调整生物钟，适应周期性变化。

Short Answer: NO MORE THAN FIVE WORDS

Matching:

- 自然周期对动物生理的影响主要是光和四季
- 白天和黑夜的交替是地球自转引起的
- 月亮的变化是月亮、地球和太阳引起的
- 四季是地球绕太阳公转引起的

110. 地球变暖

◆ **文章大意**

全球气候变暖，冰川（glacier）融化（thaw），以及一些由此带来的自然变化和科学家们的预测等等。

◆ **题型**

List of Headings; Sentence Completion; TRUE/FALSE/NOT GIVEN

111. 雪崩

◆ **文章大意**

雪崩（avalanche）的发生机制，如何避免。

◆ **题型及答案**

Matching; Sentence Completion

Sentence Completion:

Weak; 35级（degree）;（35–40级山坡易发生雪崩）windward; anchor; water; breaks away

112. 控制闪电

◆ 文章大意

控制闪电（lightening）的方法；减少闪电的危害。科技性强。

113. 伦敦烟雾

◆ 文章大意

这是一篇关于伦敦大雾使人丧命的调查研究，文章字数很少，有大量人名和时间。英国的空气污染导致产生一种浓雾，然后有位科学家就研究这个问题，还有一个组织也在研究这个问题，在政府提出空气质量监督以前就提出了大雾这种东西对人的危害，当时政府没在意。最后说如果不注意这种现象还会出现。

◆ 题型及答案

Matching; Summary; TRUE/FALSE/NOT GIVEN

第一题Matching，有七个选项，问每个选项在哪个段落提到。

A 段，没有跟选项相关。B段，选煤（coal）的使用增加。C段，选天气对烟的影响。D段，选烟对紧急情况处理效率的影响。E段，选对零售（retail）的影响。F段，选1952跟雾相关的死亡人数。G段，选烟尘的消散（dispersal of smog）。H段，选消除危险的规定（regulation of removing danger）。

Summary: traffic；fumes；cardiac；four

TRUE/FALSE/NOT GIVEN

建筑物的燃烧加重了大雾，答案是NOT GIVEN。

人们离开车因为无法呼吸，答案是FALSE。

关于郊区的车3天后怎么样了，文中根本没有出现，答案是FALSE。

有些人是因为吸入硫酸而死，答案是TRUE。

114. 欧洲森林保护

◆ 文章大意

第一段写欧洲国家都认识到了保护森林的重要性，所以开会讨论这个问题。第二段讲森林对于人类的三个重要功能。第三段讲森林保护政策应该怎样。第四段讲解决这个问题的几个途径，如：要保护所有欧洲的森林资源；要保护树种；共享有关森林火灾的信息；加强、提供资金等。

◆ 题型及答案

Matching; Multiple Choice; TRUE/FALSE/NOT GIVEN

Matching: 森林保护的六个解决方案

- systematically gather information
- all kinds of species of forest should be preserved

- forest fire
- mountain forest
- treat forest disease
- coordinated action

Multiple Choice: 文章的主题

欧洲的森林保护问题

TRUE/FALSE/NOT GIVEN:

- 人类只有在21世纪才能认识到森林的生物功能（biological function）。—— FALSE（文章有明确对应，人类从最初萌芽阶段就知道森林的某些功能，有些是最近几个世纪才知道的，但这些功能以后肯定会更加重要。题干中有only）
- 地中海国家的森林保护问题将在下次会议讨论。—— NOT GIVEN（因为文章中虽然提过地中海国家的森林保护问题在这次会议不讨论，但下一句马上说谁也不能确定以后讨不讨论。所以无法确定是不是下次会议讨论）
- 某国家的森林保护被排除在会议议题之外，因为它不是欧盟国家。—— FALSE（文章有明确说法，此国的森林保护问题局限于某些地区，而不是各国共有的问题）
- 森林保护政策应该局限于各国的国界。——FALSE（文章明确表明要跨越国家的界限）
- 会议规定森林保护政策一定要根据具体情况而有所调整，也就是要与时俱进。——TRUE

115. 海滩侵蚀

◆ 文章大意

关于海边沙子（sand）变少的文章。海岸侵蚀（beach erosion），现在沙滩上的沙变少了。每次海洋飓风对城市的破坏就加大了。沙子变少形成的原因，造成的影响，由它引发的一系列的现象分析及解决方法。

◆ 题型

Sentence Completion; TRUE/FALSE/NOT GIVEN

116. 人对自然进化的影响

◆ 文章大意

地球生物的进化和发展。动物进化有慢有快，人类的活动导致环境破坏，生物进化有的难，有的又很容易。人口、水资源、污染都可以解决，唯独绝种的生物无法复活。微生物绝种的后果。人口越来越多，地方越来越少，大动物不好生存进化，大动物面临着威胁。大动物死了无所谓，但如果一半昆虫（insect）死了，后果不堪设想。

◆ 题型

Summary; Matching; TRUE/FALSE/NOT GIVEN

Matching: 信息与段落匹配

117. 海底热源

◆ 文章大意

海底火山早已经被发现，1993年一艘叫Alvin的潜艇潜入海底进行研究。后来全世界不断发现海底火山，大部分海底火山在两千多米深的海底。

接着文章介绍这种现象形成的过程。岩浆怎样活动，怎样到地壳下，怎样混合化学物、矿物，怎样喷涌出来。举例提到黑烟（black smoke），它样子像蘑菇，就因为含有某种矿物。由于所含矿质（minerals）的不同，这种现象会呈现两种颜色，叫黑/白烟。这种现象储存了大量热量，海底大部分的热能储存于此。而且化学矿物质（chemical minerals）也很多。很多人认为在这样的恶劣环境里，没有生物能存活。但这里有细菌存在，它们在热能不断上涌的海流中寻获营养物质。就好像覆盖在陆地的植物，在阳光下存活，并供给其他生物食物。因为有细菌的存在，使这里形成了独特的深海生物群落。他们有一种特别的生存方式叫共栖（symbiosis），也就是说它们相互依存，是互利的关系。其中特别提到管虫（tube worm），它没嘴、没胃、没有任何消化系统，靠体内的细菌（bacteria）产生的碳水化合物生存。又提到一种生物，它的特别之处就在于共栖的能力很强，极具研究价值。但是由于人们不易对它进行实地考察，而在实验室中又养不活这种生物。科学家们仍然在努力研究这个生物群落的共栖现象，希望可以将其沿用到陆地上来。

◆ 题型及答案

Summary; Multiple Choice; YES/NO/NOT GIVEN

Summary:

冷的海水通过地壳（crust）的裂缝（cracks）与高温岩石接触变得过热（overheated），岩石也被熔化，形成岩浆，会吸收矿物（minerals），然后通过出口（vent）喷出，遇冷会沉淀（deposited）。海底排气口改变了温度和海水的化学物质，巨大的管虫靠细菌生活。

Multiple Choice:

- 曾经发现一个很大的黑色火山，有三层楼高、10米宽，像一个分层的蘑菇（three stories high，10 meters across，like a layer mushroom）
- Which one is true? ——世界各地都有海底火山